IMCK
A14(tig)
8.99

Child Dev

Learning to Think

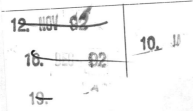

Child Development in Social Context

Other volumes in the series:

Volume 1 Becoming a Person
Edited by Martin Woodhead, Ronnie Carr and Paul Light

Volume 3 Growing up in a Changing Society
Edited by Martin Woodhead, Paul Light and Ronnie Carr

This Reader is part of an Open University course and is, therefore, related to other material available to students. Opinions expressed in it are not necessarily those of the course team or of the university. This disclaimer also applies to the use of sexist language within the articles.

If you would like to study this course, please write to The Central Enquiries Office, The Open University, Walton Hall, Milton Keynes MK7 6AA, for a prospectus and application form. For more specific information write to The Higher Degrees Office at the same address.

Child Development in Social Context 2

Learning to Think

A Reader edited by
Paul Light, Sue Sheldon and
Martin Woodhead
at The Open University

London and New York
In association with The Open University

First published 1991
by Routledge
11 New Fetter Lane, London EC4P 4EE

Simultaneously published in the USA and Canada
by Routledge
a division of Routledge, Chapman and Hall, Inc.
29 West 35th Street, New York, NY 10001

Typeset by Witwell Ltd, Southport
Printed and bound in Great Britain by Mackays of Chatham PLC, Kent

British Library Cataloguing in Publication Data
Child development in social context.
   Vol. 2, Learning to think
   1. Children. Development. Cultural factors
   I. Light, Paul II. Sheldon, Sue III. Woodhead, Martin
   IV. Open University
   155.4

   ISBN 0–415–05824–4
   ISBN 0–415–05825–2 pbk

Library of Congress Cataloging-in-Publication Data
Child development in social context.
      p. cm.
   Readings compiled for the Open University's MA in
Education, course E820.
      Includes bibliographical references and index.
      Contents: v. 2. Learning to think/edited by Paul Light,
   Sue Sheldon, and Martin Woodhead.
      ISBN 0–415–05824–4 (Hb. : v. 2) —
      ISBN 0–415–05825–2 (Pb. : v. 2)
      1. Child development. I. Light, Paul. II. Sheldon,
   Sue. III. Woodhead, Martin. IV. Open University.
   HQ767.9.C4448   1990   90–8834
   305.231—dc20   CIP

Contents

Figures

Tables

Preface

Child Development in Social Context is a module of the Open University's taught MA in Education. This is the second of three volumes of readings specially selected to serve as students' major source material. They should provide suitable reading for all psychology students, as well as teachers and others concerned with child development and education. These readings cover a range of topics from infancy through to the primary school years. They illustrate the increasing attention now being paid by developmental psychologists to social context and social relationships as fundamental in shaping the course of development, the processes of learning and thinking, and the construction of personal identity and educational achievement.

The emphasis on social context in developmental psychology is evident at various levels. In terms of methodology, there is growing dissatisfaction with artificial experimental procedures. Bronfenbrenner (1977) was prompted to remark: 'much of contemporary developmental psychology is the science of the strange behaviour of children in strange situations with strange adults for the briefest possible periods of time'. Whereas in the past developmental psychologists tended to model their work on the physical sciences, referring at conferences to 'research going on in my lab', many are now spending time squatting in the corners of sitting-rooms and classrooms making naturalistic observations of everyday life in families and schools. Of course there is still a place for controlled experiments, and modern research technologies have greatly amplified the power of the researcher's observations. This is especially true in the field of infancy, where frame-by-frame analysis of fleeting everyday encounters between young children and their parents has greatly enriched our understanding of interrelationships between the responsiveness of caregivers and the emerging competencies of children. This line of work is well illustrated by many of the articles in the first volume of the series, *Becoming a Person*.

Taking account of context is not only a matter of adopting sensitive research methods. As Richards and Light (1986: 1) put it: 'social context is . . . intrinsic to the developmental process itself'. It isn't just 'the icing on the cake, it is as much a part of its structure as the flour or eggs'. This is nowhere more clearly illustrated than in changing perspectives on cognitive development during the past decade. Piaget's theory has informed a popular image of the child as a solitary thinker struggling to construct a personal understanding of the mathematical and logical properties of the physical world. But this image is now giving way to a view of the child being initiated into shared cultural understandings through close relationships with parents and teachers, as well as siblings and peers. Viewing children's learning and thinking as embedded in social relationships owes much to the insights of Vygotsky. It is the major theme of this second volume of the series, *Learning to Think*.

The co-existence of these very different paradigms of child development is a reminder of psychology's ambivalent position as a science. While the psychologist may rightly keep one foot firmly in the exactitude of the laboratory, the other foot is entangled in more ephemeral cultural ideas about the nature and needs of children. Major psychological accounts of the child have not originated independently of social and educational practices, nor arguably should they. The problems arise when scientific statements become ethical imperatives, or when descriptive accounts became normative (Kessen 1979). This tendency is well illustrated by the role of psychological theory in reinforcing social attitudes to child care in and out of the family. This issue, along with studies of development in that more recent cultural invention, the school, is amongst the topics of the third volume in the series, *Growing up in a Changing Society*.

The underlying theme of all these volumes is that the study of the individual child, once taken to be the solid bedrock on which to build psychological knowledge, turns out to be a shifting sand. Children are physically distinct and separated off, but psychologically they are embedded in a particular society and culture. Clearly in adopting this perspective, there are dangers of substituting for an untenable universalistic model of human development an extreme culturally relativistic model which, as Campbell has acknowledged, carries the risk of 'ontological nihilism' (cited in Edelstein 1983). In defence, there is no dispute that children inherit a distinctive human nature. However the expression of that nature depends on another distinctive inheritance, human society and culture.

In one sense the new emphasis on context in child development represents a long-overdue *rapprochement* between the individualism of psychology, the social structural concerns of sociology and the cultural descriptions of anthropology. The idea that individuals are shaped by the social order is of course the 'bread and butter' of introductory sociology courses. But just as psychology has remained myopic about the significance of social influences, so sociology has failed to look seriously beyond such favourite general concepts as 'socialization' and 'social reproduction', in search of a more thorough understanding of the process of interpenetration between the social and the individual. The problem has been characterised by Super and Harkness (1981) by analogy with the well-known perceptual conflict between figure and ground popularized by 'gestalt' psychologists. Hopefully the current shift towards a more context-sensitive psychology will restructure the gestalt sufficiently that we shall, before long, be able to hold figure and ground, individual and social context, simultaneously in perspective.

REFERENCES

Bronfenbrenner, U. (1977) 'Toward an experimental ecology of human development', *American Psychologist* 32: 513–31.

Edelstein, W. (1983) 'Cultural constraints on development and the vicissitudes of progress', in F. S. Kessel and A. W. Siegel (eds) *The Child and Other Cultural Inventions*, New York: Praeger.

Kessen, W. (1979) 'The American child and other cultural inventions', *American Psychologist* 34: 815–20.

Richards, M. and Light, P. (1986) *Children of Social Worlds*, Cambridge: Polity Press.

Super, C. M. and Harkness, S. (1981) 'Figure, ground and gestalt: the cultural context of the active individual', in R. M. Lerner and N. A. Busch-Nagel (eds) *Individuals as Producers of Their Own Development*, New York: Academic Press.

Part one

Perspectives on development and instruction

Introduction

A very rough and ready history of psychology of cognitive development (at least in the English-speaking world) might run as follows. In the 1960s the 'discovery' (or rediscovery) of Piaget was the major factor, marking the ascendancy of a constructivist perspective over associationist and psychometric traditions in this field. In the 1970s Piaget's work was subject to a much more critical appraisal. Criticism focused on the 'individualism' inherent in Piaget's approach, on his claim for the universality of stages of mental development, and on the abstract, content-independent way in which cognitive processes were conceived. In the 1980s, renewed interest in Vygotsky's work reflected the need to recognize, within a constructivist framework, the role of cultural transmission of knowledge, skills and understanding. The transmission of culture lies at the heart of cognitive development, just as much as of social development. Vygotsky provides a framework within which *learning* is sharply focused: development is no longer separate from or transcendent to learning, but occurs through it.

The chapters in this first part allow both Piaget and Vygotsky to speak for themselves. The extract from Piaget (Chapter 1) dates from the 1960s. In it, he outlines his theory of the development of mental operations and, more unusually, touches on some of its implications in the field of education. Davis's (Chapter 2) article takes stock of the current position, arguing that Piaget's influence remains a major one in the 'psychology of education', and that this influence or relevance may indeed be reinforced in the context of new developments in curriculum and assessment. The Vygotsky extract (Chapter 3) which follows dates from 1930–1, and offers a clear statement of his central developmental argument concerning the social origins of the capacity for reflective thought. In particular, he discusses the role of language and, more broadly, 'signs' in the movement from the inter-mental to the intra-mental domain. Finally, Tharp and Gallimore (Chapter 4) offer a contemporary exegesis of aspects of Vygotsky's theory, especially the concept of a 'zone of proximal development' and its implications for our understanding of the processes of teaching and learning.

1 Advances in child and adolescent psychology

Jean Piaget
Source: Piaget, J. (1969) *Science of Education and the Psychology of the Child*, Harlow: Longman.

[. . .] There are some subjects, such as French history or spelling, whose contents have been developed, or even invented, by adults, and the transmission of which raises no problems other than those related to recognizing the better or worse information techniques. There are other branches of learning, on the other hand, characterized by a mode of truth that does not depend upon more or less particular events resulting from many individual decisions, but upon a process of research and discovery during the course of which the human intelligence affirms its own existence and its properties of universality and autonomy: a mathematical truth is not dependent upon the contingencies of adult society but upon a rational construction accessible to any healthy intelligence; an elementary truth in physics is verifiable by an experimental process that is similarly not dependent upon collective opinions but upon a rational approach, both inductive and deductive, equally accessible to that same healthy intelligence. The problem then, where truths of this type are concerned, is to decide whether they are better acquired by means of educational methods of transmission analogous to that which is more or less successful in the case of knowledge of the first type, or whether a truth is never truly assimilated as a truth except insofar as it has first been reconstructed or rediscovered by means of some activity adequate to that task.

[. . .] If we desire, in answer to what is becoming an increasingly widely felt need, to form individuals capable of inventive thought and of helping the society of tomorrow to achieve progress, then it is clear that an education which is an active discovery of reality is superior to one that consists merely in providing the young with ready-made wills to will with and ready made truths to know with. Though, even if one is setting out to train conformist minds that will keep to the already mapped out paths of accepted truths, the question remains one of determining whether the transmission of established truths is more efficiently carried out by using processes of simple repetition or by a more active form of assimilation.

And, in fact, it is to this problem, though without having deliberately set out to solve it, that child psychology [. . .] is now able to give a more complete answer than before. And this answer bears on three points in particular, all three of them of decisive importance with regard to the choice of didactic methods and even to the working out of educational programs: the nature of intelligence or knowledge, the role of experience in the formation of ideas, and the mechanism of social or linguistic communications between adult and child.

THE FORMATION OF THE INTELLIGENCE AND THE ACTIVE NATURE OF KNOWLEDGE

In an article written recently for the *Encyclopaedia Britannica*, R. M. Hutchins affirms that the principal aim of education is to develop the intelligence itself, and above all to teach how to develop it 'for as long as it is capable of further progress,' which is to say, of course, far beyond the age at which one leaves school. Whether the ends allotted to education, either openly or in secret, consist in subordinating the individual to society as it is or working toward a better society, everyone will doubtless accept Hutchins' formula. But it is also quite clear that this formula does not mean very much unless one can be quite precise about what intelligence consists of, for although the notions of common sense on this subject are as uniform as they are inexact, those of the theoreticians vary sufficiently to inspire the most divergent forms of pedagogy. It is therefore indispensable to consult the facts in order to find out what intelligence is, and psychological experiment has no means of answering that question other than by characterizing that intelligence according to its modes of formation and development. Fortunately, however, it is precisely in this field that child psychology has provided us with most new results [. . .].

The essential functions of intelligence consist in understanding and in inventing, in other words in building up structures by structuring reality. It increasingly appears, in fact, that these two functions are inseparable, since, in order to understand a phenomenon or an event, we must reconstitute the transformations of which they are the resultant, and since, also, in order to reconstitute them, we must have worked out a structure of transformations, which presupposes an element of invention or of reinvention. Whereas the older theories of intelligence (empirical associationism, etc.) emphasized understanding

[. . .] and looked upon invention as the mere discovery of already existing realities, more recent theories, on the other hand, increasingly verified by facts, subordinate understanding to invention, looking upon the latter as the expression of a continual construction process building up structured wholes.

The problem of intelligence, and with it the central problem of the pedagogy of teaching, has thus emerged as linked with the fundamental epistemological problem of the nature of knowledge: does the latter constitute a copy of reality or, on the contrary, an assimilation of reality into a structure of transformations? The ideas behind the knowledge-copy concept have not been abandoned by everyone, far from it, and they continue to provide the inspiration for many educational methods, even, quite often, for those intuitive methods in which the image and audio-visual presentations play a role that certain people tend to look upon as the ultimate triumph of educational progress. In child psychology, many authors continue to think that the formation of the intelligence obeys the laws of 'learning', after the model of certain Anglo-Saxon theories of learning exemplified by those of Hull: repeated responses of the organism to external stimuli, consolidation of those repetitions by external reinforcements, constitution of chains of association or of a 'hierarchy of habits' which produce a 'functional copy' of the regular sequences of reality, and so forth.

But the essential fact that contradicts these survivals of associationist empiricism, the establishing of which has revolutionized our concepts of intelligence, is that knowledge is derived from action, not in the sense of simple associative responses, but in the much deeper sense of the assimilation of reality into the necessary and general coordinations of action. To know an object is to act upon it and to transform it, in order to grasp the mechanisms of that transformation as they function in connection with the transformative actions themselves. To know is therefore to assimilate reality into structures of transformation, and these are the structures that intelligence constructs as a direct extension of our actions.

The fact that intelligence derives from action, an interpretation in conformity with the French-speaking psychological tradition of the past few decades, leads up to this fundamental consequence: even in its higher manifestations, when it can only make further progress by using the instruments of thought, intelligence still consists in executing and coordinating actions, though in an interiorized and reflexive form. These interiorized actions, which are still actions nevertheless insofar as they are processes of transformation, are nothing other than the logical or mathematical 'operations' that are the motors of all judgment, or reasoning. But these operations are not just any interiorized actions, and they present, moreover, insofar as they are expressions of the most general coordinations of action, the double character of being reversible (every operation includes an inverse, as with addition and subtraction, or a reciprocal, etc.), and of coordinating themselves in consequence into larger total structures (a classification, the sequence of whole number, etc.). It follows from this that intelligence, at all levels, is an assimilation of the datum into structures of transformations, from the structures of elementary actions to the higher operational structures, and that these structurations consist in an organization of reality, whether in act or thought, and not in simply making a copy of it.

DEVELOPMENT OF MENTAL OPERATIONS

It is the continuous development, leading from initial sensorimotor actions to the most abstract mental operations, that child psychology has attempted to describe in the past thirty years, and the facts obtained in numerous countries, as well as their increasingly convergent interpretations, today provide those educators who wish to employ them with a number of sufficiently consistent elements of reference.

The origin of our intellectual operations is thus to be sought for as far back as an initial stage of the development characterized by sensorimotor actions and intelligence. With perceptions and movements as its only tools, without yet being capable of either representation or thought, this entirely practical intelligence nevertheless provides evidence, during the first years of our existence, of an effort to comprehend situations. It does, in practice, achieve the construction of schemata of action that will serve as substructures for the operational and notional structures built up later on. At this level, for example, we can already observe the construction of a fundamental schema of conservation, which is that of the permanence of solid objects, these being looked for from nine to ten months onward (after essentially negative phases in this respect) behind screens cutting them off from any actual perceptual field. Correlatively, we can also observe the formation of structures that are already almost reversible, such as the organization of the displacements and positions within a 'grouping' characterized by the possibility of forward and backward or circling movements (reversible mobility). We can watch the formation of causal relationships, linked first of all to the action proper alone, then progressively objectified and spatialized through connection with the construction of the object, of space, and of time. One of the facts that helps to verify the importance of this sensorimotor schematism for the formation of future mental operations is that in those born blind, as we know from the research of Y. Hatwell, the inadequacy of the initial schemata leads to a lag in development of three to four years and more in the formation of the more general operations, and lasting until adolescence, whereas children who become blind at a later age suffer a much less considerable retardation.

At about the age of two, a second period lasting until the seventh or eighth year begins. The onset of this second period is marked by the formation of the symbolic or semiotic function. This enables us to represent objects or events that are not at the moment perceptible by evoking them through the agency of symbols or differentiated signs. Symbolic play is an example of this process, as are deferred imitation, mental images, drawing, etc., and, above all, language itself. The symbolic function thus enables the sensorimotor intelligence to extend itself by means of thought, but there exist, on the other hand, two circumstances that delay the formation of mental operations proper, so that during the whole of this second period intelligent thought remains preoperational.

The first of these circumstances is the time that it takes to interiorize actions as thought, since it is much more difficult to represent the unfolding of an action and its results to oneself in terms of thought than to limit oneself to a material execution of it: for example, to impose a rotation on a square in thought alone, while representing to oneself every ninety degrees the position of the variously colored sides, is quite different from turning the square physically and observing the effects. The interiorization of actions thus presupposes their reconstruction at a new level, and this reconstruction may pass through the same stages as the previous reconstruction of the action itself, but with a much greater time lag.

In the second place, this reconstruction presupposes a continual decentering process that is much broader in scope than on the sensorimotor level. During his first two years of development (the sensorimotor period), the child has already been obliged to accomplish a sort of Copernican revolution [. . .] On the level of reconstructions in thought the same holds true, but on a much broader scale, and with another difficulty added: the child must not only situate himself in relation to the totality of things, but also in relation to the totality of people around him, which presupposes a decentering process that is simultaneously relational and also social, and therefore a transition from egocentrism to those two forms of coordination, the sources of operational reversibility (inversions and reciprocities).

Lacking mental operations, the child cannot succeed during this second period in constituting the most elementary notions of conservation, which are the conditions of logical deductibility. Thus he imagines that ten counters arranged in a row become greater in number when the spaces between them are increased; that a collection of objects divided in two becomes quantitatively greater than the initial whole; that a straight line represents a greater distance if it is broken in two; that the distance between A and B is not necessarily the same as that between B and A (especially if there is a slope); that a quantity of liquid in glass A increases when poured into the narrower glass B, etc.

At about seven or eight years of age, however, there begins a third period in which these problems and many others are easily resolved because of the growing interiorization, coordinating, and decentering processes, which result in that general form of equilibrium constituted by operational reversibility (inversions and reciprocities). In other words, we are watching the formation of mental operations: linking and dissociation of classes, the sources of classification; the linking of relations $A < B < C \ldots$ the source of seriation; correspondences, the sources of double entry tables, etc.; synthesis of inclusions in classes and serial order, which gives rise to numbers; spatial divisions and ordered displacements, leading to a synthesis of them which is mensuration, etc.

But these many budding operations still cover no more than a doubly limited field. On the one hand they are still applied solely to objects, not to hypotheses set out verbally in the form of propositions (hence the uselessness of lecturing to the younger classes in primary schools and the necessity for concrete teaching methods). And, on the other hand, they still proceed only from one thing to the one next to it, as opposed to later combinative and proportional operations, which possess a much greater degree of mobility. These two limitations have a certain interest and show in what way these initial operations, which we term 'concrete,' are still close to the action from which they derive, since the linkages, seriations, correspondences, etc., carried out in the form of physical actions also effectively present these two types of characteristics.

Finally, at about eleven to twelve years of age, there begins a fourth and final period of which the plateau of equilibrium coincides with adolescence. This period is characterized in general by the conquest of a new mode of reasoning, one that is no longer limited exclusively to dealing with objects or directly representable realities, but also employs 'hypotheses', in other words, propositions from which it is possible to draw logical conclusions without it being necessary to make decisions about their truth or falsity before examining the result of their implications. We are thus seeing the formation of new operations, which we term 'propositional', in addition to the earlier concrete operations: implications ('if . . . then'), disjunctions ('either . . . or'), incompatibilities, conjunctions, etc. And these operations present two new fundamental characteristics. In the first place, they entail a combinative process, which is not the case with the 'groupings' of classes and relationships at the previous level, and this combinative process is applied from the very first to objects or physical factors as well as to ideas and propositions. In the second place, each proportional operation corresponds to an inverse and to a reciprocal, so that these two forms of reversibility, dissociated until this point (inversion of classes only, reciprocity of relationships only) are from now on joined to form a total system in the form of a group of four transformations [. . .]

MATURATION AND EXERCISE OF THE INTELLIGENCE

The development of intelligence, as it emerges from the recent research just described, is dependent upon natural, or spontaneous, processes, in the sense that they may be utilized and accelerated by education at home or in school but that they are not derived from that education and, on the contrary, constitute the preliminary and necessary condition of efficacity in any form of instruction [. . .] This spontaneity that characterizes the development of operational ability is attested to by the comparative studies that have been carried out in various countries (for example, the operations of conservation have been found both in illiterate Iranian country children and in deaf-mutes, the latter suffering a slight organizational retardation, but less than blind children).

It might therefore be supposed that intellectual operations constitute the expression of neural coordinations that develop as a function of organic maturation alone. Because the maturation of the nervous system is not completed until about the fifteenth or sixteenth year, it therefore seems evident that it does play a necessary role in the formation of mental structures, even though very little is known about that role.

The fact that a condition is necessary, however, does not mean that it is sufficient, and it is easy to show that the maturation of the organism is not the only factor at work in the development of operational ability: the maturation of the nervous system does no more than open up possibilities, excluded until particular age levels are reached, but it still remains to actualize them, and that presupposes other conditions, of which the most immediate is the functional exercise of the intelligence bound up with actions.

The proof of this limited character of the role of physical maturation is that, though the stages of development we have described always succeed one another in the same order, as do their substages, which is clear enough proof of the 'natural' and spontaneous character of their sequential development (each one being necessary for the preparation of the following one and for the completion of the preceding one), they do not, on the other hand, correspond to absolute ages; on the contrary, accelerations or delays are observed according to differences of social environment and acquired experience. Canadian psychologists working in Martinique, for example, using my own operational tests, have discovered time lags of up to as much as four years in this respect, and in children whose primary school program is identical with that used in France.

THE FACTORS OF ACQUIRED EXPERIENCE

There has been an ever increasing emphasis during the past few years on a point that I feel can never be sufficiently stressed, which is that there exists a fundamental lacuna in our teaching methods, most of which, in a civilization very largely reliant upon the experimental sciences, continue to display an almost total lack of interest in developing the experimental attitude of mind in our students. It is therefore a matter of no little educational interest to examine what child psychology has been able to teach us in recent years about the role of acquired experience in the development of intelligence and about the development of spontaneous experimentation.

On the first point, we know today that experience is necessary to the development of intelligence, but that it is not sufficient in itself, and above all that it occurs in two very different forms between which classical empiricism failed to distinguish: physical experience and logico-mathematical experience.

Physical experience consists in acting upon objects and in discovering properties by abstraction from those objects: for example, weighing objects and observing that the heaviest are not always the largest. Logico-mathematical experience (indispensable during the stages at which operational deduction is still not possible) also consists in acting upon objects, but the processes of abstraction by which their properties are discovered are directed, not at the objects as such but at the actions that are brought to bear on the objects: for example, placing pebbles in a row and discovering that their number is the same whether we move from left to right or right to left (or in a circle, etc.); in this case, neither the order nor the numerical sum were properties of the pebbles before they were laid out or before they were counted, and the discovery that the sum is independent of the order (= interchangeability) consists in abstracting that observation from the actions of enumerating and ordering, even though the 'reading' of the experiment was directed at the objects, since those properties of sum and order were in fact introduced into the objects by the actions.

As for physical experiment, that remains fairly simple-minded for a long while in the child, as indeed it did until the seventeenth century in the history of Western civilization itself, and consists at first merely in classifying objects and putting them into relationships or correspondence with one another by means of 'concrete' operations, though without any systematic dissociation of the factors involved. This direct way of approaching reality, which is nearer to immediate experience than to experimentation proper, sometimes suffices to lead the experimenter to the discovery of certain causal relationships: for example, when at about seven or eight years the child comes to additive operations and the notions of conservation that spring from them, he will also come to understand that the sugar dissolved in a glass of water does not cease to exist, as he had at first thought, but is preserved in the forms of tiny invisible grains whose sum is equal to the total quantity of sugar cubes immersed, etc. But in the majority of cases concrete operations are insufficient for the analysis of phenomena. With propositional operations, on the other hand, and above all the combinativity they make possible, between the ages of eleven to twelve and fourteen to fifteen we find the formation of an experimental spirit: faced with a fairly complex phenomenon (flexibility, oscillations of a pendulum, etc.) the child seeks to dissociate the factors and to introduce variations into each one in isolation by neutralizing the others, or to make systematic combinations between them, etc. Our schools often have no idea of the possible developments to be achieved from such aptitudes, and we shall return later to the essential pedagogic problem raised by their existence.

EDUCATIONAL COMMUNICATION AND EQUILIBRATION

Apart from the factors of maturation and experiment, the acquisition of knowledge naturally depends upon educational or social communications [. . .], and for a long while it was solely to this process that the traditional school confined its attention. Psychology in no way wishes to neglect such communication but sets itself to study questions that affect it and that may have been supposed to be long since resolved: does the success of such communication depend solely upon the quality of the presentation made by the adult himself of what he desires to inculcate in the child, or does it presuppose in the latter the presence of instruments of assimilation whose absence will prevent all comprehension?

As far as the action of experiment upon the development of knowledge is concerned, it has long since become commonplace to show how far the mind is from being a *tabula rasa* upon which ready-made connections may then be imprinted at the will of the external environment: it is observable, on the contrary, and recent researchers have increasingly confirmed this, that all experiment necessitates a structuration of reality, in other words, that the recording of any external datum presupposes instruments of assimilation inherent in the activity of the subject. But when it is a question of adult speech, transmitting or seeking to transmit knowledge already structured by the language or the intelligence of the parents or the teachers themselves, then people may suppose preliminary assimilation to be sufficient, so that the child need do no more than incorporate this predigested intellectual nourishment as it is presented, as though the process of transmission did not require a fresh assimilation, in other words, a restructuration dependent this time upon the activities of the hearer. In a word, whenever it is a question of speech or verbal instruction, we tend to start off from the implicit postulate that this educational transmission supplies the child with the instruments of assimilation as such simultaneously with the knowledge to be assimilated, forgetting that such instruments cannot be acquired except by means of internal activity, and that all assimilation is a restructuration or a reinvention.

Recent researchers have demonstrated this in the field of language itself. A child at the preoperational stage between five and six years, having observed the equality in length of two rulers when they are superimposed, will say that one of them is longer than the other if one of its ends is pushed out a few centimeters beyond its fellow, because the term 'longer' is understood (notionally as well as semantically) in an ordinal and not a metric sense, and therefore in the sense of 'reaching further'. Similarly, faced with a series A < B < C, the child will say that A is little, C is big, and B is in between, but will have great difficulty in accepting that B is at the same time bigger than A and smaller than C, because the qualities of 'bigness' and 'littleness' are for a long while incompatible, etc. In a word, language is not sufficient to transmit a logic, and it is understood only thanks to logical instruments of assimilation whose origin lies much deeper, since they are dependent upon the general coordination of actions or of operations.

The main conclusions that the varied researches of child psychology have offered pedagogy in the last few years are thus related to the very nature of intellectual development. On the one hand, this development is essentially dependent upon the activities of the subject, and its constant mainspring, from pure sensorimotor activity through to the most completely interiorized operations, is an irreducible and spontaneous operativity. On the other hand, this operativity is neither preformed once and for all nor explicable solely by the external contributions of experiment or social transmission: it is the product of successive constructions, and the principal factor in this constructivism is an equilibration achieved by autoregulations that make it possible to remedy momentary incoherences, to resolve problems, and to surmount crises or periods of imbalance by a constant elaboration of fresh structures that the school can either ignore or encourage according to the methods it employs.

2   Piaget, teachers and education: into the 1990s

Alyson Davis

INTRODUCTION

British education, especially primary education, has been exceptional in the extent to which individual schools and teachers have held autonomy on matters concerning what is taught, the way it is taught and indeed how or whether such teaching is assessed. Consequently, there exists remarkable variation from one school to another and from one class to another, in terms of the teaching practices and learning experiences which children receive. During the 1990s, however, this situation will change drastically. The 1988 Education Reform Act (ERA) has seen the introduction of a National Curriculum such that all our state schools are now sharing a common curriculum and assessment procedures.

It goes without saying that the 1988 Act is having a major impact on children, teachers and parents alike, and the educational debate surrounding the National Curriculum and related issues continues (see Lawton and Chitty 1988). My purpose here is not to add to the arguments about whether the National Curriculum is a 'good' or a 'bad' thing but to consider the implications of parts of the 1988 Act and the relationship between psychology and pedagogy in this context.

To anticipate my discussion more specifically, I shall argue that one key implication of the National Curriculum is that teachers are being asked increasingly to take on the role of 'developmental psychologist' in the classroom as they implement the National Curriculum and assess children's performance in school. The specificity of the National Curriculum means that not only are teachers expected to have a good grasp of each child's attainment and understanding but also will have to be able to *justify* those claims by backing them up with specific evidence of the child's knowledge. The task asked of teachers will be made easier if they are familiar with the basic principles of developmental psychology, how theories and evidence within psychology have influenced educational thinking and practice and the potential implications of research for good educational practice.

I hope to make the case that there already exist some fundamental links between developmental psychology and education but that these are rarely made explicit. However, the National Curriculum puts this issue high on the agenda. I begin with an overview of the relationship between developmental psychology and educational practice and theory. Then I look at the National Curriculum itself, paying particular attention to both its content and to the assessment procedures in relation to psychological theory. In the last section, I examine some ways in which psychology and education might continue to exploit their mutual common ground. Many of the examples I shall cite are taken from primary-aged children since this is where the research has been most concentrated. However, most of the points I shall make are not restricted to young children and apply equally to children of secondary school age.

PIAGET, TEACHERS AND PSYCHOLOGY

As part of an introductory session on the inservice courses I run for experienced teachers I ask them to write down the names of theorists they learnt about during their initial training, what they remember about the theories and what influence their knowledge has had on their classroom practice. Their answers are revealing: to the first question 'Piaget' is typically a unanimous reply, 'pouring water from one jar to another' is a common response to the second and 'nothing' or 'I'm not sure' is the majority response to the third. Not a very convincing start to a course which will go to some lengths to analyse Piagetian influence on psychology and education. However, all is not lost, since the next move is to ask this same group of teachers to make explicit *their* theories of child development by probing matters such as: 'What do you see as the main differences between 8-year-old children and 4-year-old children?', 'How do children learn?', 'Why do some children learn faster than others?', and 'What influence do parents have on development?' The answers to these questions are, not surprisingly, much more diverse, but these 'personal theories' paint a picture of children remarkably similar to Piaget's general principles of child development. Children are seen as being self-motivated, active learners who think qualitatively differently from adults and whose development is influenced (but not entirely so) by environmental experience such as the quality of family and school life.

Why then is there such a mismatch? Why don't these teachers report that it is their knowledge of Piagetian theory which nourished these ideas about children? Our simple answer is that these ideas have not been explicitly influenced by studying Piaget's ideas, and instead form part of a more general educational philosophy about the nature of children's development, stemming from early educators such as Froebel and Montessori who happen to share common principles with Piagetian ideas about development. I can accept this default explanation without too much concern. Many commentators, Piaget included, have argued that the general principles of Piagetian theory were not new in educational circles, but were formalizations of existing ideas. However, it is the fact that Piaget's theory is a theory of *child development* backed up by supporting evidence which makes the potential influence of Piaget on education of vital importance. Even if the content of what teachers teach children is dictated by a curriculum imposed on those teaching it, the *way* in which teachers go about their work is likely to be highly influenced by their beliefs about the nature of children and how they develop. How teachers build up those beliefs is an empirical question (see Smith 1989) but most initial training courses for teachers concentrate on asking teachers to examine their assumptions about children, looking at theories of child development as well as dealing with purely curriculum matters.

Aside from any arguments concerning Piaget's influence on any individual teacher is the larger question of his influence on educational thinking and practice in general. There are two main ways in which this is evident. The first I have already touched on, in terms of his theory's capacity to give scientific credibility to popular existing notions about the nature of children's development and consequently the best way to promote their learning. The second concerns the way that Piaget's work has been used as a justification to alter the actual content of the curriculum itself.

GENERAL PRINCIPLES OF PIAGET'S THEORY

Rather than give a résumé of Piaget's theory in this section I shall identify those general principles which are most relevant to education in considering the general nature of children's development.

Piaget saw children as *actively* constructing their own development, through their interactions with the environment. The importance of direct activity holds true for the young infant as much as the older child, and even at later stages of development when children are able to rely on mental images and language, thinking itself is seen by Piaget as 'internalised action'. This interactive emphasis on development stands in direct contrast to behavioural accounts (such as Skinner 1953) where the child is essentially viewed as a passive recipient of environmental influences. These ideas about the centrality of the child's own direct experiences map neatly onto educational notions about the need for children's own direct involvement in learning: that they should be given 'concrete experiences', that they should be able to 'discover' things for themselves and so on. Thus more traditional approaches to learning in which the child's role is passive (such as rote learning, or the use of Skinnerian type 'teaching machines'), are contrary to the basic characteristics of children's learning and development within the Piagetian framework. Within this view then the teacher's role becomes a rather indirect one in which they provide the child with the optimal experience and environment to foster the child's natural capacity to develop and learn.

Another aspect of Piaget's approach relevant to education is the fact that development is *stage-like*. Development is seen as involving progression through three main stages or periods (sensori-motor intelligence, concrete operations and formal operations) each of which is characterized by increasingly logical underlying structures and increasing organization. One important consequence of this is that children are seen as qualitatively different sorts of thinkers from adults and their adolescent peers. Thus what distinguishes infants from young children from adults is not simply the amount of experience they have had but the whole way that thinking is determined by the different stages in development. The young child is not only less knowledgeable but will view her entire world quite differently depending on the limitations of the mental structures governing thinking at any one point in time (Piaget 1962). Again, this stands in marked contrast to a behavioural view in which children are considered as immature, inexperienced adults.

The stress on the stage-like nature of cognition has given support to notions of 'readiness' – children will only learn effectively if their educational experiences are suitably matched to their current level of understanding. It is interesting to note here the overlap with the key concept in child-centred approaches that one should 'start with the child'. Indeed, some authors (e.g. Tamburrini 1981) see this qualitative distinction between children at different stages as being so central that this in itself is evidence enough that a teacher should have:

Considerable knowledge of Piagetian theory if he is learning to elicit a pupil's conclusions and level of understanding and then to decide on whether there are strategies that might extend the child's understanding or rectify his misunderstanding.

(Tamburrini 1981: 321)

In sum, then, there are general aspects of Piaget's views on child development which over the years have been used to support educational ideas of progressive education. Perhaps the most influential educational source in which these ideas were aired was in the publication of the Plowden Report (1967) *Children and Their Primary Schools* which emphasized that 'knowledge of the manner in which children develop is of prime importance, both in avoiding educationally harmful practices and in introducing effective ones'. This government seal of approval for the relevance of child development did much to institutionalize the shift from 'chalk and talk' approaches to education to a child-centred one.

Piaget and the Curriculum

So far I have referred to the generalities of Piagetian psychology without specific reference to the curriculum itself. In this section I shall outline some of the ways in which Piaget's ideas infiltrated the content of what children are taught and their associated teaching methods.

Perhaps the most extreme case of an attempt to put Piaget literally in the curriculum is exemplified by Kohlberg and Mayer (1972) who argued that it was possible and desirable to base the school curriculum directly on Piagetian stages. This attempt to take Piaget literally is also reflected in the numerous attempts to standardize Piagetian tasks into 'tests' of intelligence. However, as Ginsburg (1981) points out, such moves are inappropriate and unlikely to be successful:

an attempt to base education on the teaching of the Piagetian stages is an unfortunate misapplication of the theory. A more useful approach is the modification of the curriculum in line with knowledge of the Piagetian stages, without, however, placing undue emphasis on them and without allowing them to circumscribe one's approach.

(Ginsburg 1981: 317)

Ginsburg's reservations about the direct insertion of Piaget into the curriculum should, I believe, be taken seriously. Piaget's tests were devised by him as ways of exploring children's thinking and not as ways of promoting their learning. It would then be quite inappropriate to confuse assessment methods with teaching methods.

This said, there are examples from particular curriculum areas where Piaget's work has, in some instances, been taken literally. I have in mind here mathematics and science education. Piaget's interest was in the development of cognition, specifically logico-mathematical development. It is not surprising, therefore, that it is in the field of mathematics that Piaget had such a dramatic impact. Furthermore, his own method of collecting supporting evidence for this theory, the clinical method, involved setting children tasks and questioning children about their solutions to these problems to assess the child's underlying mental structures. In school mathematics, as much as in any area of curriculum, we see Piaget's theory *and* his methods being put into educational practice. For example Copeland (1979), in his book *How Children Learn Mathematics: Teaching Implications of Piaget's Research*, suggests that the mathematics curriculum should be organized and taught so that children are given experience of Piagetian tasks (such as number conservation and seriation) in order to establish their level of understanding and thus promote their learning.

While it is difficult to assess just how many schools took on board these kinds of recommendations, at a more general level the Piagetian influence in primary school mathematics was clearly evident in the development of the Nuffield Mathematics Project in the 1960s which to this day is a popular mathematics scheme used in many schools in this country. In contrast to Copeland's approach, however, the Nuffield scheme focused more on the generalities of Piaget's theory rather than the prescription of actual Piagetian tasks as the basis for teaching:

> The stress is on *how* to *learn*, not on what to teach. Running through all the work is the central notion that the children must be set free to make their own discoveries and think for themselves, and so achieve understanding, instead of learning off mysterious drills.
> (Nuffield Mathematics Project 1967)

Moreover, a very influential text book on primary mathematics, Williams and Shuard (1986), begins with an overview of Piaget's theory and the value of Piagetian principles to mathematics. Primary school teachers might be forgiven for supposing that Piaget was the answer to all their (and their children's) problems.

PIAGET AND EDUCATION: THE PARADOX

So far, I have pinpointed those areas in which education welcomed Piaget with relatively open arms. But before looking at more recent developments in psychology and education it is appropriate to discuss the paradox in Piaget's relationship with education. The fact remains that, despite the enormous interest in his ideas by educationists, Piaget kept himself relatively distant from educational issues. With a few notable exceptions (e.g. Piaget 1971), Piaget had rather little to say about the educational implications of his work and where he did comment it was not necessarily in a way that shed a very positive light on the teaching profession. As Bryant (1984) suggests, 'I suspect that at bottom Piaget had little respect for the teacher's business' (p. 251). How might this paradox be explained? One reason is straightforward enough. Piaget simply did not see education as *his* business; it was not his primary concern and he therefore devoted little energy to these issues. This in turn stems from a central tenet of his theory, that, 'learning is subordinate to development' (Piaget 1967). Development is seen as gradual changes reflected in stages; learning is more specific and determined by the stages themselves. His reluctance to acknowledge the developmental significance of specific learning may arise as much from his concern to avoid any account which resembled a behaviourist approach than from his general theoretical framework.

There is another, rather large issue in Piaget's story which leads one to wonder why teachers ought to even contemplate taking him seriously and that is the issue of *language*. Without language, classrooms would be very strange places indeed. Teachers rely on language to communicate with children, explain things to them and probe their understanding. Yet Piaget really did not consider that much could be gained from purely verbal conversation, since he held that language merely reflects cognitive achievement rather than controls it. Again, this could be seen as minimalizing the teacher's role.

Why then do teachers show such tolerance of Piaget's view of learning and language? For my own part, I suspect that teachers are prepared to buy this side of the argument because they too tend to see their role as being the promotion of the general educational development of the child rather than the imparting of specific knowledge. In other words, teachers are prepared to accept that their impact on children is more often indirect than as direct sources of specific knowledge.

These concerns about Piaget's account are not restricted to educationists – far from it. They have been aired by many developmental psychologists concerned to address its weaknesses and gaps in order to produce a theoretical framework which can match the increasingly large amount of empirical data on young children's thinking and language. It is to this topic which I turn in the next section.

RECENT APPROACHES IN DEVELOPMENTAL PSYCHOLOGY

In 1978 Margaret Donaldson's book, *Children's Minds*, was published. This book was to have a major impact for several reasons. For developmental psychology it marked the bringing together of findings from the 'Cognition Project', a large-scale investigation of children's thinking based on experimental techniques based at Edinburgh University, which, taken together, emphasized the importance of language in children's thinking along with evidence of children's very early intellectual competence. While Donaldson's work is frequently cited as a critique of Piagetian theory, the research itself owes much to his work, as Donaldson herself acknowledges: 'While the early chapters of the book propose certain reinterpretations, much that is said later is, I believe, in no way incompatible with Piaget's views and has certainly been influenced by them in positive ways' (p. 9).

Interestingly, the 'later' part which Donaldson refers to above is the section where she deals with the educational implications of the research reported in *Children's Minds*. This brings me to the second reason why the book represented such a landmark in the relationship between psychology and education. *Children's Minds* was the first really influential book which took on board educational implications of developmental research. It was not just a prescription that teachers need to read Piaget but tried to integrate developmental findings with educational concerns at both a specific and a general level. Donaldson shows how context-bound young children's thinking is. Their ability to solve problems depends on a variety of factors over and above the children's skill: the way in which problems are presented, the language used in 'testing' children, the child's interpretation of the task and the interpersonal relationship between adult and child.

The evidence which Donaldson reviews shows that young children are remarkably competent thinkers when that thinking takes place in an 'embedded' context – one which makes 'human sense'. Children's difficulties arise when they are required to solve problems in 'disembedded' contexts which lack the everyday human sense on which their thinking relies. It is in these situations that children fail to show the characteristic logical weaknesses common to Piaget's account of young children's thinking and reasoning. But as Donaldson argues, disembedded or context-free thinking is precisely the type of thinking that schools require of children in mathematics, reading and so on. Disembedded thinking is the very stuff that schooling is made of, and so, she argues, it should be. This is an important point, for Donaldson doesn't argue that we ought to alter the aims of education. Rather she argues that we should make the process of education more amenable to children by recognizing the difficulties they are likely to face when taking on board new ways of thinking which differ radically from their preschool experience. Thus at the heart of Donaldson's argument is a plea that teachers should understand more about the nature of children's thinking, and this of course is a psychological issue.

I would suggest that there are two reasons why teachers should gladly welcome her proposals. The first is that the portrait of the young child's mind which Donaldson paints fits in well with teachers' professional experience of working with children. Teachers know that children's success depends on their correct interpretation of what is being asked, their ability to draw on direct experience and the careful use of language. However, what teachers frequently do not have is any systematic evidence of how these factors operate. That evidence is given in *Children's Minds*.

The second reason is that, alongside that evidence, Donaldson offers some specific suggestions about how these findings should be implemented in educational practice. She argues that in the course of learning to read children not only become literate but develop skills relevant to all aspects of their thinking. Of course, literacy has always been seen as central to early education in its own right and few teachers are likely to argue against the importance of teaching children to read. But Donaldson's view goes beyond this in suggesting that literacy forces the individual to stand back and think about language and therefore has implications for how children can begin to see their own thinking in general. Thus the metacognitive skills in reading spill over to other areas of thinking and thus help the child along the path of disembedded thinking. In short, *Children's Minds* was more than 'psychology for teachers', it was a real and successful attempt at 'psychology *and* teachers'. This pulling together of education and psychology is reflected in the direction which more recent developmental research has taken in looking at issues of increasing educational relevance which are explored in later articles in this reader.

THE NATIONAL CURRICULUM

The educational debate surrounding the National Curriculum centres on three issues. The first is the general issue of whether or not a common curriculum is a desirable educational move in itself; the second issue concerns the appropriateness of the specific *content* of the curriculum as it is laid down; and the third issue relates to the question of assessing such a scheme. Psychological questions touch on all of these, but for our purposes I shall select issues which bear on points already made in this article to examine the potential impact of the National Curriculum on teachers as developmental psychologists.

The government's expectation is that at primary level the majority of time should be devoted to English, mathematics and science as the core subjects of the National Curriculum. There are also seven 'foundation subjects': a modern foreign language (secondary schools only), technology, history, geography, art, music and physical education. Not surprisingly, questions about the appropriateness of the selection of the subjects themselves, the implications for other subject areas and the demands on teacher time are hotly disputed (see, for example, Lawton and Chitty, 1988, for a critical review) but are beyond the scope of this article.

To date the government has published three documents, one in each core subject, which specify the content of the curriculum to be taught. Each of the core subject areas (mathematics, science and English) was devised by working parties comprising 'experts' in the field alongside educational specialists. These curriculum guidelines are the very basis on which teachers are asked to plan, organize and teach, and as public documents they are also available for parents. Thus for the first time, the curriculum from entry to formal schooling to school leaving age is literally 'on the table'.

However, these guidelines can only really be understood in the light of another document, the TGAT report (DES 1987). TGAT, or Task Group on Assessment and Testing, provides the framework for the structure of the curriculum by specifying the principles by which the National Curriculum is to be assessed. The principles of TGAT acknowledge the importance of assessment as being 'at the heart of the process of promoting children's learning' while recognizing the fears of parents and teachers that assessment may begin to dictate the curriculum itself. The starting point of the National Curriculum is with *attainment targets*. These targets describe the skills, understanding and range of knowledge the children will be expected to achieve as they progress through the school system. Each target has within it a description of *levels of attainment* from 1 to 10 which cover the precise knowledge and skills relevant to children at different ages and stages of progression with level 1 being the first initial level and level 10 being the highest. The expectation is that the average 7-year-old should be around level 2; by age 11, level 4; age 14, level 6; and at 16, level 7 or beyond (see Figure 2.1).

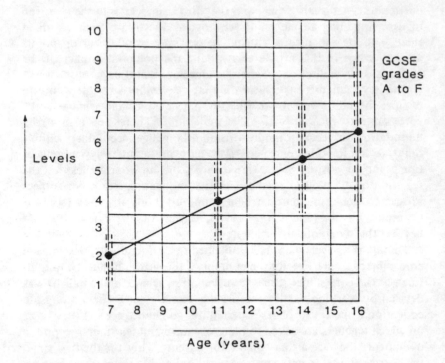

Figure 2.1   Sequence of pupil achievement of levels between ages 7 and 16

These ages – 7, 11, 14 and 16 – represent the ages at which children will be assessed. Assessment itself will take two main forms: Standard Assessment Tasks (SATs) and teacher assessment. The precise details of these assessments are to date unpublished but TGAT and later DES documentation has suggested that the SATs should assess attainment in a range of foundation subjects so that the administration of any three SATs should allow the child's performance on each Attainment Target to be assessed so that he or she can be awarded a level of achievement for each and every target; in the three core subjects. It is envisaged that teachers will be able to choose from a bank of SATs those that best match the kind of work which has been carried out in the classroom so that assessment might be as unobtrusive as possible. Furthermore, these SATs are to be based on examples of 'good classroom practice' and as such should be quite different from traditional forms of testing and assessment.

Children's learning which is not readily testable by standard tasks will be assessed by the teacher's own assessment. Again, the details of this are as yet unavailable. Neither is there final agreement as to the relative weighting of SATs and teacher assessment. However, what is clear from this brief description is that the responsibility for the assessment of children's achievement lies clearly with the classroom teacher when children are assessed at the four key stages. Before I can discuss the demands that this will make on teachers it is necessary to look at the attainment targets themselves. Those for mathematics in particular provide a basis for the points I should like to make. The mathematics curriculum comprises some fourteen attainment targets each containing statements of attainment applicable to the ten levels of attainment. These are summarized in Figure 2.2.

Attainment targets 2, 3 and 4 on number provide a convenient starting point for examining the psychological basis of the content of the National Curriculum. There are several aspects of interest, including the actual content of the curriculum itself and also the assumed developmental progression from one level to the next. Level 1, attainment target 2 (number) specifies that pupils should be able to 'count, read, write and order numbers to at least 10, understand the conservation of number'. Level 2 states that they should 'read, write and order numbers to at least 100', and at level 3 this should incorporate numbers up to 1,000. Likewise, for attainment target 3 (also on number) the progression through levels 1 to 3 is as follows: 'add or subtract, using objects where the numbers involved are no greater than 10' (level 1); 'use addition and subtraction facts up to 10' (level 2); and 'know and use addition and subtraction number facts to 20' (level 3).

Some of this, of course, will be readily recognizable to teachers and psychologists. For example, the progression from level to level does seem to represent increasing difficulty, but of what sort? Suppose one were an avid Piagetian; one's first reaction might be relief that number conservation appears as a prerequisite for any kind of dealings with number. Similarly, one might applaud the fact that in carrying out problems of addition and subtraction it is acknowledged that the child will succeed in using actual objects before manipulating abstract rules.

However, beyond this the developmental progression is rather bizarre. Neither Piaget nor more recent researchers have found evidence that distinctions between 10, 100 and 1,000 have any psychological significance. Indeed quite the contrary. The evidence we have about the young children's mathematical thinking is that they show remarkable competence in dealing with addition and subtraction of numbers less than 5 or 6 (even in the absence of objects) but then flounder on larger numbers (e.g. Gelman and Gallistel 1978; Hughes

KNOWLEDGE, SKILLS, UNDERSTANDING AND USE OF NUMBER, ALGEBRA AND MEASURES

AT1	Using and applying mathematics	Use number, algebra and measures in practical tasks, in real-life problems, and to investigate within mathematics itself.
AT2	Number	Understand number and number notation.
AT3	Number	Understand number operations (addition, subtraction, multiplication and division) and make use of appropriate methods of calculation.
AT4	Number	Estimate and approximate in number.
AT5	Number/Algebra	Recognize and use patterns, relationships and sequences, and make generalizations.
AT6	Algebra	Recognize and use functions, formulae, equations and inequalities.
AT7	Algebra	Use graphical representation of algebraic functions.
AT8	Measures	Estimate and measure quantities, and appreciate the approximate nature of measurement.

KNOWLEDGE, SKILLS, UNDERSTANDING AND USE OF SHAPE AND SPACE AND DATA HANDLING

AT9	Using and applying mathematics	Use shape and space and handle data in practical tasks, in real-life problems, and to investigate within mathematics itself.
AT10	Shape and space	Recognize and use the properties of two-dimensional and three-dimensional shapes.
AT11	Shape and space	Recognize location and use transformations in the study of space.
AT12	Handling data	Collect, record and process data.
AT13	Handling data	Represent and interpret data.
AT14	Handling data	Understand, estimate and calculate probabilities.

Figure 2.2 Attainment targets and associated statements of attainment for key stages 1–4

1986). Thus the 'small' versus 'large' number divide in psychological terms is around less than 5 versus more than 5. Distinctions between 100 and 1,000 are not psychologically pertinent. Note further that a child who can, for example, carry out subtraction on very small numbers is basically unclassifiable on the levels as they are stated in the attainment targets outlined above. One point following from this is that even in an area such as mathematics where attainment targets are relatively easy to define, there are going to be real difficulties in assessing children's knowledge (see Davis, 1990, for a review of these issues). However, the main point I should like to make is that the assessment of children's performance (responsibility for which lies with individual teachers) does require teachers to understand the nature of children's mathematical thinking. The teacher cannot arbitrarily assign children to levels, but must rely on knowledge about the child's understanding and performance in mathematics in order to assign children to the various levels.

Perhaps the overriding reason why knowledge of children's thinking and development is a prerequisite for the kinds of assessment required by the National Curriculum is that the system is fundamentally criterion-referenced. In other words the aims of the assessments are that children's performance and understanding of specific attainment targets are to be specified irrespective of the performance of other children. Thus the teacher is not being asked (at least not directly) to compare one child's performance against another child's so that these might be norm-referenced. Instead the aim is to specify the achievements of the individual child so that these can be used as the basis for future teaching and learning. This then stands in direct contrast to teachers' more familiar experience of the psychometric tradition, whereby IQ tests and reading tests focused on child–child comparisons. And it is this common ground of the criterion-referenced basis of the National Curriculum and its overlap with principles of developmental psychology which bodes well for the future.

Many teachers view the principle of criterion-referenced assessment as a welcome substitute for norm-referenced testing, but acknowledge the difficulties peculiar to the new system. Norm-referenced tests had the advantage that they are relatively easy to administer and interpret, in that scores can be calculated and checked against standardized tables and so on. In contrast, criterion-referenced testing is rarely 'pre-packaged' in this way. Instead the onus is on the teacher to make decisions about how to interpret responses in a variety of contexts and make decisions about exactly what behaviour constitutes evidence of any given knowledge or understanding. It is this very criterion-referenced nature of the National Curriculum which requires teachers to take on the role of psychologist in the classroom.

The dialogue between psychology and education will have to be extended in the future if these demands are to be met successfully. What is needed is a true interchange and not simply psychologists 'telling teachers what to do'. I hope I have shown that as we move further into the 1990s teachers and psychologists share a common frame of reference from which to interpret and influence the National Curriculum.

REFERENCES

Bryant, P. E. (1984) 'Piaget, teachers and psychologists', *Oxford Review of Education* 10(3): 251–9.

Copeland, R. W. (1979) *How Children Learn Mathematics*, third edn, New York: Macmillan.

Davis, A. M. (1990) 'The language of testing', in K. Durkin and B. Shire (eds) *Language and Mathematics Education*, Milton Keynes: Open University.

Department of Education and Science (1987) *National Curriculum: Task Group on Assessment and Testing: a Report*, London: HMSO.

Donaldson, M. (1978) *Children's Minds*, London: Fontana.

Gelman, R. and Gallistel, C. R. (1978) *The Child's Understanding of Number*, Cambridge MA: Harvard University Press.

Ginsburg, H. P. (1981) 'Piaget and education: the contributions and limits of genetic epistemology', in I. E. Sigel, D. M. Brodzinsky and R. M. Golinkoff (eds) *New Directions in Piagetian Theory and Practice*, New Jersey: Lawrence Erlbaum.

Hughes, M. (1986) *Children and Number: Difficulties in Learning Mathematics*, Oxford: Blackwell.

Kohlberg, L. and Mayer, R. (1972) 'Development as the aim of education', *Harvard Educational Review* 42: 449–98.

Lawton, D. and Chitty, C. (1988) *The National Curriculum*, London: Kogan Page.

Nuffield Mathematics Project (1967) *Mathematics Begins*, London: Newgate Press.

Piaget, J. (1962) *Judgment and Reasoning in the Child*, London: Routledge & Kegan Paul.

Piaget, J. (1967) 'Development and learning', in E. Victor and M. S. Lerner (eds) *Readings in Science Education for the Elementary School*, New York: Macmillan.

Piaget, J. (1971) *Science of Education and the Psychology of the Child*, London: Longman.

Plowden Report (1967) *Children and Their Primary Schools*, London: HMSO.

Skinner, B. F. (1953) *Science and Human Behaviour*, New York: Macmillan.

Smith, L. (1989) 'Primary teachers' beliefs about children's development', paper presented at the British Psychological Society, Developmental Section Conference, University of Surrey, September.

Tamburrini, J. (1981) 'Some educational implications of Piaget's theory', in S. Modgil and C. Modgil (eds) *Jean Piaget: Consensus and Controversy*, London: Holt Rinehart Winston.

Williams, E. M. and Shuard, H. (1986) *Primary Mathematics Today*, London: Longman.

3 Genesis of the higher mental functions

L. S. Vygotsky

Source: Leontyev, A., Luria, A. and Smirnoff, A. (eds)
(1966) *Psychological Research in the USSR*, vol. 1, Moscow:
Progress Publishers.*

The analysis and structure of the higher mental processes bring us
close to elucidating the basic problem of the entire history of the
child's cultural development, elucidating the genesis of the higher
forms of behaviour, i.e., the origin and development of the mental
forms which constitute the subject of our study.

If we examine the concept of development, as it appears in modern
psychology, we shall see that it still contains many factors which
modern investigations must overcome.

The first of these factors, the sad survival of prescientific thinking in
psychology, is the latent, vestigial preformism in the theory of child
development. Old conceptions and erroneous theories disappear from
science, leaving traces, vestiges in the form of habits of thought.
Despite the fact that the science about the child has long since rid itself
of the view that the child differs from an adult only in bodily
proportions, only in size, this conception has been retained by child
psychology in a concealed form. Not a single work in child psychology
can now openly repeat the long disproved ideas that the child is an
adult in miniature, and yet this view persists and can still be found in
concealed form in almost every psychological investigation.

From the point of view of child psychology the entire process of
development can be conceived extraordinarily simply; it consists in a
quantitative increase in size of that which is given from the very onset
in the embryo, the embryo gradually enlarging, growing and thus
developing into a mature organism. This point of view has long since

---

* The corresponding chapter in this work, 'Development of the higher mental functions'
(pp. 35–45), is in turn an 'abridged translation' (by D. Myshne) of L. S. Vygotsky's
extensive study written under the same title in 1930–1. The complete work was
published in L. S. Vygotsky's book, *Development of the Higher Mental Functions*,
Moscow, Publishing House of the R.S.F.S.R. Acadamy of Pedagogical Sciences, 1960,
pp. 13-223.

been discarded by embryology and is only of historical interest. And yet in psychology this point of view continues to exist in practice, although it has also long since been abandoned in theory.

Theoretically psychology long ago gave up the idea that the child's development is a purely quantitative process. Everybody agrees that we are dealing with a much more complex process which is not exhausted by quantitative changes alone. But in practice psychology has yet to disclose this complex process of development in all its completeness and grasp all the qualitative changes and transformations which reshape the child's behaviour in the process of development.

If we were to characterise by one general proposition the basic demand made of modern investigation by the problem of development, we could say that it consists in studying the positive peculiarity of the child's behaviour.

Psychology is now faced with the problem of grasping this real peculiarity of the child's behaviour in all the completeness and wealth of its actual expression, and of producing a positive picture of the child's personality. But this positive picture becomes possible only if we radically change our conception of the child's development and if we take into account that it is a complex dialectical process which is characterised by complex periodicity, disproportion in the development of various functions, metamorphoses or qualitative transformations of some forms into others, complex interlacement of processes of evolution and involution, complex crossing of external and internal factors, and a complex process of surmounting difficulties and of adaptation.

Another factor, the surmounting of which must clear the way to modern genetic investigation, is the concealed evolutionism which still dominates child psychology. Evolution, or development by means of gradual and slow accumulation of various changes, continues to be regarded as the only form of the child's development which exhausts all the known processes forming part of this general conception. Essentially the discourses on child development contain a concealed analogy with the process of plant growth.

Child psychology will have nothing to do with those sudden, leaplike revolutionary changes with which the history of child development is replete and which are so often encountered in the history of cultural development. To naïve consciousness, evolution and revolution seem incompatible. For it, historical development continues only as long as it proceeds along a straight line. Where there is a revolution, a disruption of historical tissue, a leap, naïve consciousness sees only catastrophe, downfall and a precipice. There history ends for it for the entire period until it takes the straight and even road again.

Scientific consciousness, on the contrary, regards revolution and evolution as two interconnected and mutually-supposing forms of development. The leap performed in the development of the child at the moment of such changes is regarded by scientific consciousness as a point in any line of development as a whole.

This proposition is of particular importance to the history of cultural development since, as we shall see below, the history of cultural development occurs to an enormous extent through such sudden, leaplike changes taking place in the child's development. The very essence of cultural development consists in the clash between the developed and the primitive forms which characterise his own behaviour.

The immediate conclusion from this is a change in the usual point of view concerning the processes of the child's mental development and a change in the conception of the character of construction and course of these processes. All processes of child development are usually conceived as stereotypical processes. In this sense, the sample of development, its model, as it were, with which all the other forms are compared, is embryonal development. This type of development depends the least on the external environment and the term 'development' may be applied to it, with good reason, in its literal sense, i.e. unfolding in the embryo in a limited form of possibilities. And yet embryonal development cannot be considered the model for any and all processes of development in the strict sense of the word. It may rather be conceived as its result or consequence. It is already a stabilised, completed and more or less stereotypical process.

Suffice it to compare with this process of embryonal development the process of evolution of the animal species, the real origin of the species, as it was disclosed by Darwin, to see that there is a fundamental difference between the former and the latter types of development. Species came into being and perished, were modified and developed in the struggle for existence, in the process of adaptation to their surroundings. If we were to draw an analogy between the process of child development and some other process of development, we should rather choose evolution of the animal species than embryonal development. Child development least of all resembles a stereotypical process screened from external influences; here the development of and changes in the child take place in an active adaptation to the external environment.

Ever-new forms arise in this process, and it is not merely links of an already formed chain which are stereotypically reproduced. Any new stage in the development of the embryo, contained already in a potential form in the preceding stage, occurs by virtue of the unfolding of these internal potentials; it is not so much a process of development as a process of growth and maturation. This form, this type, is also represented in the child's mental development; but in the history of cultural development a much more important part is played by the second form, the second type, according to which the new stage arises not from the unfolding of the potentials contained in the preceding stage, but from actual clashes between the organism and its environment, and from living adaptation to the environment.

We regard the idea that the structure of the development of behaviour in some respect resembles the geological structure of the earth's crust as one of the theoretically most fruitful ideas, which genetic psychology is mastering before our very eyes. Investigations have established the presence of *genetically different strata* in human behaviour. In this sense the 'geology' of human behaviour is undoubtedly a reflection of the 'geological' origin and development of the brain.

If we turn to the history of development of the brain, we shall see that, as the higher centres develop, the lower, older, centres do not just move aside, but continue to work as subordinate instances under the direction of the higher centres so that in an intact nervous system they cannot usually be set apart.

Another regularity in the development of the brain is what may be called a *passing of the functions upward*. The subordinate centres do not fully retain the initial type of functioning they had in the history of development, but transfer an essential part of their former functions upward, to the new centres being constructed over them. Only when the higher centres are damaged or functionally weakened do subordinate centres become independent and show elements of their ancient type of functioning which they have retained.

Thus we see that, as the higher centres develop, the lower centres persist as subordinate centres and that the brain develops according to the laws of stratification and addition of new storeys over the old ones. An old stage does not die away when a new one arises, but is eliminated by the new one, is dialectically negated by it, passing into the new one and existing in it. Similarly an instinct is not destroyed, but is 'eliminated' in conditioned reflexes as a function of the old brain in the functions of the new. Similarly a conditioned reflex is 'eliminated' in intellectual action, simultaneously existing and not existing in it. Science is faced with two entirely equal problems. It must be able to disclose the lower in the higher, but it must also be able to reveal the maturation of the higher from the lower.

The history of development of signs brings us to a much more general law governing the development of behaviour. The essence of this law is that in the process of development the child begins to practice with respect to himself the same forms of behaviour that others formerly practiced with respect to him. The child himself learns the social forms of behaviour and applies them to himself. With regard to the sphere under consideration we might say that this law does not anywhere prove so effective as in the use of the sign. The sign is always primarily a means of social relation, a means of influencing others, and only then a means of influencing oneself. Many factual relations and dependences which form this way have been established in psychology. By way of example we may point out the circumstance which was in its time mentioned by Baldwin and has now been developed in Piaget's investigation. This investigation has shown that there is an indubitable genetic connection between the child's arguments and his reflections. This is confirmed by the child's logic itself. The proofs first arise in the arguments between children and are then transferred within the child, connected by the form of manifestation of his personality. The child's logic develops only with the increasing socialisation of the child's speech and all of the child's experience. In this connection it is interesting to note that the genetic role of the collective changes in the development of the child's behaviour, that the higher functions of the child's thinking first manifest themselves in the collective life of children and only then lead to the development of reflection in the child's own behaviour. Piaget has found that precisely the sudden transition from preschool age to school age leads to a change in the forms of collective activity and that on this basis the child's own thinking also changes. 'Reflection' says this author, 'may be regarded as inner argumentation. We must also mention speech, which is originally a means of communication with the surrounding people and only later, in the form of inner speech, is a means of thinking, in order that the applicability of this law to the history of the child's cultural development should become perfectly justified.'

But we would say very little about the significance of this law if we could not show the concrete forms in which it manifests itself in the sphere of cultural development.

If we consider this law, we will see very clearly why all that is internal in the higher mental functions was at one time external. If it is true that the sign is initially a means of communication and only then becomes a means of behaviour of the personality, it is perfectly clear that the cultural development is based on the use of signs and that their inclusion in the general system of behaviour initially occurred in a social, external form. In general we may say that *the relations between the higher mental functions were at one time real relations among people*. I act with respect to myself as people act with respect to me. As verbal thinking is a transfer of speech within, as reflection is a transfer of argumentation within, so can the mental function of the word, as Janet has shown, never be explained other than by using for the explanation a vaster system than man himself. The original psychology of the functions of the word is a social function, and, if we want to trace the function of the word in the behaviour of the personality, we must consider its former function in the social behaviour of people.

We are not deciding beforehand the question of how essentially correct the theory of speech suggested by Janet is. We merely want to say that the method of investigation suggested by him is entirely incontestable from the point of view of the history of the child's cultural development. According to Janet, the word was originally a command for others, then it passed through a complex history consisting of imitations, change in functions, etc., and was only gradually separated from the action. Janet holds that it is always a command and that is why it is the principal means of mastering behaviour. That is why, if we want to elucidate genetically whence comes the volitional function of the word, why the word subordinates to itself the motor reaction, and whence comes the power of the word over behaviour, we shall inevitably arrive in the ontogenesis, as well as in the phylogenesis, at its actual commanding function. Janet says that behind the power of the word over the mental functions stands the actual power of a superior over an inferior and that the relations of the mental functions must be ascribed to the actual relations among people. Regulation of other people's behaviour by means of the word gradually leads to elaboration of verbalised behaviour of the personality itself.

But speech is the central function of social relations and of the cultured behaviour of the personality. That is why the history of the personality is particularly instructive and the transition within from without, to the individual function from the social is here especially clear. It is not without reason that Watson sees the essential difference between internal and external speech in that internal speech serves for individual and not for social forms of adaptation.

If we examine the means of social intercourse, we shall find that the relations among people are also of two kinds. Both direct and mediated relations among people are possible. The direct relations are those based on instinctive forms of expressive movement and action.

One animal influences another either by means of actions or by means of instinctive automatic expressive movements. Contact is established through touch, cries or looks. The entire history of the early forms of the child's social contact is replete with examples of this kind, and we see contact established by means of a cry, grasping at the sleeve, and looks.

On a higher stage of development, however, are the mediated relations among people, and their essential indication is the sign by means of which communication is established. It goes without saying that the higher form of communication mediated by the sign grows out of the natural forms of direct communication, but they are essentially different just the same.

Thus imitation and division of functions among people form the main mechanism of modification and transformation of the functions of the personality itself. If we examine the initial forms of labour, we shall see that in them the function of execution and the function of control are separated. The important step in the evolution of labour is that what the slave-driver and the slave do is combined in one person. This, as we shall see below, is the main mechanism of voluntary attention and labour.

In this sense all of the child's cultural development goes through three main stages which, by using the dismemberment introduced by Hegel, we may describe as follows:

Let us examine, for example, the history of development of the pointing gesture which, as we shall see below, plays an extraordinarily important part in the development of the child's speech and is generally in larger measure an old basis for all higher forms of development. By investigating its history we shall find that in the beginning the pointing gesture is merely an unsuccessful grasping movement aimed at an object and signifying forthcoming action. The child tries to grasp too distant an object, but its hand reaching for the object remains hanging in the air and the fingers make grasping movements; this situation is the point of departure for the entire subsequent development. Here for the first time arises the pointing movement which we may with good reason conditionally call a pointing gesture in itself. Here is only the child's movement objectively pointing at the object and nothing else.

When the mother comes to the aid of the child and comprehends his movement as a pointing gesture the situation essentially changes. The pointing gesture becomes a gesture for others. The child's unsuccessful grasping movement give rise to a reaction not from the object, but from another person. The original meaning to this unsuccessful grasping movement is thus imparted by others. And only afterwards, on the basis of the fact that the child associates the unsuccessful grasping movement with the entire objective situation, does the child himself begin to treat this movement as a pointing gesture. Here the function of the movement itself changes: from a movement directed toward an object it becomes a movement directed toward another person, a means of communication, the grasping is transformed into a pointing. Owing to this the movement itself is reduced and a form of pointing gesture is elaborated about which we may with good reason say that it is already a gesture for oneself. However, this movement becomes a gesture for oneself not otherwise than by being at first a pointing in itself, i.e., by objectively possessing all the necessary functions for pointing and a gesture for others, i.e., by being comprehended as a pointing by the surrounding people. The child is thus the last to realise his own gesture. Its meaning and function are created first by the objective situation and then by the people surrounding the child. Thus, the pointing gesture first begins to indicate by movement that which is understood by others and only later becomes a pointing gesture for the child himself.

Thus we may say that *we become ourselves through others* and that this rule applies not only to the personality as a whole, but also to the history of every individual function. This is the essence of the process of cultural development expressed in a purely logical form. The personality becomes for itself what it is in itself through what it is for others. This is the process of the making of the personality. Here for the first time in psychology the problem of correlations of the external and internal mental functions appears in all its enormous importance. Here, as was already mentioned, it becomes clear why all the internal was external, i.e., was for others what it is now for oneself. Any higher mental function necessarily goes through the external stage in its development because it is originally a social function. It is the centre of the whole problem of internal and external behaviour.

For us to say 'external' about a process is to say 'social'. Any higher mental function was external because it had been social before it became an internal, mental function proper; it was formerly a relation between two people: the means of influencing others or a means of influencing the personality by others.

In a child it is possible to trace step by step the alternation of these three main forms of development in the function of speech. To begin with, the word must have meaning, i.e., a relation to a thing, there must be an objective relation between the word and what it means. If this is absent, further development of the word is impossible. Then this objective connection between the word and the thing must be functionally utilised by the adult as a means of communication with the child. Only then does the word become meaningful for the child itself. Thus the meaning of the word first objectively exists for others and only afterwards begins to exist for the child himself. All the main forms of speech communication between the adult and the child later become mental functions.

We might formulate the general genetic law of cultural development as follows: *any function in the child's cultural development appears on the stage twice, on two planes, first on the social plane and then on the psychological*, first among people as an *intermental category* and then within the child as an *intramental category*. This equally applies to voluntary attention and logical memory, formation of concepts and development of volition. We have good reason to consider this proposition a law in the full sense of the word, but it stands to reason that the passage within from without transforms the process itself, changes its structure and functions. Behind all higher functions and their relations genetically stand social relations, real relations of people. Hence one of the main principles of our will is the principle of division of functions among people, division in two of that which is now blended in one, experimental unfolding of the higher mental process into the drama which is taking place among people.

We might therefore designate the main result to which we are brought by the history of the child's cultural development as a sociogenesis *of the higher forms of behaviour*.

The word 'social' applied to our subject is very important. In the first place, it means in the broadest sense of the word that all the cultural is social. Culture is a product of man's social life and social activity, and the very statement of the problem of cultural development behaviour therefore already brings us directly on to the social plane of development. We might further point out that the sign which is outside the organism is like a tool separated from the personality and is essentially a social organ or social agency. We might, furthermore, say that all the higher functions have formed not in biology, not in the history of pure phylogenesis, and that the very mechanism underlying the higher mental functions is a copy of the social. All the higher mental functions are interiorised relations of a social order, the basis of the social structure of the personality. Their composition, genetic structure and mode of action, in a word, all of their nature, is social; even when transformed into mental processes it remains quasi-social. Even when alone man retains the functions of communication.

4 A theory of teaching as assisted performance

R. Tharp and R. Gallimore

Source: Tharp, R. and Gallimore, R. (eds) (1988) *Rousing Minds to Life: Teaching, Learning and Schooling in Social Context,* New York: Cambridge University Press.

THE DEVELOPMENT OF COGNITION IN SOCIETY

[. . .] Schools have much to learn by examining the informal pedagogy of everyday life. The *principles* of good teaching are not different for school than for home and community. When true teaching is found in schools, it observes the same principles that good teaching exhibits in informal settings.

Long before they enter school, children are learning higher-order cognitive and linguistic skills. Their teaching takes place in the everyday interactions of domestic life. Within these goal-directed activities, opportunities are available for more capable members of the household to assist and regulate child performances. Through these mundane interactions, children learn the accumulated wisdom and the cognitive and communicative tools of their culture. They begin to develop functional cognitive systems; they begin to generalize their new skills to new problems and to novel aspects of familiar situations; they learn how to communicate and think.

In this formal socialization, neither communication nor cognition is the subject of direct instruction. Children's participation is sustained by the adults assuming as many of the strategic functions as are necessary to carry on (Wertsch 1979, 1985b). Children often are unaware of the goal of the activity in which they are participating, but at the earliest levels this is not necessary to learning. The caretakers' guidance permits children to engage in levels of activity that could not be managed alone. The pleasures of the social interaction seem sufficient to lure a child into the language and cognition of the more competent caregiver (Bernstein 1981).

The process begins early, much earlier than was once thought, and takes place mainly without the conscious awareness of the participants

(Ochs 1982). Without awareness, a caregiver may engage in a collaborative enterprise with the most profound implications for the development of a participating child. Revealed in the interpersonal exchanges are the precursors of cognitive and communicative functions that will some day be self-regulated by the child. [. . .] and it is through such mundane interactions that children learn the cognitive and communicative tools and skills of their culture. This insight from Vygotsky has the most profound implications for how we think about development and teaching:

> From the very first days of the child's development his activities acquire a meaning of their own in a system of social behaviour and, being directed towards a definite purpose, are refracted through the prism of the child's environment. The path from object to child and from child to object passes through another person. This complex human structure is the product of a developmental process deeply rooted in the links between individual and social history.
>
> (Vygotsky 1978: 30)

Thus, to explain the psychological, we must look not only at the individual but also at the external world in which that individual life has developed. We must examine human existence in its social and historical aspects, not only at its current surface. These social and historical aspects are represented to the child by people who assist and explain, those who participate with the child in shared functioning:

> Any function in the child's cultural development appears twice, or in two planes. First it appears on the social plane, and then on the psychological plane. First it appears between people as an inter-psychological category, and then within the child as an intrapsychological category. This is equally true with regard to voluntary attention, logical memory, the formation of concepts, and the development of volition.
>
> (Vygotsky 1978: 163)

The process by which the social becomes the psychological is called *internalization*: 'The process of Internalization is not the *transferral* of an external activity to a preexisting, internal "plane of consciousness": It is the process in which this plane is *formed*' (Leont'ev 1981: 57). The individual's 'plane of consciousness' (i.e., higher cognitive processes) is formed in structures that are transmitted to the individual by others in speech, social interaction, and the processes of cooperative activity. Thus, individual consciousness arises from the actions and speech of others.

However, children reorganize and reconstruct these experiences. The mental plane is not isomorphic with the external plane of action and speech. As the external plane is internalized, transformations in structure and function occur. In this regard, Vygotsky's thought is closer to that of Piaget than to others. For example, Vygotsky expressly denies Watson's assumption that the internal speech of thinking is identical with external speech save for the vocalization. A child does learn to speak by hearing others speak – indeed, learns to think through hearing others speak – but as private speech sinks 'underground' into thought, it is abbreviated and finally automatized into a form that bears little surface resemblance to speech itself. This transformation of form is a part of the developmental process.

The child is not merely a passive recipient of adult guidance and assistance (Baumrind 1971; Bell 1979; Bruner 1973); in instructional programs, the active involvement of the child is crucial (Bruner 1966). To acknowledge the inventive role of the child in transforming what is internalized, some developmentalists have begun to use the term *guided reinvention* – a term that connotes both social learning and cognitive reconstructivist arguments. Fischer and Bullock (1984) credit Vygotsky for having best anticipated the guided reinvention perspective, which expressly excludes the extreme positions found in some versions of modern social learning and cognitive-stage theories. Guided reinvention

> acknowledges the social learning theorists' insistence that social guidance is ubiquitous. It also acknowledges, however, the Piagetian insight that to understand is to reconstruct. Thus, guided reinvention elaborates the theme that normal cognitive development must be understood as a collaborative process involving the child and the environment.
>
> (Fischer and Bullock 1984: 112–13)

In summary, the cognitive and social development of the child (to the extent that the biological substrate is present) proceeds as an unfolding of potential through the reciprocal influences of child and social environment. Through guided reinvention, higher mental functions that are part of the social and cultural heritage of the child will move from the social plane to the psychological plane, from the intermental to the intramental, from the socially regulated to the self-regulated. The child, through the regulating actions and speech of others, is brought to engage in independent action and speech. In the resulting interaction, the child performs, through assistance and cooperative activity, at developmental levels quite beyond the individual level of achievement. In the beginning of the transformation to the intramental plane, the child need not understand the activity as the adult understands it, need not be aware of its reasons or of its articulation with other activities. For skills and functions to develop into internalized, self-regulated capacity, all that is needed is performance, through assisting interaction. Through this process, the child acquires the 'plane of consciousness' of the natal society and is socialized, acculturated, made human.

THE ZONE OF PROXIMAL DEVELOPMENT

Assisted performance defines what a child can do with help, with the support of the environment, of others, and of the self. For Vygotsky, the contrast between assisted performance and unassisted performance identified the fundamental nexus of development and learning that he called the zone of proximal development (ZPD). It is conventional and correct to assess a child's developmental level by the child's ability to solve problems unassisted – this is the familiar protocol of standardized assessment, such as the Standford-Binet. The child's *learning*, however, exceeds the reach of the developmental level and is to be found by assessing those additional problems that the child can solve with social assistance.

The distance between the child's individual capacity and the capacity to perform with assistance is the ZPD, which is

> *the distance between the actual developmental level as determined by individual problem solving and the level of potential development as determined through problem solving under adult guidance or in collaboration with more capable peers.* The zone of proximal development defines those functions that have not yet matured but are in the process of maturation, functions that will mature tomorrow but are currently in an embryonic state. These functions could be termed the 'buds' or 'flowers' of development rather than the 'fruits' of development.
>
> (Vygotsky 1978: 86; italics in original)

In contemporary neo-Vygotskian discussions, the concept of the ZPD has been extended to a more general statement, in which the 'problem solving' of the preceding quotation is understood to mean performance in other domains of competence (Cazden 1981; Rogoff and Wertsch 1984). There is no single zone for each individual. For any domain of skill, a ZPD can be created. There are cultural zones as well as individual zones, because there are cultural variations in the competencies that a child must acquire through social interaction in a particular society (Rogoff 1982). Boys in Micronesia, where sailing a canoe is a fundamental skill, will have a ZPD for the skills of navigation, created in interaction with the sailing masters. A girl in the Navajo weaving community will have experiences in a zone not quite like any ever encountered by the daughters of Philadelphia. Whatever the activity, in the ZPD we find that assistance is provided by the teacher, the adult, the expert, the more capable peer. Through this assistance,

> learning awakens a variety of internal developmental processes that are able to operate only when the child is interacting with people in his environment and in cooperation with his peers. Once these processes are internalized, they become part of the child's independent developmental achievement.
>
> (Vygotsky 1978: 90)

Distinguishing the *proximal zone* from the *developmental level* by contrasting assisted versus unassisted performance has profound implications for educational practice. It is in the proximal zone that teaching may be defined in terms of child development. In Vygotskian terms, teaching is good only when it '*awakens and rouses to life those functions which are in a stage of maturing, which lie in the zone of proximal development*' (Vygotsky 1956: 278; quoted in Wertsch and Stone 1985; italics in original).

We can therefore derive this general definition of teaching: *Teaching consists in assisting performance through the ZPD. Teaching can be said to occur when assistance is offered at points in the ZPD at which performance requires assistance.*

By whom performance is assisted is less important than that performance is achieved, and thereby development and learning proceed. To the extent that peers can assist performance, learning will occur through that assistance. In terms of pedagogy, assistance should be offered in those interactional contexts most likely to generate joint performance.

Vygotsky's work principally discusses children, but identical processes can be seen operating in the learning adult. Recognition of this fact allows the creation of effective programs for teacher training and offers guidance for organizational management of systems of assistance. Developmental processes, arising from assisted performance in the ZPD, can be observed not only in the ontogenesis of the individual

but also in the microgenesis of discrete skills as they develop throughout the life course. [. . .]

PATHS THROUGH THE ZONE

The transition from assisted performance to unassisted performance is
not abrupt. We can again use the example of an interaction between a
father and a daughter who cannot find her shoes; the father asks
several questions ('Did you take them into the kitchen? Did you have
them while playing in your room?'). The child has some of the
information stored in memory ('not in the kitchen; I think in my
room'); the father has an interrogation strategy for organizing retrieval
of isolated bits of information in order to narrow the possibilities to a
reasonable search strategy. The child does not know how to organize
an effective recall strategy; the father knows the strategy, but he does
not have the information needed to locate the shoes. Through
collaboration, they produce a satisfactory solution. When the child is
older, perhaps the father will have to say less ('Well, think of where
you last saw the shoes'), leaving the more specific interrogation to the
now self-assisting strategies of the child. This example of memory
function provides an account of the origins of what are typically called
metacognitive processes (Brown 1978; Wertsch 1978).

The developmental stages of higher cognitive, communicative, and
social functioning always involve new systemic relationships among
more basic functions. Vygotsky's discussions of higher-order mental
processes all emphasize the shifting nature of such relationships during
the course of development (Vygotsky 1987). Attentional processes
may be used as an example. In the first days of school, children can
solve even simple problems only if attentional processes are brought
into a new relationship with perception and memory. The attention
capacity of the child entering kindergarten may be in the ZPD, so that
a 5-year-old is capable of attending to teacher instruction and
direction, but only if a rich diet of teacher praise is available. The
teacher praise assists the child's attending by both cueing and reinforcing it. With time, the amount of praise required may be expected to
decline (Tharp and Gallimore 1976). As the capacity for attending
advances through the ZPD, assistance often is provided by peers, who
may remind a daydreamer that attention to the teacher is wise. For
most pupils, after the third grade, assistance by either teachers or peers
is rarely needed; attention processes can be invoked when the situation
is judged appropriate; they have become self-regulated.

The development of any performance capacity in the individual also represents a changing relationship between self-regulation and social regulation. We present problems through the ZPD in a model of four stages. The model focuses particularly on the relationship between self-control and social control.

THE FOUR STAGES OF THE ZPD

Stage I: Where performance is assisted by more capable others

Before children can function as independent agents, they must rely on adults or more capable peers for outside regulation of task performance. The amount and kind of outside regulation a child requires depend on the child's age and the nature of the task: that is, the breadth and progression through the ZPD for the activity at hand.

Wertsch (1978, 1979, 1981, 1985) has pointed out that during the earliest periods in the ZPD, the child may have a very limited understanding of the situation, the task, or the goal to be achieved; at this level, the parent, teacher, or more capable peer offers directions or modeling, and the child's response is acquiescent or imitative. Only gradually does the child come to understand the way in which the parts of an activity relate to one another or to understand the meaning of the performance. Ordinarily, this understanding develops through conversation during the task performance. When some conception of the overall performance has been acquired through language or other semiotic processes, the child can be assisted by other means – questions, feedback, and further cognitive structuring. Consider a child perplexed by the myriad pieces of a puzzle. Thus, the adult might say, 'Which part of the puzzle will you start to do?' The child may respond by putting in all the wheels, and thus see a truck take shape. Such assistance of performance has been described as *scaffolding*, a metaphor first used by Wood, Bruner, and Ross (1976) to describe the ideal role of the teacher. Greenfield (1984) noted that the characteristics of the carpenter's scaffold indeed provide an apt analogy for the teaching adult's selective assistance to a child. She added that scaffolding is similar to the concept of 'behavior shaping,' except in one important way. Shaping simplifies a task by breaking it down into a series of steps toward the goal. Scaffolding, however, does not involve simplifying the task; it holds the task difficulty constant, while simplifying the child's role by means of graduated assistance from the adult/expert (Greenfield 1984).

Scaffolding is a concept that has been of unusual importance to the study of child development. However appealing this metaphor may be, the field has advanced to the point that a more differentiated concept can be developed. For example, scaffolding suggests that the principal variations in adult actions are matters of quantity – how high the scaffold stands, how many levels it supports, how long it is kept in place. But many of the acts of the adult in assisting the child are qualitatively different from one another. 'Sometimes, the adult directs attention. At other times, the adult holds important information in memory. At still other times, the adult offers simple encouragement' (Griffin and Cole 1984: 47).

The various means of assisting performance are indeed qualitatively different. By discussing these different means of assisting performance, we have the opportunity to connect neo-Vygotskian ideas with a broader literature of American and British psychology.

For the present, we can discuss the issue in terms of the various kinds of assistance that are regular features of Stage I. Rogoff (1986) discusses some of these issues in terms of *structuring situations*. Even before interacting with the child, a parent or teacher assists by an age grading of manipulanda: the choice of puzzles, the selection of kindergarten tasks, and the selection of appropriate tools and materials for an apprentice are all important features of assisting performance.

In addition to grading manipulanda, the assistor provides a 'grading' of tasks, by structuring tasks into sub-goals and sub-sub-goals. The Saxe, Gearhart, and Guberman (1984) work on assisting children to learn to count is an example of structuring a teaching situation by careful task analysis and sub-goal selection, until the entire script is assembled back from its parts.

During Stage I, a child (or an adult learner) may not conceptualize the goal of the activity in the way that the adult assistor does (Figure 4.1). A child's initial goal might be to sustain a pleasant interaction or to have access to some attractive puzzle items, or there might be some other motive that adults cannot apprehend. As interaction proceeds, different goals and sub-goals emerge and change as the participants work together. The adult may shift to a subordinate or superordinate goal in response to ongoing assessment of the child's performance. The child's goals will also shift in response to adult help and their growing intersubjectivity. In a careful analysis of such interactions, Saxe and associates concluded that because the goal structure is located

> neither in the head of the mother nor in that of the child, this goal structure is negotiated in the interaction itself. Thus, the emergent goal structure simultaneously involves the child's understandings

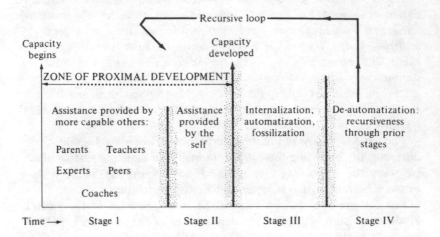

Figure 4.1   Genesis of performance capacity: progression through the ZPD and beyond

and the historical achievements of culture as communicated by the mother. . . . As children generate coherent means to achieve these socially negotiated goals, they create for themselves a system of representation that reflects achievements that have been generated in our culture's social history.

(Saxe *et al.* 1984: 29)

The shifting of goals by the adult to achieve intersubjectivity is the fundamental reason that a profound knowledge of subject matter is required of teachers who seek to assist performance. Without such knowledge, teachers cannot be ready to promptly assist performance, because they cannot quickly reformulate the goals of the interaction; they cannot map the child's conception of the task goal onto the superordinate knowledge structures of the academic discipline that is being transmitted. This fundamental aspect of interaction in the ZPD will emerge repeatedly in our analysis of teaching and the development of teaching.

During Stage I, we see a steadily declining plane of adult responsibility for task performance and a reciprocal increase in the learner's proportion of responsibility. This is Bruner's fundamental 'handover principle' – the child who was a spectator is now a participant (Bruner 1983: 60). The developmental task of Stage I is to transit from other-regulation to self-regulation. The transit begins while performance is still being carried out on the interpyschological plane of functioning, because the child can begin to use language exchanges with the adult to engender assistance. For example, in the analysis of joint puzzle-solving, the child can begin to ask the adult for strategic direction (e.g., 'Which part do I do next?') (Wertsch 1979: 19).

Indeed, by asking questions and adopting other sub-routines of the adult's assistance, children gradually take over the actual structuring of the task and thereby acquire not only the performance but also the process of transfer of the performance (Rogoff 1986). The adult's task is to accurately tailor assistance to the child by being responsive to the child's current effort and understanding of the task goal. By asking 'Which part do I do next?' the child begins to influence the level of help provided. *This assists the adult to assist.* Children, and other learners, are never passive recipients of adult or teacher input. As infants, they attracted adult attention through cries, smiles, and other responses. 'Rocking and walking are not only effective ways of calming babies but also provide them with adult legs to move on and with access to new scenes of regard that yield information about the environment' (Rogoff, Malkin and Gilbride 1984: 32).

'Legs' of a different kind are needed to solve puzzles, learn to read, and acquire all the other skills that have their origins in social interaction. But at each stage, the developing child contributes to the success of an activity. Asking for strategic direction is, in this sense, no different than the infant's cry that makes locomotion possible. In both cases, the child's partial performance provides adult assistance, thus permitting an achievement not possible without the collaborating other.

The task of Stage I is accomplished when the responsibility for tailoring the assistance, tailoring the transfer, and performing the task itself has been effectively handed over to the learner.

Of course, this achievement is gradual, with progress occurring in fits and starts. The line between any two stages in the diagram of the ZPD is represented as a zone itself.

Stage II: Where performance is assisted by the self

If we look carefully at the child's statements during this transition, we see that the child

has taken over the rules and responsibilities of both participants in the language-game. These responsibilities were formerly divided between the adult and child, but they have now been taken over completely by the child. The definitions of situation and the patterns of activity which formerly allowed the child to participate in the problem-solving effort on the interpsychological plane now allow him/her to carry out the task on the intrapsychological plane.

(Wertsch 1979: 18)

Thus, in Stage II, the child carries out a task without assistance from others. *However, this does not mean that the performance is fully developed or automatized.*

This point can be seen most clearly at the level of individual, ontogenetic development. In neo-Vygotskian theory, whether we consider the genesis of a particular performance capacity (microgenesis) or the development of an individual (ontogenesis), the same four stages describe the preponderance of self-control/social-control relationships. During Stage II, the relationships among language, thought, and action in general undergo profound rearrangements – ontogenetically, in the years from infancy through middle childhood. By the age of 2 years or so, child behavior can be inhibited by adult speech ('Don't kick!'). In the next stage of development, this same *self*-instruction ('Don't kick!') also inhibits the kicking impulse. Control is passed from the adult to the child speaker, but the control function remains with the overt verbalization. The transfer from external to internal control is accomplished by transfer of the manipulation of the sign (e.g., language) from others to the self.

The phenomenon of self-directed speech reflects a development of the most profound significance. According to Vygotsky, and his follower Luria, once children begin to direct or guide behavior with their own speech, an important stage has been reached in the transition of a skill through the ZPD. It constitutes the next stage in the passing of control or assistance from the adult to the child, from the expert to the apprentice. What was guided by the other is now beginning to be guided and directed by the self.

There is now substantial experimental and observational evidence (Gallimore *et al.* 1986; Tharp, Gallimore, and Calkins 1984; Watson and Tharp 1988) that a major function of self-directed speech is 'self-guidance, that its developmental origins have to do with early social experiences, and that it increases under task circumstances involving obstacles and difficulties' (Berk and Garvin 1984: 24; Berk 1986). Developmental analysis places self-assistance as a stage in the ZPD.

Self-control may be seen as a recurrent and efficacious method that bridges between help by others and fully automated, fully developed capacities. Meichenbaum (1977) sought to teach self-instruction to children with deficient self-control. 'Impulsive' children were taught to instruct themselves with cognitive strategies (e.g., 'Go slow and be careful') before and during a variety of performance tasks; they demonstrated improved performance in such tasks as paper-and-pencil mazes. For children older than 6 years, semantic meaning efficiently mediates performance (Gal'perin 1969). Children also employ self-directed vocalization to assist performance under conditions of stress of task difficulty (Berk 1986; Berk and Garvin 1984; Kohlberg, Yaeger and Hjertholm 1968; Roberts 1979; Roberts and Mullis 1980; Roberts and Tharp 1980).

Thus, for children, a major function of self-directed speech is self-guidance. This remains true throughout lifelong learning. At the microgenetic level, when we consider the acquisition of some particular performance capacity, adults during Stage II consistently talk to themselves, and indeed assist themselves in all ways possible. The self-conscious, systematic use of self-directed assistance strategies is one of the most vigorous movements in applied psychology (Watson and Tharp 1988).

Self-speech is more than instrumental in skill acquisition; it is itself an aspect of cognitive development of the most profound sort (Diaz 1986); it forms the basis for writing and thus is transformed into the highest forms of communication available to the literate life (Elsasser and John-Steiner 1977).

Stage III: Where performance is developed, automatized, and 'fossilized'

Once all evidence of self-regulation has vanished, the child has emerged from the ZPD into the *developmental stage* for that task. The task execution is smooth and integrated. It has been internalized and 'automatized'. Assistance, from the adult or the self, is no longer needed. Indeed 'assistance' would now be disruptive. It is in this condition that instructions from others are disruptive and irritating; it is at this stage that self-consciousness itself is detrimental to the smooth integration of all task components. This is a stage beyond self-control and beyond social control. Performance here is no longer developing; it is already developed. Vygotsky described it as the 'fruits' of development, but he also described it as 'fossilized', emphasizing its fixity and distance from the social and mental forces of change.

Stage IV: Where de-automatization of performance leads to recursion back through the ZPD

The lifelong learning by any individual is made up of these same regulated, ZPD sequences – from other-assistance to self-assistance – recurring over and over again for the development of new capacities. For every individual, at any point in time, there will be a mix of other-regulation, self-regulation, and automatized processes. The child who can now do many of the steps in finding a lost object might still be in the ZPD for the activities of reading, or any of the many skills and processes remaining to be developed in the immature organism.

Furthermore, once children master cognitive strategies, they are not obligated to rely only on internal mediation. They can also ask for help when stuck, for example, in the search for lost items of attire. During periods of difficulty, children may seek out controlling vocalizations by more competent others (Gal'perin 1969). Again, we see the intimate and shifting relationship between control by self and control by others.

Even for adults, the effort to recall a forgotten bit of information can be aided by the helpful assistance of another, so that the total of self-regulated and other-regulated components of the performance once again resembles the mother-and-child example of shared functioning. Even the competent adult can profit from regulation for enhancement and maintenance of performance.

Indeed, enhancement, improvement, and maintenance of performance provide a recurrent cycle of self-assistance to other-assistance. A most important consideration is that *de-automatization and recursion* occur so regularly that they constitute a Stage IV of the normal developmental process. What one formerly could do, one can no longer do. This de-automatization may be due to slight environmental changes or individual stress, not to mention major upheavals or physical trauma. The analogy between microgenesis and ontogenesis is again clear; at the end of life, capacities fall into general decline. After de-automatization, for whatever reason, if capacity is to be restored, then the developmental process must become recursive.

The first line of retreat is to the immediately prior self-regulating phase. We have already discussed how children doing more difficult problems talk to themselves about it more, and quite competent adults can recall talking themselves through some knotty intellectual problem or through the traffic patterns of a strange city. Making self-speech external is a form of recursion often effective in restoring competence. A further retreat, to remembering the voice of a teacher, may be required. 'Hearing the voice of the teacher' has been shown to be one of the middle stages in the development of complex skills (Gallimore *et al.* 1986). Intentionally recurring to that point in the zone – consciously reconjuring the voice of a tutor – is an effective self-control technique.

But in some cases no form of self-regulation may be adequate to restore capacity, and a further recursion – the restitution of other-regulation – is often required. The readiness of a teacher to repeat some earlier lesson is one mark of excellent teaching. The profession of assisting adults (psychotherapy) is now a major Western institution. In all these instances, the goal is to reproceed through assisted performance to self-regulation and to exit the ZPD again into a new automatization.

RESPONSIVE ASSISTANCE

In the transition from other-assistance to self-assistance (and automatization) there are variations in the means and patterns of adult assistance to the child. At the earlier phases, assistance may be frequent and elaborate. Later, it occurs less often and is truncated. Adult assistance is contingent on and responsive to the child's level of performance. In the earliest stages, when the child does not comprehend the purpose of an activity or see the connection between component steps, adult help tends to be relatively narrow in focus: 'Pick up the blue one, and put it next to the yellow one.' As the child's comprehension and skill increase, adults begin to abbreviate their help (Rogoff and Gardener 1984; Wertsch and Schneider 1979). The adult may say something like 'OK, what else could you try?'. Such a truncated bit of help may prompt the child to take another look at the model of the puzzle, or scan the finished part, or poke through the pile of pieces for a different one. In narrative retelling, the adult may ask if the child remembers any more of the story, whereas earlier queries were about more specific details ('What did the other brother do?') (McNamee 1979).

If the truncated guidance fails, the adult may add additional hints, testing to find that minimum level of help the child needs to proceed. This continual adjustment of the level and amount of help is *responsive to the child's level of performance and perceived need*. Assisting adults appear to keep in mind the overall goal of the activity, to stay related to what the child is trying to do. New information or suggestions are made relevant to furthering the child's current goal, and at the same time furthering the overall goal.

The tuning of adult assistance appears to begin quite early. For example, Cross (1977) studied 16 children ranging in age from 19 to 32 months. Although the average difference among their mean lengths of utterance (MLU) was only two words, correlations between mothers' speech adjustments and child speech levels ranged from 0.65 to 0.85. More significantly, the best predictor of mother adjustments to child utterances was the mean of the 50 longest utterances (out of 500), *not* the MLU for the entire 500. The mothers' MLUs were, on average, about three morphemes longer than their children's and less than half a morpheme longer than the children's longest utterances. The mothers probably were tracking their children's best performance, which probably was at or near the capacity level for the age of the children. This suggests that mothers' contingent speech adjustments are well 'tuned' to the leading edge of child communicative competence – to the ZPD of social communication.

For older children, responsive adult assistance can become quite varied within a single episode of collaborative activity – and the reciprocity of adult–child interactions quite complex. Attempts by assisting adults to assess a child's readiness for greater responsibility often are subtle and embedded in the ongoing interaction, appearing as negotiations of the division of labor. For example, in Rogoff's study (1986), at the beginning of sessions, mothers often provided redundant information to ensure correct performance; this decreased over the session, as in the study of Wertsch and Schneider (1979). Mothers and children used hesitation, glances and postural changes, as well as errors by the children, to adjust relative responsibilities for problem-solving. For example, one mother encouraged her child to determine where the next item went. When the child hesitated, the mother turned slightly toward the correct location. When the child still hesitated, the mother glanced at the correct location and moved the item slightly toward its intended location. Finally, she superficially rearranged other items in the correct group, and with this hint the child finally made the correct placement. Thus, the mother encouraged greater responsibility by the child and masked her assistance as random activity rather than correction of error, adjusting her support to the child's level of understanding.

However, patient, contingent, responsive, and accurately tuned adult assistance does not always occur. A major variable here is the nature of the task or performance. If efficient production is needed, the adult will likely be more directive and less tolerant of such costly child errors as failing to correctly care for animals on which the family's survival is partly dependent (Wertsch, Minick and Arns 1984).

In joint productive activities of some importance, a child's participation may be relatively passive – observing the adult/expert carry out the task, and joining in to help at those points where the child's skill matches the task demands. This is the classic pattern of informal teaching that has been described in the anthropological literature for 50 years (Fortes 1938).

But when the development of independent child skill is defined as a goal, the pattern of assistance provided by the adult is more responsive, contingent, and patient. The adult graduates the assistance, responsive to the child's performance level: the more the child can do, the less the adult does (Wertsch *et al.* 1984).

This illuminates an important pedagogical principle. 'Assistance' offered at too high a level will disrupt child performance and is not effective teaching. Once independent skill has been achieved, 'assistance' becomes 'interference'. For this reason, our definition of teaching emphasizes that *teaching can be said to occur when assistance is offered at points in the ZPD at which performance requires assistance.* Careful assessment of the child's abilities, relative to the ZPD and the developmental level, is a constant requirement for the teacher. This becomes imperative when we remember that the processes of development are recursive.

Assisted performance: child, parent, and teacher

As common as assisted performance is in the interactions of parents and children, it is uncommon in those of teachers and students. Study after study has documented the absence in classrooms of this fundamental tool for the teaching of children: assistance provided by more capable others that is responsive to goal-directed activities.

The absence of assisted performance in schools is all the more remarkable because most teachers are members of the literate middle class, where researchers have most often found such interactions. Why is it that this adult–child pattern – no doubt a product of historical, evolutionary processes – is so seldom observed in the very setting where it would seem most appropriate? Such interactions can be found in every society, in the introduction of children to any task. But this basic method of human socialization has not generally diffused into schools. Why?

There are two basic reasons. First, to provide assistance in the ZPD, the assistor must be in close touch with the learner's relationship to the task. Sensitive and accurate assistance that challenges but does not dismay the learner cannot be achieved in the absence of information.

Opportunities for this knowledge, conditions in which the teacher can be sufficiently aware of the child's actual, inflight performing, simply are not available in classrooms organized, equipped, and staffed in the typical pattern. There are too many children for each teacher. And even if there is time to assess each child's ZPD for each task, more time is needed – time of interaction, for conversation, for joint activity between teachers and children. Occasionally, now and through history, these opportunities have existed: the classical Greek academies, Oxford and Cambridge, the individual tutorial, the private American school with classes of seven or less. But all involve a pupil-teacher ratio that exceeds the politicians' judgment of the taxpayers' purse. Public education is not likely to reorganize into classrooms of seven pupils each.

This does not make the case hopeless. Emerging instructional practices do offer some hope of increased opportunities for assisted performance: the increased use of small groups, maintenance of a positive classroom atmosphere that will increase independent task involvement of students, new materials and technology with which students can interact independent of the teacher.

There is a second reason that assisted performance has not diffused into the schools. Even when instructional practices allow for increased use of assisted performance, it will not necessarily appear as a regular feature of a teacher's activity. It may not be practiced even by those teachers who are from homes and communities where, outside of school, such interactions are commonplace. It will not necessarily be forthcoming from teachers who themselves provide assisted performance for their own children. Even with the benefits of modern instructional practice, there is still too large a gap between the conditions of home and school. Most parents do not need to be trained to assist performance; most teachers do.

REFERENCES

Baumrind, D. (1971) 'Current patterns of parental authority', *Developmental Psychology Monographs* 4: 99–103.

Bell, R. Q. (1979) 'Parent, child, and reciprocal influences', *American Psychologist* 34: 821–6.

Berk, L. E. (1986) 'Relationship of elementary school children's private speech to behavioral accompaniment to task, attention, and task performance', *Developmental Psychology* 22: 671–80.

Berk, L. E. and Garvin, R. (1984) 'Development of private speech among low-income Appalachian children', *Developmental Psychology* 20: 271–86.

Bernstein, L.E. (1981) 'Language as a product of dialogue', *Discourse Processes* 4: 117–47.

Bruner, J. S. (1966) *Toward a Theory of Instruction*, Cambridge, MA: Harvard University Press.

Bruner, J. S. (1973) 'Organization of early skilled action', *Child Development* 44: 1–11.

Bruner, J. S. (1983) *Child's Talk: Learning to Use Language*, New York: Norton.

Cazden, C. B. (1981) 'Performance before competence: Assistance to child discourse in the zone of proximal development', *Quarterly Newsletter of the Laboratory of Comparative Human Cognition* 3(1): 5–8.

Cross, T. G. (1977) 'Mothers' speech adjustments: The contribution of selected child listener variables', in C. E. Snow and C. A. Ferguson (eds) *Talking to Children: Language Input and Acquisition*, pp. 151–88, Cambridge: Cambridge University Press.

Diaz, R. M. (1986) 'The union of thought and language in children's private speech', *Quarterly Newsletter of the Laboratory of Comparative Human Cognition* 8(3): 90–7.

Elsasser, N. and John-Steiner, V. P. (1977) 'An interactionist approach to advancing literacy', *Harvard Educational Review* 47: 355–69.

Fischer, K. W. and Bullock, D. (1984) 'Cognitive development in school-aged children: Conclusions and new directions', in W. C. Collins (ed.) *Development During Middle Childhood: The Years from Six to Twelve*, pp. 70–146, Washington, DC: National Academy Press.

Fortes, M. (1938) 'Education in Taleland', *Africa 1*, 11(4): 14–74.

Gallimore, R., Dalton, S. and Tharp, R. G. (1986) 'Self-regulation and interactive teaching: The impact of teaching conditions on teachers' cognitive activity', *Elementary School Journal* 86(5): 613–31.

Gal'perin, P. (1969) 'Stages in the development of mental acts', in M. Cole and I. Malzman (eds) *A Handbook of Contemporary Soviet Psychology* pp. 249–73, New York: Basic Books.

Greenfield, P. M. (1984) 'A theory of the teacher in the learning activities of everyday life', in B. Rogoff and J. Lave (eds), *Everyday Cognition: Its Development in Social Contexts*, pp. 117–38, Cambridge, MA: Harvard University Press.

Griffin, P. and Cole, M. (1984) 'Current activity for the future: The Zo-ped', in B. Rogoff and J. V. Wertsch (eds) *Children's Learning in the 'Zone of Proximal Development' (New Directions for Child Development*, no. 23, pp. 45–64), San Francisco: Jossey-Bass.

Kohlberg, L., Yaeger, J. and Hjertholm, E. (1968) 'Private speech: Four studies and a review of theories', *Child Development* 39: 691–736.

Leont'ev, A. N. (1981) 'The problem of activity in psychology', in J. V. Wertsch (ed.) *The Concept of Activity in Soviet Psychology*, pp. 37–71, Armonk, NY: M. E. Sharpe.

McNamee, G. D. (1979) 'The social interaction origins of narrative skills', *Quarterly Newsletter of the Laboratory of Comparative Human Cognition* 1(4): 63–8.

Meichenbaum, D. (1977) *Cognitive Behavior Modification: An Integrative*

Approach, New York: Plenum Press.

Ochs, E. (1982) 'Talking to children in western Samoa', *Language in Society* 11: 77–104.

Roberts, R. N. (1979) 'Private speech in academic problem-solving. A naturalistic perspective', in G. Zivin (ed.) *The Development of Self-regulation through Private Speech*, pp. 295–323, New York: Wiley.

Roberts, R. N. and Mullis, M. (1980) 'A component analysis of self-instructional training', paper presented at the annual convention of the Western Psychological Association, Honolulu.

Roberts, R. N. and Tharp, R. G. (1980) 'A naturalistic study of children's self-directed speech in academic problem-solving', *Cognitive Research and Therapy* 4: 341–53.

Rogoff, B. (1982) 'Integrating context and cognitive development', in M. E. and A. L. Brown (eds) *Advances in Developmental Psychology*, vol. 2, pp. 125–70, Hillsdale, NJ: Lawrence Erlbaum Associates.

Rogoff, B. (1986) 'Adult assistance of children's learning', in T. E. Raphael (ed.) *The Contexts of School-based Literacy*, pp. 27–40, New York: Random House.

Rogoff, B. and Gardener, W. (1984) 'Adult guidance of cognitive development', in B. Rogoff and J. Lave (eds), *Everyday Cognition: Its Development in Social Contexts*, pp. 95–116, Cambridge, MA: Harvard University Press.

Rogoff, B., Malkin, C. and Gilbride, K. (1984) 'Interaction with babies as guidance in development', in B. Rogoff and J. V. Wertsch (eds) *Children's Learning in the 'Zone of Proximal Development'*, (*New Directions for Child Development*, no. 23, pp. 30–44), San Francisco: Jossey-Bass.

Rogoff, B. and Wertsch, J. (eds) (1984) *Children's Learning in the 'Zone of Proximal Development'*, (*New Directions for Child Development*, no. 23,) San Francisco: Jossey-Bass.

Saxe, G. B., Gearhart, M. and Guberman, S. R. (1984) 'The social organization of early number development', in B. Rogoff and J. V. Wertsch (eds) *Children's Learning in the 'Zone of Proximal Development'* (*New Directions for Child Development*, no. 23, pp. 19–30), San Francisco: Jossey-Bass.

Tharp, R. G. and Gallimore, R. (1976) 'The uses and limits of social reinforcement and industriousness for learning to read' (technical report no. 60), Honolulu: Kamehameha Schools/Bishop Estate, Kamehameha Early Education Program.

Tharp, R. G., Gallimore, R. and Calkins, R. P. (1984) 'On the relationships between self-control and control by others', *Advances en Psicologia Clinical Latinamericano* 3: 45–58.

Vygotsky, L. S. (1956) *Izbrannie psibhologicheskie issledovania* (selected psychological research), Moscow: Izdatel'stvo Akadamii Pedagogicheskikh Nauk.

Vygotsky, L. S. (1978) *Mind in Society: The development of Higher Psychological Processes*, in M. Cole, V. John-Steiner, S. Scribner and E. Souberman (eds and trans.), Cambridge, MA: Harvard University Press.

Vygotsky, L. S. (1987) *Collected Works of L. S. Vygotsky: vol. 1: Problems of General Psychology* (trans. N. Minick; series eds Robert W. Reiber and Aaron S. Carton), New York: Plenum Press. (Original work published in 1982 in Russian.)

Watson, D. R. and Tharp, R. G. (1988) *Self-directed Behavior* (fifth edn), Monterey, CA: Brooks/Cole.

Wertsch, J. V. (1978) 'Adult–child interaction and the roots of metacognition', *Quarterly Newsletter of the Laboratory of Comparative Human Cognition* 2(1): 15–18.

Wertsch, J. V. (1979) 'From social interaction to higher psychological process: A clarification and application of Vygotsky's theory, *Human Development* 22: 1–22.

Wertsch, J. V. (1981) *The Concept of Activity in Soviet Psychology*, Armonk, NE: M. E. Sharpe.

Wertsch, J. V. (ed.) (1985) *Vygotsky and the Social Formation of Mind*, Cambridge, MA: Harvard University Press.

Wertsch, J. V., Minick, N. and Arns, F. A. (1984) 'The creation of context in joint problem-solving', in B. Rogoff and J. Lave (eds) *Everyday Cognition: Its Development in Social Contexts*, pp. 151–71, Cambridge, MA: Harvard University Press.

Wertsch, J. V. and Schneider, P. J. (1979) 'Variations of adults' directives to children in a problem solving situation', unpublished manuscript, Evanston, IL: Northwestern University.

Wertsch, J. V. and Stone, C. A. (1985) 'The concept of internalization in Vygotsky's account of the genesis of higher mental functions', in J. V. Wertsch (ed.) *Culture, Communication and Cognition: Vygotskian Perspectives*, pp. 162–79, New York: Cambridge University Press.

Wood, D. J., Bruner, J. S. and Ross, G. (1976) 'The role of tutoring in problem solving', *Journal of Child Psychology and Psychiatry* 17(2): 89–100.

Part two

Teaching and learning interactions

Introduction

It is perhaps a caricature of Piaget's view to say that he envisaged children as lone scientists, grappling single-handedly with the secrets of nature, rediscovering knowledge afresh with each generation. But the emphasis which he placed upon individual activity and discovery tended to marginalize any concern with the processes of social 'reproduction' or transmission of knowledge from one generation to the next. However, the greater part of the child's task might reasonably be described as discovering *what other people already know*.

The chapters which make up this second part of the volume address the processes by which this is achieved. All are influenced by the Vygotskian perspective introduced in Part one. Rogoff (Chapter 5) focuses on 'spontaneous' interactions, especially parent–child interactions, in the early years and on the ways in which these provide for the construction of joint or shared understandings. Wood (Chapter 6) describes a more experimental approach to the study of teaching–learning interactions. He compares and contrasts the informal teaching which typically goes on in the home and the more formal and 'contrived' teaching which goes on in the school. Wood's emphasis on the contingency of the teacher's behaviour upon that of the learner reflects a more general feature of this approach – namely that it concentrates on the direct interpersonal interactions between a teacher and an individual learner. The article which follows, by Edwards and Mercer (Chapter 7), more explicitly recognizes that teachers are characteristically dealing with children in classroom groups, and addresses the question of how the forms of discourse adopted in such settings allow 'common knowledge' to be built up.

The final chapter in this section, by Light and Perret-Clermont (Chapter 8), examines the productivity of interactions *between learners* in shaping their understanding of a task. In fact the sources of this work are Piagetian rather than Vygotskian: in his early work at least, Piaget saw peer conflict as a significant factor in overcoming children's intellectual egocentrism. Light and Perret-Clermont argue, however, that the resulting experimental demonstrations may tell us less about the role of conflict than about how social norms and expectations influence children's cognitive responses.

5 The joint socialization of development by young children and adults*

Barbara Rogoff
Source: Lewis M, and Feinman, S. (eds) (1989) *Social Influences and Behaviour*, New York: Plenum.

The young child is often thought of as a little scientist exploring the world and discovering the principles of its operation. We often forget that while the scientist is working on the border of human knowledge and is finding out things that nobody yet knows, the child is finding out precisely what everybody already knows.

(Newman 1982: 26) [. . .]

INTRODUCTION

First to be considered is how such joint involvement can be conceptualized. Then the main part of the chapter describes features of adult–child interactions as well as non-interactive arrangements made between adults and children, in order to examine differing aspects of the joint socialization of children's development. Finally, cultural variations and universals in the goals and means used by young children and adults that may bring about the child's entry into skilled participation in the culture are addressed.

The chapter builds on Vygotsky's concept of the *zone of proximal development*, in which child development is viewed as a social activity with children participating in activities beyond their competence through the assistance of adults or more experienced peers. In social interaction in the zone of proximal development, children are able to participate in activities that are beyond their capabilities when working independently. Through such social guidance, children are presumed to gradually internalize the skills that were practiced with adult support so that they can be performed independently (Vygotsky 1978; Wertsch 1979). Thus the zone of proximal development is a

*The issues raised in this chapter are more fully explored in Rogoff, B. (1990) *Apprenticeship in Thinking: Cognitive Development in Social Context*, New York: Oxford University Press.

dynamic region of sensitivity to learning experiences in which children develop, guided by social interaction.

In Vygotskian theory, children's interaction within the zone of proximal development is part of a larger sociocultural theory that places human skills and achievements in the context of the technologies, practices, and values available through cultural history. These sociocultural technologies and skills include inventions such as literacy, mathematics, mnemonic skills, and approaches to problem-solving and reasoning. In effect, cultural inventions channel the skills of each generation, with individual development mediated by the guidance of people who are more skilled in their use. Children are introduced to the culture through the guidance of its more experienced members (Laboratory of Comparative Human Cognition 1983; Rogoff 1982; Rogoff, Gauvain and Ellis 1984; Vygotsky 1978).

Cole (1981) suggests that the zone of proximal development is where culture and cognition meet. It is in this sensitive zone that variations in social interaction may be expected to yield adaptations of individuals to their specific cultural surroundings. Their adaptations will simultaneously show features that are similar across many cultural contexts, based on cross-cultural commonalities in the processes of communication and of child development, and variations according to the specific goals and means available for appropriate development in each culture.

The chapter extends the concept of zone of proximal development by stressing the *interrelatedness* of children's and adults' roles, in a process of *guided participation*. The thesis is that the rapid development of young children into socialized participants in society is accomplished through a finely tuned combination of children's skills and the guidance of adults (or older children). The elaboration presented in this chapter, while consistent with the Vygotskian approach, differs in its emphasis on the role of children as active participants in their own socialization. They do not simply receive the guidance of adults, they seek, structure, and even demand the assistance of those around them in learning how to solve problems of all kinds. The aim of this chapter is to stress the complementary roles of children and adults in fostering children's development.

Young children appear to come equipped with ways of ensuring proximity and involvement with more experienced members of society, and of becoming involved with their physical and cultural surroundings. The infants' strategies (if one ignores connotations of intentionality) appear similar to those appropriate for anyone learning in an unfamiliar culture: stay near a trusted guide, watch the guide's activities and get involved when possible, and attend to any instruction the guide provides.

Infants' strategies are complemented by features of adult–child interaction that are well adapted to the gradual immersion of children in the skills and beliefs of the society. Adults arrange the occurrence of children's activities and facilitate learning by regulating the difficulty of the tasks and by modelling mature performance during joint participation in activities. While adults may rarely regard themselves as explicitly teaching infants or young children, they routinely adjust their interaction and structure children's environments and activities in ways consistent with providing support for their learning.

In elaborating the concept of the zone of proximal development, Rogoff and Gardner (1984) emphasized that while more experienced people play an important role in socialization, this role is meshed with the efforts of children to learn and develop. Rogoff (1986) proposed that guided participation with school-children involves adults leading children through the process of solving a problem, and the child participating at a comfortable but slightly challenging level:

> Adults provide guidance in cognitive development through the arrangement of appropriate materials and tasks for children, as well as through tacit and explicit instruction occurring as adults and children participate together in activities. Adults' greater knowledge and skill allow them to assist children in translating familiar information to apply to a new problem, and to structure the problem so that the child can work on manageable subgoals. The effectiveness of adults in structuring situations for children's learning is matched by children's eagerness and involvement in managing their own learning experiences. Children put themselves in a position to observe what is going on; they involve themselves in the ongoing activity; they influence the activities in which they participate; and they demand some involvement with the adults who serve as their guides for socialization into the culture that they are learning. Together, children and adults choose learning situations and calibrate the child's level of participation so that the child is comfortably challenged.

> (Rogoff 1986: 38)

This chapter extends these ideas by focusing on processes of guided participation with younger children. The themes include how adults facilitate the development of infants and toddlers, how children themselves channel their own development and the assistance they receive, and similarities and variations in the processes of social guidance that may occur in varying cultures. First, however, it is necessary to examine the notion of the interrelatedness of the individual child's role and that of the social context – including the adults and older children that provide guidance.

MUTUALITY OF INDIVIDUAL EFFORT AND SOCIAL FACILITATION

This section examines alternative conceptualizations of how mutual involvement of adults and children may contribute to development. It has been common in developmental psychology to focus attention alternatively on the contribution of either partner, in examining how adults teach children, or how children develop independently. This chapter argues for the necessity of considering the mutual involvement of children and the social world in understanding child development. But such mutual involvement could be understood in different ways. In order to explore ways of conceptualizing the mutual roles of adults and children in fostering children's development, it is useful to draw a relationship with the parallel question of nature and nurture, which has long interested psychologists. By analogy, we may regard the role of the child as 'nature' and the role of social partners as 'nurture'.

The history of psychology has long pitted nature against nurture, with questions of how much of development should be credited to one and how much to the other. This traditional view places nature and nurture in opposition. Most developmentalists, as one reads in early chapters of introductory texts, are no longer trying to figure out if development is 'more nature' or 'more nurture'. Instead, they view nature and nurture as interacting to produce development: development does not occur solely through individual effort or preprogramming, nor does it occur entirely under the direction of the environment.

However, the notion of interaction often involves an assumption that the interacting entities are separable (*see* Rogoff 1982). In other words, nature and nurture in such a view can be regarded as independent influences – definable in terms not involving each other – that happen to co-occur.

In contrast to the idea that nature and nurture are separate but interacting influences on development, the present chapter is built on the premiss that nature and nurture (i.e. the child and the social world) are not separable. They are mutually involved to an extent that precludes regarding them as independently definable. In this view, development is made up of both individual efforts or tendencies and the larger sociocultural context in which the individual is embedded and has been since before conception. Thus biology and culture are not viewed as alternative influences but as aspects of a system in which individuals develop.

This stance is reflected in Vygotsky's efforts (Wertsch 1985) to study development in terms of four interrelated levels. The level with which developmental psychologists traditionally deal is termed ontogenetic development – changes in thinking and behaviour associated with age. But this is merely a grain of analysis differing from the other three: phylogenetic development is the slowly changing species history that leaves a legacy for the individual in the form of genes. Sociocultural development is the changing cultural history that leaves a legacy for the individual in the form of technologies such as literacy, number systems, and computers, as well as value systems, scripts, and norms for the handling of situations met by the individual. Microgenetic development is the moment-to-moment learning by individuals in particular problem contexts, built upon the individual's genetic and sociocultural background. In this system, the roles of the individual and the social world are seen as interrelated in the levels of analysis reflecting learning, ontogenetic development phylogenetic development, and sociohistorical development.

A similar concept of embeddedness of nature and nurture is found in Piaget's work. As Furth (1974) explains, contrary to popular belief, Piaget's theory does not stress the importance of nature. Rather, the individual's development in Piagetian theory is based on the species-typical genetic background *and* the species-typical environment, which together form the basis of the individual's effort to construct an understanding of reality. It should be noted that despite the theoretical adherence of both Vygotsky and Piaget to the idea that nature and nurture are inseparable supports for individual development, both theorists chose to emphasize one or the other aspect for further elaboration in their theories. Thus, Piaget nodded to the role of social arrangements of the environment – and variations in the species environment – while elaborating upon the individual's independent construction of a notion of the world. Vygotsky, on the other hand, allowed an important role for the individual's active efforts in becoming a socialized but stressed the sociocultural arrangements that facilitate the individual's socialization. Vygotsky suggested that rather than deriving explanations of psychological activity from the individual's characteristics plus secondary social influences, psychologists should focus on the social unit of the activity and regard individual functioning as derived from that.

The present chapter attempts to keep the roles of both the individual and the social environment in focus, to acknowledge that they build integrally on each other. This perspective is consistent with other work on socialization in the early years (Brazelton 1982; Papousek, Papousek, and Bornstein 1985; Schaffer 1984). Wartofsky (1984) argues for the importance of keeping both angles in view at once – that children are embedded in a social world and that children are active participants in their own development:

> The child is *not* a self-contained homunculus, radiating outward in development from some fixed configuration of traits, dispositions, or preformed potencies; and . . . the world, in turn, is not some eternal and objective network of causal factors converging on the neonate to shape an unresisting, passive blob to its external, pregiven structures. To put this positively: the child is an agent in its own *and* the world's construction, but one whose agency develops in the context of an ineluctably social and historical praxis, which includes both the constraints and potentialities of nature and the actions of other agents. Nurture, in short, is both given *and* taken; and so is Nature.
>
> (Wartofsky 1984: 188)

SOCIAL FACILITATION OF INDIVIDUAL DEVELOPMENT

Working from observations of adults instructing children aged 6 to 9 years, Rogoff and Gardner (1984) proposed that guided participation involves the following activities:

1 providing a bridge between familiar skills or information and those needed to solve a new problem,
2 arranging and structuring problem-solving, and
3 gradually transferring the responsibility for managing problem-solving to the child.

These activities seem relevant for the guidance of younger children as well. This section elaborates on these three features of adults' and young children's arrangements for socialization and development. It stresses the entwinement of adults' and children's activities, the active role of both participants, and the possibility that teaching and learning can occur tacitly (as well as explicitly) in the arrangements and interaction between adults and young children.

The end of this chapter considers cross-cultural universals and variations, but until then, the terms 'adult' and 'child' refer to the adults and children who have been observed in North American and Western European research – largely middle-class and English-speaking.

Providing bridges between familiar skills or information and those needed in novel situations

Adults help young children find the connections between what they already know and what is necessary to handle a new situation (D'Andrade 1981; Erickson 1982). For older children this may involve specifying exactly how the new situation resembles the old. For example, in a classification task (Rogoff and Gardner 1984), some mothers made comments such as 'You need to put the things together that go together, just like on Sesame Street when they say "three of these things belong together".'

For very young children, the bridging role of adults involves assisting children in understanding how to act in new situations by provision of emotional cues regarding the nature of the situation, nonverbal models of how to behave, verbal and nonverbal interpretations of behaviour and events, and verbal labels to classify objects and events. All of these adult activities are coupled with young children's efforts (intentional or not) to pick up information about the nature of situations and their caregivers' interpretations.

Emotional and nonverbal communication

From the first year of life, children look to adults to interpret situations that are ambiguous from the child's point of view, in a process termed *social referencing* (Feinman 1982; Gunnar and Stone 1984). Interpretations offered by adults inform infants about the appropriate approach to take to a new situation. For example, if a child is crawling toward its mother and reaches what appears to be a drop-off, the child searches the mother's face for cues regarding the safety of the situation. If the mother's emotional expression indicates fear, the child does not proceed, but if the mother has an encouraging expression, the child carefully crawls across clear glass suspended a foot above what appears to be the floor (Score *et al.* 1985).

Young children are so skilled in obtaining information from glances, winces, and mood that one of the greatest challenges of testing preschoolers is to avoid nonverbal actions that may be construed as cues. Children press for and use such cues even when given standardized intelligence tests (Mehan 1976).

Such referencing is facilitated by the ability that appears by 8 to 12 months of age to obtain information from the direction in which caregivers point and gaze (Bruner 1983; Butterworth and Cochran

1980). The development of such skill is supported by the efforts of mothers to regulate joint attention during the first year. If an infant appears not to understand a pointing gesture, mothers facilitate the baby's comprehension by touching the indicated object (Lempers 1979). As early as 3 months of infants' age, mothers attempt to achieve joint reference by introducing an object between themselves and the baby as a target for joint attention, using a characteristic intonation and shaking the object (Bruner 1983). From ages 6 to 18 months, infants are more than four times as likely to engage in joint attention when interacting with their mothers as when interacting with a peer (Bakeman and Adamson 1984). Bakeman and Adamson attribute this pattern to the mother's socialization of reference, 'embedding it within the interpersonal sphere well before infants can structure this integration by themselves' (p.1,288). Thus the infant's use of social referencing builds on earlier skills and social guidance, providing more advanced means to gather information regarding their mothers' (and others') interpretations of new situations.

Mothers and other adults may at times intentionally attempt to communicate a particular understanding of a new situation through managing their emotional and nonverbal communication. For example, at a doctor's office a mother may try to mask her apprehension when her baby is receiving an injection, in order to minimize the baby's reaction to the situation. Or parental management of cues may enter into instruction in potentially frightening situations, as suggested in the following advice to parents on teaching 3-week-old babies to swim in the bathtub:

> Your attitude toward water is important. An infant who sees her mother wince in terror every time she floats in deep water is not going to have a very confident picture of the strange situation. Since panic is the single most deadly factor in water, parents should be acutely aware of their responsibility in teaching their child a healthy respect for water. . . . If you show enjoyment of the water, she will imitate your excitement and pleasure. . . . Lift your baby into the water, and rest her on your bent knees, facing you. Dip your hands into the water, and pat your baby's body to help her adjust to the water temperature. Talk and smile constantly throughout the entire session. Gradually lower your knees until the baby is completely submerged in the water, head resting comfortably on your knees, body on your thighs. Take this part slowly, allowing enough time for your baby to become acquainted with the water.
>
> (Poe 1982: 12, 20)

Such intentional communication of how to interpret a situation may be rare. But in a less self-conscious fashion, adults handling babies seem almost inevitably to provide interpretation for the baby's actions, their own actions, and events in the environment (Shotter and Newson 1982). For example, mothers may respond to the baby's attempts to push an approaching spoon away with a running commentary such as 'You getting full? Try another bite, Mama wants you to grow up big and strong.' For babies learning to eat from a spoon, adults frequently provide supplementary cues regarding the appropriate action for the child – they can be observed to open their own mouths wide at the time the baby is to do the same (Valsiner 1984). To ensure a happy response to a potentially startling event, adults make an exaggerated face of surprise and enjoyment, for example, commenting 'isn't that funny'? when concerned that a Jack-in-the-box might startle a baby (Rogoff, Malkin, and Gilbride 1984).

Words as a cultural system for bridging

In addition to such interpretive comments and actions, the provision of a language system teaches children the meanings and distinctions important in their culture. Labels categorize objects and events in ways specific to the language of the child's culture. Roger Brown pointed out this function of language learning in his comments about the Original Word Game:

The Original Word Game is the operation of linguistic reference in first language learning. At least two people are required: one who knows the language (the tutor) and one who is learning (the player). In outline form the movements of the game are very simple. The tutor names things in accordance with the semantic custom of his community. The player forms hypotheses about the categorical nature of the things named. He tests his hypotheses by trying to name new things correctly. The tutor compares the player's utterances with his own anticipations of such utterances and, in this way, checks the accuracy of fit between his own categories and those of the player. He improves the fit by correction. In concrete terms the tutor says 'dog' whenever a dog appears. The player notes the phonemic equivalence of these utterances, forms a hypothesis about the non-linguistic category that elicits this kind of utterance and then tries naming a few dogs himself. . . . In learning referents and names the player of the Original Word Game prepares himself to receive the science, the rules of thumb, the prejudices, the total expectancies of his society.

(Brown 1958: 194, 228)

Clearly, the Original Word Game requires two active partners. Language development is facilitated by social involvement as well as deriving from the child's natural propensity to learn language. In this view, Chomsky's Language Acquisition Device cooperates with Bruner's Language Acquisition Support System, which 'frames or structures the input of language and interaction to the child's Language Acquisition Device in a manner to "make the system function" ' (Bruner 1983: 19). Consistent with this emphasis on the social supports for language acquisition are Moerk's (1983) careful analyses of maternal language input to Roger Brown's subject Eve. Eve's mother provided sufficiently rich and frequent input, with semantic and linguistic redundancy, and contingent instructional relationships between mother's and child's utterances, for her framing of Eve's language development to be considered an important contribution to the child's efforts to learn language.

The process of communication, itself a social activity, can be regarded as the bridge between one understanding of a situation and another. For an adult and child to communicate successfully, the adult must search for common reference points, translating the adult's understanding of the situation into a form that is within the child's grasp (Rogoff 1986; Wertsch 1984). Adults insert their interaction into the ongoing activity of an infant, waiting for the infant to be in the appropriate state and providing verbal and nonverbal commentary on the object or event to which the baby is already attending (Kaye 1982; Schaffer 1984).

Adjustment of the adult's perspective in the service of communication is also apparent in the way adults occasionally misclassify an atypical exemplar of a category in order to avoid confusing toddlers about the basic nature of the category. For example, adults may agree that a whale is a fish, or that an electric outlet is 'hot'. Bruner (1983, based on Deutsch and Pechmann) suggests that the fact that a physicist mother is unlikely to share an identical concept of 'electricity' with her 4-year-old does not matter as long as their shared meaning is sufficient to allow their conversation about shocks to continue. This effort to communicate draws the child into a more mature understanding that is linked to what the child already knows. In the process of communicating, adults tie new situations to more familiar ones, drawing connections from the familiar to the novel through the adult's verbal and nonverbal interpretation.

Structuring situations for child involvement

Choice and structuring of situations

Adults frequently make arrangements for children, selecting activities and materials they consider appropriate for children at that age or interest level (Laboratory of Comparative Human Cognition 1983; Valsiner 1984). Such choices may frequently be made without the intention of providing a specific learning experience, but may also be designed explicitly for the socialization or education of the child. Whiting (1980) cogently states the responsibility of parents and other adults for arranging children's learning environments:

> The power of parents and other agents of socialization is in their assignment of children to specific settings. Whether it is caring for an infant sibling, working around the house in the company of adult females, working on the farm with adults and siblings, playing outside with neighbourhood children, hunting with adult males, or attending school with age mates, the daily assignment of a child to one or another of these settings has important consequences on the development of habits of interpersonal behavior, consequences that may not be recognized by the socializers who make the assignments.
>
> (Whiting 1980: 111)

By making such choices and adjusting tasks and materials to children's competence and needs, adults tacitly guide children's development. Parents designate some objects as appropriate for children, following the recommendations of toy manufacturers and cultural lore. For example, children of different ages are presented with books adjusted to their interests and skills: cardboard or plastic picture books, paper picture books with a few words, books with pictures and text, books with pure text. Adults determine the activities in which children's participation is allowed or discouraged, such as chores, parental work and recreational activities, television shows, the birth of a sibling, or the death of a grandparent. Adults arrange the social environment to promote or avoid certain relationships, by assigning child care to a sibling, grandparent, or baby sitter, and encouraging or discouraging particular playmates.

It would be misleading to consider the choice of activities to be the sole responsibility of adults. Children are very active in directing adults towards desirable or away from undesirable activities. Children's preferences are clear in their refusal to enter some activities, and their insistence on others. Their attempts to communicate desire for involvement in specific activities begins during the last half of the first year of life. Rogoff, Malkin, and Gilbride (1984) cite an example of a 9-month-old attempting to get an adult to work a Jack-in-the-box. The baby began by pushing the box across the floor toward the adult, and patted the top of the box when the adult asked 'What'? The adult responded to the baby's actions as a request, and asked 'Should we make Jack come out?' The adult tried to get the baby to turn the handle (an action too difficult for this 9-month-old); and the baby responded with a series of frustrated yet determined moves – whining and fumbling with the box – that expressed his desire to have the box opened. Finally the adult began to turn the handle and the baby immediately relaxed. The adult asked sympathetically, 'Is that what you wanted?' and the baby stared at the handle and let out a big sigh of relief.

Structuring situations through division of responsibility

In addition to arranging the structuring learning activities by providing access and regulating the difficulty of tasks, adults structure children's involvement in learning situations by handling more difficult aspects of the task themselves and organizing the child's involvement with the more manageable aspects of the activity. In engaging the child in an appropriate handling of the situation, the adult creates a 'scaffolded' or supported situation in which the child can extend current skills and knowledge to a higher level of competence (Wertsch 1979; Wood, Bruner and Ross 1976). Note that while the term scaffold could imply a rigid structure or one that does not involve the child, most users of the term include notions of continual revisions of scaffolding to respond to children's advancements. Bruner (1983) characterizes scaffolding in language development as the adult acting on a motto of 'where before there was a spectator, let there now be a participant' (p. 60).

An example of adult support is provided by the way adults structure children's developing narration skills by asking appropriate questions to organize children's stories or accounts (McNamee 1980). If the child stops short or leaves out crucial information, the adult prompts, 'What happened next?' or 'Who else was there?' Such questions implicitly provide children with the cues they need to internalize as they develop narration skills. Adults' questions fill in the outline of what narratives involve. Building on Bruner's perspective, McNamee (1980) suggests that 'if story schemas exist for young children, they hover in the air between adults and children as they converse' (p. 6).

Adults interacting with children may structure tasks by determining the problem to be solved, the goal, and how the goal can be segmented into manageable subgoals. For example, the joint clean-up of a toddler's room may require the adult (even with a co-operative toddler) to define the goal of cleaning up the room, to segment the task into subgoals such as picking up dirty clothes and putting toys in their proper places, and to determine the specifics of each subgoal (e.g. can you find all the blocks and put them in the box?). The adult's structuring of the problem may be tailored to the child's level of skill. With a novice, the adult may take responsibility for managing the subgoals as well as making sure the overall goal is met. A more experienced child may take responsibility for the subgoals, and eventually for the whole task. Such changes in the division of responsibility are an important feature of guided participation, in which the child becomes increasingly responsible for managing the situation as skills increase.

Transfer of responsibility for managing situations

Children take on increasing responsibility for managing situations over the course of years as well as through the process of becoming familiar with a particular task. Effective transfer of responsibility for managing a situation requires adults to be sensitive to children's competence in particular tasks so that responsibility is given when the child is able to handle it. Similarly, such decisions require knowledge (again, it may be tacit) of what skills and knowledge are needed in order to be able to independently handle that situation, and are facilitated by knowledge of the course of development of skill in handling that particular situation. In addition to adults' adjustment of support according to children's skills, children are active in arranging for participation at an appropriate level.

Adults' adjustment of support

Scaffolding requires revision as the child gains in understanding. One form of scaffolding involves providing sufficient redundancy in messages so that if a child does not understand one aspect of the communication, other forms are available to make the meaning clear. As children develop greater understanding, adults and older children adjust the level of scaffolding necessary to support the young child's learning and performance by reducing the level of redundancy.

For example, mothers assisting preschoolers in a counting task adjusted the level of their assistance to children's correctness (Saxe, Gearhart, and Guberman 1984). When children made accurate counts, mothers shifted their directives to a more superordinate level in the task structure so that children had more responsibility for determining the subgoals regarding how to obtain one-to-one correspondence, and when children counted inaccurately, mothers shifted to a subordinate level in the task structure, taking over management of the subgoals themselves.

In early parent–child communication, adults facilitate infants' language acquisition by supporting verbal messages with enough redundant nonverbal information to ensure understanding (Greenfield 1984). As infants become able to comprehend verbal messages, adults decrease the nonverbal information. Messer (1980) observed that maternal discourse was organized in episodes referring to specific objects, and within the episodes the mothers provided great redundancy regarding which thing was the object of reference. This organization of maternal speech was greatest for younger children, again suggesting that the structure of maternal communication provides a continually modified scaffold for learning.

Researchers in pre-linguistic development have noted that adults carry on conversations with infants in which the adult's role as conversational partner is adjusted to the baby's repertoire:

> The mothers work to maintain a conversation despite the inadequacies of their conversational partners. At first they accept burps, yawns, and coughs as well as laughs and coos — but not arm-waving or head movements — as the baby's turn. They fill in for the babies by asking and answering their own questions, and by phrasing questions so that a minimal response can be treated as a reply. Then by seven months the babies become considerably more active partners, and the mothers no longer accept all the baby's vocalizations, only vocalic or consonantal babbles. As the mother raises the ante, the child's development proceeds.
>
> (Cazden 1979: 11)

Caregivers simplify their own language, they repeat and expand upon infants' contributions, and they provide visual supports and redundant information to assist an infant's understanding (Bruner 1981, 1983; Hoff-Ginsberg and Shatz 1982; Messer 1980; Moerk 1983; Snow 1977; Zukow, Reilly, and Greenfield 1982). Mothers report that their conversations with 2-year-olds help the children learn to talk (Miller 1979).

The modification of discourse by adults speaking to infants and young children may provide support for children's conversation and language learning. In the earliest months, the restriction of parental baby talk to a small number of melodic contours may enable infants to abstract vocal prototypes (Papousek, Papousek, and Bornstein 1985).

Caregivers make the context of statements explicit by clarifying their own and the child's intentions and specifying the referents of a statement (Ochs 1979). Such provision of background knowledge is reduced as children gain language facility. The structure of mother—child discourse allows children to participate in conversations that are beyond their competence in discourse and may help children advance their skills (Bernstein 1981). Some evidence regarding the impact of adult language input on children's language development is discussed in a later section on the influence of guided participation.

Children's role in arranging participation

While it is certainly true that adults carry great responsibility in socialization – they are more knowledgeable and have authority – children are also very active in gaining skill through social interaction. Children participate by indicating their readiness for greater responsibility or even by managing the transfer of information. Adults do not simply solve problems and report their solutions, nor do children passively observe adults and extract the relevant information spontaneously. An adult assesses a child's current understanding of the material and adjusts the scaffolding to support the child's developing skill, while the child simultaneously adjusts the pace of instruction and guides the adult in constructing the scaffold.

An example of an infant seeking a more active role is found in Rogoff, Malkin, and Gilbride's (1984) description of an adult and a 12-month-old working a Jack-in-a-box together. Initially, the adult performed all aspects of manipulating the toy (turning the handle to get the bunny out of the box, and pushing the bunny back into the box), while the baby concentrated solemnly on the actions. In the second episode of play with the Jack-in-a-box, the baby attempted to push the bunny back in the box, and the adult encouraged, 'close it up', while helping the baby push the lid down. In the third episode, the baby began to participate in cranking the handle, and in the fourth episode the baby seemed to demand some independence in managing the handle while the adult encouraged this involvement:

The baby grabbed the box on its sides and shoved it back and forth on the tray, and the adult paused in cranking. The baby looked at the crank and slowly reached for it, confirming the adult's interpretation that he had been demanding a turn. Putting the baby's hand on the crank and turning the crank, the adult said, 'Okay now, you do it'.

(Rogoff *et al.* 1984: 40-1)

Over the course of this interaction, the baby eventually participated in winding the handle, pushing the bunny back in the box, and closing the box, while the adult supported the baby's involvement by winding the handle to near the end of the cycle and assisting the baby in holding the lid down on the springy bunny.

Negotiations regarding level of participation and the nature of the activity can be managed by babies through eye contact, joint attention, smiles or cries, and posture changes. Babies can indicate interest by looking eagerly toward an object or event, leaning forward and gesturing toward the object or event with arms, and making enthused grunts. In a negative situation, or if the adult seems not to understand the baby's cues, the baby's activity may change from joint attention to listlessness, then gaze aversion, and finally to turning entirely away. Kaye (1977) found that 6-month-old infants' actions, especially gaze aversion, controlled their mothers' efforts to teach them to reach around a barrier.

In addition to their contribution to managing joint interaction, young children influence their participation in adults' ongoing activities that may not have interaction with the child as a focus. Children's attempts to learn from adult activities may go unnoticed by parents, who are likely to view children's attempts to 'help' or be involved in adult activities as just an inevitable aspect of childhood. During the first year, babies seem to be automatically interested in whatever object an adult is handling, and try to grasp it themselves. An adult's manipulation of a toy facilitates contact by 11- to 13-month-olds with the same toy, with markedly similar actions performed on the toy (Eckerman, Whatley, and McGhee 1979). Toddlers follow their parents around the house, trying to be involved in ongoing activities. Rheingold (1982) found that children aged 18 to 30 months spontaneously and energetically helped their parents or a stranger in the majority of the household chores that the adults performed in a laboratory or home setting. Many of the parents reported that they commonly circumvented their child's efforts to participate at home by trying to do chores while the child was napping, to avoid the child's 'interference'.

The propensity to seek proximity to and involvement with adults assists infants and toddlers in acquiring information about the environment and about the activities of the person who is followed (Hay 1980). Their eagerness to be involved may force a busy parent to give them some role in activities, allowing them to stir the batter, put tape on the present, carry the napkins to the table, help turn the screwdriver, and so on.

In such activities, the adult's and child's roles are likely to fit the characteristics of guided participation. For pragmatic reasons, the adult may try to keep the child from getting involved in an aspect of the activity that is too far beyond the child's skill, e.g., to avoid broken eggs, torn wrapping paper, or damage to the child or to objects. Nevertheless, the child is likely not to be satisfied with an aspect of the job that is too simple, and will insist on greater involvement if given an obvious make-work role. Thus even in interaction with a reluctant adult, the adult and child together may contribute to the child's learning through guided participation.

An example of how a child's insistence on involvement may be instrumental is provided by my daughter, who at age 3½ years was interested in sewing. I was getting ready to leave the house, and noticed that a run had started in the foot of my stocking. My daughter volunteered to help sew the run, but I was in a hurry and tried to avoid her involvement by explaining that I did not want the needle to jab my foot. I began to sew, but could hardly see where I was sewing because my daughter's head was in the way, peering at the sewing. Soon she suggested that I could put the needle into the stocking and she would pull it through, thus avoiding sticking my foot. I agreed and we followed this division of labor for a number of stitches. When I absent-mindedly handed my daughter the needle rather than starting a stitch, she gently pressed my hand back toward my foot, and grinned when I glanced at her, realizing the error. The same child at 4 years of age asked me, as we worked in the kitchen, 'Can I help you with the can opener by holding onto your hand while you do it? . . . That's how I learn'. These incidents illustrate the eagerness with which children approach the possibility of learning through involvement with adult activities, as well as their active role in the 'instruction'. The child arranges for participation in the activity, and the adult tacitly (sometimes unwillingly) provides access and information.

Does guidance participation influence learning and development?

Thus far, I have suggested that the integrated role of children seeking involvement and structuring their participation, and of adults providing information and arranging for children's activities, may in part be responsible on a day-to-day basis for the rapid progress of children in becoming socialized participants in the intellectual and social aspects of their society. But the existence of such interaction and arrangements between adults and children does not prove that they are influential in children's learning and development.

I would argue, however, that guided participation does play a role in children's learning and development. So much of what children are able to do requires being embedded in their culture. They would certainly not learn English without exposure to that language, nor would they develop scripts for restaurants, peek-a-boo, or book reading without involvement in those activities, as observers or participants. Many of the skills that developmental psychologists study are tied closely to the technology (e.g. books, number system, language, logic, television) of the culture in which children develop and which children learn to master, with the assistance of people who already participate skillfully in culturally important activities.

A variety of studies find an association between children's experiences and their independent skills. In Rogoff, Malkin, and Gilbride's (1984) observations of adults and infants playing with a Jack-in-the-box, the infants' understanding of the game script and skill in manipulating the toy improved over the course of repeated episodes in single sessions. Babies who participated in monthly games of roll-the-ball with their mothers were able to return the ball almost two months earlier than they returned any items in a standard test of infant development (Hodapp, Goldfield, and Boyatzis 1984). The extent to which mothers expand on infants' pointing gestures by labeling objects is associated with the number of object names in the child's vocabulary (Masur 1982), and the pattern of joint adult–child construction of propositions from one-word utterances appears to form the foundation of children's combinations of words (Scallon 1976).

Several studies provide evidence that an important function of social interaction with adults may be the direction of young children's attention. Attention may be an important individual activity that can be channeled by the highlighting of events by social partners. Mothers who more frequently encourage their 4-month-olds' attention to objects, events, and environmental properties have babies with greater speaking vocabularies and Bayley scores at age 12 months, even when the effect of 4-month infant vocalization and the effect of 12-month maternal stimulation are partialed out (Papousek, Papousek, and Bornstein 1985). In an experiment in which the level of maternal focusing of attention was increased (by having an encouraging observer comment on the effectiveness of the mother's naturally occurring efforts to stimulate her infant), infants showed greater exploratory competence as much as two months after the intervention (Belsky, Goode, and Most 1980). Active involvement of a supportive parent or experimenter in children's exploration of novel objects, compared with these adults' more passive presence, led to more active object exploration by 3- to 7-year-olds (Henderson 1984a, 1984b).

It is hardly surprising that children learn what they are taught; it is but a short extension to argue that on a day-to-day basis what children learn and are taught contributes to the development of what they know. In this perspective, development is built upon learning and, at the same time, learning is based on development. Children contribute to their own development through their eagerness and management of learning experiences as well as through their employment of the knowledge they already have at hand. At the earliest ages this 'knowledge' includes their reflexes and aspects of behavior necessary for eating and protection, as well as primordial schemas for social interaction and learning systems such as language. Soon, however, their inborn behavioural repertoire is modified with experience to reflect their history of learning experiences in the knowledge they bring to each new situation.

CULTURAL UNIVERSALS AND VARIATIONS IN GUIDED PARTICIPATION

Most research on the zone of proximal development, guided participation, scaffolding, and adult–child interaction has involved middle-class parents and children in North America and Britain. How then do the processes observed in such samples relate to the broader spectrum of child-rearing practices around the world? How do observations made in non-industrial societies compare with and extend the theory? In this final section, some speculations are offered regarding cultural universals and variations in the processes of guided participation.

Universality of guided participation

The general outline of guided participation may appear in diverse cultural groups. Caregivers around the world are likely to play an instrumental role in helping children extend their existing knowledge to encompass new situations. Caregivers and children around the world are likely to devote attention to the arrangements of activities for children, and to revise children's roles in activities as their skill and knowledge develop. They are likely to participate in joint activities that serve the function of socializing children to more mature roles in their culture.

Ethnographic accounts of teaching and learning in different cultures suggest that adults structure children's activities and provide well-placed instruction in the context of joint activities, and that children are active participants in their own socialization (Fortes 1938; Greenfield 1984; Rogoff 1986; Ruddle and Chesterfield 1978). Children participate in the cultural activities of their elders, with adjustment of their responsibilities according to their own initiative and skill. Adults may provide guidance in specific skills in the context of their use. For example, toddlers in India learn at an early age to distinguish the use of their right and left hands, as the former is the clean hand used for eating, and the latter is the 'dirty' hand used for cleaning oneself after defecation.

> If a child did not learn to eat with the right hand by participation and observation, a mother or older sister would manipulate the right hand and restrain the left until the child understood and did what was required. One of the earliest lessons taught a child of one-and-a-half to two years of age was to distinguish between the right and left hand and their distinctly separate usages. . . . Although we judged that the Indian style of eating required considerable manipulative skill, we observed a girl, not quite two, tear her chapati solely with her right hand and pick up her vegetable with the piece of chapati held in the right hand.
>
> (Freed and Freed 1981: 60)

It is notable that the caregivers relied on children's participation as well as structuring the situation, and the children achieved an impressive understanding of the difficult concept required to differentiate right and left. Joint participation and learning through social activity may be especially available to young children, who spend so much of their time in intimate contact with the activities and interpretations of more skilled members of their culture.

Cultural variations in what is learned and the means of transmission

Though the process of guided participation may have widespread use in socialization of children around the world, there are striking cultural differences in such adult–child interaction as well. Different cultural groups vary in the skills and values that are fostered, as well as the means used to transmit these culturally appropriate skills and values.

Differences in skills and values promoted

The most important differences across cultures in the social guidance of development involve variation in the skills and values that are promoted. Relevant skills (e.g. reading, weaving, sorcery, healing, eating with the right hand) vary from culture to culture, as do the objects and situations available for the practice of skills and the transmission of values.

Cross-cultural psychologists and sociocultural theorists have argued that basic to the differences in behavior across cultural (or historical) groups are the tools developed for the solution of problems (Cole and Griffin 1980; Rogoff, Gauvain, and Ellis 1984; Vygotsky 1962, 1978). For example, there is speculation that modes of remembering and classifying information vary as a function of the possibility of making lists (Goody 1977), and that the presence of literacy and Western schooling influence the specific cognitive skills that are practiced and learned (Rogoff 1981b; Scribner and Cole 1981). Mathematics skills vary as a function of the technology available – notches on sticks, paper and pencil long division, or hand calculators. Currently, speculations abound regarding the effect computers have on the thinking of children who learn to use them (Papert 1980). Television's effects on children's thinking and social skills has long been a matter of discussion. Such technologies have been termed 'cultural amplifiers', and their function is an integral part of the practice of the skills developed in each culture (Cole and Griffin 1980).

Skills for the use of cultural amplifiers such as literacy are socialized by parents of very young children even before children have contact with the technology itself. Middle-class United States parents teach their children 'literate' forms of narrative in preschool discourse, as they embed their children in a way of life in which reading and writing are an integral part of communication, recreation, and livelihood (Cazden 1979; Taylor 1983). Picture-books made up of durable materials are offered to babies, and bedtime stories become a part of the baby's daily routine.

A fascinating comparison of middle-class school-oriented practices for inculcating literacy with those of families from two communities whose children have difficulty in reading is available in Heath (1982). Parents in a white Appalachian milltown taught their preschool children a respect for the written word but did not involve book characters or information in the children's everyday lives; their children did well in the first years of learning to read but had difficulty when required to *use* literate skills to express themselves or interpret text. Preschool children of rural origin in a black milltown learned a respect for skillful and creative use of language but were not taught about books or the style of analytic discourse used in school; they had difficulty in learning to read which kept them from making use of their creative skills with language in the school setting. Early childhood in both of these communities did not include reading and writing in the texture of daily life, and the children experienced difficulties in the use of literacy in school.

Differences in the means by which adults and children communicate

Research indicates that adult–child communication strategies vary across cultures (Leiderman, Tulkin, and Rosenfeld 1977; Field, Sostek, Vietze, and Leiderman 1981). Such cultural variations in communication strategies would deeply influence the ways in which parents and children collaborate in the child's socialization. If such differences are not recognized, it may be easy for Western researchers to overlook the structuring and joint participation that occurs in other cultures, since it may be at variance with child-rearing practices familiar in middle-class Western settings.

The most striking cultural differences may involve the explicitness and intensity of verbal and nonverbal communication, the interactional status role of children versus adults, and the extent of reliance on face-to-face interaction.

The extent of reliance on explicit, declarative statements compared with tacit, procedural, and subtle forms of verbal and nonverbal instruction appears to vary across cultures (Jordan 1977; Rogoff 1982; Scribner and Cole 1973), with an emphasis on explicit verbal statements in cultures that emphasize Western schooling (Rogoff 1981b; Scribner 1974). Differences in use of explicit statements may also relate to cultural values regarding the appropriate use of language, subtlety, and silence, as well as to the adequacy of other forms of communication for most purposes. For example, among the Navajo, who have frequently been characterized as teaching quietly by demonstration and guided participation (e.g. Cazden and John 1971), talk is regarded as a sacred gift not to be used unnecessarily.

Though researchers have focused on talking as the appropriate means of adult–child interaction, this may reflect a cultural bias in overlooking the information provided by gaze, postural changes, and touch. United States infants have been characterized as 'packaged' babies who do not have direct skin contact with their caregiver (Whiting 1981), and often spend more than a third of their time in a room separate from any other people. This may necessitate the use of distal forms of communication such as noise. In contrast, children who are constantly in the company of their caregivers may rely more on nonverbal cues such as direction of gaze or facial expression. And infants who are in almost constant skin-to-skin contact with their mother may manage effective communication through tactile contact in squirming and postural changes. Consistent with this suggestion that vocalization may be less necessary when there is close contact between adults and infants, Freed and Freed (1981) report work by Lewis in 1977 showing that United States infants and small children are less likely to vocalize when held on the lap, and more likely to vocalize when out of the mother's arms and lap.

Another important cultural difference in adult–child communication involves the interactional status of children. In some societies, young children are not expected to serve as conversational peers with adults, initiating interactions and being treated as equals in the conversation (Blount 1972; Harkness and Super 1977). Instead, they may speak when spoken to, replying to informational questions or simply carrying out commands.

Ochs and Schieffelin (1984) suggest that there may be two cultural patterns of speech between children and their caregivers. In cultures that adapt situations to children (as in middle-class United States families), caregivers simplify their talk, negotiate meaning with children, co-operate with children in building propositions, and respond to verbal and nonverbal initiations by the child. In cultures that adapt the child to the normal situations of the culture (as in Kaluli New Guinea and Samoan families), caregivers model unsimplified utterances for the child to repeat to a third party, direct the child to notice others, and build interaction on situational circumstances to which the caregiver wishes the child to respond.

In both patterns, the child participates in activities of the society, but the patterns vary in terms of the child's versus the caregiver's responsibility to adapt in the process of learning or teaching the more mature forms of speech and action. It seems likely that the adaptation of caregivers to children may be more necessary in societies that segregate children from adult activities, thus requiring them to practice skills or learn information outside of the mature context of use (Rogoff 1981a). In societies in which children are integrated in adult activities, the child is assured a role in the action (at least as an observer) and socialization may proceed with less explicit child-centred interaction to integrate the child in the activities of society.

Efforts to instruct children may thus vary in terms of the children's responsibility to observe and analyse the task, versus the caregivers' responsibility to decompose the task and motivate the child. Dixon, Levine, Richman, and Brazelton (1984) noted that Gusii (Kenyan) mothers taught their 6- to 36-month-old infants using clear 'advance organizers' in instruction, often modeling the expected performance in its entirety, appearing to expect the task to be completed exactly as specified if the child attended to it, giving the children the responsibility for learning. This contrasted with the efforts of American mothers, who concentrated on arousing the child's interest and shaping the child's behaviour step by step, providing constant encouragement and refocusing, taking the responsibility for teaching.

Related to the cultural differences suggested here in the interactional role of children are differences that have been observed in the use of face-to-face interaction. Face-to-face interaction may be a prototype in United States research on mother–child communication due to the didactic role assumed by middle-class American mothers, relying on their own efforts to motivate children to learn, in contrast with mothers who give the responsibility for learning to the children. There appears to be cultural variation in the extent to which mothers rely on this position for communication. Mothers in many cultures commonly hold infants facing away from them (Martini and Kirkpatrick 1981; Sostek, Vietze, Zaslow, Kreiss, van der Waals, and Rubinstein 1981).

Variation in infant positioning from facing the mother to facing the same way as the mother may reflect cultural values regarding the social world in which the child is to be embedded, as well as the means by which children are socialized. Martini and Kirkpatrick (1981) note that Marquesan mothers (in the South Pacific) appeared strained and awkward when asked to interact with their babies in a face-to-face orientation. In everyday activities, babies were usually held facing outward and encouraged to interact with and attend to others (especially slightly older siblings) instead of interacting with the mother. The authors report that this is consistent with a general cultural value of embeddedness in a complex social world. Marquesan infants learn a different lesson in their socialization than do American infants engaged in face-to-face interaction, but their mothers appear to provide similarly rich guidance in developing culturally appropriate skills and values. Marquesan mothers actively arrange infants' social interactions with others; if babies appear to get self-absorbed, mothers interrupt and urge attention to the broader social environment:

> [Mothers] consistently provided the infant with an interactively stimulating world, first by interacting, next by encouraging and making effective his attempts to make contact, and finally by directing others to interact with the infant. Caregivers . . . shaped the infants' attention towards others and objects, and shaped their movements towards effective contact and locomotion. By the end of the first year, infants were becoming interactants able to accompany and learn from older children in an environment supervised by adults.
>
> (Martini and Kirkpatrick 1981: 209)

SUMMARY

This paper proposes that middle-class Western children as well as children in other cultures learn and develop in situations of joint involvement with more experienced people in culturally important activities. Adults and children collaborate in children's socialization as they negotiate the nature of children's activities and their responsibilities in participation. They work together to adapt children's knowledge to new situations, to structure problem-solving attempts, and to regulate children's assumption of responsibility for managing the process. This guidance of development includes tacit forms of communication and distal arrangements of children's learning environments, as well as explicit verbal interaction. The mutual roles played by adults and children in children's development rely both on the adults' interest in fostering mature skills and on children's own eagerness to participate in adult activities and push their own development.

These joint socialization roles may be universal, although cultures vary in the goals of socialization and the means used to implement them. Cultures vary in the explicitness of subtlety of verbal and nonverbal communication, the orientation of the infant towards parents versus siblings or other caregivers, the adaptation of children to the adult world or vice versa, and the accessibility of caregivers to infants through proximal and distal forms of communication. The variations as well as the similarities across cultures in how adults and infants interact may be instrumental in the rapid socialization of infants to be participating members of their cultures.

REFERENCES

Bakeman, R. and Adamson, L. B. (1984) 'Coordinating attention to people and objects in mother–infant and peer–infant interaction', *Child Development* 55: 1,278–89.

Belsky, J., Goode, M. K., and Most, R. K. (1980) 'Maternal stimulation and infant exploratory competence: Cross-sectional, correlational, and experimental analyses', *Child Development* 51: 1,163–78.

Bernstein, L. E. (1981) 'Language as a product of dialogue', *Discourse Processes* 4: 117–47.

Blount, B. G. (1972) 'Parental speech and language acquisition: Some Luo and Samoan examples', *Anthropological Linguistics* 14: 119–30.

Brazelton, T. B. (1982) 'Joint regulation of neonate–parent behavior', in E. Z. Tronick (ed.) *Social Interchange in Infancy*, pp. 7–22, Baltimore MD: University Park Press.

Brown, R. (1958), *Words and Things*, New York: Free Press.

Bruner, J. S. (1981) 'Intention in the structure of action and interaction', in L. P. Lipsitt (ed.) *Advances in Infancy Research*, pp. 41–56, Norwood, NJ: Ablex.

Bruner, J. S. (1983) *Child's Talk: Learning to use Language*, New York: Norton.

Butterworth, G. and Cochran, G. (1980) 'Towards a mechanism of joint visual attention in human infancy', *International Journal of Behavioral Development* 3: 253–72.

Cazden, C. (1979) 'Peekaboo as an instructional model: Discourse development at home and at school', *Papers and Reports on Child Language Development*, no. 17, Stanford CA: Stanford University, Department of Linguistics.

Cazden, C. B. and John, V. P. (1971) 'Learning in American Indian children', in M. L. Wax, S. Diamond, and F. O. Gearing (eds) *Anthropological Perspectives in Education*, pp. 252–72, New York: Basic Books.

Cole, M. (1981) 'The zone of proximal development: Where culture and cognition create each other', Center for Human Information Processing, report no. 106, San Diego: University of California.

Cole, M. and Griffin, P. (1980) 'Cultural amplifiers reconsidered', in D. R. Olson (ed.) *The Social Foundations of Language and Thought*, pp. 343–64, New York: Norton.

D'Andrade, R. G. (1981) 'The cultural part of cognition', *Cognitive Science* 5: 179–95.

Dixon, S. D., Levine, R. A., Richman, A., and Brazelton, T. B. (1984) 'Mother–child interaction around a teaching task: An African–American comparison', *Child Development* 55: 1,252–64.

Eckerman, C. O., Whatley, J. L., and McGhee, L. J. (1979) 'Approaching and contacting the object another manipulates: a social skill of the one-year-old', *Developmental Psychology* 15: 585–93.

Erickson, F. (1982) 'Taught cognitive learning in its immediate environments: a neglected topic in the anthropology of education', *Anthropology and Education Quarterly* 13: 149–80.

Feinman, S. (1982) 'Social referencing in infancy', *Merrill-Palmer Quarterly*
28: 445-70.
Field, T. M., Sostek, A. M., Vietze, P., and Leiderman, P. H. (eds) (1981)
Culture and Early Interactions, Hillsdale, NJ: Erlbaum.
Fortes, M. (1938) *Social and Psychological Aspects of Education in
Taleland*, Oxford: Oxford University Press.
Freed, R. S. and Freed, S. A. (1981) *Enculturation and Education in
Shanti Nagar*, vol. 57, no. 2, New York: Anthropological Papers of the
American Museum of Natural History.
Furth, H. G. (1974) 'Two aspects of experience in ontogeny: Development
and learning', in H. Reese (ed.) *Advances in Child Development and
Behavior*, vol. 9, pp. 47-67, New York: Academic Press.
Goody, J. (1977) *The Domestication of the Savage Mind*, Cambridge:
Cambridge University Press.
Greenfield, P. M. (1984) 'A theory of the teacher in the learning activities
of everyday life', in B. Rogoff and J. Lave (eds) *Everyday Cognition: its
Development in Social Context*, pp. 117-38, Cambridge, MA: Harvard
University Press.
Gunnar, M. R. and Stone, C. (1984) 'The effects of positive maternal affect
on infant responses to pleasant, ambiguous, and fear-provoking toys',
Child Development 55: 1,231-6.
Harkness, S. and Super, C. M. (1977) 'Why African children are so hard to
test', in L. L. Adler (ed.) *Issues in Cross-cultural Research, Annals of the
New York Academy of Sciences*, vol. 285, pp. 326-31.
Hay, D. F. (1980) 'Multiple functions of proximity seeking in infancy',
Child Development 51: 636-45.
Heath, S. B. (1982) 'What no bedtime story means: Narrative skills at home
and school', *Language in Society* 11: 49-76.
Henderson, B. B. (1984a) 'Parents and exploration: The effect of context on
individual differences in exploratory behavior', *Child Development* 55:
1,237-45.
Henderson, B.B. (1984b) 'Social support and exploration', *Child Develop-
ment* 55: 1,246-51.
Hodapp, R. M., Goldfield, E. C., and Boyatzis, C. J. (1984) 'The use and
effectiveness of maternal scaffolding in mother-infant games', *Child
Development* 55: 772-81.
Hoff-Ginsberg, E. and Shatz, M. (1982) 'Linguistic input and the child's
acquisition of language', *Psychological Bulletin* 92: 3-26.
Jordan, C. (1977) 'Maternal teaching, peer teaching, and school adaptation
in an urban Hawaiian population', Michigan: paper presented at the
meetings of the Society for Cross-Cultural Research.
Kaye, K. (1977) 'Infants' effects upon their mothers' teaching strategies', in
J.D. Glidewell (ed.) *The Social Context of Learning and Development*,
New York: Gardner Press.
Kaye, K. (1982) 'Organism, apprentice, and person', in E.Z. Tronick (ed.)
Social Interchange in Infancy, Baltimore: University Park Press.
Laboratory of Comparative Human Cognition (1983) 'Culture and cogni-
tive development', in W. Kessen (ed.) *History, Theory, and Methods*,

P. H. Mussen (ed.) *Handbook of Child Psychology*, vol. 1, pp. 294–356, New York: Wiley.

Leiderman, P. H., Tulkin, S. R., and Rosenfeld, A. (eds) (1977) *Culture and Infancy*, New York: Academic Press.

Lempers, J. D. (1979) 'Young children's production and comprehension of nonverbal deictic behaviors', *Journal of Genetic Psychology* 135: 93–102.

Martini, M. and Kirkpatrick, J. (1981) 'Early interactions in the Marquesas Islands', in T. M. Field, A. M. Sostek, P. Vietze, and P. H. Leiderman (eds) *Culture and Early Interactions*, pp. 189–213, Hillsdale, NJ: Erlbaum.

Masur, E. F. (1982) 'Mothers' responses to infants' object-related gestures: Influences on lexical development', *Journal of Child Language* 9: 23–30.

McNamee, G. D. (1980) 'The social origins of narrative skills', unpublished dissertation, Evanston, IL: Northwestern University.

Mehan, H. (1976) 'Assessing children's school performance', in J. Beck, C. Jenks, N. Keddie, and M. F. D. Young (eds) *Worlds Apart*, London: Collier McMillian.

Messer, D. J. (1980) 'The episodic structure of maternal speech to young children, *Journal of Child Language* 7: 29–40.

Miller, P. J. (1979) *Amy, Wendy, and Beth: Learning Language in South Baltimore*, Austin: University of Texas Press.

Moerk, E. L. (1983) *The Mother of Eve – as a First Language Teacher*, Norwood, NJ: Ablex.

Newman, D. (1982) 'Perspective-taking versus content in understanding lies', *Quarterly Newsletter of the Laboratory of Comparative Human Cognition* 4: 26–9.

Ochs, E. (1979) 'Introduction: What child language can contribute to pragmatics', in E. Ochs and B. Schieffelin (eds) *Developmental Pragmatics*, New York: Academic Press.

Ochs, E. and Schieffelin, B. B. (1984) 'Language acquisition and socialization: Three developmental stories and their implications', in R. Schweder and R. LeVine (eds) *Culture and its Acquisition*, Chicago: University of Chicago Press.

Papert, S. (1980) *Mindstorms*, New York: Basic Books.

Papousek, M., Papousek, H., and Bornstein, M. H. (1985) 'The naturalistic vocal environment of young infants', in T. M. Field and N. Fox (eds) *Social Perception in Infants*, Norwood, NJ: Ablex.

Poe, P. (1982) 'Beginning in the bathtub', *American Baby* 44(19): 12–20.

Rheingold, H. L. (1982) 'Little children's participation in the work of adults, a nascent prosocial behavior', *Child Development* 53: 114–25.

Rogoff, B. (1981a) 'Adults and peers as agents of socialization: A Highland Guatemalan profile', *Ethos* 9: 18–36.

Rogoff, B. (1981b) 'Schooling and the development of cognitive skills', in H. C. Triandis and A. Heron (eds) *Handbook of Cross-cultural Psychology*, vol. 4, pp. 233–94 Boston: Allyn & Bacon.

Rogoff, B. (1982) 'Mode of instruction and memory test performance', *International Journal of Behavioral Development* 5: 33–48.

Rogoff, B. (1986) 'Adult assistance of children's learning', in T. E. Raphael (ed.) *The Contexts of School Based Literacy*, New York: Random House.

Rogoff, B. and Gardner, W. P. (1984) 'Guidance in cognitive development: an examination of mother–child instruction', in B. Rogoff and J. Lave (eds) *Everyday Cognition: its Development in Social Context*, pp. 95–116, Cambridge, MA: Harvard University Press.

Rogoff, B., Gauvain, M., and Ellis, S. (1984) 'Development viewed in its cultural context', in M. H. Bornstein and M.E. Lamb (eds) *Developmental Psychology*, Hillsdale, NJ: Erlbaum.

Rogoff, B., Malkin, C., and Gilbride, K. (1984) 'Interaction with babies as guidance in development', in B. Rogoff and J. V. Wertsch (eds) *Children's Learning in the 'Zone of Proximal Development'*, pp. 31–44, San Franciso: Jossey-Bass.

Ruddle, K. and Chesterfield, R. (1978) 'Traditional skill training and labor in rural societies', *The Journal of Developing Areas* 12: 389–98.

Saxe, G. B., Gearhart, M., and Guberman, S. B. (1984) 'The social organization of early number development', in B. Rogoff and J. V. Wertsch (eds) *Children's Learning in the 'Zone of Proximal Development'*, pp. 19–30, San Francisco: Jossey-Bass.

Schaffer, H. F. (1984) *The Child's Entry into a Social World*, London: Academic Press.

Scallon, R. (1976) *Conversations with a One-year-old*, Honolulu: University Press of Hawaii.

Scribner, S. (1974) 'Developmental aspects of categorized recall in a West African society', *Cognitive Psychology* 6: 475–94.

Scribner, S. and Cole, M. (1973) 'Cognitive consequences of formal and informal education', *Science* 182: 553–9.

Scribner, S. and Cole, M. (1981) *The Psychology of Literacy*, Cambridge, MA: Harvard University Press.

Shotter, J. and Newson, J. (1982) 'An ecological approach to cognitive development: implicate orders, joint action, and intentionality', in G. Butterworth and P. Light (eds) *Social Cognition: Studies in the Development of Understanding* pp. 32–52, Sussex: Harvester.

Snow, C. (1977) 'Mother's speech research: From input to interaction', in C. Snow and C. Ferguson (eds) *Talking to Children*, New York: Cambridge University Press.

Sorce, J. F., Emde, R. N., Campos, J. J., and Klinnert, M. D. (1985) 'Maternal emotional signaling: Its effects on the visual cliff behavior of 1-year-olds', *Developmental Psychology* 21: 195–200.

Sostek, A. M., Vietze, P., Zaslow, M., Kreiss, L., van der Waals, F., and Rubinstein, D. (1981) 'Social context in caregiver–infant interaction: a film study of Fais and the United States', in T. M. Field, A. M. Sostek, P. Vietze, and P. H. Leiderman (eds) *Culture and Early Interactions*, Hillsdale, NJ: Erlbaum.

Taylor, D. (1983) *Family Literacy*, Exeter, NH: Heinemann Educational Books.

Valsiner, J. (1984) 'Construction of the zone of proximal development in adult–child joint action: The socialization of meals', in B. Rogoff and

J. V. Wertsch (eds) *Children's Learning in the 'Zone of Proximal Development'*, pp. 65-76, San Francisco: Jossey-Bass.

Vygotsky, L. S. (1962) *Thought and Language*, Cambridge, MA: M.I.T. Press.

Vygotsky, L. S. (1978) *Mind in Society: The Development of Higher Psychological Processes*, Cambridge, MA: Harvard University Press.

Wartofsky, M. (1984) 'The child's construction of the world and the world's construction of the child', in F. S. Kessel and A. W. Siegel (eds) *The Child and Other Cultural Inventions*, pp. 188-215, New York: Praeger.

Wertsch, J. V. (1979) 'From social interaction to higher psychological processes', *Human Development* 22: 1-22.

Wertsch, J. V. (1984) 'The zone of proximal development: Some conceptual issues', in B. Rogoff and J. V. Wertsch (eds) *Children's Learning in the 'Zone of Proximal Development'*, pp. 7-18, San Francisco: Jossey-Bass.

Wertsch, J. V. (1985) *Vygotsky and the Social Formation of Mind*, Cambridge, MA: Harvard University Press.

Whiting, B. B. (1980) 'Culture and social behavior: A model for the development of social behavior', *Ethos* 8: 95-116.

Whiting, J. W. M. (1981) 'Environmental constraints on infant care practices', in R. H. Munroe, R. L. Munroe, and B. B. Whiting (eds) *Handbook of Cross-cultural Human Development*, pp. 155-79, New York: Garland.

Wood, D., Bruner, J. S., and Ross, G. (1976) 'The role of tutoring in problem solving', *Journal of Child Psychology and Psychiatry* 17: 89-100.

Zukow, P. G., Reilly, J., and Greenfield, P.M. (1982) 'Making the absent present: Facilitating the transition from sensorimotor to linguistic communication', in K. Nelson (ed.) *Children's Language*, vol. 3, New York: Gardner Press.

6 Aspects of teaching and learning

David Wood

Source: Richards, M. and Light, P. (eds) (1986) *Children of Social Worlds*, Cambridge: Polity Press, pp. 191–212.

INTRODUCTION: IMAGES OF THE LEARNER AND REFLECTIONS ON THE TEACHER

Teaching is a complex, difficult and often subtle activity. Although I will be arguing that a great deal of teaching is spontaneous, 'natural' and effective, deliberate teaching of groups of children in formally contrived contexts is an intellectually demanding occupation. It is also a relatively new one. Compulsory, formal education for all has a short history and the technologies and consequences it has spawned, both material and mental, are still poorly understood and the subject of political and academic debate.

Some years ago, Greenfield and Bruner (1969) argued that the invention and widespread availability of schooling has had dramatic effects on the nature of human knowledge; not simply creating wider dissemination of facts but fundamental changes in the nature of thinking itself. Although ensuing studies of the impact of schooling on the human intellect have shown that the effects are somewhat less general than this hypothesis suggested (e.g. Cole and Scribner 1974) they have shown that schooling, in company with other technologies (notably literacy), has marked effects on various intellectual 'skills'. Donaldson (1978), in a critical examination of Piagetian theory, argues that schooling does help to create certain varieties of human reasoning, particularly a capacity to deploy powers of reasoning to solve problems that involve abstract, hypothetical entities. In such contexts, thinking out problems and understanding what is implied by them demands attention to the formal structure of the problem and cannot be achieved by appeals to common sense or plausible inferences. Thus, Donaldson concludes that schooling is the source of special ways of thinking about and operating upon the world.

One implication of this view is that teachers (broadly rather than narrowly conceived) are responsible for inculcating certain ways of thinking in children. Not only do they pass on facts and information about things but also ways of conceptualizing and reasoning. Where they succeed, teachers recreate their own ways of thinking in their pupils; where they fail they may inhibit or prevent a child's access to power within his own society.

Our knowledge of the 'psychology of teaching' is derived from several sources. The first and most obvious is from theories and studies of learning and development. Theorists of human development, notably Bruner, Vygotsky and Piaget, offer not only radically different views of what children are like, what *knowledge* is and how it develops; they sketch out radically different images of the teacher. In this chapter we will examine some of the major features of these theories in relation to the issue of what teaching *is*.

A second source of information about teaching stems from the now numerous attempts to describe and analyse teaching as it occurs in classrooms. Unfortunately, many such studies are largely atheoretical and even idiosyncratic, so it is seldom possible to utilize the data they provide to inform our arguments about theories of what teaching is. One possible reason for this is that teachers do not actually do what any of the theories dictate they should do, either because teachers are ignorant of theories or theorists are ignorant of teaching. One view is that theories developed out of psychological research cannot be used to develop categories to describe what goes on in classrooms because their relevance is limited to what happens in laboratories. There has been a good deal of debate in recent years about the status and relevance of theories about children based largely on experimental, psychological research. For example, Cole and his colleagues (1979) observed children in home-like contexts and reported that they seldom found evidence of the sorts of demands, tasks and interactions that cognitive psychologists use in the laboratory to explore learning and development. Thus, psychologists *qua* psychologists are likely to be working with very different raw material in fashioning their theories of children's thinking to that which informs the views of parents and others. Herein, perhaps, lie some reasons for different conceptualizations of the nature of children by psychologists and non-psychologists. Psychologists may be accused of having created 'straw children' and imaginary learners who haunt the psychological laboratory but not the 'real' world.

I shall be arguing, however, that the differences between children's behaviour in different contexts (e.g. laboratory versus home) are of more interest and importance than this interpretation suggests. More specifically, I will be exploring the idea that interactions between adults and children in 'spontaneous' and 'contrived' encounters are different in nature. By contrived, I mean teaching/learning/testing encounters that are deliberately brought about by those with power (e.g. teachers or psychologists) as opposed to those which 'arise' spontaneously out of adult–child contacts. I shall also work on the assumption (not totally without evidence) that most interactions at home are spontaneous and child-initiated, and those in schools or psychological laboratories are usually contrived and adult-controlled. I also suggest that when adults and children in the two different contexts appear to be working on the 'same' tasks or doing superficially similar things, the processes involved are dissimilar. The interactions follow different 'ground rules' and create different demands of both the adult and the child and this explains why children often appear to display varying levels of intellectual or linguistic competence in different situations. We will consider, for example, why children who are inquisitive and loquacious at home may show little initiative in school.

But what are 'ground rules'? Mercer and Edwards (1981) have provided some examples in a consideration of classroom interactions, drawing attention to differences between the constraints which operate in classroom and everyday discourse. For example, being able to answer questions such as 'It takes three men six hours to dig a certain sized hole. How long would it take two men to dig the same hole?' demands more than a knowledge of how to apply and execute the sums involved. One must also appreciate what constitute appropriate and inappropriate answers. Problems demanding similar decisions in everyday life (e.g. working out how long a certain job will take) might legitimately concern issues such as when the ground was last dug over; what tools are to be used; how experienced the men are and so forth. In mathematics lessons, however, such considerations are 'irrelevant'. To know what is relevant, a child has to discover or infer the rules underlying what is a very special form of discourse. Arguments, for example, about making mathematics 'relevant' are likely to founder if they simply choose 'everyday' situations and ignore the fact that the ground rules for solving everyday, practical numerical problems and abstract, formal mathematical problems are different.

If one accepts that activities occurring across contexts may be governed by different, implicit social practices and rules, then what may seem like the 'same' task in different contexts may, to children who have yet to acquire all the rules, appear very different. Several researchers (e.g. Donaldson 1978) have shown that young children often appear able to do things in some contexts but not others. They possess competence that does not always emerge in their performances. One may seek to understand such discrepancies in the fact that some contexts are more threatening, unfamiliar or less motivating to children. But it is also likely that the apparent similarities between the competence demanded in such situations are misleading. Thus, identifying the reasons why observations of teaching and learning in home, school and laboratory often yield different views of the processes involved is no simple matter. What might seem to be essentially similar tasks and activities in various contexts may well be located in quite different 'rules' of conduct and interpretation.

Another line of evidence relating to the question of what effective teaching is would seem, on first sight, to offer the most direct and compelling way of adjudicating between competing theories. A number of educational programmes have been set up, particularly in the USA, to help provide young children from economically poor homes with a 'Headstart' in their educational life by providing pre-school educational experiences (see Woodhead 1985 for an overview). There have been some successful intervention programmes. But these were inspired by a range of *different* theories of learning and development. No one theory held the day. Weikart (1973), commenting upon the success of his own, neo-Piagetian programme and those of others who had based their interventions on other theories, concludes that the important common element in success was not the curriculum *per se* nor the material it employed but the commitment and competence of its teachers! The *nature* of such competence remains obscure.

We will examine just a few aspects of what teaching competence might involve. I do not claim, however, to be more than scratching the surface of what is undoubtedly an extremely complex issue.

LEARNING AND DEVELOPMENT

I will in this part of the chapter be discussing in some detail a series of studies of the teaching–learning process that have employed a common task. The children being taught range from three to five years of age. Left to their own devices, the children would not be able to do the task at hand. Nor do they learn how to do the task if they are taught ineffectively. Given effective instruction, however, they can be taught how to do most or all of it alone (Wood and Middleton 1975).

Although the task we shall be considering is a specific and concrete one I shall argue that some aspects of the teaching–learning process it identifies are general ones which are relevant to and implicated in many naturalistic encounters between adults and children. I shall also try, however, to identify some important differences between the nature of interactions observed in such contrived teaching–learning encounters and those found in more spontaneous encounters between adults and children in homes and schools.

The conceptual framework adopted in this chapter is derived from the theorizing of Vygotsky (1978) and Bruner (1968). Vygotsky, for example, contributed the concept of a 'zone of proximal development'. This expression refers to the gap that exists for a given child at a particular time between his level of performance on a given task or activity and his potential level of ability following instruction. Vygotsky offers a conceptualization of intelligence that is radically different from that promoted either by conventional, psychometric intelligence tests or Piagetian theory. Vygotsky's theory of intelligence takes the capacity to learn through instruction as central. The intelligence of a species is determined not only by a capacity to learn but also to teach. Furthermore, two children who behave similarly in a given task situation, suggesting similar levels of competence, may in fact be quite different, in that one may prove able to benefit far more from instruction in that task than another.

Underlying this view of the role of instruction in learning are radically different conceptions of the nature of knowledge, development and maturity from those embodied in Piagetian theory. Piaget's child is an epistemologist; a natural seeker after, and architect of, his own understanding. He learns largely through his own activity in the world. He constructs progressively more powerful, abstract and integrated systems of knowing by discovering how his actions affect reality. All a teacher can do is to facilitate that understanding by providing appropriate materials and contexts for the child's actions and by helping the child to discover inconsistencies in his own views. The primary motivator of developmental change for Piaget is 'disequilibration'; a state of conflict between what the child expects as a result of his interactions with the world and what actually transpires. Knowing the stages of development and materials and activities that are likely to be relevant to the activities dictated by each stage, a teacher can facilitate developmental change by helping the child to discover implicit contradictions in his own thinking. But any contradictions must be *latent* in the child's structure of knowledge. They can be activated but not induced. There is no point and may even be harm in confronting the child with hypotheses, demonstrations or explanations that are not 'natural' to his stage of development.

Whilst there is evidence favouring the view that one basis for developmental change or learning is cognitive conflict and contradiction (e.g. Glachan and Light 1982) I will be arguing that far more is involved in effective teaching than simply providing material for the child to 'digest' or activating competing ideas that are already implicit in his thinking. We will explore the view that adult and child, working together, can construct new schemes through shared interaction. The potential effects of teaching will prove to be far greater than Piagetian theory allows. What the child develops, in this alternative conceptualization, are not mental operations derived from his actions on the world but 'concepts' that are jointly constructed through interaction with those who already embody them, together with ways of doing and thinking that are cultural practices, recreated with children through processes of formal and informal teaching.

THE NATURE OF EFFECTIVE INSTRUCTION: CONTINGENT CONTROL OF LEARNING

We are confronted with two individuals who are in asymmetrical states of knowledge about a problem facing them. The more knowledgeable, the teacher, is attempting to communicate a more informed understanding to the less knowledgeable, the learner. How are practical skills and ideas transferred from one body to the other?

Our task here is to discover an analysis of teaching and learning interactions that will enable us to relate instructional activity to the learning process. If we are successful in identifying the crucial features of effective teaching, then it should be possible to examine a range of different teaching styles or strategies and make testable predictions about their relative effectiveness.

Some years ago we attempted to meet these goals in an analysis of mother–child interactions in an experimental situation (Wood and Middleton 1975). The children involved were four years old and the task the mothers were asked to teach them was a specially designed construction toy. When a child first encountered the task, he or she saw 21 wooden blocks of varying size and shape. The mother had already been shown how these could be assembled to create a pyramid, but the child had no knowledge of the solution to the problem. The mother was asked to teach the child how to put the blocks together in any way she saw fit. She was also told that when the pyramid had been put together, it would be taken apart and the child asked to assemble it alone.

Each block in the toy is unique and will only fit into one position in the final construction, but the task was designed to incorporate a number of repeated rules of assembly. The pyramid (more accurately, a ziggurat) comprises five square levels, each a different size. The bottom level is approximately nine inches square and is constructed out of four, equally sized, square pieces. Two of these assemble by fitting a peg in one into an equally sized hole in the second. When this pair is assembled in the correct orientation, two half pegs, one on each block, are brought together. Similarly, two other blocks assemble by a hole and peg arrangement but to bring two half-holes together. When the two pairs are constructed, the peg and hole formed can be fitted together to produce a level of the pyramid. This rule of assembly is repeated with sets of blocks of diminishing size to construct four more levels. The assembly of each set of four also creates connectives to enable them to be piled on top of each other. On the 'top' of each block is a quarter section of a round peg. When each level is assembled correctly, these come together to form a peg which fits into a circular depression in the base of the level above, which is similarly created from four quarter depressions in each block. Thus, the levels can be piled to form a rigid structure. The assembly is completed by placing a single block with a depression in its base on the top level.

The blocks were designed so that any peg would fit into any hole and any level could fit onto any other. Thus, the task presents many possibilities for 'incorrect' assembly. Left to their own devices, four year olds cannot do the task but given effective instruction they can. But what does effective instruction look like? How are we to describe the maternal attempts to teach children?

Imagine we are watching a mother and child in a teaching–learning encounter with these blocks. The mother has just given an instruction. First, we determine how much *control* the instruction implicitly exerts over what happens next. Five categories are listed in Table 6.1 which, we have found in a number of studies, can accommodate any instruction a teacher might make in this situation. These vary in terms of degree of control.

The first category, general verbal prompts, includes instructions that demand activity but do not specify how the child should proceed to meet such demands. Specific verbal instructions give the child information about features of the task that need to be borne in mind as he or she makes the next move. If the teacher not only tells the child what to attend to in making his or her next move but also shows him or her what is referred to by pointing at or picking out relevant material, then the instruction is classified as Level 3. If the teacher not

Table 6.1 Levels of control

Level	Example
1 General verbal prompts	'Now you make something'
2 Specific verbal instructions	'Get four big blocks'
3 Indicates materials	Points to block(s) needed
4 Prepares for assembly	Orients pairs so hole faces peg
5 Demonstrates	Assembles two pairs

only identifies material but goes on to prepare it for assembly then the child is simply left with the problem of how to complete the operation in question. Finally, if the teacher demonstrates, he or she takes full control of the next step in the construction whilst the child, hopefully, looks on and learns.

As we come down the list, then, the instructions become more controlling, with the teacher implicitly taking more, and offering the child correspondingly less, scope for initiative.

Mothers vary enormously in the way they attempt to teach their young children how to do this task, and children also vary widely in their ability to do the task alone after instruction. Does the style of teaching affect what is learned? It does. Mothers whose children do well after instruction are those who are most likely to act in accordance with two 'rules' of teaching. The first dictates that any failure by a child to bring off an action after a given level of help should be met by an immediate increase in help or control. Thus, if the teacher, say, had provided the child with a specific verbal instruction and then found that the child did not succeed in complying with it, the appropriate response is to give more help either by indicating the material implicated in the previous instruction or by preparing it for assembly.

The second rule concerns what should happen when a child succeeds in complying with an instruction. This dictates that any subsequent instruction should offer less help than that which pre-dated success. In other words, after success the teacher should give the child more space for success (and error).

The pattern of responses by the teacher to a child's momentary successes and failures *judged in relation to the instructions which pre-dated them* is the basis for our evaluation. Every time a teacher acts in accordance with the rules she is deemed to have made a *contingent* response. Every time she does something different (e.g. fails to provide an instruction immediately after a child fails or gives one at an inappropriate level) the instruction is non-contingent. What we find is that the more frequently contingent a teacher is the more the child can do alone after instruction.

Stated simply and boldly, the rules of contingent teaching sound easy. However, even in our experimental situation involving a practical task with a single solution, it is difficult to teach all children contingently all the time. Indeed, when we trained an experimenter to teach children according to different rules we found that she was only able to follow the contingency rules about 85 per cent of the time (Wood *et al.* 1978). Monitoring children's activity, remembering what one had said or done to prompt that activity and responding quickly to their efforts at an appropriate level is a demanding intellectual feat. Effective teaching is as difficult as the learning it seeks to promote.

SCAFFOLDING THE LEARNING PROCESS

We have defined the *process* of effective instruction as the contingent control of learning. Elsewhere, using the metaphor of 'scaffolding', we have identified some of the *functions* that instruction may fulfil for the learner (Wood, Bruner and Ross 1976). Since this notion has been extended beyond laboratory studies to help describe more naturalistic teaching–learning processes, it is necessary to explore the characteristics of scaffolding and its relationship to control and contingency before moving on to consider more general aspects of teaching and learning.

One of the most influential approaches to the study of human intelligence stems from a view of a human being as a 'limited information processor'. Individuals can only take in so much information about their situation at any moment in time, so they must organize their activities over time (develop a plan) in order to assimilate and operate within that situation. The development of knowledge and skill involves the discovery of what is best paid attention to, borne in mind and acted upon in an appropriate (goal-achieving) sequence.

At the heart of this conception of human abilities is the notion of 'uncertainty'. When we find ourselves needing to act in a very unfamiliar situation, uncertainty is high and our capacity to attend to and remember objects, features and events within the situation is limited. Observation, practice, trial and error, the growing appreciation of regularities and learning, involve the progressive reduction of that uncertainty. Accompanying its reduction are increased accuracy of perception and powers of memory. Thus, experts in a task are able to observe, take in and remember more of what they experience (within the task situation) than novices.

Children, being novices of life in general, are potentially confronted with more uncertainty than the more mature and, hence, their abilities to select, remember and plan are limited in proportion. Without help in organizing their attention and activity, children may be overwhelmed by uncertainty. The more knowledgeable can assist them in organizing their activities, by reducing uncertainty; breaking down a complex task into more manageable steps or stages. As children learn, their uncertainty is reduced and they are able to pay attention to and learn about more of the task at hand.

But such assisted learning presupposes that the children are actively involved in trying to achieve task-relevant goals. Clearly, what individuals attend to and remember in a given context is dictated by their purposes and goals; relevance is relative to the purpose in mind. Children may perceive a situation differently from an adult because they face greater uncertainty and/or because they may be entertaining different ideas about the opportunities for activity offered by the task situation.

Where a child is already involved in the pursuit of a goal or the fulfilment of an intention, then provided that the would-be teacher is able to discover or infer what that goal is, the child may be helped to bring it off. In formal or contrived situations, where the teacher decides what purpose the child must pursue, *task induction* becomes a primary scaffolding function and a *sine qua non* for effective learning. Children also face additional problems in contrived encounters because, given that they are compliant, they have to discover what their intentions are supposed to be.

How does one invoke intentions or a sense of goal directedness in the young child? More specifically, can demonstrations or verbal instructions be used effectively to invoke relevant activity? Clearly, showing children things or asking them to perform activities that they are currently unable to do will only be successful if the child understands enough of what was said or shown to lead to relevant, if not fully successful, task activity. Instruction must, to use Vygotsky's term, operate within the learner's 'zone of proximal development'. For such a concept to be useful, perception must, in some way, help to lead or constrain action and understanding.

I suggest that young children often think they understand and are capable of doing what an adult shows or tells them when, in fact, they do not. Young children, in short, often overestimate their own abilities. However, children's beliefs about their own competence lead to intentional activity and trap them in problem-solving; into trying to do what they think they can do. Provided that effective help is forthcoming, the child may be led to construct new skills. These, in turn, accompany modified perceptions of what is seen and heard. The learner comes closer to mature understanding. Put another way, both demonstrations and verbal instructions can be used to define problem spaces within which adult and child can work co-operatively and contingently to promote learning. Perhaps a few examples will illustrate this argument.

In the experimental situation already outlined we found that three-year-old children showed signs of *recognizing* what was an appropriate task goal before they were able to *achieve* that goal. For instance, they appreciated the fact that four dissimilar blocks could be put together to create a single and more parsimonious *Gestalt*. They would usually attempt to reproduce such a configuration after a demonstration. When their attempted constructions did not look similar to that demonstrated, they would usually take them apart and try again. However, they almost never took apart a construction that did look like the model; evidence both that they possessed some sense of what was task-relevant and that their activities were goal-directed.

Although purely verbal instruction proved an ineffective teaching strategy, every child so taught did begin by attempting to do what was requested. We suggest that the young child possesses sufficient linguistic competence to derive plans from verbal instructions which are partially but not fully understood. Thus, when told to 'Put the four biggest ones together' they never selected the smallest blocks and usually attempted to fit pegs into holes. Although they did not realize, early in the instructional session, all the constraints that were implicated in such general verbal instructions, they understood enough of what they implied to lead them into task-relevant activity.

Even when children do not fully understand what we show them or ask of them, they may believe that they understand and understand enough to lead them into task-relevant, if initially unsuccessful, action. We suggest, then, that a learner's *incomplete* understanding of what he or she is shown and told (what is perceived) is a vital basis for learning through instruction. Perhaps incomplete but relevant understanding of what children see adults doing and hear them saying is at the heart of what Vygotsky termed the 'zone of proximal development'.

Once the learner is involved in task-relevant activity other scaffolding functions become operative. I have already said that young children, like all of us, are limited in how much they can attend to and remember in problematic situations. There is also evidence that, left to their own devices, they are unlikely to realize whether or not they have actually examined a situation 'fully' (Vurpillot 1976). Pre-school children do not search exhaustively or systematically for evidence that might be relevant to what they are trying to do; tending to make up their minds on the basis of a limited inspection of the situation at hand (in contrived problem situations, at least).

There is also evidence, again from contrived situations, that young children are unlikely to 'rehearse' what they are trying to remember. Thus, their powers of memory may be limited not only by an uncertain world but also because they have yet to learn (or to be taught) how best to remember what they seek to retain.

Given children's propensity to attend to a limited range of features of problematic situations and, perhaps, their immature strategies for deliberate memorization, a teacher will often have to scaffold their immediate actions. They may, for example, *highlight* crucial features of the task situation that have been ignored or forgotten. In so doing, they also help the child to *analyse* the task. They may act as an external source of memory and planning for the child, either by prompting recall of a previous activity or, more subtly, by holding constant the fruits of past activities whilst the child concentrates his or her limited resources on another domain. For example, children in our task situation would often put together two pieces and then try to add a third one. The blocks are so designed that it is extremely difficult to put together four pieces without first constructing the two pairs. By directing the child's attention away from the first-assembled pair or by keeping hold of it whilst the child attempted to assemble the second pair, the instructor helped the child by breaking down a goal into a series of less-complex sub-goals.

Scaffolding functions effectively support and augment learners' limited cognitive resources, enabling them to concentrate upon and master manageable aspects of the task. With experience, such elements of the task become familiar and the child is able to consider further related task elements. Contingent control helps to ensure that the demands placed on the child are likely neither to be too complex, producing defeat, nor too simple, generating boredom or distraction.

TEACHING: NATURAL AND CONTRIVED

So far, we have been exploring the concepts of scaffolding, control and contingency in contrived encounters between adults and children in laboratory settings. We have also been dealing with very specific, short-term learning outcomes in a well-structured, concrete task with a specific 'right' answer. Are such concepts useful in more naturalistic situations? Are the effects of contingent teaching task specific or does it engender more general effects?

In this section, I will explore some attempts to extend the concepts of scaffolding and contingency to adult–child interactions in studies of language acquisition to see how far their use in this, more naturalistic research, involves more than a metaphorical relationship with their use in more formal, specific contexts.

Bruner's (1983) account of the development of the pre-verbal foundations of language acquisition extends the concept of scaffolding to the analysis of mother–child interactions. He argues that the development of early linguistic competence in the child depends upon the (informal) teaching roles played by the adult. The development of the infant's communication abilities takes place within frequently recurring 'formats' of interaction. Initially, such formats (families of interactions such as simple games, feeding sessions, nappy changing etc., which take on a predictable pattern), are largely regulated by the adult and are the basis of what Bruner terms 'Language Acquisition Support Systems'. The frequent repetition of formats provides infants with opportunities to discover and exploit regularities in their experiences. But adults play the major role in initiating and structuring the early interactional formats. Bruner writes:

> If the 'teacher' in such a 'system' were to have a motto, it would surely be 'where before there was a spectator, let there now be a participant'. One sets the game, provides a scaffold to assure that the child's ineptitudes can be rescued by appropriate intervention, and then removes the scaffold part by part as the reciprocal structure can stand on its own.
>
> (Bruner 1983: 60)

Whilst he sees adults taking the leading role in the construction of such systems of support, it seems that what is involved is not so much a process of *directing* the child but one more akin to 'leading by following'. Once the child's involvement has been gained and he is inducted into activity that can be orchestrated into an emerging system of interaction, adults tend to make what they do contingent upon their interpretation of what is likely to be the current focus of interest or relevance to the child. Thus, 'it becomes feasible for the adult partner to highlight those features of the world that are already salient to the child and that have a basic or simple grammatical form'. To the extent that adults make where they look and what they do and say contingent upon their interpretation of the child's current interest, what they are likely to be putting into words is relevant to what is in the child's mind. Thus, adults help to bring the infant's experience of the world and linguistic communication about that world into contact.

Bruner's use of the concepts of scaffolding and contingency shares formal similarities with the processes described in the analysis of contrived teaching. The task of inducting the infant into what is to become a predictable format of interaction; supplementing and orchestrating the child's role in the interaction by actions designed to highlight critical features of the joint task or activity; reducing degrees of freedom for action (buffering from distraction) to encourage the infant to focus on critical aspects of the situation; trying to hand over increasing responsibility for the execution of actions that have been constructed with the child; attempts to perform such functions in a manner that is contingent upon the child's activities, are important features of the teaching process, whether natural or contrived. Whilst I would argue, however, that the scaffolding functions are common to both types of activity with children of very different ages, the means whereby such functions are achieved change with the developing competence of the infant. Induction, for example, changes from a process that we might term 'capture' to one of 'recruitment'. This change occurs in response to the (co-ordinated) development of planning and self-consciousness in the child.

For example, in the early encounters described by Bruner and others, what might initially be a 'chance' or unintentional act by the child may be highlighted and responded to by the adult 'as if' it were an intended component of an envisaged performance. Such highlighting can be achieved by the adult performing a marked, exaggerated action or *display* that is contingent upon and follows closely in time behind the infant's activity. To the extent that this display captures the infant's attention and interest, it may evoke a repetition of the child's initial activity. Initially spontaneous, unpremeditated movements by the baby may thus form the basis for the emergence of intentional acts of communication.

A number of studies have highlighted the degree of 'fit' between both the content and timing of events that are likely to grasp the infant's attention and the 'natural' or spontaneous displays of adults (or even very young children) *en face* with the infant (e.g. Brazelton 1982). The adult achieves induction of the infant by *capturing* his attention.

With older children, induction is easier in some contexts and more difficult in others. Once attention and interest can be solicited by verbal invitations or demonstrations, the teacher may evoke intentional action towards a goal from the child. As early as nine to 18 months, young children also display some knowledge of the fact that the adult can be *recruited* to help them in an activity that they are unable to bring off alone (Geppert and Kuster 1983). By 30 months, teaching–learning encounters may be solicited by either party. But, around the same age, infants also show evidence of wishing, at some times, to maintain the independence of their own actions; of wanting to 'do it myself'.

Although, as we have seen, it is possible to induce the pre-schooler into joint problem solving, evidence from naturalistic observations in the home indicates that most encounters between young children and their parents are of the children's own choosing. In short, they tend to solicit rather than be inducted into most exchanges with parents.

The evidence comes from Wells (1979) who found, from audio-taped recordings of exchanges between parents and their three year olds at home, that 70 per cent of interactions were initiated by the child. Thus, what adults and child are likely to be working on, attending to and talking about is still largely determined by the *child's* interests.

Wells's analyses also indicate that parents who respond contingently to the child's utterances by elaborating, developing and negotiating about what they mean are more likely to engender conditions for establishing mutual understanding and the development of linguistic competence in the child. Although his analyses do not make explicit use of concepts such as scaffolding and control he does employ the term contingency in a similar way. I suggest that his findings are consistent with the view that effective scaffolding and control are factors that influence the development of linguistic competence in children. To extend this argument, however, I need to make reference to other research in which the notions of control and contingency have been exploited to study the effects of different styles of talking to children on the child's performances in school contexts.

ASKING AND TELLING: WHO IS CONTINGENT UPON WHOM?

We are studying two complex systems that know things: teacher and child. We believe that these two systems are in asymmetrical states, in that the teacher knows more than the child and has responsibility for transferring that knowledge. But the asymmetry is not entirely one-sided. The child also knows things about the world and himself that the teacher does not know. The desire to make teaching 'relevant', 'learner centred', to 'start where the learner is at' or to be contingent upon their attempts to learn is implicated in most theories of learning and development (Wood 1980b). Thus, teachers must also seek to understand what the child knows if they are to help develop, extend, clarify and integrate that knowledge.

Wells's studies, in company with research by Tizard and her colleagues (Tizard and Hughes 1984) suggest that pre-school children tend to initiate interactions, ask questions and seek information more readily at home than at school. Much of their 'epistemic' activity is directed towards achieving explanations about facts of everyday life and is occasioned by happenings in the local culture. The parent tends to be in a privileged position in relation to these requests and demands, being a *part* of that culture. Their practices and talk are embedded in which it is that the child seeks to know. Further, their privileged access to the child's history provides a basis for intersubjectivity. Their implicit hypotheses about what is likely to have motivated an epistemic act from the child; what the child is already likely to have experienced in relation to it, to know, think and feel about it, are more likely than those of strangers to prove workable or enactable.

Thus, the conditions that promote the quest for knowledge from the child are often present in the home and the needs of the child are most likely to be interpretable to those who know them. Conditions for the generation of a contingent learning environment are more likely to be endemic to the home or local culture in a way that they are not to school. Thus, the pre-school child at nursery or school is less likely to be prompted to wonder about the 'why's' and 'wherefore's' of what is going on, which is perhaps why their discourse often centres on the happenings of the moment and thus seems 'context-dependent'. Where children *do* talk about things outside the classroom, not surprisingly, it tends to be to mention significant others in their daily life (relatives), or the events, happenings, promises and surprises that occur at home (Wood, McMahon and Cranstoun 1980).

Children, then, 'present' themselves differently at home and at school. Even when teachers set out to work with individual children, they face considerable difficulties in establishing a contingent interaction because children generally give them relatively few epistemic offerings to be contingent upon. Thus, task induction becomes a more demanding activity for the teacher than the parent (and, by the same token, for a psychologist in a laboratory setting: Wood 1983). Other factors also operate against the establishment of child-initiated, adult-contingent encounters. One is group size. At home, the presence of a third person, particularly a younger sibling, is likely to promote talk between parent and child about the actions, needs and morality of another (Dunn and Kendrick 1982). Children, in their second year of life, begin to wonder about the nature of other people. At school, however, surrounded by numbers of relative strangers, observations by children about the 'psychology' of other people around are relatively rare (Wood *et al.* 1980). Faced with groups of children, the teacher encounters purely numerical difficulties in any effort to promote and sustain productive encounters with individuals. Management of self, time and resources becomes an important feature of the teaching role. Any attempts to instruct or inform are thus embedded within a wider set of roles and objectives.

The common teacher response to these difficulties is to initiate and sustain interactions not by showing or telling but by demanding and asking. Both demands and questions are exercises in *control*. In a number of different studies several classroom observers have noted the very high frequency of teacher questions. Such studies range from preschoolers to children about to leave school (Wood and Wood 1985). Furthermore, teacher questions tend to display a number of 'special' characteristics. They are often specific, demanding a narrow range of possible 'right' answers (e.g. MacLure and French 1981; Tizard *et al.* 1976; Wood *et al.* 1980). Teachers often know the answers to the questions they ask, and children, by four years of age, possess the ability to recognize this fact, in some contexts at least (Wood and Cooper 1980). Furthermore, the readiness of children to talk about what they know is likely to be inhibited by such questions.

Several reasons have been given for the frequency and nature of teacher questions. Questioning groups is one strategy whereby (at best) the minds of all involved can be focused on the same idea or topic. Questions are one tactic for the achievement of 'group intersubjectivity'. When a child is not forthcoming with numerous, spontaneous epistemic acts, then questions will usually achieve a response and, therefore, may be used as tactics for initiating and, perhaps, modelling epistemic inquiry. Speculating further, it might be the case that the use of questioning represents a historical reaction to 'talk and chalk' or 'didactic' methods of education. Questioning may be seen as a tactic designed to engage the child actively in the teaching–learning process. Rather than 'passively' sitting and listening to the teacher's declarations the child should be enjoined, through questions, to wonder and think about the topic at hand.

Whatever the rationale or 'cause' of frequent questioning by teachers, I would argue that the strategy is counter-productive.

If we accept the fact that, particularly with young children, what we seek to show them and tell them demands a knowledge of what they can already do and what and how they think about the task at hand, how are we to encourage them to display their knowledge? Focusing for the moment on mainly verbal exchanges, I suggest the following 'operationalized' definition of knowledge display. Children will ask questions about the topic, revealing their uncertainty and what they seek to know. They will take up openings to contribute to and comment upon the topic at hand. They may go beyond a direct answer to the teacher's questions to add additional information, ideas or observations that they consider supplement or qualify their answers. Further, if, as Wells argues, adult and child need to negotiate their perspectives on and objectives in a given domain, we may find that a child responds to the teacher's questions with requests for clarification or to negotiate the conditions under which they are prepared to answer.

These aspects of children's discourse define a set of conditions in which the teacher can gain access to the *child's* thoughts and uncertainties about opinions and attitudes towards the topic at hand.

These conditions are inhibited to the extent that teachers manage the interaction through questions. The more they question the less children say. Children's contributions (even when an opportunity is given) become rarer and more terse the more questions are asked (e.g. Wood and Wood 1983). Children are only likely to go beyond the force of teachers' questions to give additional ideas and explanations if questions are relatively infrequent. In some contexts at least, they are less likely to seek information through questions themselves when the teacher is asking a lot of questions.

Pupils tend to take single 'moves' in dialogue with the teacher. Whereas teachers display a number of offerings in their turns (e.g. accepting what a child has said, offering a contribution to the discourse and immediately asking a question) pupils are most likely to make a single type of move. Thus, if the teacher terminates his or her utterance with a contribution (i.e. statement, opinion, speculation) children are likely to respond with a contribution of their own; more so if the teacher's contributions are frequent. Similarly, if a teacher accepts or acknowledges what a child says but offers no further question or observation, the child is likely to continue with the topic at hand. There are also a number of second-order effects of teaching style. The less a teacher interrogates children, the more likely they are to listen to, make contributions about and ask questions of what the other children say (Griffiths 1983; Wood and Wood 1983). Such findings occur both as correlations between teaching style and pupil responses in natural classroom discourse and can be brought about in experimentally contrived encounters in which teachers vary their style of responding to groups of children (Wood and Wood 1983, 1984).

The extent to which a child reveals his or her own ideas and seeks information is thus inversely proportional to the frequency of teacher questions – and this finding embraces studies of pre-school children through to 16 year olds, deaf children and children acquiring English as a second language.

Some of the teachers who have participated in experimentally contrived classroom sessions in which they have modified their style of talking to children by asking fewer questions, becoming less controlling and giving more of their own views and opinions have commented that they found out things about the children's experiences, views and ideas that they did not know and would not have thought to ask questions about (Lees 1981). Questions may solicit the information demanded by the teacher and serve as specific probes and checks for retention of information or of a child's capacity to draw inferences. As tools for finding out things that a child thinks or knows that are not already anticipated or known by the teacher they are ineffective, at least when used in excess. If it is a teacher's goal to discover 'where the child is at' in order to respond contingently to their ideas and thoughts, the established 'register' of the classroom is generally ineffective in achieving this goal. Teachers can, however, engender sessions in which children show more initiative, if they are prepared to ask fewer questions and say more about their own ideas and views. Just as effective teaching of practical skills demands a contingent combination of showing and telling, so the extension of children's understanding through discourse demands an integration of the declarative and interrogative voice.

There is now an extensive and growing literature on the 'effective use of questioning' (e.g. Blank *et al.* 1978). Although the issue of what constitutes a 'good' and timely question is not resolved and the literature on the effects and effectiveness of questions has produced somewhat equivocal results, a few general points and reasonable speculations are emerging from the literature. First, as we saw above, several researchers have concluded that too many teacher questions are 'closed' and lead children to search for specific right answers rather than into processes of reasoning and weighing evidence. Second, teachers tend to leave relatively short pauses after their questions before taking back control of the interaction. When they are helped to extend these pauses (from one to three seconds) the frequency and level of student response increase (Rowe 1974; Swift and Gooding 1983). It seems that pupils usually need more time to think about their answers to teacher questions than teachers normally allow. Questions to which the teacher already knows the answer are also common. Thus, the implicit theory of learning involved is one in which the teacher knows all the answers and the child's task is simply to find them. Sigel and his colleagues (Sigel and McGillicuddy-Delisi, in press) analysing discourse between parents and children, have shown, for example, that more open-ended, demanding parental questions (which, in Sigel's terms 'distance' the child from and encourage him to reflect upon his immediate experiences and concerns) are positively correlated with various measures of the child's intellectual development, whereas more closed questions are not. Similarly, Redfield and Rousseau (1981), in a review of questioning, concluded that the use of questions high in 'cognitive demand' by teachers has a positive effect on student achievement.

Unfortunately, however, studies in this area usually concentrate on comparisons of different types of questions and fail to explore any effects of different levels of teacher contributions of statements. In a small-scale study (Wood and Wood 1983) we found that where a teacher offers contributions that are high in level of presentation (e.g. speculations, opinions, reasoning, etc.) children are likely to respond in kind. Questions high in cognitive demand (similar to the definitions of Blank *et al.* 1978) also solicit high cognitive responses from children but at the cost of inhibiting follow-through, elaboration or spontaneous comments from them. Where teachers, in one sense, answer their own putative questions to provide possible answers, opinions and so on, children as young as four years of age reciprocate by adopting a similar cognitive–linguistic stance and remain relatively active and forthcoming at the same time.

High control of interactions by teachers in natural or contrived encounters, in laboratory, home or school, are likely to inhibit overt epistemic activity from children. Furthermore, the fact that children are not contributing ideas, asking questions or elaborating on their answers to the teacher's questions, but spending the vast majority of their time in complying or answering questions means that their thinking (unless they 'drop out' of the interaction) is almost entirely contingent upon the demands of the teacher. If teachers are not gaining knowledge from the children, then they have few opportunities for making any questions, comments or ideas that they have contingent upon the children's own thoughts, for these are simply not revealed or displayed.

The role played by children in teaching–learning encounters is fundamentally constrained by the way in which teachers manipulate control. If a child is not active, forthcoming and curious about the task at hand, the main cause of this inactivity may lie not in some 'inner resource' lacked by the child, but in the level of control and ensuing lack of opportunity for contingent instruction determined by the manner in which the teacher orchestrates the interaction.

TEACHING AS EPISTEMIC INQUIRY

Teaching is usually defined as the *transmission* of knowledge and the inculcation of skills and understanding. Such definitions seem reasonable but are inadequate and even misleading. Teaching also involves learning; it provides opportunities for the acquisition of knowledge. It is epistemic activity. Furthermore, the knowledge obtained from acts of teaching informs the process of effective teaching.

Piaget has characterized the child as a 'natural' epistemologist. We have not rejected this basic stance but argued that the epistemological activity of the child is, and often must be, enveloped within that of a teacher. Piaget has also demonstrated how the study of the systematic and 'universal' errors that children make can be exploited to investigate the nature and development of knowledge. Similarly, I have suggested that the study of 'errors after instructions' is a primary basis for learning about the learner, learning, what is being learned and teaching. An instruction from a teacher is, potentially, an epistemic probe as well as an attempt to prompt epistemic activity in the child. If it is treated as a hypothesis about the child's 'zone of proximal development', for example, then a failure to comply by the child suggests that the hypothesis may be invalid and that he or she needs more help. Conversely, success serves as a signal to the teacher to update her hypothesis about where the child is 'at' and, hence, to revise future instruction; in Bruner's economic metaphor to 'up the ante'. Teachers may utilize the fate of their own instructions as a basis for learning and revising their 'theory' of the child and what he or she is learning. The tremendous difficulties in doing this in school environments, however, often preclude such contingent instruction, and demand, essentially, that it is the child who must make his or her thinking contingent upon that of the teacher. If children are able and willing to be contingent upon the thought processes and actions of another, then learning may proceed. If they are not, then it seems unlikely that learning will follow.

Although we have been stressing the importance of teaching and exploring the complex questions of what effective instruction involves, this does not imply that effective teaching is a sufficient or always a necessary condition for learning. We have not been advocating a return to classical learning theory nor rejecting the now extensive evidence which shows that young children form hypotheses, infer and generalize rules to make creative and productive use of their experiences. But I have tried to identify some factors in natural and contrived encounters that serve to facilitate or inhibit such epistemic activities by the young child. Such a view leads us, for example, to attribute failure or lack of progress by a learner not simply to factors located 'in' the child but to constraints that arise as an emergent property of teacher–learner interactions. These, in turn, are tightly constrained by the nature of the institutions that we have invented to bring teachers and learners together. If we find ourselves dissatisfied with the interactions that take place in such institutions, measured against what we take to be the optimum contexts for learning, then we must question not simply the teacher's 'skills' but the form of the institution within which we expect these to be deployed.

REFERENCES

Blank, M., Rose, S. A. and Berlin, L. J. (1978) *The Language of Learning: the Preschool Years*, New York: Grune and Stratton.

Brazelton, T. B. (1982) 'Joint regulation of neonate-parent behavior', in E. Z. Tronick (ed.) *Social Interchange in Infancy: Affect, Cognition and Communication*, Baltimore, Mld: University Park Press.

Bruner, J. S. (1968) *Toward a Theory of Instruction*, New York: Norton.

Bruner, J. S. (1973) 'The organisation of early skilled action', *Child Development* 44: 1–11.

Bruner, J. S. (1983) *Child's Talk: Learning to Use Language*, Oxford: Oxford University Press.

Cole, M. and Scribner, S. (1974) *Culture and Thought: a Psychological Introduction*, New York: Wiley.

Cole, M., Hood, L. and McDermott, R. (1979) *Ecological Niche Picking*, New York: Rockefeller University Monographs.

Donaldson, M. (1978) *Children's Minds*, London: Fontana.

Dunn, J. and Kendrick, C. (1982) *Siblings: Love, Envy and Understanding*, London: Grant McIntyre.

Geppert, U. and Kuster, U. (1983) 'The emergence of "wanting to do it oneself": a precursor of achievement motivation', *International Journal of Behavioral Development* 6: 355–70.

Glachan, M. and Light, P. (1982) 'Peer interaction and learning: can two wrongs make a right?', in G. Butterworth and P. Light (eds) *Social Cognition: Studies of the Development of Understanding*, Brighton: Harvester.

Greenfield, P. M. and Bruner, J. S. (1969) 'Culture and cognitive growth', in

D. A. Goslin (ed.) *Handbook of Socialisation Theory and Research*, New York: Rand McNally.

Griffiths, A. J. (1983) 'The linguistic competence of deaf primary school children', Ph.D. thesis, University of Nottingham.

Lees, J. M. (1981) 'Conversational strategies with deaf children', M.Phil. thesis, University of Nottingham.

MacLure, M. and French, P. (1981) 'A comparison of talk at home and school', in G. Wells (ed.) *Learning Through Interaction: the Study of Language Development*, London: Cambridge University Press.

Mercer, N. and Edwards, D. (1981) 'Ground rules for mutual understanding', in N. Mercer (ed.) *Language in School and Community*, London: Edward Arnold.

Murphy, C. M. and Wood, D. J. (1981) 'Learning from pictures: the use of pictorial information by young children', *Journal of Experimental Child Psychology* 32: 279-97.

Piaget, J. and Inhelder, B. (1969) *The Psychology of the Child*, London: Routledge & Kegan Paul.

Redfield, D. L. and Rousseau, E. W. (1981) 'A meta-analysis of experimental research on teacher questioning behavior', *Review of Educational Research* 51: 237-45.

Rowe, M. B. (1974) 'Wait-time and rewards as instructional variables, their influence on language, logic and fate control. I. Wait time', *Journal of Research in Science Teaching* 11: 81-94.

Sigel, I. and McGillicuddy-Delisi, I. (in press) 'Parents as teachers to their children', in A. Pellegrini and T. Yawkey (eds) *The Development of Oral and Written Language*, Norwood, NJ: Ablex.

Swift, J. N. and Gooding, C. T. (1983) 'Interaction of wait time, feedback and questioning instruction on middle school science teaching', *Journal of Research in Science Teaching* 20: 721-30.

Tizard, B. and Hughes, M. (1984) *Young Children Learning: Talking and Thinking at Home and School*, London: Fontana.

Tizard, B., Philips, J. and Plewis, I. (1976) 'Staff behaviour in pre-school centres', *Journal of Child Psychology and Psychiatry* 17: 251-64.

Vurpillot, E. (1976) *The Visual World of the Child*, London: George Allen & Unwin.

Vygotsky, L. S. (1978) *Mind in Society: the Development of Higher Psychological Processes*, Cambridge, Mass.: Harvard University Press.

Walkerdine, V. (1982) 'From context to text: a psychosemiotic approach to abstract thought', in M. Beveridge (ed.) *Children Thinking Through Language*, London: Arnold.

Weikart, D. P. (1973) Cited in Brainerd, C. J. (1983) 'Modifiability of cognitive development', in S. Meadows (ed.) *Developing Thinking: Approaches to Children's Cognitive Development*, London and New York: Methuen.

Wells, G. (1979) 'Variation in child language', in P. Fletcher and M. Garman (eds), *Language Acquisition*, Cambridge: Cambridge University Press.

Wood, D. J. (1980a) 'Teaching the young child: some relationships between social interaction, language and thought', in D. Olson (ed.) *Social Foundations of Language and Cognition: Essays in Honor of J. S. Bruner*, New York: Norton.

Wood, D. J. (1980b) 'Models of childhood', in A. J. Chapman and D. M. Jones (eds) *Models of Man*, London: The British Psychological Society.

Wood, D. J. (1983) 'Teaching: natural and contrived', *Child Development Society Newsletter*, no. 32, London: Institute of Education.

Wood, D. J., Bruner, J. S. and Ross, G. (1976) 'The role of tutoring in problem solving', *Journal of Child Psychology and Psychiatry* 17: 89–100.

Wood, D. J. and Cooper, P. J. (1980) 'Maternal facilitation of 4–5 year old children's memory for recent events', *Proceedings of the XXIInd International Congress of Psychology*, Leipzig, East Germany: International Union of Psychological Science.

Wood, D. J. and Middleton, D. J. (1975) 'A study of assisted problem solving', *British Journal of Psychology* 66: 181–91.

Wood, D. J., McMahon, L. and Cranstoun, Y. (1980) *Working with Under-fives*, London: Grant McIntyre.

Wood, D .J., Wood, H. A. and Middleton, D. J. (1978) 'An experimental evaluation of four face-to-face teaching strategies', *International Journal of Behavioral Development* 1: 131–47.

Wood, D. J., Wood, H. A., Griffiths, A. J., Howarth, P. and Howarth, C. I. (1982) 'The structure of conversations with 6- to 10-year-old deaf children', *Journal of Child Psychology and Psychiatry* 23: 295–308.

Wood, D. J. and Wood, H. A. (1985) 'Teacher questions and pupil initiative', paper to the American Educational Research Association, Chicago, USA.

Wood, H. A. and Wood, D. J. (1983) 'Questioning the pre-school child', *Educational Review* 35: Special Issue (15), 149–62.

Wood, H. A. and Wood, D. J. (1984) 'An experimental evaluation of five styles of teacher conversations on the language of hearing-impaired children', *Journal of Child Psychology and Psychiatry* 25: 45–62.

Woodhead, M. (1985) 'Pre-school education has long effects: but can they be generalized?, *Oxford Review of Education* 11: 133–55.

7 Reconstructing context: the conventionalization of classroom knowledge

Derek Edwards and Neil Mercer

Source: Edwards, D. and Mercer, N. (1989) 'Reconstructing context: the conventionalization of classroom knowledge', *Discourse Processes* 12: 91–104.

> Ultimately, social contexts consist of mutually shared and ratified definitions of situation and in the social actions persons take on the basis of these definitions.
>
> (Erickson and Schultz 1981: 148)

The 'context' of any utterance or stretch of discourse is more complex and more interesting than it first appears to be. At the simplest level, context can be defined as the surrounding speech, or text. And perhaps to this definition can be added the surrounding circumstances of persons, time, and place in which the discourse is created. But the implication remains that context is something finite and observable, available for scrutiny in the transcript or the video recording. Things are not so convenient. Although the investigators might have the luxury of access to recordings and transcripts, the participants themselves, like the referees whose decisions are examined in television's slow-motion replays, must rely on what they perceive, understand, and remember at the time. It is a commonplace of cognitive psychology that perception, remembering, and understanding are not processes that have a straightforward, veridical relationship to the world. But, the fact that the investigator's recourse to context was only, in the first place, made in an effort to understand the communications of the participants leads to the conclusion that this apparent luxury of a privileged vantage point could be illusory. Context is not concrete for the observer, but intersubjective for the participants.

In Vygotsky's (1978; cf. Wertsch 1985) terms, context is 'intermental,' a function of the joint actions and understandings of the communicators. Vygotsky was not much concerned with the context and continuity of discourse but, rather, with the social, intermental origins of individual thought. He strove to develop a cultural–historical account of the nature of thinking and knowledge, of the 'higher mental processes.' This concern with the cultural basis of knowledge, and more specifically with its linguistic and semiotic basis, was an important feature of Vygotsky's psychology, which, though neglected by subsequent generations of cognitive psychologists, he shared with one of the founders of that discipline, Sir Frederick Bartlett (1932). Much of Bartlett's work was devoted to exploration of the cultural basis of thinking and remembering, especially with the process of 'conventionalization,' through which cultural symbols, signs, and texts, and the mental schemata that used them, took on their recognized properties. In an extended discussion of this and other aspects of Bartlett's work, Edwards and Middleton (1987) show that it was the sociohistorical process through which symbolic materials become conventionalized, not merely some version of schematic information processing, that Bartlett was trying to reproduce in his well-known studies of serial remembering in individuals.

> The method of serial reproduction, famous as a paradigm for the study of memory, was essentially designed to capture the process of conventionalization. Remembering was for Bartlett not simply the recalling of experience, but rather a fundamentally symbolic process both rooted in and constitutive of culture, forming and formed by symbols and meanings transmitted in texts and pictures.
>
> (Edwards and Middleton 1987: 79)

So, the Vygotskian approach encourages an examination of the process of classroom education as a joint enterprise involving teacher and learner in the establishment of a common understanding. Bartlett's psychology offers the notion that what develops between teacher and pupil might be conceived of as a collective memory, a joint version of things encoded symbolically, in which shared understandings become established through the development of a common language and a common discursive context. The study of classroom discourse therefore offers an appropriate basis for looking at how classroom understandings are constituted socially.

Studies of classroom discourse have concentrated, for the large part, upon the structured nature and sequencing of talk (e.g. Sinclair and Coulthard 1975), and on the role of this talk in the social organization of classrooms (e.g. Edwards and Furlong 1978; Mehan 1979). They offer a version of classroom talk in which what occurs is revealed as a cooperative negotiation of meanings from moment to moment as the interaction proceeds. But as Griffin and Mehan (1981) have stressed, 'interlocutors have a history' (p. 191). This paper concerns the development of shared knowledge rather than the micro social order. It is a matter of emphasis, the psychologist's concern rather than the sociologist's. Not that these disciplines can or should sustain their usual distance. In fact, the authors agree with Griffin and Mehan that

> There is no evidence, as far as we know, that the process or structures proposed as acceptable analyses of the cognitive, academic or content aspects of lessons would be any different from the processes or structures involved in the social aspects. . . . The increments to a child's skills, concepts or information base that a lesson is designed to facilitate are not available for the teacher to offer, or for the child to grasp, or for the analyst to locate except as they are instantiated in the social negotiations of the speech event.
>
> (Griffin and Mehan 1981: 191)

For pupils in school, the only knowledge that counts is that which is, or can be, communicated (cf. Mercer and Edwards 1981).

Transcripts of classroom dialogue will be examined, looking for some features of how the participants establish a shared understanding of the curriculum, what has been called a 'common knowledge' (Edwards and Mercer 1987). The specific features of concern here are those that might have interested Bartlett, the *reconstructive rememberings*. As the discourse proceeds, it carries and builds with it a basis of shared understandings in terms of which the participants are able to make joint sense of what they are saying and doing, of how these things should be understood and talked about, and of what constructions to put upon experience. This *intermental context* is precisely that – intermental, defined, created, and assumed by the participants, rather than simply available to the investigators through flipping back through the pages of transcript. The aim of this study is to demonstrate a conception of educational knowledge (and by implication, other sorts of knowledge too), as socially constructed and reconstructed, conventionalized and historical, socialized and socializing. The historical and socializing aspects derive from two further, and related, facts about our school classroom data:

1 The preexistence of the curriculum and of the great historical accumulation of fact and method, procedure and assumption from which this is drawn.
2 The teacher's role in controlling and guiding the learning process, as authoritative representative of the educated culture.

These two aspects are considered to have been neglected in discourse-analytic and ethnomethodological studies of classroom talk.

CONTEXT AS COMMON KNOWLEDGE

The video recordings of classroom lessons derive from a larger study in state schools in the Midlands of England, with teachers and groups of 9- to 10-year-olds. They were made in sequences of three lessons that successively developed some particular topic (e.g., how to do computer graphics using LOGO, or experiments on the science of pendulums). This facilitated the gain of some information about how collective knowledge was built from lesson to lesson, as well as within lessons.

This building process was most apparent at the beginning of lessons. Sequence 1 is the opening talk from the first of three lessons on computer graphics. In this and subsequent sequences of dialogue, diagonal slashes represent pauses (one for pauses less than 2 sec, two for longer ones). Notes on situational features, actions, and gestures are in the right-hand column.

Sequence 1: Introducing the lesson

T: Right/this is our new computer/the four eighty zed. You haven't seen this one before. Erm when you've used computer programs before/ what's happened is that the words have come up on the screen/or the instructions/for you/have come up on the screen/and you've just answered the questions/and typed in/what the/ computer wanted you to do. This program is different. In this program the computer doesn't know what to do. You've got to tell it what to do/so you have got to instruct the computer.	(An RML 480Z micro). Teacher gestures with arm toward screen.

The teacher began the lesson by introducing the pupils to their new computer and immediately established a context for it in terms of their previous experience with computers in the classroom. Lessons typically began in this manner, with introductions to the work to be done and continuity links established with what had been done previously. Thus Lesson 2, recorded a week later, began with a back reference to where the previous computer lesson had left off.

Sequence 2: Building upon the previous lesson

T: Now you've got your programs from last
week have you/to show me what you're   T reminding pupils of
Pupils: Yes.   instruction she gave
T: (continuing) going to do/with angles not   last week.
nintey degrees./We had to try something
else didn't we? What did you find most
difficult Susan? What's yours?

Besides these opening links, explicit references were also made during
lessons to what had been done and said earlier. Sequence 3 lists the
teacher's back references from the last of three lessons on making clay
pottery. (This is a different teacher, pupils, and school).

Sequence 3: Back references to shared experience and talk

- What did I tell you about thin bits? What happens when they dry?
- What did I tell you about eyes?
- Can you remember what you forgot to do Patricia/when you put
  that little belt thing round?
- Look when you put its eyes in./I did tell you this before Lorraine.
- John/you seem to have forgotten everything you've learned don't
  you?
- Don't forget/if it's too wide chop it off.

In Sequence 3, the teacher's remarks to John and Lorraine reflect the
fact that constructing a continuity of shared knowledge can be a
problematic process. Indeed, all of the cases listed in Sequence 3
occurred in the context of some difficulty arising with regard to the
understanding that teacher and pupils had established up to that
point in the lesson. That is, the teacher was most likely to point out
that knowledge was, in her opinion, shared when pupils were acting
as though it were not. When the pupils seemed not to have grasped
some significant principle, procedure, or instruction, the teacher
would remind them that this matter had, in fact, been dealt with
previously.

It has been suggested that this association of explicit references to
past shared experience, including previous discourse, with occasions
on which the commonality of knowledge appears to be in doubt is a
general feature of conversation, not something peculiar to school

classrooms. It has been observed in adult conversation in educational and noneducational settings (Edwards and Middleton 1986; Mercer and Edwards 1987) and in parent–child conversation during early language learning (Edwards and Goodwin 1986). In the classroom, however, such explicit appeals to significant aspects of past shared experience might have an important pedagogical function. As transactions between child and adult, they occur in Vygotsky's 'zone of proximal development', at precisely the points at which common knowledge is being created. It is the teacher's role to draw children's attention to such matters, and so establish knowledge that is both common and communicable. The next sequence illustrates this very clearly.

Sequence 4: Continuity: What have you been doing all along?

T: Now/how are you fixing them on Katie?

Katie: Putting them/well its (. . .)   Katie mutters
                                              hesitantly.
T: Now/what do you think you should do
   what have you been doing all along every
   time you've joined anything?

Katie: Putting grooves in it.

T: Putting grooves in it/haven't you and
   water/ grooves and water/the water to fill
   up the grooves/on both bits of clay./You
   must do it/ otherwise it will dry/and when
   it's dry like those are dry/those ears will
   just be lying on the floor/or the table.
   Take them off/otherwise you'll be very   Katie refits the ears.
   sad./You've got to do things the right way
   round with clay or they just don't work.

Sequence 4 is taken from the second of three pottery lessons. The teacher noticed that Katie was having problems and so intervened and appealed explicitly to a continuity of shared experience: 'What have you been doing all along?' The exchange succeeded in focusing Katie's awareness on what the teacher perceived to be the salient part of her actions, this, then, becoming the necessary shared mental context for the teacher's explanation of why those actions were important – 'You must do it/otherwise it will dry.' One might argue that this is an essential element of good teaching: explanation is built upon an appeal to shared experience, or rather to selected aspects of joint experience and activity, made explicit through the discourse.

It would seem, then, that the teachers' use of explicit recaps was to ensure that pupils had developed a joint understanding, with the teachers, of the significant aspects of what had been said and done. The establishment of this *legitimized* version of shared past experience could then become the basis of further teaching, a shared mental context for what was to follow. This is a process particularly well illustrated in the next sequence, taken from the second of a series of lessons on solvents (in this case, on the effects of different household washing products on stained fabrics). It is an abbreviated part of a lesson introduction that went on for about 10 minutes. Omitted discourse has been indicated thus: (. . .). In it, the teacher is attempting to establish continuity among what has happened in the previous lesson, the present situation, and what the children will go on to do next.

Sequence 5: Past, present and future

T: Now the other day we were talking about which washing powder was going to wash best. And when we began talking about it you gave me some positive firm answers./What made you say what you did say?   To Tom.

Tom: Well//we used a popular television things

T: Yes erm//well you were thinking about the ones that were advertised on television./Yes/ What did you say first of all? Which washing powder did you think was going to wash best?

Tom: Persil

T: What did you think?   To Ellie.

Ellie: Persil.

T: Persil. Somebody said Daz./Who was that? (. . .) And you were thinking *then* about what your mothers said.

Pupils: Yeh.

T: And what your mothers used.

Pupils: Yeh.

T: Weren't you? (. . .) Then we went on and we looked at what the manufacturers said on the packets about their products and you then thought that which washing powder was going to wash best?

Mary: Ariel.

T: Ariel. And what made you say that Ariel

Mary: It digests dirt and stains (. . .)   Mary interrupts T.
T: Yes it digests dirt and stains (. . .) *Now   *T turns to equipment
   when you're staining your fabrics, you've   laid out on table.
   got your stains out here.// How much
   stain are you going to use?
Ellie: Two blobs//two blobs of five on the
   cloth.
T: You're going to make two separate areas
   of five drops not squirts. And then (. . .)

RECONSTRUCTING A COLLECTIVE MEMORY

It should not be thought that the establishment of collective classroom memories was a process dominated merely by communicative necessity, nor the pursuit of an accurate record of events. It was also an arena in which what might actually have happened could be creatively reinterpreted in the light of what ought to have happened, a process guided in turn by the teacher's privileged position as one who knew in advance what truths were there to be discovered. The teachers studied made use of a variety of powerful discursive devices (for an account of these, see Edwards and Mercer 1987), through which, despite an overtly child-oriented, invitational, and eliciting style of talking to pupils, a tight rein could nevertheless be kept upon what was collectively done, thought, and understood. These devices ranged from the obvious, such as controlling pupils' contributions; sanctioning who should speak, when, and about what; ignoring unwelcome contributions and selectively encouraging others, to the very subtle, such as introducing understandings or versions of events via presupposition and implication, effectively defining them as 'given', to be taken as understood, as not open to question.

Through another such device, that of 'reconstructive paraphrasing', the teacher was able to impose a preferred vocabulary, or conventional description, merely by paraphrasing her repetition of what a pupil had just said. But the most extensive reconstructions were those that occurred typically at the beginnings and ends of lessons, when teacher and pupils were establishing what was to count as common knowledge, how the context of shared experience, upon which subsequent teaching and learning would proceed, should be defined. The concentration here will be on these latter sorts of events, in which the process of creating a joint version of events, a joint understanding, can be seen as one of symbolic conventionalization of knowledge, controlled by the teacher.

Sequence 6 occurred in Lesson 2 on the pendulum, when the teacher was recapping, via the familiar sorts of IRF elicitations (see Mehan 1979; Sinclair and Coulthard 1975), Lesson 1. Both teacher and pupils took advantage of the opportunity to offer a more acceptable version of events. The teacher was in the process of asking each pair of pupils to recount what they had discovered in their respective experiments.

Sequence 6: Recapping the main empirical findings

T: Jonathan/you and Lucy.
Jonathan: Well we tried different weights/on the
    end of the*/on the end of the pen thing   *Pauses, points
    whatever you call it.   to pendulum.
T: And how did you change the weight? What
    did you use?
    Jonathan: Erm/washers.   Points with pencil
       at pendulum.
T: That's right yes.
Jonathan: And did them at the same height each
    time/and then/they all came out/the same.
T: Which surprised you didn't it?
Jonathan: Yeh.   Jonathan nods.

It had been Jonathan and Lucy's task to vary the weight of the pendulum bob, using different numbers of metal washers, and to measure the effect this had on its period of swing (the time taken to swing to and fro). As the teacher knew, but the pupils did not, the weight variable ought to have no effect on the period of swing. After some negotiation with the teacher in Lesson 1, this had been agreed upon as what had indeed been 'found'. The most notable reconstruction in Sequence 6 is Jonathan's declaration that he and his partner had varied weight alone, that they had changed the number of washers 'and done them at the same height (angle) each time'. What had actually happened was that angle of swing, as well as weight of the bob, had been varied, a fact that the teacher had clearly witnessed but chose at the time (in Lesson 1) to ignore. This was important for scientific reasons. It had never been established whether or not the proper experimental controls had been observed when altering the two variables. By Lesson 2, the experimental principle of altering variables one at a time had been grasped (though its rationale remained unexplained), and pupils and teacher were now prepared to collude in a blatant revision of what had actually occurred in Lesson 1.

In the same vein, Jonathan's claim that the results surprised him was a direct contradiction of his declaration in Lesson 1 that the results were precisely as he had predicted. Indeed, his reconstruction in Lesson 2 of what he had done and thought in Lesson 1 now incorporated the subsequently confirmed hypothesis: 'I thought it might go faster because it has a different weight'. These discrepancies are not treated as mere errors of recall or, for that matter, of honesty. Indeed, surrounded as he was by witnesses and video-recording paraphernalia, there would seem little point in such motives. Here is the collective establishment of a common version of events, the construction of a small piece of conventional wisdom.

Also in Lesson 2, Sharon and Karen were called upon to recount their experiment, the one that varied angle of swing.

Sequence 7: Reconstructing a principle of equal intervals

T: Right we started off at/what was this one?

> T indicates leftmost position on x-axis of graph displayed on OHP.

Sharon: Forty degrees

T: Forty?

> T pointing to next position (55°).

Sharon: Fifty-five degrees.

T: Yes:

> T pointing to 70519, then to 85° marks on x-axis of graph.

Sharon: Seventy degrees and eight-five degrees.

T: Yes/erm/did you follow any particular pattern? Is there any reason why you chose those angles or did you just sort of chalk/

Sharon: Fifteen degrees difference.

T: Good girl fifteen degrees difference between the two. That's valuable when you're doing and experiment/to try and establish some sort of a pattern/in the numbers/or the erm timing or/ whatever it is that you're using. Try and keep the pattern the same/ the interval* the same/ for example between the degrees.

> T looking around group, using up-turned hand with finger tips joined (precision gesture). *T holds palms of hand a fixed interval apart and moves them sideways through the air.

The clear impression to be gained from Sequence 7 is that Sharon and Karen chose angles that were equal distances apart, 15°, as a matter of proper scientific procedure. This time the text of Lesson 1 (Sequence 8) will be examined to see what actually happened. In fact, the four angles had first been marked without measurement on the top of the pendulum, and then, only after the experiment was completed, were estimated, under the teacher's guidance, to be equidistant at intervals of 15°. The girls had in fact determined their various angles of swing earlier in the lesson by uncalibrated trial and error, constrained, not by any principle of scientific measurement, but by the angles at which the string was found to snag on the pendulum upright.

Sequence 8: How the equal intervals were measured

Sharon: We're stuck.
T: You're stuck Sharon?

> T gets up and moves round table to Sharon and Karen.

Sharon: We're going to find (. . .)
T: What love?

> T moving into position in front of Sharon and Karen's pendulum.

Sharon: I'm going to find the angles/and/
T: The angles that you've used
Karen: We can't get the protractor on there.

> Karen pointing to top plate of pendulum where lines are marked at different angles.

T: Well what I always do in cases like that I usually guess.

> Sharon turns away laughing.

Karen: I know that that one's roughly ninety degrees.
T: What one would that one be Karen?
Karen: That's roughly ninety degrees.

> Karen pointing to the uppermost line.

> Karen still pointing.

T: Roughly/is it quite ninety or would it be [more/less?
Karen: [Not quite/just less I think.

> (Square brackets mark simultaneous speech).

T: So what then?

Karen: Just/

Sharon: Eighty-five?   Sharon to Karen.

Karen: Yeh.

T: Come on then/eighty-five/Now
   what   Sharon, T and Karen bend
                                  forward, watching as Sharon
                                    writes on her notepad.

   about this one at the bottom then?
   That's ninety.   T points in turn to bottom
                                    line and then to top (90°
                                    line).

Karen: That one's ninety. That one's
   roughly forty-five.   Karen points appropriately to
                                    top and bottom lines in turn.

T: More or less than forty-five?

Karen: Less.

T: Less than forty-five so/

Karen: Forty.

T: Forty.//   Rising intonation; all bend
                                    forward and watch again as
                                    Sharon writes on the pad.

   And what about the ones in   T and Karen look up at top
   between?   plate.

Karen: Well/that's going to be/   Karen points to 3rd line
                                    down.

Sharon: That one will be seventy
   then//
                                    Sharon points up towards
                                    2nd line down then writes on
                                    pad.

Karen: So that one must be about/   T walks over to Antony and
                                    David as Karen and Sharon
                                    work out the remaining
                                    angle, between 70 and 40.

Sharon: Thirty.

Karen: Thirty-five?   (Note that 30 and 35 are both
                                    less than 40°; these
                                    impossible estimates were
                                    later surreptitiously replaced
                                    by '55°')

The conventionalization of classroom knowledge can be seen in the way that what began as a casual positioning of marks on the pendulum was constructed in Lesson 1, and further refined in Lesson 2, into the guiding scientific principle of using equidistant measurement intervals. Clearly, notwithstanding the edifice of Piagetian developmental psychology, it would be inadvisable to place too much emphasis on the importance of what pupils learn simply from their own activity and experience. At least as important is the conventional sense put upon that experience, the words that define and communicate it, the principles encapsulated in the words, and the reworking of events that those words carry. Furthermore, the social basis of what pupils come to understand is founded not only upon the intrinsically social nature of discourse, but also upon the nature of the relationship between teacher and pupil. In the various lessons that have been observed, it was largely the teacher who provided the criteria of conventionality, the terms and versions to be adopted, while eliminating others from the common vocabulary and all the time governing the discursive process in which particular descriptions and versions of events were established. The establishment of a conventional wisdom was contingent upon an exercise of power.

CONCLUSION: INTERMENTAL CONTEXTS AND COLLECTIVE MEMORY

In agreeing on a reconstructed version of classroom knowledge and experience, pupils are indeed active participants in the process. But their role is not the same as the teacher's. The eventual conventionalizations of remembered experience are those that the teacher knew in advance, or could at least judge when they arose, to be 'right'. In his account of the creation of conventions, David Lewis (1969) shows how social rituals, the conventionalized and implicit bases of social encounters, are initially explicated and later become implicit, or 'understood', through reiteration. This is the sense of 'ritual' invoked by Goffman (1971) and by Griffin and Mehan (1981). Although there are intriguing similarities, it is Bartlett's (1932) notion of conventionalization that is closer to the one pursued here, being concerned more explicitly with the cultural–historical dimension of psychological representations and depictions of events. From the cultural perspective, much of the knowledge that children must acquire is older than they are, originates from outside of the classroom and beyond their discourse with the teacher, and operates as a constraint and guide, through the teacher's mediating agency, to the significance of classroom discoveries and experiences.

The role of memory, or remembering, in school has a long and controversial pedigree. It is associated most strongly with what has become known as the 'traditional', or 'transmissional' sort of education, in which children were required to rehearse verbatim their multiplication tables, pages of classical poetry, conjugations and declensions, dates of battles and kings and treaties, mathematical formulae and derivations, the number of pounds in a ton or yards in a furlong. With the advent of the more 'child-centered', 'progressive' sorts of pedagogy, the importance of brute memory has been diminished. According to this more modern educational philosophy, children are to be guided along a more personal path of development, and it is as much a process of growth from within as of learning what is given. Knowledge is created, constructed by the learner, not merely passively acquired from textbooks and teacher talk, nor written upon some tabula rasa. But it is not rote learning that has been examined here. The study of educational discourse as the development and shaping of collective accounts and understandings has much to offer our conception of schooling. Indeed, it is the key to reconciling the active, exploratory conception of learning with the one strength that the older, traditional sort of pedagogy possessed: a recognition of culture, of the preexistence of knowledge. Children do not just happen to reinvent the knowledge of centuries.

The notion of memory, or remembering, as the rote learning of materials has little relevance to modern educational practice. The notion of a developing consensus of shared knowledge is much more interesting. The idea that education involves collective remembering, discourse-based construction, and conventionalization of experience, has two complementary foundations. One is that educational knowledge has the properties of a ready-made culture that precedes the coming together of teacher and pupils. The other is the process of collective remembering itself, the building of a context and continuity of shared knowledge as joint activity and discourse proceed. In developing a shared vocabulary for experience and understanding, and a jointly held version of events in the classroom, teacher and pupils construct together a framework of educational knowledge that reflects both sides of the process, that is, pupils' experiences in the classroom and the principles and categories of understanding that the curriculum, or the teacher's preconceptions, have set as the agenda to be learned.

REFERENCES

Bartlett, F. C. (1932) *Remembering: A Study in Experimental and Social Psychology*, Cambridge: Cambridge University Press.

Edwards, A. D. and Furlong, V. J. (1978) *The Language of Teaching*, London: Heinemann.

Edwards, D. and Goodwin, R. Q. (1986) 'The language of shared attention and visual experience: A functional study of early nomination', *Journal of Pragmatics* 9: 475–93.

Edwards, D. and Mercer, N. M. (1987) *Common Knowledge: The Growth of Understanding in the Classroom*, London: Methuen.

Edwards, D. and Middleton, D. J. (1986) 'Conversation and remembering: Constructing an account of shared experience through conversational discourse', *Discourse Processes* 9: 423–59.

Edwards, D. and Middleton, D. J. (1987) 'Conversation and remembering: Bartlett revisited', *Applied Cognitive Psychology* 1: 77–92.

Erickson, F. and Schultz, J. (1981) 'When is a context? Some issues and methods in the analysis of social competence', in J. L. Green and C. Wallat (eds) *Ethnography and Language in Educational Settings*, Norwood, NJ: Ablex.

Goffman, E. (1971) *Relations in Public: Microstudies of the Public Order*, Harmondsworth, England: Penguin Books.

Griffin, P. and Mehan, H. (1981) 'Sense and ritual in classroom discourse', in F. Coulmas (ed.) *Conversational Routine: Explorations in Standardized Communication Situations and Prepatterned Speech*, The Hague: Mouton.

Lewis, D. K. (1969) *Convention: A Philosophical Study*, London: Oxford University Press.

Mehan, H. (1979) *Learning Lessons: Social Organization in the Classroom*, Cambridge, MA: Harvard University Press.

Mercer N. M. and Edwards, D. (1981) 'Ground rules for mutual understanding: Towards a social psychological approach to classroom knowledge', in N. M. Mercer (ed.) *Language in School and Community*, London: Edward Arnold.

Mercer, N. M. and Edwards D. (1987) 'Knowledge development in adult learning groups', *Open Learning* 2: 22–8.

Sinclair, J. McH. and Coulthard, R. M. (1975) *Towards an Analysis of Discourse: The English Used by Teachers and Pupils*, London: Oxford University Press.

Vygotsky, L. S. (1978) *Mind in Society: The Development of Higher Psychological Processes*, London: Harvard University Press.

Wertsch, J. V. (1985) *Vygotsky and the Social Formation of Mind*, London: Harvard University Press.

8 Social context effects in learning and testing

Paul Light and Anne-Nelly Perret-Clermont
Source: Gellatly, A., Rogers, D. and Sloboda, J. (eds) (1989) *Cognition and Social Worlds*, Oxford: Clarendon Press.

INTRODUCTION

Within academic developmental psychology the dominant view of cognitive development has always had a more or less maturationalist flavour. In the 1940s and 1950s cognitive development was frequently characterized as unfolding through stages regulated by internal biological mechanisms (e.g. Gessell 1943). In the 1960s and 1970s, under the influence of Piaget, this conception was elaborated into a view of intelligence as a progressive construction involving feedback. The basic ingredients of development (the body with its physiological and psychological regulatory processes) are given at birth. Development proceeds step by step, and involves the integration of the child's experiences into cognitive functioning. However, such integration is constrained by the fact that the child's capacity for experience is itself determined by his or her present intellectual structures or schemas.

This conception of cognitive development bears all the hallmarks of 'cognitivist' approaches in psychology generally. It is focused very heavily upon the *individual* and upon the characteristics of the individual's endogenous mental organization at different stages of development. Development consists essentially in the stage-by-stage construction of new logical or 'operational' competences. Procedures developed by Piaget and his associates were refined and formalized in order to provide precise diagnostic tests for these various competences. Conservation (the understanding that number, volume, weight, etc. remain invariant across various transformations) emerged for Piaget as perhaps the most critical element in the genesis of operational thought (e.g. Piaget 1968: 121), and the conservation test became one of the 'trade marks' of the Piagetian approach in developmental psychology and education. In the present chapter we shall use the conservation test as a case study in an examination of emerging alternatives to the long-dominant maturationalist/Piagetian view.

Any essentially maturational view of cognitive development necessarily relegates social factors (language and social experience in the family, the peer group, the school, etc.) to a secondary role. Such factors may facilitate or inhibit but they have no genuinely constitutive function. By contrast, in the alternative 'sociogenic' traditions reaching back to the work of G. H. Mead and Vygotsky, cognitive development is treated as essentially a social–cultural product. A combination of social and symbolic factors associated with the family, the school, peer groups, mass media, social ritual, and work and play activities are constitutive of cognitive processes. Language is seen as having a crucial part to play. Since the mid 1970s the developmental literature has reflected a marked revival of interest in this approach, with both theoretical and empirical interest centring more and more clearly on the conception of cognitive development as a social/symbolic process. Interestingly, many students of the social conditions of learning and development have found in the conservation test a useful microcosm for the study of socio-cognitive processes. Thus if conservation has continued to hold a central place in the concerns of psychologists, it is partly because it serves as a useful bridge or point of connection between contemporary socio-cognitive work and the large corpus of Piagetian work built up over recent decades.

In the sections which follow we shall focus first on a line of predominantly Swiss research concerned with the developmental potential of child–child interaction in the context of conservation. Then we shall review some predominantly British work in which the conservation test has been examined as a social interaction between tester and child, governed by 'conversational' rules. In the latter part of the chapter we shall explore the recent signs of convergence between these two lines of research and will argue a case for seeing cognitive development (and in particular conservation) in terms of a socially grounded process of co-construction of meanings.

PEER INTERACTION AND CONSERVATION

In some of his early work (especially *The Moral Judgment of the Child* 1932) Piaget had suggested a privileged role for child–child interaction in 'decentring' the child's thought. At very much the same time Mead (in *Mind Self and Society* 1934) and Vygotsky (in *Thought and Language* 1934/1962) emphasized the establishment of shared meanings in interaction and the role of play and 'inner speech' in the development of thought. It took some forty years for these ideas to spawn any strong tradition of empirical work on cognitive development. Paradoxically, perhaps, the conservation test, itself a product of Piaget's later much more individualistic psychology, provided one of the main vehicles for this development.

In the mid-1970s in Geneva, Doise, Mugny, and Perret-Clermont embarked on a series of experimental studies designed to address the issue of the role of peer interaction in cognitive development (Doise, Mugny, and Perret-Clermont 1975; Perret-Clermont 1976). This work (together with parallel work elsewhere in Europe, e.g. Carugati, De Paolis, and Mugny 1979; Rijsman, Zoetebier, Ginther, and Doise 1980) involved a three-step procedure. First, individual children, typically 4- to 7-year-olds, were pre-tested. Then some were assigned to pairs or small groups for an interaction session, while others (controls) worked alone. Finally, all children were individually post-tested.

In the case of conservation of liquids (Perret-Clermont 1980), for example, the experimental procedure might take the following course. At the pre-test stage a conservation of liquid test is administered to each child individually. Two identical glasses are filled to the same level and the child is asked whether they each contain the same amount. When he or she has agreed that they do, the contents of one are poured into, say, a taller, thinner glass. The child is then asked whether the two glasses still contain the same amount of liquid. Justifications are sought. Other more or less closely related conservation procedures may also be included in the pre-test. About a week later, each child who failed to conserve at pre-test is allocated to an interaction or control condition. The interaction session might for example involve being paired with another child (conserver or non-conserver) in order to 'play a game' involving sharing out juice equally. The adult experimenter gives one child a glass which is taller and thinner than the other child's and tells the non-conserving child to pour out equal shares. A third glass, identical to one of the others, is available for their use. The 'game' ends when the children agree that they both have the same amount to drink. The post-test session a week later mirrors the pre-test.

The results of such studies (e.g. Perret-Clermont 1980; Perret-Clermont and Schubauer-Leoni 1981) show that, under certain circumstances, children who participated in the interaction session show significantly more pre- to post-test progress than control subjects who do not have the opportunity to interact with a peer. Pairing with a partner who presented the *correct* response did not appear to be a necessary condition for progress. Other studies using different conservation tasks or other types of task involving spatial transformations or co-ordinations have obtained similar results (e.g. Ames and Murray 1982; Doise and Mugny 1981; Glachan and Light 1982).

The interpretation of these findings was principally in terms of *socio-cognitive conflict*. In the peer interaction situation, according to this explanation, the child is confronted with alternative and conflicting solutions which, while not necessarily offering the correct response, suggest some relevant dimensions which the child might otherwise have neglected. Moreover, the social context in which these conflicting solutions are proffered is of such a character that each child has to take account of his or her partner's view in order to pursue the social interaction in which they are jointly involved.

Progress occurs through a conflict of centrations which can only be resolved by the achievement of a new 'decentred' cognitive schema which can account for the various points of view. Thus socio-cognitive conflict can occur whenever partners to an interaction offer differing solutions, whether or not any of these solutions is correct.

Socio-cognitive conflict is an inherently social mechanism, in that progress is envisaged as resulting from inter-individual conflict (conflict between the viewpoints of different persons) rather than from intra-individual cognitive conflict or dissonance. However, while this interpretation offers a clear role for social interaction, such interaction remains essentially an 'external' factor, stimulating the child's cognitive development but not determining its content or direction. Put in very simple terms, maybe the child, in this interpretation, does not progress towards operational thinking entirely on his or her own, but only needs a little help from a friend.

There were indications right from the outset that children's responses in these three-step experiments were influenced by wider socio-cultural factors (Mackie 1980; Perret-Clermont 1980; Perret-Clermont and Mugny 1985), but rather than pursue these at this stage we shall introduce in the next section a separate strand of work, also developed through the late 1970s and early 1980s, which approached the role of social interaction in a rather different way.

THE CONSERVATION TEST AS AN INTERACTIONAL SETTING

Doise, Mugny, and Perret-Clermont, in the works to which we have been referring, have been grappling with the problem of how children *learn* to conserve. A rather different concern has been central to the work of Donaldson (1978), and others in Britain and the United

States, who have been concerned primarily with how children's understanding of conservation can be validly *assessed*. For this reason, their experimental work has typically involved single-session testing rather than the three-step procedures described in the previous section.

McGarrigle and Donaldson's (1975) 'Conservation accidents' paper remains probably the best known in this literature, and exemplifies very clearly the central concern with how the child represents or understands *what is going on* in the conservation test. Four- and five-year-olds were given a variety of conservation tests in the usual way and, as expected, few showed any understanding of conservation. However, they were also tested using a variation of the procedure in which instead of the transformation of materials (the curling up of string in a length conservation task or the bunching up of counters in a number conservation task) being achieved by a deliberate and focused act of the adult experimenter, it resulted from an apparently haphazard or mischievous action of a teddy bear. 'Naughty teddy' was in actual fact manipulated by the experimenter, but McGarrigle and Donaldson hoped by using it to avoid a misleading suggestion which they felt was implicit in the usual procedure. They suggested that the usual conservation testing procedure created an ambiguity, since whereas the experimenter referred verbally (in his questions), to, let us say, number, he referred nonverbally (through his actions in transforming the materials) to a different factor such as spacing or length of rows. Certainly the use of the naughty teddy bear to achieve the transformations resulted in substantially higher levels of correct response.

Other ways have also been found of rendering the transformation of materials 'incidental' to the proceedings. Light, Buckingham, and Robbins (1979) used a badly chipped beaker as a reason for pouring the contents from one container to another. This produced correct conservation judgements from 70 per cent of a sample of 5- and 6-year-olds, compared to 5 per cent success in a control sample tested in the usual way. Similar results have been obtained by Hargreaves, Molloy, and Pratt (1982), Miller (1982) and others.

The central argument underlying these studies was that the young child's non-conserving responses may reflect not so much a misunderstanding of the effects of the transformation (i.e. a lack of grasp of conservation) as a misunderstanding of the experimenter's *intentions*. The confusion is not so much conservational as conversational. From the perspective of an analysis of the conservation task as a piece of discourse, the way that the transformation of materials is handled is by no means the only important factor. Rose and Blank (1974) pointed out that typically in a conservation task the pre- and post-transformation questions are exactly the same. It seemed possible that repetition of the question by the experimenter might lead the child to suppose his or her first answer to have been wrong, and therefore to change the response. Or alternatively, the repetition of the question after the transformation might lead the child to suppose that the transformation must, after all, have been relevant to the question. Rose and Blank showed that, although normally all children answer the pre-transformation question (the question about initial equality of amounts) correctly, simply leaving it out led to a significant increase in the level of correct responding to the crucial post-transformation question. Rose and Blank (1974) used number conservation, and although attempts to replicate this study have not always succeeded, it has been replicated successfully by Samuel and Bryant (1984) not only for number but for several other conservation tasks.

In another analysis of the 'conversational assumptions' which might influence the child's responses to the conservation task, Perner and colleagues (Perner, Leekam, and Wimmer 1984) have drawn attention to the shared knowledge which exists between experimenter and child. The child knows that the amounts were equal before transformation – and the initial questioning ensures that he or she and the experimenter *both* know about this. This being so, Perner argues, the child cannot readily treat the post-transformation question as a straightforward request for information, since everything that the child knows, the experimenter also obviously knows. Of course the experimenter is really interested not in the equality or otherwise of amount, but rather in *what the child knows*. Perhaps the child's difficulty lies in dealing, not with conservation *per se*, but with this type of 'examination' question which, as Elbers (1986) has argued, involves a significant departure from the patterns of communication to which the child will be accustomed at this age. Perner *et al.* (1984) offered some evidence that, as would be predicted from this argument, the child's difficulty can be alleviated by introducing a second experimenter, apparently naive to the pre-transformation state of affairs, to ask the post-transformation question. Such a 'naive experimenter' can ask about the equality or inequality of amounts as a straightforward request for information, since after the transformation the equality or otherwise is far from obvious perceptually.

Light, Gorsuch, and Newman (1987) have recently confirmed this observation in a study with 5- and 6-year-olds, tested in pairs. The task began with a heap of dried peas on a table. The children had to help the experimenter to divide this heap into two equal piles. The experimenter put the peas from one pile into one glass container and those from the other pile into another, differently shaped container, and then asked whether there was the same 'amount of peas' in each. Less than 20 per cent of children responded correctly. However, another sample of children followed exactly the same procedure except for an interruption which occurred just after the peas had been placed in the glass containers. Another adult, already familiar to the child, popped her head round the door and said that the experimenter was wanted on the telephone. The incoming adult then took over the experimenter's role and asked the crucial conservation question. Even though the wording of the question was exactly the same, over 50 per cent of children succeeded in this condition.

This experiment also provided an opportunity to test the efficacy of another factor which had more or less surreptitiously crept in to a number of previous studies (e.g. Light *et al.* 1979). This concerns the introduction of a *game* between the participants, in which the requirements of fair competition make equality of amounts an important issue. The Light *et al.* (1987) study just described had an alternative format, in which before the heaps of peas were divided up the pairs of children were told that they were going to play a game which involved moving the peas into a target bowl (by sucking them with straws), and that the one who finished first would be the winner. During the initial division into two piles the importance of fairness was reiterated, but otherwise the procedure and the questions were as described earlier. In this game format over 50 per cent succeeded in the single experimenter condition and over 70 per cent when the second experimenter was introduced to ask the post-transformation question. Statistical analysis of the results of this experiment showed significant main effects both for standard versus game context and for the one-versus two-experimenter conditions, with no significant interaction between these effects.

In this section we have considered a family of related empirical studies of conservation testing, which have demonstrated that various more or less subtle 'discourse cues' available in the testing situation can have a major impact on the child's reading of the situation, and on his or her response to it. There is certainly room for doubt as to whether correct judgements given in response to these various modified tasks necessarily indicate a full grasp of the principles of conservation. Donaldson (e.g. 1978) has tended to take the view that the modified procedures show that many 4-, 5-, and 6-year-olds really do understand about conservation, and that their failure in standard Piagetian tests reflects the inherently misleading and confusing nature of these tests. Others (e.g. Light *et al.* 1979) have been more sceptical, arguing that children's correct responses in the modified contexts of task presentation cannot be regarded as independent of the support which those contexts offer. Some broader issues relevant to this debate will be discussed in the final section of the chapter, but first we shall turn our attention back to the peer interaction/socio-cognitive conflict research introduced in the previous section. Our purpose is to outline recent developments in this research, and in particular to explore the ways in which it has converged with the (originally rather separate) research tradition which has been the subject of the present section.

SOCIAL INTERACTION AND THE CO-CONSTRUCTION OF MEANINGS

We sketched out earlier the basic three-step experimental paradigm used in cognitive development. The 'continental' (mostly Genevan) work, up to 1980, concentrated upon identifying the conditions under which cognitive changes occurred (*see* Mugny, Perret-Clermont, and Doise 1981, for a review). In particular, studies were directed at establishing the cognitive prerequisites necessary for progress, the efficacy of different combinations of cognitive level in the pair or group, the importance of assigning particular roles to individuals in the group, and so on.

To counter the criticism that children were merely learning the right response to conservation problems by superficial imitation or cueing, considerable attention was given to demonstrating that at post-test the children who had made gains were able to satisfy all the various Piagetian criteria for conservation. These include justification of responses, generalization to related tests, and durability of gains. So the question of whether success on the standard conservation post-tests was indicative of an understanding of conservation was addressed in detail. By contrast, the complementary question as to whether *failure* on standard conservation pre- and post-tests was indicative of an *absence* of an understanding of conservation attracted little attention.

This issue of the significance of failure on the standard task, which is so obviously raised by the work discussed in the previous section, did come to the surface in one aspect of the Genevan peer interaction work, namely that concerned with socio-cultural differences. Perret-Clermont (1980) observed that working-class children tended to perform significantly less well than middle-class children in conservation pre-tests, but that in the experimental groups this class difference largely or entirely disappeared by post-test. Differential benefit from interaction has also been shown in more recent work in Neuchatel. For example, Nicolet (personal communication) has found recovery from initial disadvantage as a result of the peer interaction session in children from rural (farming) backgrounds compared with those whose parents have more urban occupations.

An explanation of such findings in Piagetian terms might be that the initial disadvantage of working-class children reflected a social milieu less conducive to the development of cognitive structures, and that the interaction sessions provided the requisite stimulation to allow rapid development. But this is hardly convincing. How could an interaction session of perhaps 10 minutes duration compensate for a 'deficient social milieu', and bring about such a profound cognitive advance almost instantly? An alternative approach to interpretation of such findings is to suppose that perhaps the initial pre-test differences may reflect not so much a class difference in the children's understanding of conservation, but rather a class difference in their understanding of the test situation itself.

Grossen (1988) has recently confirmed the finding that at around 5 years of age, in both conservation of number and (in a separate sample) conservation of liquid quantity, twice as many middle-class as working-class children respond correctly. Role-playing techniques reveal that conservers and non-conservers understand the task differently and their verbal justifications of questions and answers differ not only on cognitive grounds.

Also in Neuchatel, Bell (personal communication) has obtained rather similar results with respect to occidental and non-occidental children in context of an international school. Success rates were substantially higher amongst the former, but there were various indications that this arose from differences in the extent to which the children were able to achieve a shared understanding with the experimenter about the topic and nature of the discourse. For example, the non-occidental children more often asked questions about why the experimenter was pouring the juice, and they more frequently justified their responses in terms which were seemingly irrelevant (or at least would seem so to the classically trained Piagetian experimenter expecting 'logical' interpretation).

Another pointer to the fact that the conservation test is not functioning as a neutral 'litmus test' of logical reasoning comes from the observation that differences in the presentation of the test have differential effects for different social class groups. Thus Perret-Clermont and Schubauer-Leoni (1981) showed that for a middle-class sample it did not make any difference whether a liquid conservation task was presented in terms of juice having to be shared between two identical dolls or between the experimenter and the child. For the working-class sample not only did the children do worse overall, but they also found the dolls condition significantly more difficult. Grossen (1988) found similar results in a conservation of liquid task in which the type of beaker received by the non-conserving child was manipulated in such a way that in one condition the non-conserving child always had the illusion of having *more* juice than his or her partner (advantage condition) and in the other always *less* juice (disadvantage condition). The results show that the conditions of beakers attribution did not have the same effects for every social class and that the working-class subjects were the only ones to react to the difference of conditions, giving more conserving judgements in the disadvantage condition.

The issue of *sharing*, and the associated norms of equality and of fairness, may themselves be very important factors contributing to the efficacy of peer interaction in stimulating correct conservation responses. We saw evidence in the previous section on contextual modifications of the conservation test that setting the test within the context of a competitive game, with explicit reference to the norm of fairness, led to significantly better results. As indicated in the second section of this chapter, the typical procedure for a peer interaction experiment involves explicit reference to establishing equal shares. Even where this is not explicitly the objective of the peer interaction session, the issue of fairness will almost inevitably arise (at least implicitly) whenever children are working together on the distribution of quantities. Thus it may be that the efficacy of the peer interaction procedure arises not (or not only) from the socio-cognitive conflict mechanism outlined earlier, but from the introduction of a norm of equality which serves to support correct responses which are then carried over to the individual post-test.

This interpretative shift has indeed been evident in much of the recent European work. The concept of 'social marking' has been introduced to describe the way in which the ease or difficulty of a cognitive task can be affected by the extent to which it can be mapped on to social norms or rules with which the child is familiar (e.g. Doise and Mugny 1981; Doise 1985; Girotto 1987; Roux and Gilly 1984). In the case of conservation the importance of the norm of equality is becoming increasingly apparent. Doise, Rijsman, Van Meel, Bressers, and Pinxten (1981) showed that pairs of 'nonconserving' children given a series of liquids conservation tests were significantly more likely to succeed if they were told at the outset that since they deserved equal rewards they should have equal amounts of juice. This superiority carried over to individual post-test.

Nicolet and Iannaconne (1988) found that the norm of fairness did not act '*in vacuo*' nor did the setting of the conservation task in the context of a game suffice to produce high levels of conservation, but that the impact of the recall of the norm depended on the type of interpersonal relationship (co-operative or competitive) experienced previously in the game. Zhou (1987) has independently obtained very much the same results.

Doise *et al.* (1981) also included an individual condition in their study. Here the child worked alone with the experimenter, but an emphasis on equality of rewards was introduced in terms of equality with another child 'who will come in a minute'. This condition proved to be just as effective as its two-child counterpart. This finding perhaps serves to highlight the difference between the position we have now arrived at and that described (in terms of socio-cognitive conflict) at the end of our second section. Socio-cognitive conflict is, as we suggested earlier, a mechanism which reflects the importance of the 'social other' as embodying an alternative perspective to the child's own. Social marking, by contrast, is a mechanism which does not require the physical presence of others, but it is social in the wider and perhaps more fundamental sense that the child's social experience elicited by symbolic means (e.g. the evocation of a norm) provides the framework within which the problem is understood.

Work with the 'three-step' experimental paradigm is actively continuing, at Neuchatel and elsewhere. For example Perret-Clermont and Brossard (1985) have been examining where (or at whom) the subjects *look* at critical points in the procedure. But (as is evident from this example) the interpretative framework within which these three-step studies are viewed has shifted substantially. Ten years ago we were thinking primarily in terms of conflicts of pre-operational centrations within the pair or group of interacting children – an essentially cognitive analysis still. Today our concern is more with the ways in which just the fact of interacting with others (*inclusive* of being confronted with different centrations) transforms the experience of the situation for the children. Moreover, we are conscious that not only in the 'interaction session' but also in the pre- and post-tests the child is in an interactive setting, and in these situations too the child's experience in the test is modulated in subtle ways by the conditions of his or her encounter with the experimenter. And we are alive to at least some of the ways in which the wider network of roles and relationships from which we draw our 'subjects' will impinge upon their readings of the situations we create for them (Hinde, Perret-Clermont, and Stevenson-Hinde 1985).

CONCLUSION

Where does all this work leave conservation? To some extent we have just used the conservation task as a convenient point of departure, or point of reference, for studies of the operation of interpersonal/ contextual cues in testing and learning situations. But much more interesting is the way in which some of these cues (especially the notion of fairness at the outset of a game, or of equality of reward) *map on* to the conservation problem specifically, providing a rationale for it and supporting a correct reading of the questioner's intent. We would like to suggest that these various 'mappings', between the logic of the conservation task on the one hand and the practical social activities of exchanging and sharing on the other, may be important not just for the expression of an understanding of conservation but for the genesis of that understanding.

If for a moment we widen our perspective on 'the social context' we can see the child as being, in effect, an apprentice to his or her culture. The child is immersed in a language and a culture which are themselves grounded in practical and social human purposes. The concepts of amount, number, area, volume, weight, and so on exist in that language and culture because they have long served just such practical purposes, associated with sharing, distributing, or transacting various commodities. And the various conservations are *embodied* in these concepts, since they refer precisely to those properties which are conserved across particular kinds of transformation.

Conservation concepts can thus be thought of not as transcendent logical entities but as historically elaborated products of certain practical and social purposes (Light 1986; Russell 1978). The conservation of liquids task to which we have made such extensive reference in this chapter, is really neither a matter of logic nor of exact science. When we pour juice from one beaker to another we conveniently forget differential evaporation, or the residues left behind in the 'empty' beaker. We disregard such things because for practical purposes the amounts can be regarded as the same. In this case the 'practical purposes' concern the sharing out of the juice.

In general terms, then, our argument is that in mastering conservation the child's task is to gain access to certain subtle, culturally elaborated abstractions. Although these are embodied in language, they are not 'merely linguistic'. The language that we use cannot readily be sanitized or separated from the practical purposes to which it relates. Language is not just a matter of agreements in meaning, but also of agreements in doing (shared forms of life, in the Wittgensteinian sense). Thus the child's task in mastering conservation concepts is arguably only possible to the extent that he or she is able to share in the purposes and practices to which these concepts relate. We have seen that where children's interpretation of the meaning of the situation is supported in this way, they can often give correct judgements. Rather than worrying too much about the status of these precocious judgements as 'true' indicators of the 'presence' of conservation we should perhaps concentrate on what these modifications of the conservation task have to tell us about the way in which children can be inducted into such socially supported correct performances, which bridge from the familiar to the unfamiliar, from the known to the unknown.

In this chapter we have reviewed two lines of research on conservation which have been prominent in the last ten or fifteen years. What we have taken from the British and American work of the late 1970s and early 1980s is a concern with interpersonal and discursive cues in the assessment context. What we have taken from the 'continental' work of the same period is a concern with social mechanisms of cognitive change. The more recent work which we have discussed illustrates both the convergence of these two lines of research and the emergence of an alternative conception of *what develops*. Here, in place of a Piagetian focus on cognitive development as a sequence of emerging logical competences, pragmatic, intersubjective agreements-in-meaning are seen as lying at the heart of the developmental process.

REFERENCES

Ames, G. and Murray, F. (1982) 'When two wrongs make a right: promoting cognitive change by social conflict', *Developmental Psychology* 18: 894–7.

Carugati, F., De Paolis, P. and Mugny, G. (1979) 'A paradigm for the study of social interactions in cognitive development', *Italian Journal of Psychology* 6: 147–55.

Doise, W. (1985) 'Social regulations in cognitive development', in R. Hinde, A. N. Perret-Clermont and J. Stevenson-Hinde (eds) *Social Relationships and Cognitive Development*, Oxford: Oxford University Press.

Doise, W. and Mugny, G. (1981) *The Social Development of the Intellect*, Oxford: Pergamon Press.

Doise, W., Mugny, G. and Perret-Clermont, A.-N. (1975) 'Social interaction and the development of cognitive operations', *European Journal of Social Psychology* 5: 367–83.

Doise, W., Rijsman, J., Van Meel, J., Bressers, I. and Pinxten, W. (1981) 'Sociale marketing en cognitieve ontwikkelling', *Pedagogische Studien* 58: 241–8.

Donaldson, M. (1978) *Children's Minds*, London: Fontana.

Elbers, E. (1986) 'Interaction and instruction in the conservation experiment', *European Journal of Psychology of Education* 1: 77–89.

Gessell, A. (1943) *Infant and Child in the Culture of Today*, New York: Harper.

Girotto, V. (1987) 'Social marking, socio-cognitive conflict and cognitive development', *European Journal of Social Psychology* 17: 171–86.

Glachan, M. and Light, P. (1982) 'Peer interaction and learning: can two wrongs make a right?', in G. Butterworth and P. Light (eds) *Social Cognition*, Brighton: Harvester.

Grossen, M. (1988) 'La construction sociale de l'intersubjectivité entre adulte et enfant en situation de test', Ph.D. thesis, Université de Neuchâtel.

Hargreaves, D., Molloy, C. and Pratt, A. (1982) 'Social factors in conservation', *British Journal of Psychology* 73: 231–4.

Hinde, R., Perret-Clermont, A.-N. and Stevenson-Hinde, J. (eds) (1985) *Social Relationships and Cognitive Development*, Oxford: Oxford University Press.

Light, P. (1986) 'Context, conservation and conversation', in M. P. M. Richards and P. H. Light (eds) *Children of Social Worlds*, pp. 170–90, Cambridge: Polity Press.

Light, P., Buckingham, N. and Robbins, A. (1979) 'The conservation task as an interactional setting', *British Journal of Educational Psychology* 49: 304–10.

Light, P., Gorsuch, C. and Newman, J. (1987) 'Why do you ask? Context and communication in the conservation task', *European Journal of Psychology of Education* 2: 73–82.

Mackie, D. (1980) 'A cross cultural study of intra and inter-individual conflicts of centrations', *European Journal of Social Psychology* 10: 313–18.

McGarrigle, J. and Donaldson, M. (1975) 'Conservation accidents', *Cognition* 3: 341–50.

Mead, G.H. (1934) *Mind, Self and Society*, Chicago: University of Chicago Press.

Miller, S. (1982) 'On the generalisability of conservation', *British Journal of Psychology* 73: 221–30.

Mugny, G., Perret-Clermont, A.-N., and Doise, W. (1981) 'Interpersonal coordinations and sociological differences in the construction of the intellect', in G. Stephenson and J. Davis (eds) *Progress in Applied Social Psychology* 1, Chichester: Wiley.

Nicolet, M. and Iannacomme, A. (1988) 'Norme sociale d'équité et contexte relationnel dans l'étude du marquage social', in A.-N. Perret-Clermont and M. Nicolet (eds) *Interagir et Connaitre*, Coussett: Delval.

Perner, J., Leekam, S. and Wimmer, H. (1984) 'The insincerity of conservation questions', paper presented to B.P.S. Development Section Annual Conference, Lancaster, September.

Perret-Clermont, A.-N. (1976) 'L'interaction sociale comme facteur du développement cognitif', doctoral thesis, University of Geneva.

Perret-Clermont, A.-N. (1980) *Social Interaction and Cognitive Development in Children*, London: Academic Press.

Perret-Clermont, A.-N. and Brossard, A. (1985) 'On the interdigitation of social and cognitive processes', in R. Hinde, A.-N. Perret-Clermont, and J. Stevenson-Hinde (eds) *Social Relationships and Cognitive Development*, Oxford: Oxford University Press.

Perret-Clermont, A.-N. and Mugny, G. (1985) 'Effets sociologiques et processes didactiques', in G. Mugny (ed.) *Psychologie Sociale du Développement Cognitif*, Bern: Peter Lang.

Perret-Clermont, A.-N. and Schubauer-Leoni, M. (1981) 'Conflict and cooperation as opportunities for learning', in W. P. Robinson (ed.) *Communication in Development*, London: Academic Press.

Piaget, J. (1932) *The Moral Judgement of the Child*, London: Routledge & Kegan Paul.

Piaget, J. (1968) *Six Psychological Studies*, London: University of London Press.

Rijsman, J., Zoetebier, A., Ginther, A., and Doise, W. (1980) 'Sociocognitief conflict en cognitieve ontwikkeling', *Pedagogische Studien* 57: 125–33.

Rose, S. and Blank, M. (1974) 'The potency of context in children's cognition', *Child Development* 45: 499–502.

Roux, J.-P. and Gilly, M. (1984) 'Aide apportée par le marquage social dans une procedure de résolution chez des enfants de 12–13 ans', *Bulletin de Psychologie* 38: 145–55.

Russell, J. (1978) *The Acquisition of Knowledge*, London: Macmillan.

Samuel, J. and Bryant, P. (1984) 'Asking only one question in the conservation experiment', *Journal of Child Psychology and Psychiatry* 25: 315–18.

Vygotsky, L. (1934/1962) *Thought and Language*, Cambridge, MA: MIT Press.

Zhou, R. (1987) 'Marquage social, conduites de partage et construction de la notion de conservation', unpublished PhD thesis, Aix-en-Provence: University of Provence.

Part three
Tools for thought

Introduction

Technological tools can serve to 'amplify' human capacities. The telephone and the television are two examples which obviously affect the possibilities for the communication and sharing of information and 'culture' in a wide sense. The computer is an instance of a new technology which seems to have even more direct implications for the way in which we develop and utilize our mental faculties.

Behind these new technologies lie older technologies, which we tend to take so much for granted that we cease to recognize them as culturally elaborated techniques and see them as simply 'natural'. Amongst these are various forms of external representation through which human thought can be expressed, developed, communicated and extended. Drawing, written language and number offer three cases in point.

The first chapter in this section is extracted from a compendious review of children's art by Somerville and Hartley (9) and deals with aspects of the development of children's drawing. Much has been learned in recent years about the development of representational strategies, but, as this review indicates, rather less attention has been paid to the communicative role of drawings in development.

The next chapter by Meadows (10) concerns writing. Here again we are dealing with 'marks on paper', and the developmental relationships between drawing and writing are clearly close ones. Writing is a 'second-order' symbol system, in as much as the marks on paper represent language rather than reality. But as Meadows points out, writing is by no means just 'written down speech'; the form of representation imposes its own limitations and offers its own possibilities.

The third chapter in this section by Hughes (11) is about young children's understanding of number. Again, attention is given to the significance of the written representations involved, and their developmental relationship to drawing and writing. Hughes focuses particularly on the problems posed for the young child by the translation between concrete situations and the formal codes of arithmetic.

Finally, Light and Blaye (Chapter 12) discuss the advent of microcomputers on the educational scene, identifying some of the claims and expectations regarding the effects of this new technology on children's thinking, and suggesting that some very different 'effects' may be emerging 'effects which have less to do with the generation of powerful abstract cognitive skills and more to do with the support of effective collaborative learning.

9   Art

S. Somerville and J. Hartley

Source: Dillon, R. and Sternberg, R. (eds) (1986) *Cognition and Instruction*, Orlando: Academic Press.

[. . .]

THE ORIGINS OF SYMBOLIC REPRESENTATION

The commonly accepted view of how representation begins has been that children initially produce graphic products as an unplanned by-product of motor activities with a pencil or crayon (e.g. moving it back and forth, or in a circular path, or jabbing it repeatedly on a page). For example, Kellogg (1969) has argued that children's early scribble patterns (produced from about 1½ or 2 years) take a number of regular forms and are gradually transformed into distinguishable shapes and then into various complexes (e.g. the mandala) that eventually form the building blocks of the earliest representational drawings (at about 3 or 4 years). Similarly, Gardner (1980) has emphasized that the 1- to 2-year-old's interest is in the contrasting motor activities that produce dots, smooth lines, or jagged patterns, rather than in the products of those motions on the page. Although there are occasional earlier signs, 'the linkage of the world of graphic activity to the universe of experience does not occur until the age of three' (Gardner, 1980: 46). In this respect, children's graphic skills have been said to lag behind developments in play, block building, and the creation of stories or musical tunes. Whereas these other activities are used to signify events in the real world as soon as the capacity for symbolic activity is attained (i.e. at about 18 to 24 months of age; cf. Piaget 1951, 1954), 'the forms that are drawn remain just forms, still unconnected to the world of objects and experiences beyond' (Gardner 1980: 45). However, in the light of several recent studies this view now seems a controversial one.

Golomb (1981) has questioned whether representational drawings are produced only after the mastery of various nonpictorial patterns and shapes has occurred. In a study in which 2- to 7-year-olds were asked to draw human figures, animals, a tree, a house, and other items, Golomb found that 39% of 2-year-olds produced at least one representational drawing (most often a human) and that the 3-year-olds were able to comply with a variety of representational requests. These representational drawings, in common with those of the older children, were marked by characteristic preferred orientations for different items (e.g. sideways and horizontal for a snake, front facing and upright for a human). Golomb therefore argued that children are aware of the representational possibilities of graphic activity at a very early age and that 'objects in the real world rather than . . . practice with designs determine the selection of representational forms and models' (p. 41).

This position is also supported by the work of Freeman (1977, 1980), who found that 2-year-olds, if asked, were able to make appropriate additions to a partially drawn human figure to represent, for example, an ear or a nose. However, these same children were unable to initiate complete representational drawings of a human figure on their own. Matthews (1983) has argued on the basis of detailed consideration of the drawings of several 2-year-olds (interpreted with the help of contextual and verbal information) that even at this young age the child's graphic products represent actions and the figurative appearances of objects. Although it is extremely difficult to obtain conclusive evidence about the precise beginnings of representation in drawings, it seems likely-that children are sensitive at least to the potential for differential representation of different objects soon after they begin to place marks on the page.

Gardner and his colleagues (Gardner 1983; Gardner and Wolf 1983; Wolf 1983) provided new insights into the early development of symbolic skills through a longitudinal study of nine children over a period of six years, beginning at the age of 1 year. The investigators assessed these children's developing use of seven different symbol systems at very frequent intervals. The seven symbol systems were 'language (particularly story telling and metaphor), symbolic play, two-dimensional representation, three-dimensional representation (primarily block-building), bodily expression, music and number' (Gardner 1983: 4). They then analyzed and compared developments occurring within these different systems and postulated three successive 'waves of symbolization' beginning approximately one year apart, the first at the age of about 2 years.

They suggested that the first wave depends on the child's early capacity to structure his or her experience with the world in terms of events, and is signaled by the child's use of language and symbolic play to represent this structured knowledge. At this early stage there is somewhat inappropriate transfer of this type of symbolization to other systems; for example, the child may use a marker to enact the action of 'driving' across the paper when asked to draw a picture of a truck. The second wave of symbolization involves an important step for graphic representation, because the patterns or spatial properties of events or displays which the child experiences are now mapped onto the symbolic system. Now an object such as a truck will be represented by a closed shape, perhaps with additional shapes for the wheels. These mappings are restricted to elementary topological features of the spatial relations (cf. Piaget and Inhelder 1967) and do not include precise representations of the relative sizes, numbers, or interval properties of items belonging, for example, to an ordered series. In a third wave of symbolization, beginning at about 4 years, the child begins to represent metric properties such as the relative sizes of objects and the intervals between notes in a musical scale (Wolf 1983).

In summary, in the period from 2 to 4 years the child is engaged in an effort to connect the forms and marks that he or she can produce to the subject matter of his or her world. As N. R. Smith (1979) has pointed out, this struggle to achieve a balance between the potentials of the artistic materials and the intended portrayal of a subject is common to the work of all artists, be they children or adults. At about 4 years of age the child enters a period of artistic productivity that is unparalleled by any other developmental period in its exuberance and air of mastery (Gardner 1980). In the next several years the child acquires, modifies, and perfects an impressive repertoire of strategies for graphic and other forms of representation. The next section examines the developments which occur during this remarkable period, dealing first with the cognitive rules and strategies and then with the aesthetic aspects.

REPRESENTATIONAL STRATEGIES IN THE YOUNG CHILD

[. . .]

Parts and what they represent

Children's earliest representational drawings are composed of parts, each represented by a line or shape. An encircling shape is often used to signify the collection of various parts into a whole. The most famous of children's early representations are the 'tadpole' figures in which a closed, irregular shape has certain features contained inside it and others extending outward. These are perhaps the earliest representations of human and other animal forms. There have been arguments about the interpretation of tadpole figures. Some investigators have seen them as revealing children's insensitivity to the spatial relations between body parts (e.g. Piaget and Inhelder 1967), while other investigators have argued that they represent more global visual concepts of the body (Arnheim 1974). Goodnow (1977) has drawn attention to the great variety of shapes, line forms, and connections between them that children use in these early representations of the human figure. By presenting human figures that are partially drawn and asking young children to add to them, several investigators have also shown that the placement, size, and orientation of new parts will be influenced by the positions, relative sizes, and other features of the parts which are already present (e.g. Freeman 1975, 1980; Goodnow 1977; Goodnow and Friedman 1972).

Interpreters of these early representational attempts have tended to fall into two camps, one emphasizing the cognitive deficits or limitations in information-processing capacity that might lead to missing or strangely connected parts (e.g. Freeman 1980), the other stressing that the drawings represent visual concepts and should not be misconstrued as attempted 'copies' of an original form (Arnheim 1974; Golomb 1981). The same issue has arisen in studies of children's reproductions of geometric shapes and of three-dimensional objects such as houses or cubes. Early investigators in this area interpreted children's failures to produce accurate copies as indicative of deficiencies in their understanding of spatial relations (e.g. Lewis 1963; Piaget and Inhelder 1967). More recently, however, researchers have been concerned to emphasize that drawings cannot be taken as direct indicators of children's knowledge of spatial relations (Kosslyn *et al.* 1977) or of their knowledge of how to transform two- and three-dimensional relations in the real world into a two-dimensional graphic representation (Phillips *et al.* 1978; Willats 1981, 1983).

For example, Phillips *et al.* (1978) found that 7-year-old children copied the same two-dimensional pattern differently under conditions where it was seen as representing a three-dimensional object (cube) and conditions where it was seen as a two-dimensional pattern of lines. Thus the children's concepts of what the drawing was intended to represent (i.e. its denotational purpose) had a distinct effect on the copies they made. Somewhat paradoxically, their copies more accurately reflected the Euclidean relationships between lines when the drawing was not seen as a cube. In their copies of the cube children introduced 'distortions', perhaps in order to denote the fact that a cube would normally rest flat on a surface rather than standing on one corner. In a different study which supports this interpretation, Willats

(1981, 1983) has argued that the drawings of various three-dimensional solids by 5- to 11-year-olds illustrate the parallel development of two systems of representation. The first (*transformational*) system governs the transformation of one set of spatial relations into another and is relatively independent of what the elements in the drawing might stand for. For example, there are a number of projection systems which a person might use to transform a three-dimensional set of relations into a two-dimensional set. The second (*denotational*) system is concerned with what type of element can stand for what, that is, with rules governing the denotation of parts of an object or scene by lines, shapes or regions in a drawing. For example, a line can conventionally be used to denote an edge or crack, but not a boundary between colors (Kennedy 1983). Willats found that in a denotative sense the young child initially uses two-dimensional regions of a drawing to denote three-dimensional objects, and lines to represent surfaces (Willats 1981, 1983). He also found that, with development, changes occur both in the projection system used to transform spatial relations (Willats 1977a, 1977b) and in the denotational correspondences found in the drawings.

One of the most dramatic changes in the drawings of young children is the change from the separate placement of adjoining or collected parts to the execution of a single-outline figure. Drawings of the human figure in which a single contour combines two or more parts of the body into one begin to appear at 5 or 6 years and are most common in the drawings of children at about the age of 7 years (Goodnow 1977). There is a similar developmental change from the use of separate lines to the use of a continuous line when children copy a many-sided shape such as a square. Goodnow pointed out that this change from the production of separate parts to the execution of an all-embracing line represents a major intellectual as well as artistic step because 'the child must mentally have constructed not simply a list of parts but a number of interacting relationships between them' (1977: 35). She also examined the planning and production problems that result from the adoption of a single-outline strategy. For example, if the single outline includes arms and five fingers for each hand, it is inevitable (due to problems of motor control) that the fingers and perhaps the arms as well will become out of proportion with the rest of the body. Goodnow argued that as a consequence of these production problems the hands and even the arms are sometimes omitted from young children's outline drawings of a human figure. She also made the important point that these omissions and/or exaggerations of regions of the body have been misinterpreted by adults as indicating, for example, that the child is preoccupied with certain parts or functions.

Sequences and rules governing the placement of parts

The first group of production rules or strategies dealt with what the parts in a drawing might represent. A second type of representational strategy prescribes sequential steps or placement rules which govern the composition of separate parts into a unified whole. Goodnow (1977) reported one study in which 50 out of a total of 79 'tadpole' drawings by 3- to 5-year-olds were executed in the order 'circle, some face details, then legs' (p. 56). In 21 of these 50 drawings the child then stopped, producing a figure without arms. However Goodnow (1977), Freeman (1980), and Bassett (1977) have all reported departures from this top-to-bottom ordering, in addition to the many cases of conformity. Similarly, there are particular patterns followed by many young children in the execution of a sun with radial lines, or in the copying of letters and letter-like forms (Goodnow 1977; Goodnow and Levine 1973). Furthermore, the preferred patterns tend to change with age, for example, from a right-to-left to a left-to-right order for drawing two arms or two legs (Goodnow 1977), or from a shape-copying strategy that minimizes the ambiguity about where to start each line to one in which all verticals are drawn top to bottom and all horizontals left to right (Ninio and Lieblich 1976). Children's differential tendencies to use strategies such as these are likely to lead to discernible differences between the drawings of one child and another. Because no strategy is followed universally, there will be differences between children of the same age as well as differences between younger and older children. These differences provide a plausible foundation for the development of individual artistic styles in young children.

A series of intricate investigations by Van Sommers (1983, 1984) has revealed a great deal about the cognitive and motor sources of regularities to be found in the drawing actions of children and adults. One of his studies provided detailed documentation of some individual strategies employed by 20 children aged 5 to 6 years. Each child produced at least 10 drawings of each of 12 objects (some from life, some from memory) over a period of several months. The objects drawn from life included a pair of scissors, a light bulb, and a tennis shoe; those drawn from memory included a bicycle, a television set, and a baby in a pram. The strokes used by each child to execute each drawing were recorded on videotape, and the production sequences were then analyzed in detail. Van Sommers found evidence that individual children evolved and retained a distinctive graphic 'schema' for organizing the parts of their drawings of each different object (e.g. for one child the bicycle might consist of three major parts – the two wheels and the frame). For each object there was a 'strong family resemblance amongst the productions of a single child' (Van Sommers 1983: 7). He also found a great deal of variation in the order in which the major and minor parts of the drawings of the same object were executed by a given child on different occasions, despite the similarities between the finished products. For example, the order and direction in which the same lines were drawn were not constant across successive drawings of the same object, and there were small additions and deletions made to the drawings on different occasions. Thus the consistency over time in each child's portrayal of the same object could not be accounted for by the repeated use of a fixed sequence of motor movements. Instead, the child used an extremely flexible production process to arrive at a representation which was generated by a structured graphic schema. For example, from a detailed examination of one 6-year-old's repeated drawings of a clear light bulb. Van Sommers drew the conclusion that 'the whole process of depicting the lamp is a mosaic of graphic devices developed and mobilized in various combinations throughout the sequence' (1984: 219). These findings strongly suggest that the young child is a master of rather than a slave to the idiosyncratic sequencing strategies which he or she may adopt when depicting a particular subject.

Young children also show an awareness of various rules governing the placement of one part of a drawing in relation to others. Pre-schoolers will avoid placing hair on a head if it threatens to cross the figure's arms, even to the point of drawing a hat instead (Goodnow 1977). Goodnow suggested that for the young child it is important for each part to preserve its own boundaries. Winner (1982) has pointed out that even when the young child's drawings do not portray spatial relations between the parts with accuracy, there is a 'visual logic' to the placement of parts on the page: 'The layout of forms on the page creates an ordered and balanced two-dimensional composition' (p. 152). This aspect of young children's placement of parts is perhaps most striking in certain types of drawings of three-dimensional objects which do not represent overlap or occlusions, but lay out the various sides of the object as flat, two-dimensional shapes. Goodnow (1977) referred to these as 'aerial perspective' drawings. Willats (1981) as drawings with 'oblique' projection rules, and Kosslyn *et al.* (1977) as 'diagrammatic' layouts of the object. Arnheim (1974) has emphasized the artistic merit and acceptability (especially in non-Western cultures) of such two-dimensional compositions that are not drawn from a consistent viewpoint.

When young children do depart from a strategy involving the segregation of the parts in their drawings, they often produce so-called transparency drawings (e.g. a person's legs are 'seen' through the clothing, or the contents of a house 'seen' through the wall). In these drawings the occluded and occluding parts are overlaid on one another, again creating an unusual visual effect that has also been sought by adult artists (Winner 1982). A variation on drawings with overlay are those in which parts of the foreground are 'cut away' to enable objects which would be occluded to be shown. An illustration of this is provided by the drawing of a sailboat and some fish by a 7-year-old boy, shown in Figure 9.1, in which the ocean is cut away to reveal the boat, which in turn has a transparent side through which details of the cabin interior can be seen. This drawing also illustrates the use of multiple perspectives in the same drawing: the fish are seen from above and the boat from the side, while the small representations of the skipper, the crew, and the helm are drawn from the front.

Children's strategies of placing parts of a drawing in a segregated arrangement or overlaid upon each other or with sections cut away to reveal what is behind are eventually replaced by attempts to capture three-dimensional spatial relations using a variety of perspective cues. Willats (1977a, 1977b) has found that children progress through a number of stages of perspective representation, several of which do not correspond to the conventional system that was devised at the time of the Renaissance and is now accepted as 'realistic'. He suggested that the developmental progression occurring between 5 years of age and late adolescence illustrates children's changing cognitive attempts to solve the perspective problem. Children do not simply copy the accepted representations they see around them, although their later attempts at solution are apparently influenced by the conventional system.

There are other types of placement rules that young children follow, for a time, in their drawings. These rules complement and interact with those described. For example, some time after the child produces drawings in which each item has a separate place but in which there is no overall coordination of spatial relations between the items, drawings with a groundline appear (e.g. Goodnow 1977; Kellogg 1969). Objects are now related to one another by being drawn on or above the groundline, often in a no-man's land between one line for the ground and another for the sky. Eventually these two lines become

Figure 9.1 Drawing of a sailboat and fish by a boy 7 years old, illustrating cut away parts, transparency, and the use of multiple perspectives.

one, making a dividing horizon between earth and sky (typically with the two regions colored differently) and creating depth effects not present in younger children's representations (Winner 1982).

Another family of placement rules concerns the orientation of objects and their parts with respect to each other and to the page (Freeman 1980; Goodnow 1977). For example, the young child considers that the eyes of a human face should not be centered in the head, but should be closer to one edge with the body attached to the outside of the opposite edge. A 4- or 5-year-old's tendency to follow this rule can lead to figures drawn upside-down or floating sideways on a page, constrained by the initial placement of the eyes (Goodnow and Friedman 1972). Even children older than this have difficulty with the angular relations between parts of a drawing. The well-known examples of chimneys drawn perpendicular to roofs or trees drawn perpendicular to the sides of a hill are difficult to interpret. They may perhaps illustrate children's early tendencies to adopt a local or internal frame of reference rather than an external, absolute one (e.g. Freeman 1980; Piaget and Inhelder 1967) and/or their biases toward perpendicularity and the bisection of angles in their drawings (Bremner and Taylor 1982; Ibbotson and Bryant 1976; Perner, Kohlmann and Wimmer 1984). Alternatively, they may reflect quite different concerns, such as that the chimney should have two equal sides and thus conform to a good shape.

The discussion of rules and principles for drawing to this point has assumed that there is a single graphic system of representation to be acquired by the child. The situation is actually more complex than this, as is seen in the next section.

Different representational systems

Children must become acquainted with a number of different conventional systems governing which particular marks or shapes can stand for what in a drawing. For example, when used in different contexts a wavy line can represent a water surface, the smoke emanating from a chimney, or, in a metaphorical way when drawn behind a figure, movement. Similarly a rectangular shape can represent the walls of a house or can be used to separate one step from the next in a diagrammatic account of house building.

Davis and Fucigna (1983) have suggested two major developmental steps in the young child's mastery of different representational systems. First, by the age of about 4 or 5 years the child has mastered the basic distinctions between the methods of representing depth or motion in different symbol systems (e.g. block building, drawing, gesture). Whereas a 2-year-old 'drawing' a car might 'drive' the marker across the page (i.e. use a gesture), a 5-year-old draws the shape for a car, with lines to represent the movement. And whereas a 3-year-old might turn the page over to draw the back of the house on the other side (a method reminiscent of block building), a 5-year-old depicts the whole house on one side. However, Davis and Fucigna argued that within any given symbol system, such as drawing, the 5-year-old does not distinguish between the different 'channels' which the activity of representation may take. Although children at this age show some awareness that marks on the page are sometimes pictures, sometimes maps or diagrams, and sometimes written stories or lists, their own attempts to produce these different representations are unsuccessful imitations that do not follow the accepted conventions.

For example, a 5-year-old's maps are pictorial rather than designed to convey information about spatial landmarks and their layout (see also Goodnow 1977).

It is not until the second step occurs at the age of about 7 or 8 years that the child realizes that an X is sufficient to represent a house on a map, but not in a picture, or that an aerial perspective is appropriate for a map, a frontal perspective for a picture. These developments in the graphic system are paralleled by differentiations occurring within other symbol systems: For example, language skills may be channeled toward either an eye-witness account or a story version of the same events.

Goodnow (1977, 1978) has interpreted similar developmental changes as indicative of children's progressive mastery and modification of various equivalence relations. She argued that the child initially establishes very simple equivalences, such as that a closed shape can represent a person, an object, or perhaps a sound. These basic equivalences are gradually modified to produce, for example, animals that are human equivalents with longer ears and/or with a different orientation of parts on the page, or to produce maps which are constructed by the assembly of a number of different shapes. Of particular interest are the developmental changes Goodnow (1978) found in the modifications that children introduce to convey movements of various kinds. In this study, when 5- to 10-year olds were asked to draw a person bending to pick up a ball or a person running fast, the younger children made at most a few simple modifications to their customary (upright, stationary) 'equivalents' for the human figure. For example, the 'bending' figure remained upright and front-facing, with an arm elongated to make contact with the ball, or modifications to the person were avoided entirely by simply enlarging the ball so that it touched the hand. As they became older, children were more likely to modify the person to show bending at the neck, waist, and/or knee, different positioning of the arms, and an overall side view of the person. Similar developmental changes were found in the additions (e.g. 'streaming' lines) and modifications (limb orientation, bending, etc.) that the children used to portray a figure running fast.

In summary, these studies have revealed a great deal about the varied, continually changing strategies for graphic representation with which young children work. There is ample evidence in these studies to explain the child's own enjoyment of and fascination with graphic activity. [. . .]

CHILDREN'S GRAPHIC PRODUCTION

There has been something of a revolution in our thinking about young children's drawings, akin to the vast changes in our understanding of their language which have been brought about by studies of their early speech (e.g. Brown 1973; Bruner 1974; Halliday 1975). Researchers who are in sympathy with Arnheim's (1969) conviction that visual thinking is underemphasized in Western cultures, as a result of these cultures' preoccupation with linear, verbal forms of thought, have made several attempts to reveal the structure and sophistication of visual knowledge. To underscore the fact that visual knowledge involves a representational system of equal importance to language, language has often been used either explicitly or implicitly as a metaphor for the new conceptual approaches to graphic representation.

The first example is the work of Goodnow and others (Goodnow and Levine 1973; Ninio and Lieblich 1976) in which the authors have spoken of the rules that guide the young child's production of various forms as 'syntactic' rules, amounting to a 'grammar of action'. By this they mean that the child may try to draw letter-like forms, for instance, using a series of strokes starting in a particular place (e.g. the top left corner) and drawing verticals first (top to bottom) and horizontals next (left to right). Many of the typical errors made by young children when they draw letters can be explained by their tendency to use rules of this type. As a second example, Willats (1981) has argued, by direct analogy with language acquisition, that the 'errors' to be found in children's developing graphic representations are brought about by the application of certain rules for transformation or denotation. His evidence came from an analysis of developmental changes in children's attempts at two-dimensional representations of three-dimensional objects or scenes. Finally, efforts to understand the cognitive strategies or visual 'schemata' that generate the flexible but rule-governed graphic productions of the child (e.g. Freeman 1980; Golomb 1981; Goodnow 1977; Van Sommers 1984) bear a strong resemblance to accounts of the child's developing grammatical competence in language. Generating a variety of sentences which are semantically and/or syntactically related requires cognitive skills similar to those required for the generation of related drawings. The importance of these analyses for education is that they have demonstrated that the child's intuitive knowledge about graphic representation embodies some understanding of the use of rules or generative schemes. It is this aspect of children's intuitive understanding which it is important to recognize in designing more formal instruction.

However, children's intuitive graphic knowledge consists of more than just 'syntactic' production rules, and the educational implications are correspondingly more subtle and complex. To extend the language analogy, there are also semantic, narrative, and more general pragmatic aspects to children's early graphic skills. We argue that this is manifested, in part, in the discernible individual styles of the 4- to 7-year-old. However, before examining evidence about school-age children, we first discuss the earliest semantic and communicative aspects of graphic activity, because it is here that the educational process must begin.

At a very early age the young child understands that communicative acts can be performed by drawing (e.g. Gardner 1980; Winner 1982). This is indicated by the verbal labels given to scribbles, dots, and other products of motor activity. These acts seem analogous to the child's primitive speech acts that serve various communicative purposes prior to the acquisition of grammatical linguistic knowledge (e.g. Dore 1975; Halliday 1975). Gardner (1980) has also pointed out the similarity between the 2-year-old's tendency to engage in sequences of loosely connected drawing activities and the tendency to rehearse and embellish a repertoire of verbal forms.

Many investigations have attested to the adult's sensitivity to early linguistic communications by the child and to the importance of this sensitivity for language acquisition (e.g. Bruner 1974; Ratner and Bruner 1978; Trevarthen 1979). A particularly informative example, for the present discussion, is Mervis and Canada's (1981; see also Mervis and Mervis 1982) study of mothers' behavior in relation to their children's early semantic categories. Over a period of 9 months Mervis and Canada observed mothers' tendencies to accept, reject, or attempt to modify their infants' overgeneralized uses of words (e.g. *truck* for any vehicle, *ball* for any round object). They found that mothers initially accepted and encouraged their children's use of terms to refer to 'child-basic' categories, that is, to categories that did not correspond to any groupings of items that would be made by an adult. One child, for example, used the word *ball* to refer to a round candle, a wooden bead, and an unshelled walnut. Mervis and Canada found that at opportune moments in later play interactions with their children the mothers attempted to relabel these objects with their 'adult-basic' names (e.g. *candle*), but if the children rejected the new labels the mothers reverted to the child-basic usage themselves. Mervis and Canada concluded that the mothers played an essentially supportive role in their children's lexical acquisitions. The generation, differentiation, and revision of categories was under the control of the conceptual system of the child, not the adult.

There have been no comparable enquiries into the capacity an adult might have to interpret, respond to, and interact with a very young child in a graphic exchange. Gardner (1980) observed that a kind of contagion occurred between his own motor movements with a pen and those of his son at the age of 20 months. That is, the two of them tended to copy and extend the jabbing or circling motions made by the other to produce marks on the page. However there have been few systematic investigations of early communicative activity using graphic representation. Matthews' (1983) analysis of what 2-year-olds are attempting to represent in their drawings, Golomb's (1981) demonstration that 3- and to some extent 2-year-olds respond differentially to differing requests for representational drawings, and Freeman's (1977) evidence that 2-year-olds can add parts appropriately to human-figure representations constitute a beginning in this regard.

Even where children at a somewhat more advanced age are concerned, the attention given to the semantic or communicative aspects of their drawings has still been sparse. N. R. Smith (1979) described a 4-year-old's step-by-step forging of the connections between forms and intended meanings in a single drawing of an airplane. Gardner (1980) examined the progressions over several years in young children's portrayals of their favorite subject matter; for one child the subject matter was Batman and related characters, and for another it was horses. Gardner, Wolf, and Smith (1982) drew attention to the fact that two children of the same age may use graphic activities in quite different communicative ways. They contrasted the drawings of one 3½-year-old, for whom the lines on the page conveyed everything that was intended, with the drawings of another for whom the graphic forms were merely part of an overall communicative act, forming an accompaniment of 'backdrop' to verbal, narrative activities. Again, there has been little systematic investigation of the potential for communicative graphic activity between adult and child in the period between 2 and 4 years, that is, in the period when a basic mastery of graphic forms is achieved. This is in stark contrast with language skills, where much is known about the child's early semantic, pragmatic, and communicative competence (e.g.Ervin-Tripp and Mitchell-Kernan 1977; Snow and Ferguson 1977). A more complete understanding of what children mean to convey in their first years of graphic activity would undoubtedly provide better foundations for instruction in the early school years.

More evidence is available about the expressive and communicative aspects of drawings by the 4- to 7-year-old. In the first place, we know that the child of this age has a reliable method of generating representations of the human figure, including methods of adjusting aspects such as the size and orientation of the whole or the parts to be consistent with other constraints in the drawing (e.g. Freeman 1980; Goodnow 1977). We also know that there are some types of modification of basic forms (e.g. changes designed to portray movement) that the young child attempts only infrequently in drawing. When they are attempted, it is also likely to be by the use of unconventional methods. This is reminiscent of young children's early attempts at difficult linguistic transformations and inflections. Earlier we discussed evidence which shows that young children make diverse but consistent attempts at drawings of the same subject matter (e.g. a bicycle) over a period of months (Van Sommers 1984). These attempts are reminiscent of the young child's exploration of the semantic relations between words which have long been acquired, but whose meanings and whose use in different contexts are still capable of elaboration and change (Bowerman 1978). These parallels between the early development of graphic and linguistic skills suggest that we might discover quite a lot about how children learn to draw by examining how they learn to use other representational systems such as language. In fact, as we mentioned earlier, Gardner and his colleagues (Gardner 1982; Gardner and Wolf 1983) have begun to unravel the complex relationships between early developments in a number of symbolic systems.

The next important point about developments in the early school years is that there is an interplay between the rules available for generating forms, on the one hand, and the types of meanings or expressive qualities that the child wants the drawing to have, on the other. It is particularly striking that the 7-year-old will produce quite different copies of the same configuration of lines when those lines represent a three-dimensional object (a cube) as against a two-dimensional pattern (Phillips *et al.* 1978). These findings suggest that there are certain meanings or ideas connected with a cube, such as the fact that it will sit flat on a surface rather than balancing on one corner, which the child seeks to incorporate in a representation, even though this may interfere with the reproduction of lines and angles which could otherwise be represented accurately (as a 'pattern').

Willats' (1981, 1983) studies have also drawn attention to the fact that the drawings of young children are determined by rules for simply denoting or referring to certain features (edges, surfaces, etc.) in addition to rules for transforming spatial relations in the external world into spatial relations on the page. In young children's first attempts at maps and diagrams there is a similar tendency to do more than represent just the spatial relations between elements or the temporally ordered steps in an assembly. In a map, for example, the drawing may also represent events on a journey from one place to another or may include a pictorial display of landmarks that could be denoted adequately in a nonpictorial way (Davis and Fucigna 1983; Goodnow 1977).

These findings, taken as a whole, suggest that the young child's intuitive understanding of graphic representational methods includes not only rule-governed or conventional aspects (e.g. a line can represent an edge or a path on a map) but also figural, expressive aspects (e.g. a cube is a solid object, which rests in certain positions). There is also evidence to suggest that each child evolves his or her own characteristic ways of achieving a marriage between rule-governed production techniques and the meanings or expressive qualities which he or she intends the drawings to have (N. R. Smith 1979; Van Sommers 1984). This is also shown, indirectly, by the finding that young children exhibit individual styles, recognizable to adults, and by the further finding that traces of a child's style at 5 years of age may be apparent in drawings which are made up to 2 years later (Hartley *et al.* 1982; Somerville 1983). There is, of course, the problem that a child at this age may not be aware of, or able to assess, exactly what his or her graphic representations convey to others (Gardner 1980; Korzenik 1977). And the complementary problem is that what adults read in a drawing by a young child might not necessarily have been intended (Winner 1982). In principle, at least, the interpretive difficulties of the adult can be overcome by more sensitive investigations of the young child's representational systems, such as those which we discussed earlier.

Eisner (1976) suggested that there has been a pervasive tendency to underestimate what children entering school are capable of learning, in the arts as well as in other disciplines. Kellogg (1969) argued that educators have tended to create a gulf between child art and adult art, placing too great an emphasis on the teaching of conventional methods of pictorial representation to the child. Traditionally, in her view, the assumption has been that it is desirable to replace the child's intuitive methods of graphic representation with the more conventional, pictorial, representations that are preferred by adults. In fact, Kellogg (1969) considered that 'among those art educators concerned with elementary school programs, the importance of pictorialism is stressed to a degree that amounts almost to a repudiation of possible aesthetic values in child art' (p. 148).

A more adequate understanding of young children's representational systems has been provided by Kellogg's (1969) extensive observations and categorizations of early graphic products and by the subsequent research which her analyses did much to inspire. Although our understanding of the intricacies of these representational systems and their development is by no means complete, there is sufficient information about the typical strategies, rules, and aesthetic concerns of the young school-age child to form a basis for the design of instruction in graphic production. It seems reasonable to hope that instruction designed with children's intuitive representational systems in mind might mitigate the loss of enthusiasm and creative spontaneity that often occurs in the early school years. [. . .]

REFERENCES

Arnheim, R. (1969) *Visual Thinking*, Berkeley: University of California Press.

Arnheim, R. (1974) *Art and Visual Perception*, Berkeley: University of California Press.

Arnheim, R. (1981) 'Style as a Gestalt problem', *The Journal of Aesthetics and Art Criticism* 39: 281–9.

Bassett, E. M. (1977) 'Production strategies in the child's drawing of the human figure: Towards an argument for a model of syncretic perception', in G. Butterworth (ed.) *The Child's Representation of the World*, pp. 49–59, New York: Plenum.

Bowerman, M. (1978) 'Systematizing semantic knowledge: Changes over time in the child's organization of word meaning', *Child Development* 49: 977–87.

Bremner, J. G. and Taylor A. J. (1982) 'Children's errors in copying angles: Perpendicular error or bisection effect?', *Perception* 11: 163–71.

Brown, R. (1973) *A First Language: The Early Stages*, Cambridge, MA: Harvard University Press.

Bruner, J. S. (1974) 'From communication to language: A psychological perspective', *Cognition* 3: 255–87.

Davis, M. and Fucigna, C. (1983) 'Mapping and drawing: Two channels of graphic symbolization', paper presented at the biennial meeting of the Society for Research in Child Development, Detroit.

Dore, J. (1975) 'Holophrases, speech acts and linguistic universals', *Journal of Child Language* 2: 21–40.

Eisner, E. W. (1976) 'What we know about children's art – and what we need to know', in E. W. Eisner (ed.) *The Arts, Human Development and Education*, pp. 5–18, Berkeley: McCutchan.

Ervin-Tripp, S. and Mitchell-Kernan, C. (eds) (1977) *Child Discourse*, New York: Academic Press.

Freeman, N. H. (1975) 'Do children draw men with arms coming out of the head?' *Nature* 254: 416–17.

Freeman, N. H. (1977) 'How young children try to plan drawings', in G. Butterworth (ed.) *The Child's Representation of the World*, pp. 3–29, New York: Plenum.

Freeman, N. H. (1980) *Strategies of Representation in Young Children*, New York: Academic Press.

Gardner, H. (1973) *The Arts and Human Development*, New York: Wiley.

Gardner, H. (1980) *Artful Scribbles: The Significance of Children's Drawings*, New York: Basic.

Gardner, H. (1982) 'Nelson Goodman: The symbols of art', in H. Gardner (ed.) *Art, Mind and Brain: A Cognitive Approach to Creativity*, pp. 55–64, New York: Basic.

Gardner, H. (1983) 'The nature of symbolic skills', paper presented at the biennial meeting of the Society for Research in Child Development, Detroit.

Gardner, H. and Wolf, D. (1983) 'Waves and streams of symbolization: Notes on the development of symbolic capacities in young children', in D. R. Rogers and J. A. Sloboda (eds) *The Acquisition of Symbolic Skills*, pp. 19–42, New York: Plenum.

Gardner, H., Wolf, D. and Smith, A. (1982) 'Max and Molly: Individual differences in early artistic symbolization', in H. Gardner (ed.) *Art, Mind and Brain: A Cognitive Approach to Creativity*, pp. 110–27, New York: Basic.

Golomb, C. (1981) 'Representation and reality: the origins and determinants of young children's drawings', *Review of Research in Visual Arts Education* 14: 36–48.

Goodnow, J. J. (1977) *Children Drawing*, Cambridge, MA: Harvard University Press.

Goodnow, J. J. (1978) 'Visual thinking: Cognitive aspects of change in drawings', *Child Development* 49: 637–41.

Goodnow, J. J. and Friedman, S. (1972) 'Orientation in children's human figure drawings', *Developmental Psychology* 7: 10–16.

Goodnow, J. J. and Levine, R. A. (1973) 'The "grammar of action": Sequence and syntax in children's copying', *Cognitive Psychology* 4: 82–98.

Halliday, M. A. K. (1975) *Learning How to Mean*, London: Arnold.

Hartley, J. L., Somerville, S. C., Jensen, D. V. C. and Eliefja, C. C. (1982) 'Abstraction of individual styles from the drawings of five-year-old children', *Child Development* 53: 1,193–1,214.

Ibbotson, A. and Bryant, P. E. (1976) 'The perpendicular error and the vertical effect', *Perception* 5: 319–26.

Kellogg, R. (1969) *Analyzing Children's Art*, Palo Alto, CA: Mayfield.

Kennedy, J. M. (1983) 'What can we learn about pictures from the blind?', *American Scientist* 71: 19–26.

Korzenik, D. (1977) 'Saying it with pictures', in D. Perkins and B. Leondar (eds) *The Arts and Cognition*, pp. 192–207, Baltimore: Johns Hopkins University Press.

Kosslyn, S. M., Heldmeyer, K. H. and Locklear, E. P. (1977) 'Children's drawings as data about internal representations', *Journal of Experimental Child Psychology* 23: 191–211.

Lewis, H. P. (1963) 'Spatial representation in drawing as a correlate of development and a basis for picture preference', *Journal of Genetic Psychology* 102: 95–107.

Matthews, J. (1983) 'Children drawing: Are young children really scribbling?', paper presented at the British Psychological Society International Conference on Psychology and the Arts, Cardiff.

Mervis, C. B. and Canada, K. (1981) 'Child-basic categories and early lexical development', paper presented at the biennial meeting of the Society for Research in Child Development, Boston.

Mervis, C. B. and Mervis, C. A. (1982) 'Leopards are kitty-cats: Object labeling by mothers for their thirteen-month-olds', *Child Development* 53: 267–73.

Ninio, A. and Lieblich, A. (1976) 'The grammar of action: "Phrase structure" in children's copying', *Child Development* 47: 846–9.

Perner, J., Kohlmann, R. and Wimmer, H. (1984) 'Young children's recognition and use of the vertical and horizontal in drawings', *Child Development* 55: 1, 637–45.

Phillips, W. A., Hobbs, S. B. and Pratt, F. R. (1978) 'Intellectual realism in children's drawings of cubes', *Cognition* 16: 15–33.

Piaget, J. (1951) *Play, Dreams and Imitation in Childhood*, London: Heinemann.

Piaget, J. (1954) *The Construction of Reality in the Child*, New York: Ballantine.

Piaget, J. and Inhelder, B. (1967) *The Child's Conception of Space*, London: Routledge.

Ratner, N. and Bruner, J. S. (1978) 'Games, social exchange and the acquisition of language', *Journal of Child Language* 5: 391–401.

Smith, N. R. (1979) 'How a picture means', in D. Wolf (ed.) *Early Symbolization*, pp. 59–72, San Francisco: Jossey-Bass.

Snow, C. E. and Ferguson, C. A. (eds) (1977) *Talking to Children: Language input and acquisition*, Cambridge, England: Cambridge University Press.

Somerville, S. C. (1983) 'Individual drawing styles of three children from five to seven years', in D. R. Rogers and J. A. Sloboda (eds) *Acquisition of Symbolic Skills*, pp. 89–96, New York: Plenum.

Trevarthen, C. (1979) 'Communication and cooperation in early infancy: A description of primary intersubjectivity', in M. Bullowa (ed.) *Before Speech*, pp. 321–47, New York: Cambridge University Press.

Van Sommers, P. (1983) 'The conservatism of children's drawing strategies: At what level does stability exist?', in D. R. Rogers and J. A. Sloboda (eds) *The Acquisition of Symbolic Skills*, pp. 65–80, New York: Plenum.

Van Sommers, P. (1984) *Drawing and Cognition*, New York: Cambridge University Press.

Willats, J. (1977a) 'How children learn to draw realistic pictures', *Quarterly Journal of Experimental Psychology* 29: 367–82.

Willats, J. (1977b) 'How children learn to represent three-dimensional space in drawings', in G. Butterworth (ed.) *The Child's Representation of the World*, pp. 189–202, New York: Planum Press.

Willats, J. (1981) 'What do the marks in the picture stand for? The child's acquisition of systems of transformation and denotation', *Review of Research in Visual Arts Education* 13: 18–33.

Willats, J. (1983) 'Drawing systems revisited: The complementary roles of projection systems and denotation systems in the analysis of children's drawings', paper presented at the Conference on Graphic Representation, University of York.

Winner, E. (1982) *Invented Worlds*, Cambridge, MA: Harvard University Press.

Wolf, D. (1983) 'Event-structures: The first wave of symbolic understanding', paper presented at the biennial meeting of the Society for Research in Child Development, Detroit.

10 The development of writing

Sara Meadows

Source: This chapter is an edited version of material to
appear in *The Child as Thinker: the Development and
Acquisition of Cognition in Childhood*, London: Routledge.

Writing is an activity which integrates many different processes –
physical, linguistic, cognitive, even social and affective – in different
ways according to the writer's age, experience and purposes.
Scardamalia (1981) lists the interdependent skills involved, among
them the physical production of text through handwriting or typing,
spelling and punctuation; considerations of content, word choice,
syntax and textual connections; and considerations of overall purpose,
organisation, clarity and euphony. Each of these skills is itself of
course highly complex: each shows developmental change in what is
done and in what is expected. Some writing skills, but not all, are
intensively taught: some remain the area of expertise of comparatively
few writers.

Two aspects of writing, its nature as a physical skill and the 'ecology'
of its use, I will only mention briefly, concentrating my discussion on
the cognitive skills of writing. Writing involves the use of fine muscle
movements in varied but coordinated patterns, with visual monitoring, at a speed (in experienced writers) far faster than the brain can
send messages to the hand and receive feedback, though more slowly
than thinking or speaking. As Thomassen and Teulings (1983) remind
us, the human hand is an extraordinarily intricate and delicate
mechanism, controlled by a large number of muscles. During writing,
movements in fingers, wrists, arms and shoulders, plus movements of
the eyes (and perhaps head) for monitoring writing, have to be
coordinated. These muscle movements have to be small, quick and
precise, and because the speed of transmission of neural control
messages along the length of the arm is relatively slow, the brain
cannot wait for one movement to be completed before the next is
begun. Even at this level the brain must plan ahead to get the hand in
the right position at the right place at the right time.

To do this, we write not in single letters but in larger units. As an example, compare the ease of writing 'written backwards' with the difficulty of writing 'sdrawkcab nettirw' and note where the pauses and breaks in writing came. 'Units' may occur over longer strings than single words; we pause more between clauses than within them. For example, 'over-unitting' may produce errors. I planned the second sentence of the last paragraph, 'Writing involves the use of fine muscle movements' etc. as it is now printed, but wrote 'final' instead of 'fine', conflating 'fine' with the sound at the end of 'muscle' rather than making a semantic error. Motor skills of the highly complex sort involved in writing fluently are acquired mainly through practice. Children's fine motor coordination continues to develop throughout childhood (Laszlo and Bairstow 1985) and maturation may limit the neatness of their handwriting. Nineteenth-century pedagogy did successfully force several generations of children to write (and sew) neatly, as witness surviving copybooks and samplers sewn by what now seems remarkably young girls. However accounts in biographies and novels testify to the pains of being made to conform to strict standards of neatness, and casual observation today will show that a high proportion of people never really learn to write neatly!

Given a piece of paper and a pencil, a child in the second year of life will enjoy making marks on the paper. Initially these line and dot scribbles are probably not unsuccessful attempts to write or draw. Rather they are successful attempts to make marks on the paper where there were no marks before. 'Writing' usually follows attempts at drawing representations of objects. Vygotsky (1978) points out that writing is a second-order symbol system: the letters stand for the spoken word, which itself stands for the object. Drawings and idiosyncratic pictographs are, like spoken words, in a first-order symbolic relation to the object they represent. Such an account of writing's symbolic relations obviously implies that writing will develop after drawing has begun: writing is a special sort of drawing which represents language. As children experience written language by being read to (or reading for themselves), they learn that 'writing' consists of particular sorts of patterns arranged on the page in particular orientations – in English, horizontal lines from left to right of the twenty-six letters of the alphabet. Young children may 'write' in a scribble or string of letters running horizontally across the page, or accompanying a picture as an adult might produce a caption. Kamler and Kilarr (1983: 187–9; see also Meadows 1986: 89–91) provide a fascinating observation of a child just under five as she composes a 'story' to accompany a picture. She writes horizontal 'words' using a limited set of letters: her first word is written at the top of the page, the second nearly at the bottom, the third, fourth and fifth words are fitted in between them, and the sixth is a late addition at the bottom of the page. She composes in bursts, and reads what she has written from top to bottom of the page. Thus when she first wrote it, 'Kioe' at the bottom of her page was her second word and meant 'sat', but when she re-reads from top to bottom it is the third word and means 'mat'. She has considerable difficulty in being consistent in her matching of written word to thought-of word. Kamler and Kilarr (1983) comment that the child may be making her 'random clusters of letters' first and only later attributing meaning to them, like the child artists who seem to decide what their drawing represents after they have produced it. The demands of making the movements and marks which produce the written words are themselves considerable and may make coherent composition virtually impossible. Smith (1982) advocates writing practice free from demands for correctness in spelling, punctuation or composition which may distract from establishing automatic motor patterns. It is important to point out that children do not normally write letters untidily or incorrectly because of inadequate visual processing, but because of production difficulties: letters have to be precisely formed in direction, size, joins, spaces and so forth, and the motor control needed for this is very considerable. Practice gives a fluent production system, but children who lack one make the sort of errors and attempt the sort of solutions that they do in drawings (Freeman and Cox 1985). There is a complex interaction of the purely motor and the cognitive skills in the apparently simple making of written symbols.

Writing is embedded in a social context, and can serve a variety of purposes. Where a reader is essentially concerned with extracting meaning from a pre-existing text, with or without increase in enjoyment or knowledge, a writer may have any of a wider range of purposes: for example to inform, to entertain, to persuade, to criticize, to record, to express something personally felt, and so forth. This list is obviously similar to one listing the functions of spoken language. Recording is the major exception, as generally it is better done by writing than by speaking, and indeed some theorists suggest that writing was invented largely for record-keeping purposes (records of property and liability for taxes, regrettably: see e.g. Goody 1977, Goody and Watt 1968). Children's spoken language will have been used for most of these functions by the end of the pre-school years (Wells 1985; Meadows 1986), but they may not have experienced all these functions expressed in writing. Although most adults write sometimes, studies of the 'ecology' of writing (e.g. Griffiths and Wells 1983) show that the main functions of writing at home are in response to social or mnemonic requirements: domestic messages, family letters and shopping lists. When adults do write to express themselves, to tell stories or to record their own experience they mostly do so privately or at least away from the interruptions of pre-school children, who will thus have little writing activity to observe that involves anything other than notes of information or domestic letters. Adult literacy is positively correlated with children's literacy (Wells 1981, 1985), perhaps because the children of literate parents have both more opportunities to observe literacy and more formal and informal teaching from their parents. Tizard and Hughes (1984) describe some mothers teaching their daughters to write, sometimes as a session of letter forming or copying words, sometimes as part of an activity such as writing a letter to grandparents. The latter is probably a fairly common real-life experience for quite a lot of children. Parents may encourage (or require) children to write letters to grandparents or to people who have given presents or hospitality; thus there is a real social purpose to writing. Most available examples from young children seem to be conventional rather than expressive. There are clear rules for beginning and ending the text of letters, and since there is often a specific interpersonal reason for writing the letter, at least some of what it must contain is also specified. A thank-you letter from Z to X acknowledging a gift, Y, must include at least phrases equivalent to 'Dear X,' 'Thank you for the Y', 'from Z'. Collerson (1983) collected the letters his daughter Juliet wrote between the ages of 5 and 9, they show an increase in length via the inclusion of informative or expressive material beyond the minimum demanded by the formal letter scheme, and an increasing tendency to use written language as a means to a continuing dialogue with people who are known but too far away to speak to. The child 'learns that letters can be a means of reporting and interpreting experience, a device for exchanging information, and a method of maintaining social interaction among friends' (Collerson 1983: 92).

Writing and speaking have both similarities and differences. It may appear that writing is simply written down speaking, a pen and ink record like a tape recording, or a pen and ink production instead of a lips and larynx enactment. However this is not the case. Stubbs (1980) points out that the relationship between written and spoken language differs for different writing systems, different authorial purposes, and different cultures, but one consistent difference is that the written text has to convey its meaning more independently of paralinguistic context than spoken language has to do. The writer must construct the text without the assistance of signals from the recipient about whether the meaning is being understood, whether more or less information is needed, whether jokes are being appreciated or persuasive arguments are having the desired effect. The reader has to get meaning from the text in the absence of many of the signals that accompany spoken language: cues from the speaker's 'body language', pitch, intonation, speed of speaking, facial expression and so forth are not available in conventional written text, though devices of punctuation and typography may be used to make up for some of this loss. Writers and readers interact much more distantly than speakers and listeners. Writers cannot, alas, monitor their readers' understanding. If they wish to be effective, they must therefore compose and review their writing more carefully than most speakers need to do, lest problems in their choices of words and syntax and the overall organisation and clarity of the text, or adverse reactions by the readers to the writer's purpose and assumptions, should prevent satisfactory communication. They also need to appreciate some of the conventions that differ between spoken and written language. The text must create its own paralinguistic context, so the writer must assess what knowledge can safely be assumed and what information must be incorporated into the text. The writer must also assess what is the best order for pieces of text and present each piece unambiguously and explicitly. It may be easier for the reader to go back and read text again than it is for the listener to recall speech in order to re-examine it, but the writer cannot adjust content, order or emphasis, as the speaker can, in response to the reader's cues of understanding or failure to understand. In short, effective written language normally needs careful thought in the composing.

Given this need, and given the high importance placed on being able to compose effectively (at least at the level of writing applications for jobs), it is not surprising that a considerable amount of research has been done on composition. Martlew (1983) reviews some of the errors that poor or inexperienced writers make: they write as they speak, leaving their writing dependent on a context which the reader may not share; they plan poorly, if at all, and prepare themselves for writing too briefly to be able to produce clearly organized text; they rarely review or criticize what they have produced, and what review and self-criticism occurs almost never leads to improving the text. Some of these inadequacies no doubt arise because the whole task of considering the adequacy of the text *plus* spelling correctly *plus* writing neatly *plus* producing the right amount to satisfy the teacher overwhelms young writers. Some, however, probably stem from their uncertainty about what to do in composition, and how to do it. Frederiksen and Dominic (1981) suggest that important cognitive resources include:

> the writer's knowledge, the already established strategies and pro-
> cedures for constructing a meaning and expressing it, and the
> general characteristics of their cognitive systems such as processing
> capacity and both the automaticity and efficiency of component
> processes.
>
> (Frederiksen and Dominic 1981: 4)

Very young writers often find problems simply in generating content. They frequently produce the equivalent of one utterance on the subject, and then stop, claiming that that is all they can think of to say. Bereiter and Scardamalia (1982) demonstrate that devices of various sorts increase the amount produced. Instructions to produce a large amount, the opportunity to speak or to dictate the text instead of having to write it, instructions to continue composing leaving aside questions of difficult spelling, the provision of simple prompts such as 'on the other hand' or 'also', all increase both the number of words and the number of ideas expressed, as well as the children's satisfaction with their writing. Children clearly had not really reached the limits of what was available on the subject. They welcomed prompts and appreciated their effects. Learning to provide prompts for yourself is part of the development of writing skills.

Although not generating enough material is a problem in writing, the optimum solution is not simply to generate more irrespective of its quality, truth, relevance, suitability and so forth. It is preferable that the writer should think what to say, stay on topic, produce a coherent and intelligible whole appropriate to the audience, and to do this involves coordinating searches of memory for useful material with the various physical, linguistic and cognitive processes which I mentioned earlier. This may be comparatively straightforward when writers are recounting personal experiences or dealing with routine scripts and stories. It becomes more problematic when the task is one of making an exposition of a subject. Scardamalia and Bereiter (Bereiter and Scardamalia 1987), suggest that the predominant and 'natural' strategy is what they call 'knowledge-telling'. It is 'natural' because it uses skills developed in normal language competence and learned through ordinary social experience, but it does not go beyond them. It starts with the writer constructing a mental representation of a writing task, identifying topic and genre. The writer has some relevant knowledge on the topic (Piaget's theory, say) and on what the genre (e.g. an exam question calling for 'evaluation') involves (e.g. a tabulation of positive and negative points). The mental representation of topic and genre call up from memory an item of content, for example the experiments which assessed children's understanding of conservation. As this is relevant to the topic and to the demands of the genre it is expressed in language suitable for the essay, e.g.:

> Piaget did experiments on conservation where he asked children if spreading out a line of counters changed the number in it and young children said the number did change. However Margaret Donaldson did the experiment with a naughty teddy messing the line up and her children said the number was still the same.

This then serves as a probe for a further search of memory, so perhaps an account of other variations on the conservation situation is produced. This alternation of finding a relevant idea and expressing it continues until a sufficient quantity of text has been constructed, or memory yields no more material, or time runs out. The 'knowledge-telling' strategy for composition is comparatively rapid and automatic, and it does not involve much reflection on what is produced: the results of each probing of memory are juxtaposed like beads on a string, independent of each other and in inconsequential order.

Knowledge-telling lacks goal-related planning and significant revision, and the pouring-forth of what is known is only minimally adjusted to the precise demands of the task or to the characteristics of the reader. The text is not interconnected but made up of unrelated passages produced one after the other without reference forward or, more particularly, back. It may therefore contain repetitions and contradictions: there is evidence from reading comprehension studies (Brown *et al.* 1983; Markman 1979, 1981) that children seem to have difficulties in spotting such problems in other people's writing as well as in their own. On the other hand, knowledge-telling does guarantee a fairly easy generating of text that is on topic and does fulfil the minimum demands of the genre, and it usually leads to a quantity of text sufficiently large to satisfy task requirements. It fits, in fact, many novice writers' needs and their beliefs about what writing involves. Knowledge-telling followed by rigorous revision and ruthless discarding of weak material is a perfectly respectable technique of composing. However inexperienced writers are very unlikely to do such revision: they normally limit themselves to proofreading, word choice and checking the 'mechanics' of spelling, punctuation and grammar (e.g. Nold 1981; Brown *et al.* 1983).

Knowledge-telling is a serviceable strategy, and may persist because of that, as it is conspicuously difficult to give up strategies and theories which work well within limits in favour of a more complex strategy or theory which has greater potential but also higher 'running costs' (Brown *et al.* 1983; Karmiloff-Smith and Inhelder 1974–5), as anyone who has had to get to grips with a technological innovation such as word processing or microwave cooking will recognize. Bereiter and Scardamalia (1987) describe another writing strategy which is distinctly more complex and distinctly rarer. In it, knowledge-telling is a subordinate process within a far more radical questioning and reorganization of both content and genre. Memory search is not simply a matter of taking whatever item comes next, but involves personal elaboration of the connections and implications of items and thus the construction of reformulated representations of what is known, a heuristic search of memory (Newell and Simon 1972) not just a mechanical probing of it. Similarly the writing task itself is represented in a more complex way, with explicit considerations of the goals involved, the probable effect of the text on the expected reader, and so forth. Content and topic can influence each other. For example, if a passage seems unclear, the effort to achieve clarity may be translated into a need to examine whether the ideas to be expressed have really been fully understood; or thinking of a new item of content may change the direction of the argument or the possible conclusions to be drawn. This strategy is therefore called 'knowledge transforming'. It involves far more integration of procedures for composing, monitoring and revising, consideration of the text in terms of its overall structure, gist, and goals as well as at the microlevels of spelling and so forth, and, especially, far less automatic production of text and more self-regulation. It is harder work, more problematic, but also more rewarding. It is also, perhaps, an important means to better thinking not just better writing (Palincsar and Brown 1984) – at least *some* authors have occasionally felt that they only knew what they thought when they read what they'd written!

REFERENCES

Bereiter, C. and Scardamalia, M. (1982) 'From conversation to composition: the role of instruction in a developmental process', in R. Glaser (ed.) *Advances in Instructional Psychology*, vol. 2, Hillsdale, NJ: Erlbaum.

Bereiter, C. and Scardamalia, M. (1987) *The Psychology of Written Composition*, Hillsdale, NJ: Erlbaum.

Brown, A. L., Bransford, J. D., Ferrara, R. A. and Campione, J. C. (1983) 'Learning, remembering and understanding', in J. H. Flavell and E. M.

Markman (eds) vol. 3 of *Handbook of Child Psychology* (series ed. P. Mussen), New York: Wiley.

Collerson J. (1983) 'One child and one genre: developments in letter writing', in B. Kroll and G. Wells (eds) *Explorations in the Development of Writing*, Chichester: Wiley.

Frederiksen, C. H., Whiteman, M. F. and Dominic, J. F. (eds) (1981) *Writing: the Nature, Development and Teaching of Written Communication*, vol. 2 of *Writing: Process, Development and Communication*, Hillsdale, NJ: Erlbaum.

Freeman, N. H. and Cox, M. V. (eds) (1985) *Visual Order: the Nature and Development of Pictorial Representation*, Cambridge: Cambridge University Press.

Goody, J. (1977) *The Domestication of the Savage Mind*, Cambridge: Cambridge University Press.

Goody, J. and Watt, I. (1968) 'The consequences of literacy', in J. Goody (ed.) *Literacy in Traditional Societies*, Cambridge: Cambridge University Press.

Griffiths, M. and Wells, G. (1983) 'Who writes what and why?', in B. Kroll and G. Wells (eds) *Explorations in the Development of Writing*, Chichester: Wiley.

Kamler, B. and Kilarr, G. (1983) 'Looking at what children can do', in B. Kroll and G. Wells (eds) *Explorations in the Development of Writing*, Chichester: Wiley.

Karmiloff-Smith, A. and Inhelder B. (1974–5) 'If you want to get ahead, get a theory', *Cognition* 3: 195–212.

Laszlo, J. I. and Bairstow, P. J. (1985) *Perceptual-motor Behaviour: Developmental Assessment and Therapy*, London: Holt, Rinehart & Winston.

Markman, E. M. (1979) 'Realising that you don't understand: elementary school children's awareness of inconsistencies', *Child Development* 50: 643–55.

Markman, E. M. (1981) 'Comprehension monitoring', in W. P. Dickson (ed.) *Children's Oral Communication Skills*, New York: Academic Press.

Martlew, M. (1983) *The Psychology of Written Language: Developmental and Educational Perspectives*, Chichester: Wiley.

Meadows, S. (1986) *Understanding Child Development*, London: Hutchinson.

Newell, A. and Simon, H. (1972) *Human Problem Solving*, Englewood Cliffs, NJ: Prentice Hall.

Nold, E. W. (1981) 'Revising', in C. H. Frederiksen and J. F. Dominic (eds) *Writing: the Nature, Development and Teaching of Written Communication*, Hillsdale, NJ: Erlbaum.

Palincsar, A. and Brown, A. L. (1984) 'Reciprocal teaching of comprehension-fostering and monitoring activities', *Cognition and Instruction* 1: 117–75.

Scardamalia, M. (1981) 'How children cope with the cognitive demands of writing', in C. H. Frederiksen, M. F. Whiteman and J. F. Dominic (eds) *Writing: the Nature, Development and Teaching of Written Communica-*

Smith, F. (1982) *Writing and the Writer*, London: Heinemann.
Stubbs, M. (1980) *Language and Literacy: the Sociolinguistics of Reading and Writing*, London: Routledge & Kegan Paul.
Thomassen, A. J. and Teulings, H.-L. (1983) 'The development of handwriting', in M. Martlew (ed.) *The Psychology of Written Language*, Chichester: Wiley.
Tizard, B. and Hughes, M. (1984) *Young Children Learning*, London: Fontana.
Vygotsky, L. S. (1978) *Mind in Society*, M. Cole, V. John-Steiner, S. Scribner and E. Souberman (eds), Cambridge, MA: Harvard University Press.
Wells, C. G. (1981) 'Preschool literacy related activities and success in school', in D. R. Olson (ed.) *The Nature and Consequences of Literacy*, Cambridge: Cambridge University Press.
Wells, C. G. (1985) *Language Development in the Pre-school Years*, Cambridge: Cambridge University Press.

11 What is difficult about learning arithmetic?

Martin Hughes

Source: Donaldson, M., Grieve, R. and Pratt, C. (eds) (1983) *Early Childhood Development and Education*, Oxford: Blackwell.

Maths is like learning a foreign language, Marcie. No matter what you say, it's going to be wrong anyway.

('Peanuts')

As our society becomes more and more dependent on high levels of computer-based technology, it becomes increasingly important that children should grow up with a basic competence and familiarity with numbers, and that they should feel at home in the world of calculation and computation. Of course, there are many children who easily develop a facility with numbers. Yet there are also many children who share the sentiments of the Peanuts character above, and who approach numerical problems with a mixture of confusion and helplessness. Some of these children manage to scrape by in school, by picking up a collection of techniques, tricks and rules of thumb. These may suffice to get them through the exams, but they may be only hazily understood. Other children do not even manage this, and remain almost totally at sea.

Why do children find arithmetic so difficult? Why does it seem like a foreign language to so many of them? For some years now one of the standard responses from educationalists to such questions is that formal arithmetic has been imposed on children long before they were conceptually ready for such learning. This position has often been justified by appealing to the work of Jean Piaget and his colleagues in Geneva.

THE PIAGETIAN EXPLANATION

Piaget's explanation of young children's difficulties with number can be found in various books and articles published over a period of some thirty years. However, one particularly influential article of his appeared in *Scientific American* in 1953. The first two paragraphs of this article are worth quoting in full:

> It is a great mistake to suppose that a child acquires the notion of number and other mathematical concepts just from teaching. On the contrary, to a remarkable degree he develops them himself, independently and spontaneously. When adults try to impose mathematical concepts on a child prematurely, his learning is merely verbal; true understanding of them comes only with his mental growth.
>
> This can easily be shown by a simple experiment. A child of five or six may readily be taught by his parents to name the numbers from one to ten. If ten stones are laid in a row, he can count them correctly. But if the stones are rearranged in a more complex pattern or piled up, he no longer can count them with consistent accuracy. Although the child knows the names of the numbers, he has not yet grasped the essential idea of number: namely, that the number of objects in a group remains the same, is 'conserved', no matter how they are shuffled or arranged.

These paragraphs contain several characteristically Piagetian ideas. We find here, for example, the belief that teaching children before they are conceptually 'ready' is likely to produce only superficial learning: that true learning comes only with the child's mental growth, and that mathematical concepts cannot be taught. There is also the underlying implication that learning mathematics is not essentially difficult, for it is something which children can for the most part acquire 'independently and spontaneously'.

At the centre of Piaget's argument, however, is the idea of conservation. Piaget maintains that if children cannot conserve number – that is, if they appear not to understand that the number of objects in a group remains the same however the objects are arranged – then they are not yet ready to start on school arithmetic. Indeed, Piaget suggests that teachers should mistrust any apparent ability – such as counting – that young children bring with them to school. If the children cannot conserve then this apparent knowledge is likely to be 'merely verbal' parrot-style learning.

Many of these ideas have now become widely accepted within early mathematics education. For example, the idea that mathematical concepts are acquired through the child's mental growth – and in particular through activities involving concrete objects – is taken as virtually axiomatic by most nursery and infant school teachers. The majority of infant school mathematics schemes start off with very concrete activities, such as matching objects on a one-to-one basis, or sorting them into sets. These activities are intended to develop the young child's general concept of number, as measured by a Piagetian conservation test. It is only when children seem to have grasped the idea of number conservation that they are considered ready to start on addition and subtraction.

NEW EVIDENCE ON THE ABILITIES OF THE PRESCHOOL CHILD

If children arrive at school as limited in their concept of number as Piaget suggests, then it is clearly undesirable to proceed as if they were more advanced. However, while Piaget's ideas have become increasingly influential within early childhood education, they have been attracting increasing amounts of criticism within developmental psychology (Donaldson 1978; Gelman and Gallistel 1978). In particular, there is now a considerable amount of evidence that children starting school are by no means as limited in their number concepts as Piagetian theory maintains.

Much of this evidence is concerned with Piaget's claim that children starting school do not, on the whole, understand the idea that number is conserved when a collection of objects is displaced or rearranged. In order to understand these criticisms, we need to consider the nature of the conservation task itself. In what is generally regarded as the 'standard' number conservation procedure, a young child is confronted with two identical rows of objects placed in one-to-one correspondence (Piaget 1952). Virtually all children will agree at this stage that the two rows contain the same number of objects. The critical part of the task comes next. The adult displaces one of the rows so that it is now longer (or shorter) than the other, and asks the child if the two rows still contain the same number of objects. Piaget found that children younger than six or seven years will not, as a rule, conserve their judgements, but will incorrectly say that one row now contains more objects than the other. It is only when children reach the age of six or seven years that they will regularly conserve; that is, they will reply that the rows still contain the same number of objects despite the displacement.

There is widespread agreement that young children do in fact respond to the standard number conservation task in the way Piaget describes. However, it is increasingly being questioned whether this standard procedure is really testing what it claims to test. Several studies have now compared the standard procedure – in which the adult displaces one of the rows in a deliberate manner – with alternative procedures in which the displacement is either 'accidental' or 'incidental' (McGarrigle and Donaldson 1974; Light *et al.* 1979; Neilson and Dockrell 1982). In each of these studies, significantly more children gave the right answer with the alternative procedure than with the standard procedure. It seems that some children may fail on the standard conservation task yet still have a good understanding of number conservation.

More direct evidence that young children have coherent number concepts comes from the work of Rochel Gelman and her associates in America (Gelman 1972; Gelman and Gallistel 1978; Gelman and Tucker 1975). Much of Gelman's evidence comes from studies using an ingenious 'magic' game. In this game, children develop an expectancy that a particular array will contain, for example, three objects. The array is then surreptitiously altered in one of two ways. In one condition objects are added to or taken from the array, while in the second condition the objects are simply rearranged. In both cases, the reaction of the children to the change in the array is carefully noted.

On the basis of her magic studies, Gelman claims that children as young as three years understand the *invariance* of small number arrays (three objects or less). That is, they seem to understand that displacing the objects in an array does not affect its numerosity in the way that adding or subtracting objects does. While this is not quite the same thing as Piaget's idea of conservation (see Silverman *et al.* 1979 for further discussion of this point), it does seem that Piagetian theory cannot easily account for Gelman's findings.

Gelman also claims that many three- and four-year-old children understand the idea of addition and subtraction. In the course of a 'magic' game children who notice that objects have been removed from an array can usually say that more objects must be added if the game is to be 'fixed' (i.e. restored to its original condition), and they can often say how many objects need to be added to do this. Again, such a claim does not fit easily with Piaget's own belief that children below six or seven years do not really understand addition or subtraction (Piaget 1952: 190).

Gelman's claim that preschool children understand addition and subtraction is based on somewhat indirect evidence: her children were not actually asked to carry out additions or subtractions. More direct evidence comes from a study I have recently carried out in Edinburgh (Hughes 1981). In this study, 60 children aged between three and five years were given simple addition and subtraction problems in a variety of different forms. In one task the children watched as bricks were added to or taken from a box, and they were then asked how many bricks were now in the box. For example, they might know there were three bricks in the box to begin with, and might see two bricks being taken out but not see what was left. Their task was to work out that only one brick remained. Like Gelman, I found that if the numbers involved were small (one, two, three or zero) then the children performed surprisingly well (83 per cent correct). The children also performed well (62 per cent correct) when simple additions and subtractions were presented in a hypothetical form (e.g. 'If there were three children in a sweetshop and two went out, how many children would be left in the shop?'). Just over a quarter of the children could also carry out similar additions and subtractions when the numbers involved were slightly larger (five, six, seven and eight).

Such findings give strong support to Gelman's claim that preschool children have 'a coherent set of principles for reasoning about number', particularly if the numbers involved are small. Most children who are approaching school age, it would seem, understand the invariance of number, and can carry out simple additions and subtractions, when the numbers involved are small. Moreover, a sizeable proportion of children have similar competence with slightly larger numbers. While the abilities involved are obviously not as sophisticated as those possessed by older children or adults, they still reveal a striking degree of competence in very young children.

THE NATURE OF SCHOOL ARITHMETIC

If these conclusions are correct, then we need to think again about why young children may find difficulty with school arithmetic. The Piagetian explanation is that children are being introduced to formal arithmetic too early, at an age when they lack a coherent concept of number. It now seems that children starting school are not so incompetent with number as Piaget has made out. But if this is so, there is even more of a puzzle: if children are more competent at the outset, why do so many still have a difficulty learning school arithmetic?

Some clues to this problem come from the study of addition and subtraction mentioned above (Hughes 1981). As well as the tasks already described – involving bricks in boxes and children in sweet-shops – the children were also asked 'school arithmetic' questions such as 'What does one and two make?' Most children found these questions extremely difficult: overall, only about 10 per cent of such questions were answered correctly. Similar difficulties arose when the questions were phrased slightly differently – e.g. 'How many is one and two?', of 'What is one and two more?' It seems, in other words, that while most children approaching school age know that one brick added to two bricks makes three bricks, very few can answer questions involving 'one and two'.

At first sight this result does not seem too surprising. Questions involving 'one and two' do feel intuitively harder than those involving 'one brick and two bricks'. But what exactly does this 'hardness' consist of?

The first point to make is that questions like 'What does one and two make?' are totally unfamiliar to most preschool children. According to Corran and Walkerdine (1981), such a use of language occurs very rarely in conversations between four-year olds and their mothers at home. When number words such as 'one' and 'two' do occur, they almost invariably refer to objects: 'one cup', 'two spoons', and so on. Corran and Walkerdine argue that questions like 'What does one and two make?' are part of a very restricted form of discourse – which I will call the *formal code of arithmetic*. Unlike ordinary language, this formal code will not be acquired simply through the child's participation in everyday conversations, but will have to be learned in the more formal setting of school. Rather surprisingly, some preschool children seem to be aware of this fact. One four-year-old in the study who was asked what one and two made replied that she could not answer questions like that because she 'didn't go to school yet'.

The second point to make about the formal code of arithmetic is that statements in the code are *context-free*. They make no reference to any particular objects or entities: they are not about anything specific. Yet this property is precisely what makes arithmetic such a powerful tool for thinking and problem-solving. The formal code of arithmetic is essentially a representational device in which words such as 'one' and 'two' can represent, or stand for, a whole range of objects: one brick, two houses, and so on. The quantity is what matters: the nature of the objects is irrelevant. Statements like 'one and two makes three' get their power from this very great generality. They are not about anything in particular, yet they are relevant to just about everything.

It seems, however, that the context-free nature of arithmetic statements is the source of much of children's difficulty with them. In the following dialogue, Ram (four years, seven months) makes his puzzlement quite explicit:

Adult: What's three and one more? How many is three and one more?

Child: Three and what? One what? Letter – I mean number?
(We had earlier been playing a game with magnetic numbers and Ram is presumably referring to them here)

Adult: How many is three and one more?

Child: One more what?

Adult: Just one more, you know?

Child: I *don't* know (disgruntled).

These observations provide a new perspective on the difficulties facing young children when they first encounter formal arithmetic. The problem is not that young children are completely lacking in their number concepts, for we have already seen that this is not so. Rather the problem is that they are encountering a novel code, or representation system, which may well be like a foreign language to them. Pursuing this analogy further, what they need are procedures for *translating* between this new language and the modes of representation which they already have. In other words, the problem is one of creating links between the novel, formal language of arithmetic and their existing number knowledge.

One question of obvious importance is whether young children can create these links for themselves, or whether they need to be helped. The study described earlier (Hughes 1981) suggests that most preschool children do not spontaneously translate formal code questions, such as 'What does one and two make?', into a more concrete form. When asked these questions 'out of the blue', they usually replied by naming a number, such as 'six', which bore no obvious relationship to the question being asked. Very few children appeared to be reasoning along the following lines: 'Well I don't know what one and two makes, but I do know that one brick and two bricks makes three bricks, so maybe the answer's three.' Naturally, one would not expect preschool children to verbalize the problem in exactly this way, but their thinking might have proceeded along such lines.

At first sight this might seem to be an unlikely thing for a young child to do. However a group of young children did something very similar in a study carried out by Bob Grieve and myself (Hughes and Grieve 1980). In this study children aged five and seven years were asked questions like 'Is red bigger than yellow?' We wanted to see how young children would react when asked questions which, to us, seemed quite bizarre. To our surprise, we found that virtually all the children treated these questions seriously and constructed sensible meanings for them. One tactic they often used was to translate the questions into a specific context. For example, one child looked round the room and then replied that yellow was bigger than red 'because that red cushion there is smaller than that yellow curtain there'.

If children spontaneously translate unusual questions involving colour into specific contexts, then it is reasonable to suppose that they might be encouraged to do the same with unusual questions involving number. In an attempt to facilitate this process I presented preschool children with formal code questions either immediately before or immediately after questions about particular objects. Even with this procedure, though, the children rarely translated between the two types of question. The following dialogue with Amanda (three years, eleven months) was typical of this approach:

Adult: How many is two and one?
Child: (long pause: no response).
Adult: Well, how many bricks is two bricks and one brick?
Child: Three
Adult: OK . . . so how many's two and one?
Child: (pause) Four? (hesitantly).
Adult: How many is one brick and one more brick?
Child: Two bricks
Adult: So how many is one and one?
Child: One, maybe.

Amanda clearly sees no connection between the formal code questions and the questions concerned with bricks. Indeed, she seems to be using a strategy of giving a *different* response to the formal code questions. It is as if she is thinking 'Well I don't understand this question but I know it's not the same as the previous one, so I'll try a different answer.'

I have also tried another approach which emphasizes what is common to a whole series of addition questions about specific objects. This approach, however, was equally unsuccessful. The child in the following example is Patrick (four years, one month).

Adult: How many is two and one more?
Child: Four.
Adult: Well, how many is two *lollipops* and one more?
Child: Three.
Adult: How many is two *elephants* and one more?

Child: Three.
Adult: How many is two *giraffes* and one more?
Child: Three.
Adult: So how many is *two* and one more?
Child: (looks adult straight in the eye) Six.

It is interesting that children find questions involving colour words easier to translate into specific contexts than those involving number words. This may reflect some universal property of number as an abstract system, or it may be a particular property of our own number words, such as 'one' and 'two'. There are some cultures, for example, where the connection between the number words and the number being represented is made more directly. Menninger (1969) describes an early Indian system in which the word for 'one' was the same as the word for 'moon'; the word for 'two' the same as that for 'eyes'; that for 'four' the same as that for 'brother' (in Indian mythology Rama has three brothers); the word for 'seven' the same as that for 'head' (the head has seven openings) and so on. It is possible that young children would find it much easier to learn formal arithmetic if our own number system contained similar links between number words and concrete objects.

WRITTEN ARITHMETICAL SYMBOLISM

So far we have been concerned with formal arithmetic in its spoken form: that is when it is expressed in verbal statements like 'one and two makes three' or 'three take away two makes one'. But these same statements can of course be represented in written form, such as: $1 + 2 = 3$ or $3 - 2 = 1$.

The age at which children are introduced to this kind of written symbolism varies from country to country and from school to school. The children whose work is shown in Figure 11.1 below attended a socially-mixed school in Edinburgh, run by the local authority. Towards the end of their first year in school (age five to six years) the children are introduced to simple additions like those shown in Figure 11.1a. By the end of their second year in school (age six to seven years), they can produce the more complex additions and subtractions shown in Figure 11.1b.

Our interest in what the children were doing in their workbooks grew out of a study of their spontaneous written representations of simple number concepts. In this study, carried out by Miranda Jones and myself, we wanted to know how children would represent on

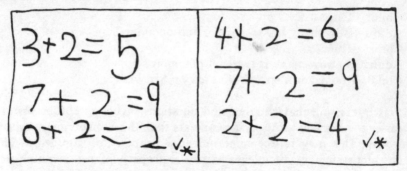

(a) Class 1 (five to six years)

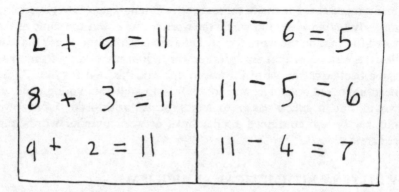

(b) Class 2 (six to seven years)

Figure 11.1   Pages from children's workbooks

paper, without any prompting from us, basic arithmetical concepts such as cardinal number (the number of objects in a group), addition and subtraction. In particular, we wanted to see whether they would use the conventional symbolism (1, 2, 3, +, -, =, etc.) which they had been taught and which they used in their workbooks, or whether they would use their own more idiosyncratic methods.

A group of 72 children between five and seven years of age were given three tasks in random order. In the *cardinal number* task, a group of bricks numbering between one and six was placed on a table. The child was given paper and pencil and asked to show how many bricks were on the table. In this task the children were also asked to represent zero: i.e., to show there were no bricks on the table. In the other two tasks, the *complete operations* and the *transformation* tasks, the children were asked to produce paper and pencil representations of simple additions and subtractions. In the *complete operations* task, the child was asked to show, for example, that there were originally three bricks on the table, that one brick was then taken away, and that two bricks were left. In the *transformation* task, the child was asked to show that a specified number of bricks had been added to or taken away from a large pile of bricks of unknown number.

The children's responses were extremely interesting. On the whole the *cardinal number* task provided few difficulties, with almost all the children providing an accurate representation of the number of bricks on the table. The most frequent response (45 per cent overall) was simply to draw the required number of bricks, with the next most frequent (38 per cent) being to write conventional numerals (1, 2, 3 . . .). Several children drew single vertical strokes or tallies for each brick, while others drew vague blob-like shapes. Some children, interestingly enough, drew the appropriate number of some different object – like one girl who said 'I'll draw houses' and drew three houses to represent three bricks (see Figure 11.2 for examples of these responses).

The two tasks which involved representing addition and subtraction proved very much harder. In the *complete operations* task, no child in any age group was able to produce an adequate representation of any of the operations, with the commonest response (69 per cent) being simply to represent the final number of bricks on the table. We had expected this task might be difficult because it required the child to represent three different quantities (the initial amount, the transformation, and the final amount). For this reason we had also included the *transformation* task, in which the child was only required to represent a single transformation – what had been done to the pile. Surprisingly enough, the *transformation* task proved just as difficult as the *complete operations* task. Most of the children (69 per cent of all responses) correctly represented the number of bricks which were added or subtracted, but very few represented whether an addition or subtraction had taken place. Only 11 children managed to differentiate between addition and subtraction in their responses, and only four of these did so in a way which might have been understood by anyone else. One seven-year-old wrote 'took 1 away' or 'add 3', while a six-year-old drew the added bricks superimposed on the pile and the subtracted bricks inside the box (see Figure 11.3). A five-year old drew a hand adding bricks to the pile, while subtracted bricks were drawn being put into the box (see Figure 11.3). Finally, another five-year old drew the bricks which were added but drew dashes to show those which had been removed.

Some children went to ingenious lengths in their attempts to

Daniel (5:11)

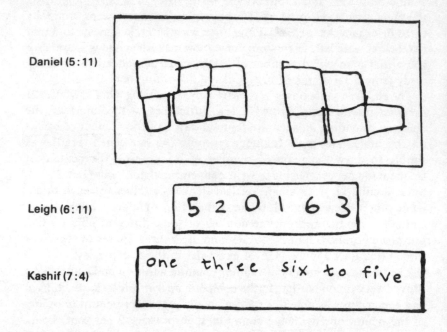

Leigh (6:11)

5 2 0 1 6 3

Kashif (7:4)

one three six to five

Emma (5:2)

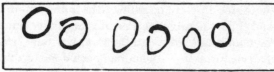

Pamela (5:1)

Figure 11.2   Responses to cardinal number task

Habib (6:5)

Denny (5:5)

Scott (7:7)

Figure 11.3 Attempts to discriminate between addition and subtraction

represent additions and subtractions. For example, one seven-year old represented bricks that were added with the appropriate number of British soldiers marching from left to right, while bricks that were subtracted were represented by Japanese soldiers marching from right to left (see Figure 11.3). Other children attempted to represent movement by drawing arrows or hands (see Figure 11.4) but these attempts almost invariably failed to convey what had happened.

The most surprising finding from the two addition and subtraction tasks however, was that *not a single child used the conventional operator signs + and − to represent addition or subtraction*. We know from the children's workbooks (Figure 11.1) that operator signs were

Rosanne (6 : 8)

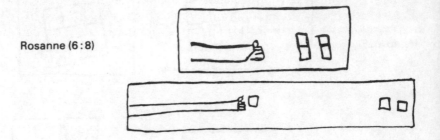

Niels (6 : 6)

Denny (5 : 5)

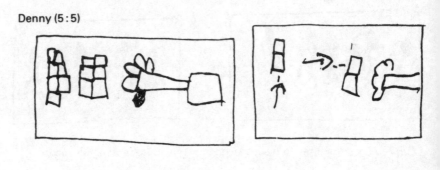

Leigh (6 : 11)

Figure 11.4 Attempts to show movement in representing addition and subtraction

being used regularly – in some cases daily – by the children from age five years upwards, yet not one child thought of solving the difficult problem of representing addition and subtraction by using these signs.

This total reluctance to use operator signs, together with the similar, but less extreme reluctance to use numerals, suggests that what the children are doing in their school workbooks may be a wholly self-contained activity, which few of them see as being relevant to the tasks they are being asked to perform. In other words, many children do not seem to realize that the arithmetical symbols which they use in their workbooks can also be used to represent quantities of objects or operations on these quantities. If this conclusion is correct, then there appears to be a serious deficiency in many children's understanding of the nature and utility of written arithmetical symbolism.

LEARNING ARITHMETIC: A NEW FRAMEWORK

It seems that if we are to make much progress in understanding why children have difficulty with arithmetic then we need a framework something like the one shown in Figure 11.5. This figure illustrates schematically the fact that a simple arithmetical statement like 'one and two makes three' can be represented in two different forms. On the left-hand side we have various concrete realizations of this addition, involving physical objects such as bricks, children in a sweetshop and so on. On the right-hand side we have the same addition expressed in the formal code, both in its spoken form: 'one and two makes three', and in its written form: 1 + 2 = 3. Linking the two forms of representation are what I have called *translation procedures*. These are perhaps the most important part of the picture.

Now being competent at arithmetic has two important components. At the most obvious level, it means being able to operate solely within

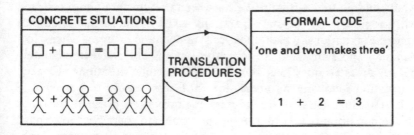

Figure 11.5 Framework for learning arithmetic

the formal code, to carry out arithmetical calculations and computations free from any concrete realizations. This aspect of arithmetical
competence was emphasized most strongly by traditional teaching
methods, and is what people nowadays have in mind when they talk of
going 'back to basics'. But there is more to arithmetical competence
than that. As the progressivists quite rightly pointed out, we do not
want children simply to churn out arithmetical statements by rote: we
want them to *understand* what they are doing, what the arithmetical
statements mean. Unfortunately, many progressivists, taking their
lead from Piaget, have taken this to mean an overemphasis on
concrete experience, and a corresponding devaluation of operating
with the formal code. In other words, the traditionalists have
emphasized the right-hand side of Figure 11.5 at the expense of the
left, while the progressivists have emphasised the left at the expense of
the right.

The framework presented here suggests the beginnings of a way out
of the 'progressivist versus traditionalist' dilemma. This framework
not only puts a more equal emphasis on *both* modes of representation,
but also gives particular importance to the links between them. These
links are important in learning the formal code, but they are also used
in solving arithmetic problems long after the code has been acquired.
Many problems, for example, come in concrete form and have to be
translated into their appropriate formal representation before they can
be solved. At the same time, we often have to translate formal
problems into concrete realizations in order to understand them fully,
or to check that a particular solution is reasonable. A truly competent
user of arithmetic should not only be able to operate within the formal
code of arithmetic, but should also be able to make fluent translations
between formal and concrete representations of the same problem.

On this analysis, the ability to translate between different modes of
representation is of central importance in arithmetical competence.
Yet much of the work described earlier suggests that this is precisely
what children find difficult. We have seen that few preschool children
will spontaneously translate questions asked in the formal code into
concrete situations which they can understand – even when, like
Amanda and Patrick, these formal questions are asked immediately
before or after questions referring to concrete situations. Clearly,
translation involving numbers does not come easily to very young
children. But neither does it seem to have been grasped by older
children in primary school. Despite being able to cover page after page
of their workbooks with addition and subtraction sums, many children were still reluctant to represent concrete events by arithmetical

symbols. Being able to manipulate the formal code does not, it would seem, guarantee that the user understands the kind of code that it is.

HOW CAN WE HELP?

An important implication of this argument is that learning arithmetic is by no means a natural and effortless process. On the contrary, in asking young children to master a novel context-free code we are requiring them to do something which runs very much counter to their 'natural' mode of thinking. Not only that, we are asking them to move in two directions at once. On the one hand, we are trying to free their thinking from the concrete, to introduce them to the power and usefulness of a context-free mode of thought. But at the same time we want to avoid doing this in a way that severs all links with the concrete, for these links are essential for understanding the representational nature of the formal code.

We must accept, then, that in introducing young children to formal arithmetic we are demanding a great deal of them. But how can the task be made easier? What principles and techniques can we offer which might make the process more successful?

Some procedures that might assist children are emerging from a study I have recently carried out. The aim of this study was to introduce arithmetical symbols to four-year-old preschool children, through the use of simple games. My purpose in doing this was two-fold. I wanted to see whether such an enterprise was possible, whether very young children could grasp the idea of using symbols at all. But I was also concerned about how the symbols were introduced: I wanted to find a way of introducing them which was not only enjoyable to the child but which provided a clear rationale as to why the symbols were being used, and why they might be helpful to the child.

This point may become clearer when I describe the games. The basic set-up involves a number of identical tins containing different numbers of 'sweets' (in fact, bricks wrapped up in silver paper). The child is shown that one tin contains one sweet, another contains two sweets, and so on. The lids are put back on and the tins shuffled round. The child is asked to guess which tin has one sweet in, and so on. After a few turns of guessing in this way, the adult introduces a set of plastic numerals, with magnets on the back, and suggests the child sticks them on the tins to help distinguish between them. Most of the children I have worked with respond readily to this suggestion. Some children respond in the way an adult might, by sticking the number 1 on the tin with one sweet in, the number 2 on the tin with two in, and so on. Other children, interestingly enough, often use the magnetic numbers in one-to-one correspondence with the sweets: they stick one number – it doesn't matter which – on the tin containing one sweet, two numbers on the tin containing two sweets and so on. Whatever form of response they use, almost all the children seem to appreciate that this helps them distinguish the tins. As Craig (four years, three months) put it: 'It's easy now, 'cos we put the numbers on!'.

Once children can use the magnetic numbers to represent the number of sweets, the game can be extended to introduce operator signs + and -. In one version, for example, the child shuts his eyes while the adult puts some more 'sweets' in one of the tins. However, the adult leaves behind a message on the lid of the tin to show what he has done. For example, he might put on + 1 to show he has added one more sweet.

The following dialogue comes from a game with Thomas (four years, no months). We started with the number 1 on the tin and one sweet inside. I explained that if I then put one more sweet in the tin I would leave the signs + and 1 on the lid; if I put in two more sweets, I would leave + 2 and so on. While Thomas's eyes were shut I put one more sweet in the tin and added the signs + 1. The tin now had 1 + 1 on the lid.

Child: (guesses with eyes shut) Three!
Adult: Open your eyes.
Child: (notices 1 + 1 on tin) I said three! (he seems to realize his guess was wrong).
Adult: How many sweets have I put in?
Child: Two . . . (pause) . . . one to begin with (points to 1 on left-hand side) and then you put in two (points to 1 on right-hand side).
Adult: No I didn't.
Child: You put in one more.
Adult: I put in one more.
Child: Which makes two!
(Thomas replaces the 1 + 1 with 2, and hides his eyes again. I put in two more sweets and put + 2 on the tin: the tin now has 2 + 2 on the lid)
Adult: Open your eyes. How many have I put in this time?
Child: (looks at 2+2 on tin) That means three . . . 'cos you started with two and then you put in one . . . two (puzzles over + 2).
Adult: I put in two more, didn't I?
Child: You put in two more, so it makes four!

While Thomas is not totally fluent at reading and interpreting the message on the tins, he seems to have grasped some of the ideas involved. He appears to understand that a message left behind in this way can tell us about events that have happened in the past: he is also on the verge, it seems, of mastering the convention that such messages are conventionally read from left to right. It is also interesting to note how he is detaching himself from thinking about the sweets and is instead thinking in terms of numbers. In the dialogue above, Thomas does not once refer to 'sweets', but instead uses terms like 'you started with two', 'you put in two more' and 'so it makes four'.

Thomas is clearly a long way from being competent at arithmetic. Nevertheless, games like these are important in demonstrating two points. First, they show that even before they go to school, children can begin to grasp the beginnings of arithmetical symbolism, provided we are careful to introduce the symbols in appropriate ways. But more importantly perhaps, the games are showing young children the usefulness of arithmetical symbols. They are demonstrating that there are situations where numbers – and operator signs – do indeed make life easier, where there is a rationale for using them, and where there is a purpose for making translations between symbols on the one hand and concrete objects and events on the other. If we can continue to keep this principle at the forefront of our teaching throughout school, then we may be able to make learning arithmetic a much easier process.

REFERENCES

Corran, G. and Walkerdine, V. (1981) 'The practice of reason, Vol. 1: Reading the signs of mathematics', unpublished mimeograph.

Donaldson, M. (1978) *Children's Minds*, London: Fontana.

Gelman, R. (1972) 'Logical capacity of very young children: number invariance rules', *Child Development* 43: 75–90.

Gelman, R. and Gallistel, C. R. (1978) *The Child's Understanding of Number*, Cambridge, MA: Harvard University Press.

Gelman, R. and Tucker, M. F. (1975) 'Further investigations of the young child's conception of number', *Child Development* 46: 167–75.

Hughes, M. (1981) 'Can preschool children add and subtract?', *Educational Psychology* 1: 207–19.

Hughes, M. and Grieve, R. (1980) 'On asking children bizarre questions', *First Language* 1: 149–60.

Light, P. H., Buckingham, N. and Robbins, A. H. (1979) 'The conservation task as an interactional setting', *British Journal of Educational Psychology* 49: 304–10.

McGarrigle, J. and Donaldson, M. (1974) 'Conservation accidents', *Cognition* 3: 341–50.

Menninger, K. (1969) *Number Words and Number Symbols*, Cambridge, MA: M.I.T. Press.

Neilson, I. and Dockrell, J. (1982) 'Conservation tasks as interactional settings', in G. Butterworth and P. Light (eds) *Social Cognition*, Brighton: Harvester Press.

Piaget, J. (1952) *The Child's Conception of Number*, London: Routledge & Kegan Paul.

Silverman, I. W., Rose, A. P. and Phillis, D. E. (1979) 'The "magic" paradigm revisited', *Journal of Experimental Child Psychology* 28: 30–42.

12 Computer-based learning: the social dimensions

Paul Light and Agnes Blaye

Source: Foot, H. C., Morgan, M. J. and Shute, R. H. (eds) (1990) *Children Helping Children*, reproduced by permission of John Wiley and Sons Limited, Chichester.

INTRODUCTION

This chapter concerns the cognitive consequences of peer interaction in the context of educational microcomputer use. The computer has, in the course of its appearance on the educational scene, acted as a multi-faceted mirror, reflecting the whole gamut of educational and psychological theories concerning the development of children's thinking. Moreover, the computer has not only lent itself well to assimilation into a wide variety of educational contexts, it also has the potential to transform those contexts.

Without attempting a comprehensive review, we propose to examine some of the broad issues surrounding individualized versus group microcomputer use, to offer an overview of the available experimental literature, and to take a look at some of the possibilities for future development in this field. We will restrict ourselves to situations of 'direct' face-to-face interaction, while acknowledging that the use of networking, of electronic mail and conferencing would all deserve a place in any full discussion of the social dimensions of children's computer use.

THE COMPUTER AS AN EDUCATIONAL TOOL: CONCEPT TO REALITY

There are a number of distinct frameworks within which the computer has been envisaged as contributing to education. One of these is the Piagetian constructivist framework, developed in this context most effectively by Papert (1980). Papert's seminal work with LOGO has done a great deal to shape microcomputer use, especially at younger age levels. He saw in programming a distinctive route toward the development of generalizable problem-solving skills ('powerful ideas'), and emphasized the individual constructive activity of the child in acquiring such skills. While Papert's vision was not of the child–computer dyad as *isolated* from other learners, there was little room for any analysis of the social dimensions of the learning process. Programming in a high-level language such as LOGO requires the pupils to have a precise and formal representation of all the necessary steps to a particular goal. The essence of Papert's view was that the writing, testing and 'debugging' of programs offers a uniquely powerful resource for the development of abstract thought and high-level problem-solving abilities. The intellectually constructive aspect of computer use, then, is to be found in the creative engagement of the child with the computer program.

While this perspective has been an influential one, the majority of contemporary school computer use is of a very different ilk. Surveys such as that by Jackson, Fletcher and Messer (1986) confirm that most computer use in primary schools involves 'drill and practice' software. The pedagogical perspective here is that the computer can provide a level of routine individual tutoring which the busy classroom teacher cannot. Any given educational task can be broken down into its elements and the individual child can be taken through a carefully graduated series of subtasks embodying these elements. The child can progress at his or her own pace, being given lots of practice to establish full mastery of each subtask. From this perspective one of the main virtues of the computer is its facility for providing direct and immediate feedback, shaping performance and ensuring a progressive build-up of understanding.

From this standpoint, the computer can be seen as an infinitely patient teaching assistant, a descendent of the Skinnerian 'teaching machine' of an earlier era. Indeed it has been said of this kind of usage that it amounts to employing the technology of the 1980s to embody the curriculum of the 1950s (Baker 1985). While the principles of programmed learning proved difficult to implement in the then-available technology, the computer with its speed and flexibility offers these principles a new lease of life.

The recent development of intelligent tutoring systems provides a new way to harness the educational potentialities of computers. What characterizes 'drill and practice' and other non-intelligent computer-assisted learning software is the lack of flexibility which results in all pupils having to undergo essentially the same teaching sequence. By contrast, an intelligent tutoring system offers the possibility of generating the teaching sequence 'online' during the educational interaction

(Elsom-Cook 1987). As a result the teaching sequence is tailored to the requirements of each pupil.

An essentially individualistic view of the learning process is fundamental to the tradition which stretches from programmed learning to intelligent tutoring systems, and *progress* in this domain has largely been measured in terms of increasingly flexible and accurate tailoring of the software to the needs of the individual learner. This in turn has provoked concern about the dangers, supposedly inherent in information technology, of losing out on the social and interactional aspects of the learning process. The worrying image of the socially isolated and withdrawn child, hunched over a computer for hours at a time, is one which has considerable currency (Baker 1985).

The reality, at least for the early school years in North America and the UK, appears to be very different. For what may prove temporary and pragmatic reasons, the indications are that, far from reducing socially interactive learning, computers in the classroom *increase* the opportunities for such learning. This is especially true in respect of child–child interaction. The most obvious factor here is the scarcity of computer hardware in schools. The survey mentioned earlier by Jackson *et al.* (1986) indicated that in the Primary sector the level of provision averaged less than one computer per class. Moreover, whereas over most curricular areas the teacher has vastly more expertise than the pupils, this is often not true in respect of computers. Here, knowledgeable pupils often become valued sources of information for other children in the class (Sheingold, Hawkins and Char 1984).

The net result of these factors is that much educational computer work takes place within relatively autonomous *groups* of pupils. Indeed, Jackson *et al*'s (1986) survey showed that primary school teachers saw learning to interact in groups as one of the main *advantages* of computer use in schools. The view of computer-related activities as incentives to social interaction has been supported by many systematic observations of work on the computer in the classroom (e.g. Hawkins 1983; Hawkins *et al.* 1982). Sheingold, Hawkins and Char (1984) reviewed a number of early studies which point to the conclusion that work with computers promotes both a high level of task-related interaction and a high probability of children calling on one another (rather than the teacher) for help. Far from preventing peer interaction, then, computer work in schools may perhaps offer a peculiarly effective environment for interaction between learners.

EMPIRICAL STUDIES OF COMPUTER USE BY CLASSROOM GROUPS

Classroom-based observational studies have suggested a similar picture for activities specific to computers (e.g. programming and word processing) and for traditional activities transferred to the computer (e.g. most drill and practice and non-intelligent CAL – Computer-Assisted Learning – software).

Cummings (1985), on the basis of an Australian study of children using a variety of CAL programs, concluded that the computer can and does provide an effective motivator for groupwork. In particular he saw computer-based work as supplying the context for the kind of genuine discussion between children which the Bullock Report (1975) considered so necessary, but which is so difficult to achieve in teacher-centred classrooms. Broderick and Trushell (1985), observing 10-year-old children using word processors, described a wealth of positive mutually supportive interactions amongst the children. Proponents of LOGO in recent years (e.g. Hoyles and Sutherland 1986; Hughes, MacLeod and Potts 1985; Hawkins 1983; Hawkins *et al.* 1982) have offered detailed observational support to the view that children working with LOGO in pairs or small groups typically show high levels of spontaneous interaction. Indeed, Hoyles and Sutherland see this as one of the major strengths of this approach to learning mathematics. They suggest that it is the context of social interaction which pushes the children towards adopting an objective attitude to the task in hand. Their ongoing studies are attempting to validate this claim through a fine-grained analysis of the interaction actually going on between pairs of children working together on LOGO over a prolonged period of time.

Hawkins and colleagues (1982) describe the interaction between pupils when they work with LOGO as sometimes taking the form of sustained collaboration on a joint project, sometimes taking the form of children seeking help and advice from one another when they are in difficulties, and sometimes involving children just 'stopping by' at the computer in passing. Not surprisingly, patterns of interaction are affected by the kind of software in use. Crook (1987) for example, observed that a piece of CAL software involving maze-solving tended to produce turn-making on a part of the children. Another piece of software involving series completion produced more differentiated interaction, with discussion of competing hypotheses. The richest discussion was promoted by an adventure game, though differences in reading ability were limiting. Similarly in word processing, children's very limited keyboard skills imposed severe restrictions on the interaction (Crook 1986).

Though suggestive, these kinds of studies cannot definitively establish the effects of such interaction upon individual children's learning. In the next section we turn to more artificial, experimental studies which have sought to do this.

EXPERIMENTAL STUDIES

One series of experimental studies has stemmed from the mainly American tradition of social-psychological research rooted in the work of Lewin and Deutsch on group dynamics and cooperation. These studies put their emphasis on cooperative organization of groups, tasks and rewards (e.g. Johnson and Johnson 1986; Johnson, Johnson and Stanne 1986) and deal mainly with CAL tasks. For example. Johnson and Johnson describe a study in which 14-year-olds worked in groups of four on a geography simulation task on the computer. In some groups the pupils were given individual goals, independently of one another. In other groups the children within the groups were instructed to work competitively, to see who was best. In the third type of group the children were instructed to work cooperatively, being assigned to specific roles in rotation. The third condition produced significantly higher levels of individual achievement on a number of measures than did either of the other two. Both the cooperative and the competitive conditions produced more positive expressed attitudes towards computers than did the individualized condition.

Johnson and colleagues suggest that such benefits of cooperation may be more evident with more complex and exploratory software of the kind they used. However, rather similar advantages for pupils working in cooperative pairs have been found with relatively simple drill and practice software (Mevarech 1987). Twelve-year-olds were studied working alone or in pairs of similar ability on arithmetic drill and practice programs. All children were individually post-tested. Those who had worked in pairs achieved significantly better results, and this was especially true amongst the low-achieving children. However, in another rather similar study involving computer-based instruction in Hebrew, only marginal and non-significant differences favouring homogeneous pairs over individuals were found (Mevarech, Stern and Levita 1987).

Another variable which could potentially play an important role is group size. Trowbridge (1987) observed 13- and 14-year-olds working on CAL software designed to teach them about electrical circuits. The pupils worked either one, two, three or four to a computer. Measures of interactional behaviour taken from videotapes of the sessions indicated that children working in twos or threes engaged in the highest levels of interaction, though those working in threes were more likely to show competitive interaction. The pairs were the most mutually supportive. The children working in pairs made the fewest incorrect entries and formulated higher-quality responses than those working in the other conditions, though post-tests failed to show significant superiority in individual learning outcome.

Whereas the work we have discussed thus far has mainly emphasized social motivational and attitudinal concomitants of interaction, treating cognitive attainments simply as an outcome measure, another body of (mainly European) experimental work has attempted a more cognitively oriented analysis of the interaction. For example, Fletcher (1985) has attempted to analyse the role of the verbalization which typically accompanies collaborative work. In a study with 9- to 11-year-olds, children worked on a computer simulation game either as individuals or in groups of three. Amongst the individuals, some were instructed to work silently while others were asked to talk aloud. On most measures, the groups performed substantially better than the silent individuals. The requirement to verbalize reasons for decisions etc. led to some improvement amongst the children working alone, leading Fletcher to conclude that overt verbalization may have at least some part to play in group facilitation of performance. However, there was no individual post-test on the task in this study, and a post-test measure of verbal knowledge concerning the task indicated no significant differences between the conditions.

Experimental studies have also been carried out involving rather more 'computer-specific' activities such as programming. Programming the computer can be thought of as a highly technical chore which, mercifully, computer users have to concern themselves with less and less these days. But it can also be thought of as the activity which most fully embodies the educational potentialities of the micro-computer. We saw this earlier with Papert, who envisaged the writing, running, debugging and developing of LOGO programs as an activity which distilled and rendered accessible to the young child a whole range of powerful, abstract ideas. Indeed, as Colbourn and Light (1987) noted, the claims Papert made for the cognitive benefits of programming (especially in terms of the child's metacognitive ability to reflect upon and articulate his or her own problem-solving abilities) bear a distinct resemblance to claims which have been made for the cognitive benefits of peer interaction. So what can we say about the effectiveness of bringing these two phenomena together and employing peer interaction in the service of learning to program?

We saw earlier that classroom observation work involving LOGO indicates its potential for supporting high levels of task-related social interaction, though the evidence that it promotes the generalizable problem-solving skills envisaged by Papert is less than convincing (Clements 1987; DES 1987; Kliman 1985). For present purposes the key question is whether there is any experimental evidence that child–child interaction facilitates the learning of programming concepts and skills. There appear to have been relatively few systemic studies in this area.

One such study involved 11- and 12-year-old children learning to use a programming language called microPROLOG (Colbourn and Light 1987; Light, Colbourn and Smith 1987). The children worked in class groups of eight over a number of sessions. Each group of eight pupils was given access to either two, four or eight microcomputers. No differences were found between these conditions in terms of children's individual grasp of microPROLOG at post-test. A significant difference between the design of this study and those of most others we have discussed is that, although in one condition the children had a microcomputer each, they were working within a group of eight pupils and could interact freely with one another. Videotapes of selected sessions indicated little difference in level of task-related child–child interaction in the 'individual', 'two to a machine' and 'four to a machine' conditions. This perhaps serves to highlight the artificiality of experimental studies in which the 'control' condition involves children working alone at the computer with no access at all to their fellow students.

Faced with this difficulty, one way forward is to rely on trying to *correlate* the amount or quality of interaction which particular learners engage in and their particular learning outcome. Webb, Ender and Lewis (1986) adopted this approach in a study of 11- to 14-year-olds learning BASIC programming in pairs over a number of sessions. They looked for evidence that the quality of social interaction and discussion in which children engaged during learning could predict achievement in terms of eventual individual programming skills. Measures were taken of the frequency of such behaviours as giving and receiving explanations, asking questions and getting replies, and verbalizing aloud. Correlations with learning outcome were calculated, partialling out variations in initial ability level. The results showed that many of the interaction measures were significantly positively correlated with some (though not all) of the learning outcome measures.

Perhaps the most systematic and theoretically coherent body of experimental work on the cognitive consequences of peer interaction has been that associated with Doise, Mugny and Perret-Clermont in Geneva and Neuchatel. While this work has not been concerned with computer-based learning, it has exercised considerable influence on work in this field. Doise and colleagues typically used a three-step experimental design involving an individual pre-test, an intervention session in which children work either alone (the control condition) or in groups (usually pairs) and finally an individual post-test. The studies which established this tradition (see for example Doise and Mugny 1984; Perret-Clermont 1980) involved children in the age range 5–7 who, in Piaget's terms, were in the process of mastering concrete operational modes of thought. Where working in pairs facilitated subsequent individual performance the mediating process was characterized as 'socio-cognitive conflict', i.e. conflict between differing wrong answers based on partial centrations, embodied socially in the differing perspectives of the two children. The social dimension of the situation was seen as providing the impetus towards resolving the conflict. Such resolution could be achieved by transcending the different centrations to arrive at a more advanced 'decentred' solution.

This analysis has been adapted by a number of researchers interested in peer-facilitation effects on non-Piagetian tasks, and several of these have involved computer-based work (Blaye 1988; Fraisse 1987; Light *et al.* 1987). In these cases, the reason for using the computer was principally that it offered advantages in controlling and manipulating task presentation, so as to facilitate detailed study of interactional effects. In some cases these manipulations involve the software, in some the hardware.

As an example of a software manipulation, Fraisse (1985, 1987) followed up a series of studies on recursive reasoning with 11- and 12-year-olds by pitting children, either alone or in pairs, against the computer. When the 'computer-opponent' was programmed to give poor (in fact random) answers the children working in pairs discussed their ideas and showed superior learning to those children who worked alone. But when the 'computer-opponent' was programmed to give perfect answers every time, the children in effect used the computer to check out their hypotheses, did not interact much with their partners, and showed no peer-facilitation of performance.

The effects of different types of hardware and interface devices upon interactive learning has not been extensively studied as yet (Wilton and McClean 1984). However, Scaife (1987) has begun to analyse children's performance with various kinds of input devices. Most such devices have clearly been designed with a single user in mind. However, it is possible to exploit them for cooperative usage, and this has been done in a number of experiments.

Blaye (1988) reports a series of studies in which 5- and 6-year-olds worked on a form/colour matrix filling task either individually or in pairs. Although the task might have been expected to engender conflicts of centration, the children worked in pairs showed only a low frequency of verbal disagreement, and there was little to suggest that such disagreements were conducive to learning. Nevertheless, experience in pairs did in some studies lead to greater individual progress than working alone. This was particularly true with a version of the task where the interaction in the pairs was structured so that one child indicated his or her choice with a lightpen and the other had to key in his or her assent via the keyboard before the instruction would be accepted by the computer.

A rather similar procedure for preserving the engagement of both children with the task was used by Light *et al.* (1987). Here pairs and individuals were presented with a problem-solving task on the computer. Superiority of the pairs condition (as judged in terms of individual post-test performance) was only shown when the keyboard was modified so as to require corresponding key entries from both partners to activate a response. Despite rather little verbal interaction of any kind, this 'dual key' condition, resulting in joint participation of both children in every move, was associated with clear peer facilitation of individual performance. As with Blaye (1988), the most likely mechanism underlying progress seems to be the destabilization of initial inefficient solution strategies, creating novel intermediate stages on the basis of which the children could see their way through to more efficient solutions.

Light and Glachan (1985) and Light and Foot (1987) have reported a number of studies of problem solving on the computer which suggest that both the likelihood of peer interaction benefits and the underlying mechanisms vary considerably from task to task. For example, whereas benefits in the 'Tower of Hanoi' task seemed to accrue from the essentially non-verbal disequilibration process referred to above, explicit verbal justification of choices seemed to be an important factor in a 'Balance Beam' task. Disagreement and argument about moves proved a good predictor of learning outcome in the code-breaking game 'Master-mind'.

It is clear from these and other studies that pairs or groups of children working at the computer do not always perform better than individuals, and even when they do this advantage is not always reflected in individual learning outcome. On the other hand it is worth remarking that *contrary* results, favouring the individual over the group, do not seem to appear in this literature. The studies we have reviewed either favour learning in groups or indicate no difference in outcome. There are no indications from these studies that, for example, the reduced 'hands on' experience associated with group use of the computer entails any disadvantages to the learner.

As to the mechanisms of group facilitation, where it occurs, it is apparent that the concept of socio-cognitive conflict which inspired much of the recent work in this field is far from adequate to explain all the effects observed. Much remains to be done in explicating the processes involved. We have seen in some of the studies that we have been considering that manipulations of computer hardware and software can be used as a way of influencing the nature of the socio-cognitive activity and hence the outcome of the interaction. How far can this be taken? To what extent can we envisage the computer actively supporting interaction amongst learners or participating as a full interactive partner in the learning process? These are some of the issues to which we shall turn in the final section of this chapter.

PROSPECTS: THE SOCIAL INTERFACE

As we noted at the outset of this chapter, the goal of intelligent tutoring systems has often been expressed in terms of *individualizing* the learning process (Elsom-Cook 1988), and to this extent it may seem to be very much opposed in spirit to any consideration of social processes in learning. But this is not necessarily the case. Woolf (1988) recently noted the 'most surprising' observation that certain experimental intelligent tutoring systems have been shown to be very effective when used with quite heterogeneous *groups* of students (in this case adults). Hennessy and colleagues are presently developing an arithmetic tutor specially designed to be used by pairs of children (Hennessy *et al.* 1987).

To pick up the idea touched upon at the end of the previous section, it is possible to envisage an intelligent tutor not only coping with pairs of learners but also as being itself a *member* of such a pair, i.e. a partner in the learning process. If it is the case that children learn certain things in and through peer group interaction, then can this process itself be modelled? The possibility of the computer playing the role of a working companion to the child, interacting in such a way as to maximize the child's learning, has recently surfaced in the Intelligent Tutoring literature. For example, Chan and Baskin (1988) propose a system in which the computer plays both the role of teacher and the role of a companion who 'learns' to perform the task at about the same level as the child, and who exchanges ideas with the child as they work together on the same material.

Many problems stand in the way of implementing such a system, not the least of which is our very imperfect understanding of how 'real' learning companions help one another. While there is a long way to go, there are real signs of convergence with some of the work being undertaken by developmental psychologists working in this field. For example, Blaye, Farioli and Gilly (1987), using Blaye's matrix-filling task mentioned earlier, experimented with a condition in which the child proposed an entry for a given cell and the computer 'partner' proposed an alternative choice. The alternative selected was based on a diagnosis of the child's proposal – if it reflected a centration on one dimension of the matrix the computer-partner suggested an (equally wrong) alternative based on the other dimension of the matrix. The results were not impressive – in fact, as we have seen, Blaye's (1988) other studies seriously question the power of socio-cognitive conflict as a mechanism for progress on this task – but the basic design illustrates well the close convergence of work in cognitive science and developmental psychology at the present time.

Similar issues arise in respect of computer-based 'help' facilities. Researchers in this area seem to be confronted with two basic observations. Firstly, children are typically very ready to use their peers as sources of help when faced with computer tasks. Secondly, when help facilities are available on the computer itself, the children seem to show little interest in them and benefit little from their use (Messer, Jackson and Mohamedali 1987; Turner 1988). These apparently conflicting results again point to the need to integrate psychological research on peer facilitation with software design work.

We need to be able to specify the ways in which children solicit and gain help from those around them while working at the computer, and then to use this knowledge of socially mediated help to inform the design of machine-based help. In the realm of adults, the need for research on learners' informal support networks when working with computers is increasingly being recognized, as indeed are the potential implications of such research for the design of effective software-based help (e.g. Bannon 1986; O'Malley 1986). Hopefully, similar research with children will generate progress towards more adaptive and 'helpful' software for children (whether working individually or collectively) before too long.

It is striking, given the inherently individualistic assumptions about the learning process which informed so much of the early work in the field of educational computing, that the social dimension of computer-based learning has come so clearly to the fore. It should allay the fears of any who still see the computer as necessarily a threat to social processes in learning. We concur with a recent OECD report that 'there is every prospect for more rather than less interchange among learners thanks to the new information technologies' (1987: 105). We hope that we have said enough to indicate why psychologists interested in 'children helping children' should be interested in educational computing. It is an area where more psychological research on the social foundations of learning is sorely needed, and where such research has a real chance of influencing children's educational experience.

REFERENCES

Baker, C. (1985) 'The microcomputer and the curriculum: a critique', *Journal of Curriculum Studies* 17: 4.

Bannon, L. (1986) 'Helping users help each other', in D. Norman and S. Draper (eds) *User Centred System Design*, Hillsdale, NJ: Erlbaum.

Blaye, A. (1988) 'Confrontation socio-cognitive et résolution de problème', unpublished doctoral thesis, University of Provence.

Blaye, A., Farioli, F. and Gilly, M. (1987) 'Microcomputer as a partner in problem solving', *Rassegna di Psicologia* 4: 109–18.

Broderick, C. and Trushell, J. (1985) 'Problems and processes – Junior School children using wordprocessors to produce an information leaflet', *English in Education* 19: 2.

Bullock, A. (1975) *A Language for Life*, London: HMSO.

Chan, T.-W., and Baskin, A. (1988) ' "Studying with the Prince": the computer as learning companion', paper presented to IT-88 Conference, Montreal, June.

Clements, D. (1987) 'A longitudinal study of the effects of LOGO programming on cognitive abilities and achievement', *Journal of Educational Computing Research* 3: 1.

Colbourn, C. J. and Light, P. H. (1987) 'Social interaction and learning using micro-PROLOG, *Journal of Computer Assisted Learning* 3: 130–40.

Crook, C. (1986) 'The use of word-processor to support writing as a joint activity', paper presented at second European Developmental Psychology Conference, Rome, September.

Crook, C. (1987) 'Computers in the classroom: defining a social context', in J. Rutkowska and C. Crook (eds) *Computers, Cognition and Development*, Chichester: Wiley.

Cummings, R. (1985) 'Small group discussions and the microcomputer', *Journal of Computer Assisted Learning* 1: 149–58.

DES (1987) 'Aspects of the work of the Microelectronics Education Programme', London: Department of Education and Science.

Doise, W., and Mugny, G. (1984) *The Social Development of the Intellect*, Oxford: Pergamon Press.

Elsom-Cook, M. (1987) 'Intelligent computer-aided instruction research at the Open University', CITE Technical Report No. 10, Milton Keynes: The Open University.

Elsom-Cook, M. (1988) 'Guided discovery tutoring and bounded user modelling', in J. Self (ed.) *Artificial Intelligence and Human Learning*, London: Chapman & Hall.

Fletcher, B. (1985) 'Group and individual learning of junior school children on a microcomputer based task', *Educational Review* 37: 251–61.

Fraisse, J. (1985) 'Interactions sociales entre pairs et découverte d'une stratégie cognitive chez des enfants de 11 ans', unpublished doctoral thesis, University of Provence.

Fraisse, J. (1987) 'Etude du rôle pertubateur du partenaire dans la découverte d'une strategie cognitive chez des enfants de 11 ans en situation d'interaction sociale', *Bulletin de Psychologie* 382: 943–52.

Hawkins, J. (1983) 'Learning LOGO together: the social context', Tech. Report 13, New York: Bank St. College of Education.

Hawkins, J., Sheingold, K., Gearhart, M. and Berger, C. (1982) 'Microcomputers in schools: impact on the social life of elementary classrooms', *Journal of Applied Developmental Psychology* 3: 361–73.

Hennessy, S., Evertsz, R., Ellis, D., Black, P., O'Shea, T. and Floyd A. (1987) 'Design specification for "Shopping on Mars" '. CITE report 29, Institute of Educational Technology, Milton Keynes: The Open University.

Hoyles, C. and Sutherland, R. (1986) 'Using LOGO in the mathematics classroom', *Computers in Education* 10: 61–72.

Hughes, M., MacLeod, H. and Potts, C. (1985) 'Using LOGO with Infant School children', *Educational Psychology* 5: 3–4.

Jackson, A., Fletcher, B. and Messer, D. (1986) 'A survey of microcomputer use and provision in primary schools', *Journal of Computer Assisted Learning* 2: 45–55.

Johnson, D. and Johnson, R. (1986) 'Computer assistefd cooperative learning', *Educational Technology*, January.

Johnson, R., Johnson, D. and Stanne, M. (1986) 'Comparison of computer assisted cooperative, competitive and individualistic learning', *American Educational Research Journal* 12: 382–92.

Kliman, M. (1985) 'A new approach to Infant and Early Primary Mathematics', DAI Research Paper 241, Edinburgh: Department of Artificial Intelligence, University of Edinburgh.

Light, P. H., Colbourn, C. J. and Smith, D. (1987) 'Peer interaction and logic programming: a study of the acquisition of micro-PROLOG', ESRC Information Technology and Education Programme, occasional paper ITE/17/87.

Light, P. H. and Foot, T. (1987) 'Peer interaction and microcomputer use', *Rassegna di Psicologia* 4: 93–104.

Light, P. H., Foot, T., Colbourn, C. and McClelland, I. (1987) 'Collaborative interactions at the microcomputer keyboard', *Educational Psychology* 7: 13–21.

Light, P. H. and Glachan, M. (1985) 'Facilitation of problem solving through peer interaction', *Educational Psychology* 5: 217–25.

Messer, D., Jackson, A. and Mohamedali, M. (1987) 'Influences on computer-based problem solving', *Educational Psychology* 7: 1.

Mevarech, Z. (1987) 'Learning with computers in small groups: cognitive and social processes', paper presented at 2nd European Conference for Research on Learning and Instruction, Tubingen, W. Germany, September.

Mavarech, Z., Stern, D. and Levita, I. (1987) 'To cooperate or not to cooperate in CAI: that is the question', *Journal of Educational Research* 80: 164–7.

OECD (1987) 'Information technologies and basic learning', Paris: Organisation for Economic Cooperation and Development.

O'Malley, C. (1986) 'Helping users help themselves', in D. Norman and S. Draper (eds) *User Centred System Design*, Hillsdale, NJ: Erlbaum.

Papert, S. (1980) *Mindstorms: Children, Computers and Powerful Ideas*, Brighton: Harvester Press.

Perret-Clermont, A.-N. (1980) *Social Interaction and Cognitive Development in Children*, London: Academic Press.

Scaife, M. (1987) 'Sensorimotor learning in children's interactions with computerised displays', final report to ESRC, no. C08250010.

Sheingold, K., Hawkins, J. and Char, C. (1984) ' "I'm the thinkist, you're the typist": the interaction of technology and the social life of classrooms', Tech. Report 27, New York: Bank St. College of Education.

Trowbridge, D. (1987) 'An investigation of groups working at the computer', in Berger, K. Pezdek and W. Banks (eds) *Applications of Cognitive Psychology: Problem Solving, Education and Computing*, Hillsdale, NJ: Erlbaum.

Turner, T. (1988) 'Cognitive development through child-computer interaction using HELP facilities', unpublished paper, Department of Psychology, University of Southampton.

Webb, N., Ender, P. and Lewis, S. (1986) 'Problem solving strategies and group processes in small groups learning computer programming', *American Educational Research Journal* 23: 243–61.

Wilton, J. and McClean, R. (1984) 'Evaluation of a mouse as an educational pointing device', *Computers and Education* 8: 455–61.

Woolf, B. (1988) 'Representing complex knowledge in an intelligent machine tutor', in J. Self (ed.) *Artificial Intelligence and Human Learning*, London: Chapman & Hall.

Part four
Context and cognition

Introduction

The chapters which make up this final part address in a variety of different ways the issue of contextual constraints on children's thinking. The recognition of a high degree of domain specificity in most aspects of thinking and reasoning, in adults as well as in children, is one notable aspect of recent psychological research. Piagetian psychology tended to see the developmental process in terms of the elaboration of more and more abstract, formal and universal modes of thought, with context simply muddying the water. Donaldson, in *Children's Minds* (1978) gave context a fuller role by suggesting that the social intelligibility of 'human sense' supplied by the contextualization of a problem supported the young child's solution of that problem. The developmental task thus came to be seen as the disembedding or decontextualization of thought. But as we have seen from many of the earlier chapters in this volume, school learning can be seen as being just as firmly contextualized as learning that takes place elsewhere.

The first chapter in this section, by Carraher, Carraher and Schliemann (13) deals directly with this issue of 'thinking in and out of school'. It shows how strikingly *in*dependent mathematical development can be in these two domains. The fact that children frequently have several very different strategies available for tackling a given type of problem is taken up in the next chapter by Siegler (14), who tries to develop a general model for characterizing the determinants of children's strategy choices.

Clough and Driver (Chapter 15) approach a different, but related issue, namely how students' informal or intuitive explanations relate to formal, school-taught explanations in the domain of science. In particular, they examine the relative consistency of these different types of explanation across analogous problems.

In the final chapter of this volume, Rogoff, Gauvain and Ellis (16) take on the major task of reviewing the available evidence concerning the impact of cultural contexts on the development of thinking. They use this evidence to argue a case for a specific learning model rather than a 'central processor model' of thinking. We cannot improve on the sentence with which they end their chapter, which makes a fitting final statement for this volume: 'Sociocultural experience and individual functioning are fundamentally tied to one another and are, thus, companions in human behavior and development' (p. 329).

REFERENCE

Donaldson, M. (1978) *Children's Minds*, London: Fontana.

13 Mathematics in the streets and in schools

Terezinha Nunes Carraher, David William Carraher and *Analúcia Dias Schliemann*
Source: *British Journal of Developmental Psychology* (1985) 3: 21–9.

There are reasons for thinking that there may be a difference between solving mathematical problems using algorithms learned in school and solving them in familiar contexts out of school. Reed and Lave (1981) have shown that people who have not been to school often solve such problems in different ways from people who have. This certainly suggests that there are informal ways of doing mathematical calculations which have little to do with the procedures taught in school.

Reed and Lave's study with Liberian adults showed differences between people who had and who had not been to school. However, it is quite possible that the same differences between informal and school-based routines could exist within people. In other words it might be the case that the same person could solve problems sometimes in formal and at other times in informal ways. This seems particularly likely with children who often have to do mathematical calculations in informal circumstances outside school at the same time as their knowledge of the algorithms which they have to learn at school is imperfect and their use of them ineffective.

We already know that children often obtain absurd results such as finding a remainder which is larger than the minuend when they try to apply routines for computations which they learn at school (Carraher and Schliemann 1985). There is also some evidence that informal procedures learned outside school are often extremely effective. Gay and Cole (1976) for example showed that unschooled Kpelle traders estimated quantities of rice far better than educated Americans managed to. So it seems quite possible that children might have difficulty with routines learned at school and yet at the same time be able to solve the mathematical problems for which these routines were devised in other more effective ways. One way to test this idea is to look at children who have to make frequent and quite complex calculations outside school. The children who sell things in street markets in Brazil form one such group (Carraher *et al.* 1982).

THE CULTURAL CONTEXT

The study was conducted in Recife, a city of approximately 1.5 million people on the north-eastern coast of Brazil. Like several other large Brazilian cities, Recife receives a very large number of migrant workers from the rural areas who must adapt to a new way of living in a metropolitan region. In an anthropological study of migrant workers in São Paulo, Brazil, Berlinck (1977) identified four pressing needs in this adaptation process: finding a home, acquiring work papers, getting a job, and providing for immediate survival (whereas in rural areas the family often obtains food through its own work). During the initial adaptation phase, survival depends mostly upon resources brought by the migrants or received through begging. A large portion of migrants later become unspecialized manual workers, either maintaining a regular job or working in what is known as the informal sector of the economy (Cavalcanti 1978). The informal sector can be characterized as an unofficial part of the economy which consists of relatively unskilled jobs not regulated by government organs thereby producing income not susceptible to taxation while at the same time not affording job security or workers' rights such as health insurance. The income generated thereby is thus intermittent and variable. The dimensions of a business enterprise in the informal sector are determined by the family's work capability. Low educational and professional qualification levels are characteristic of the rather sizable population which depends upon the informal sector. In Recife, approximately 30 per cent of the workforce is engaged in the informal sector as its main activity and 18 per cent as a secondary activity (Calvalcanti 1978). The importance of such sources of income for families in Brazil's lower socio-economic strata can be easily understood by noting that the income of an unspecialized labourer's family is increased by 56 per cent through his wife's and children's activities in the informal sector in São Paulo (Berlinck 1977). In Fortaleza it represents fully 60 per cent of the lower class[1] family's income (Calvalcanti and Duarte 1980a).

Several types of occupations – domestic work, street-vending, shoe-repairing and other types of small repairs which are carried out without a fixed commercial address – are grouped as part of the informal sector of the economy. The occupation considered in the present study – that of street-vendors – represents the principal occupation of 10 per cent of the economically active population of Salvador (Calvalcanti and Duarte 1980b) and Fortaleza (Calvalcanti and Duarte, 1980a). Although no specific data regarding street-vendors were obtained for Recife, data from Salvador and Fortaleza serve as close approximations since these cities are, like Recife, State capitals from the same geographical region.

It is fairly common in Brazil for sons and daughters of street-vendors to help out their parents in their businesses. From about the age of 8 or 9 the children will often enact some of the transactions for the parents when they are busy with another customer or away on some errand. Pre-adolescents and teenagers may even develop their own 'business', selling snack foods such as roasted peanuts, pop-corn, coconut milk or corn on the cob. In Fortaleza and Salvador, where data are available, 2.2 and 1.4 per cent, respectively, of the population actively engaged in the informal sector as street-vendors were aged 14 or less while 8.2 and 7.5 per cent, respectively, were aged 15–19 years (Cavalcanti and Duarte 1980a, 1980b).

In their work these children and adolescents have to solve a large number of mathematical problems, usually without recourse to paper and pencil. Problems may involve multiplication (one coconut cost x: four coconuts, $4x$), addition (4 coconuts and 12 lemons cost $x + y$), and substraction (Cr$500 – i.e. 500 *cruzeiros* – minus the purchase price will give the change due). Division is much less frequently used but appears in some contexts in which the price is set with respect to a measuring unit (such as 1 kg) and the customer wants a fraction of that unit: for example, when the particular item chosen weighs 1.2 kg. The use of tables listing prices by number of items (one egg – 12 *cruzeiros*; two eggs – 24, etc.) is observed occasionally in natural settings but was not observed among the children who took part in the study. Pencil and paper were also not used by these children, although they may occasionally be used by adult vendors when adding long lists of items.

METHOD

Subjects

The children in this study were four boys and one girl aged 9–15 years with a mean age of 11.2 and ranging in level of schooling from first to eighth grade. One of them had only one year of schooling; two had three years of schooling; one, four years; and one, eight years. All were from very poor backgrounds. Four of the subjects were attending school at the time and one had been out of school for two years. Four of these subjects had received formal instruction on mathematical operations and word problems. The subject who attended first grade and dropped out of school was unlikely to have learned multiplication and division in school since these operations are usually initiated in second or third grade in public schools in Recife.

Procedure

The children were found by the interviewers on street corners or at markets where they worked alone or with their families. Interviewers chose subjects who seemed to be in the desired age range – school children or young adolescents – obtaining information about their age and level of schooling along with information on the prices of their merchandise. Test items in this situation were presented in the course of a normal sales transaction in which the researcher posed as a customer. Purchases were sometimes carried out. In other cases the 'customer' asked the vendor to perform calculations on possible purchases. At the end of the informal test, the children were asked to take part in a formal test which was given on a separate occasion, no more than a week later, by the same interviewer. Subjects answered a total of 99 questions on the formal test and 63 questions on the informal test. Since the items of the formal test were based upon questions of the informal test, order of testing was fixed for all subjects.

1   The informal test

The informal test was carried out in Portuguese in the subject's natural working situation, that is, at street corners or an open market. Testers posed to the subject successive questions about potential or actual purchases and obtained verbal responses. Responses were either tape-recorded or written down, along with comments, by an observer. After obtaining an answer for the item, testers questioned the subject about his or her method for solving the problem.

The method can be described as a hybrid between the Piagetian clinical method and participant observation. The interviewer was not merely an interviewer; he was also a customer – a questioning customer who wanted the vendor to tell him how he or she performed their computations.

An example is presented below taken from the informal test with M, a coconut vendor aged 12, third grader, where the interviewer is referred to as 'customer':

Customer: How much is one coconut?
M: 35.
Customer: I'd like ten. How much is that?
M: (Pause) Three will be 105; with three more, that will be 210. (Pause) I need four more. That is . . .[2] (pause) 315 . . . I think it is 350.

This problem can be mathematically represented in several ways: 35 × 10 is a good representation of the *question* posed by the interviewer. The subject's answer is better represented by 105 + 105 +105 + 35, which implies that 35 × 10 was solved by the subject as (3 × 35) + (3 × 35) + (3 × 35) + 35. The subject can be said to have solved the following sub-items in the above situation:

(a) 35 × 10;
(b) 35 × 3 (which may have already been known);
(c) 105 + 105;
(d) 210 + 105;
(e) 315 + 35;
(f) 3 + 3 + 3 + 1.

When one represents in a formal mathematical fashion the problems which were solved by the subject, one is in fact attempting to represent the subject's mathematical competence. M proved to be competent in finding out how much 35 × 10 is, even though he used a routine not taught in third grade, since in Brazil third-graders learn to multiply any number by ten simply by placing a zero to the right of that number. Thus, we considered that the subject solved the test item (35 × 10) and a whole series of subitems (1 to 6) successfully in this process. However, in the process of scoring, only *one* test item (35 × 10) was considered as having been presented and, therefore, correctly solved.

2   The formal test

After subjects were interviewed in the natural situation, they were asked to participate in the formal part of the study and a second interview was scheduled at the same place or at the subject's house.

The items for the formal test were prepared for each subject on the basis of problems solved by him or her during the informal test. Each problem solved in the informal test was mathematically represented according to the subject's problem-solving routine.

From all the mathematical problems *successfully solved* by each subject (regardless of whether they constituted a test item or not), a sample was chosen for inclusion in the subject's formal test. This sample was presented in the formal test either as a mathematical operation dictated to the subject (e.g. 105 + 105) or as a word problem e.g. Mary bought x bananas; each banana cost y; how much did she pay altogether?). In either case, *each subject solved problems employing the same numbers involved in his or her own informal test.* Thus quantities used varied from one subject to the other.

Two variations were introduced in the formal test, according to methodological suggestions contained in Reed and Lave (1981). First, some of the items presented in the formal test were the inverse of problems solved in the informal test (e.g. 500 − 385 may be presented as 385 + 115 in the formal test). Second, some of the items in the informal test used a decimal value which differed from the one used in the formal test (e.g. 40 *cruzeiros* may have appeared as 40 *centavos* or 35 may have been presented as 3,500 in the formal test – the principal Brazilian unit of currency is the *cruzeiro*; each *cruzeiro* is worth one hundred *centavos*).

In order to make the formal test situation more similar to the school setting, subjects were given paper and pencil at the testing and were encouraged to use these. When problems were nonetheless solved without recourse to writing, subjects were asked to write down their answers. Only one subject refused to do so, claiming that he did not know how to write. It will be recalled, however, that the school-type situation was not represented solely by the introduction of pencil and paper but also by the very use of formal mathematical problems without context and by word problems referring to imaginary situations.

In the formal test the children were given a total of 38 mathematical operations and 61 word problems. Word problems were rather concrete and each involved only one mathematical operation.

RESULTS AND DISCUSSION

The analysis of the results from the informal test required an initial definition of what would be considered a test item in that situation. While, in the formal test, items were defined prior to testing, in the informal test problems were generated in the natural setting and items were identified *a posteriori*. In order to avoid a biased increase in the number of items solved in the informal test, the definition of an item was based upon *questions* posed by the customer/tester. This probably constitutes a conservative estimate of the number of problems solved, since subjects often solved a number of intermediary steps in

Table 13.1 Results according to testing conditions

| | Informal test | | Formal test | | | |
| | | | Mathematical operations | | Word problems | |
Subject	Score	No. of items	Score	No. of items	Score	No. of items
M	10	18	2.5	8	10	11
P	8.9	19	3.7	8	6.9	16
Pi	10	12	5.0	6	10	11
MD	10	7	1.0	10	3.3	12
S	10	7	8.3	6	7.3	11
Totals		63		38		61

Note: Each subject's score is the percentage of correct items divided by 10.

the course of searching for the solution to the question they had been asked. Thus the same defining criterion was applied in both testing situations in the identification of items even though items were defined prior to testing in one case and after testing in the other. In both testing situations, the subject's oral response was the one taken into account even though in the formal test written responses were also available.

Context-embedded problems were much more easily solved than ones without a context. Table 13.1 shows that 98.2 per cent of the 63 problems presented in the informal test were correctly solved. In the formal test word problems (which provide some descriptive context for the subject), the rate of correct responses was 73.7 per cent, which should be contrasted with a 36.8 per cent rate of correct responses for mathematical operations with no context.

The frequency of correct answers for each subject was converted to scores from 1 to 10 reflecting the percentage of correct responses. A Friedman two-way analysis of variance of score ranks compared the scores of each subject in the three types of testing conditions. The scores differ significantly across conditions ($\chi^2 = 6.4$, $p = 0.039$). Mann–Whitney Us were also calculated comparing the three types of testing situations. Subjects performed significantly better on the informal test than on the formal test involving context-free operations ($U = 0$, $p < 0.05$). The difference between the informal test and the word problems was not significant ($U = 6$, $p > 0.05$).

It could be argued that errors observed in the formal test were related to the transformations that had been performed upon the informal test problems in order to construct the formal test. An evaluation of this hypothesis was obtained by separating items which had been changed either by inverting the operation or changing the decimal point from items which remained identical to their informal test equivalents. The percentage of correct responses in these two groups of items did not differ significantly; the rate of correct responses in transformed items was slightly higher than that obtained for items identical to informal test items. Thus the transformations performed upon informal test items in designing formal test items cannot explain the discrepancy of performance in these situations.

A second possible interpretation of these results is that the children interviewed in this study were 'concrete' in their thinking and, thus, concrete situations would help them in the discovery of a solution. In the natural situation, they solved problems about the sale of lemons, coconuts, etc., when the actual items in question were physically present. However, the presence of concrete instances can be understood as a facilitating factor if the instance somehow allows the problem-solver to abstract from the concrete example to a more general situation. There is nothing in the nature of coconuts that makes it relatively easier to discover that three coconuts (at Cr$35.00 each) cost Cr$105.00. The presence of the groceries does not simplify the arithmetic of the problem. Moreover, computation in the natural situation of the informal test was in all cases carried out mentally, without recourse to external memory aids for partial results or intermediary steps. One can hardly argue that mental computation would be an ability characteristic of concrete thinkers.

The results seem to be in conflict with the implicit pedagogical assumption of mathematical educators according to which children ought first to learn mathematical operations and only later to apply them to verbal and real-life problems. Real-life and word problems may provide the 'daily human sense' (Donaldson 1978) which will guide children to find a correct solution intuitively without requiring an extra step – namely, the translation of word problems into algebraic expressions. This interpretation is consistent with data obtained by others in the area of logic, such as Wason and Shapiro (1971), Johnson-Laird *et al.* (1972) and Lunzer *et al.* (1972).

How is it possible that children capable of solving a computational problem in the natural situation will fail to solve the same problem when it is taken out of its context? In the present case, a qualitative analysis of the protocols suggested that the problem-solving routines used may have been different in the two situations. In the natural situations children tended to reason by using what can be termed a 'convenient group' while in the formal test school-taught routines were more frequently, although not exclusively, observed. Five examples are given below, which demonstrate the children's ability to deal with quantities and their lack of expertise in manipulating symbols. The examples were chosen for representing clear explanations of the procedures used in both settings. In each of the five examples below the performance described in the informal test contrasts strongly with the same child's performance in the formal test when solving the same item.

1 First example (M, 12 years)

Informal test

Customer: I'm going to take four coconuts. How much is that?
Child: Three will be 105, plus 30, that's 135 . . . one coconut is 35
           . . . that is . . . 140!

Formal test

Child resolves the item 35 × 4 explaining out loud:
4 times 5 is 20, carry the 2; 2 plus 3 is 5, times 4 is 20.
Answer written: 200.

2 Second example (MD, 9 years)

Informal test

Customer: OK, I'll take three coconuts (at the price of Cr$40.00 each).
           How much is that?
Child: (Without gestures, calculates out loud) 40, 80, 120.

Formal test

Child solves the item 40 × 3 and obtains 70. She then explains the procedure 'Lower the zero; 4 and 3 is 7'.

3 Third example (MD, 9 years)

Informal test

Customer: I'll take 12 lemons (one lemon is Cr$5.00).
Child: 10, 20, 30, 40, 50, 60 (while separating out two lemons at a
           time).

Formal test

Child has just solved the item 40 × 3. In solving 12 × 5 she proceeds by lowering first the 2, then the 5 and the 1, obtaining 152. She explains this procedure to the (surprised) examiner when she is finished.

4   Fourth example (S, 11 years)

Informal test

Customer: What would I have to pay for six kilos? (of watermelon at Cr$50.00 per kg).
Child: (Without any appreciable pause) 300.
Customer: Let me see. How did you get that so fast?
Child: Counting one by two. Two kilos. 100, 200, 300.

Formal test

Test item: A fisherman caught 50 fish. The second one caught five times the amount of fish the first fisherman had caught. How many fish did the lucky fisherman catch?
Child: (Writes down 50 × 6 and 360 as the result; then answers) 36.
Examiner repeats the problems and child does the computation again, writing down 860 as result. His oral response is 86.
Examiner: How did you calculate that?
Child: I did it like this. Six times six is 36. Then I put it there.
Examiner: Where did you put it? (Child had not written down the number to be carried).
Child: (Points to the digit 5 in 50). That makes 86 (apparently adding 3 and 5 and placing this sum in the result).
Examiner: How many did the first fisherman catch?
Child: 50.
A final example follows, with suggested interpretations enclosed in parentheses.

5   Fifth example

Informal test

Customer: I'll take two coconuts (at Cr$40.00 each. Pays with a Cr$500.00 bill). What do I get back?
Child: (Before reaching for customer's change) 80, 90, 100, 420.

Formal test

Test item 420 + 80.
The child writes 420 plus 80 and claims that 130 is the result. (The procedure used was not explained but it seems that the child applied a step of a multiplication routine to an addition problem by successively

adding 8 to 2 and then to 4, carrying the 1; that is, $8 + 2 = 10$, carry the one, $1 + 4 + 8 = 13$. The zeros in 420 and 80 were not written. Reaction times were obtained from tape recordings and the whole process took 53 seconds.)

Examiner: How did you do this one, 420 plus 80?
Child: Plus?
Examiner: Plus 80.
Child: 100, 200.
Examiner: (After a 5 second pause, interrupts the child's response treating it as final) Hum, OK.
Child: Wait a minute. That was wrong. 500. (The child had apparently added 80 and 20, obtaining one hundred, and then started adding the hundreds. The experimenter interpreted 200 as the final answer after a brief pause but the child completed the computation and gave the correct answer when solving the addition problem by a manipulation-with-quantities approach.)

In the informal test, children rely upon mental calculations which are closely linked to the quantities that are being dealt with. The preferred strategy for multiplication problems seems to consist in chaining successive additions. In the first example, as the addition became more difficult, the subject decomposed a quantity into tens and units – to add 35 to 105, M first added 30 and later included 5 in the result.

In the formal test, where paper and pencil were used in all the above examples, the children try to follow, without success, school-prescribed routines. Mistakes often occur as a result of confusing addition routines with multiplication routines, as is clearly the case in examples (1) and (5). Moreover, in all the cases, there is no evidence, once the numbers are written down, that the children try to relate the obtained results to the problem at hand in order to assess the adequacy of their answers.

Summarizing briefly, the combination of the clinical method of questioning with participant observation used in this project seemed particularly helpful when exploring mathematical thinking and thinking in daily life. The results support the thesis proposed by Luria (1976) and by Donaldson (1978) that thinking sustained by daily human sense can be – in the same subject – at a higher level than thinking out of context. They also raise doubts about the pedagogical practice of teaching mathematical operations in a disembedded form before applying them to word problems.

Our results are also in agreement with data reported by Lave *et al.*

(1984), who showed that problem solving in the supermarket was significantly superior to problem solving with paper and pencil. It appears that daily problem solving may be accomplished by routines different from those taught in schools. In the present study, daily problem solving tended to be accomplished by strategies involving the mental manipulation of quantities while in the school-type situation the manipulation of symbols carried the burden of computation, thereby making the operations 'in a very real sense divorced from reality' (see Reed and Lave 1981: 442). In many cases attempts to follow school-prescribed routines seemed in fact to interfere with problem solving (see also Carraher and Schliemann 1985).

Are we to conclude that schools ought to allow children simply to develop their own computational routines without trying to impose the conventional systems developed in the culture? We do not believe that our results lead to this conclusion. Mental computation has limitations which can be overcome through written computation. One is the inherent limitation placed on multiplying through successive chunking, that is, on multiplying through repeated chunked additions – a procedure which becomes grossly inefficient when large numbers are involved.

The sort of mathematics taught in schools has the potential to serve as an 'amplifier of thought processes', in the sense in which Bruner (1972) has referred to both mathematics and logic. As such, we do not dispute whether 'school maths' routines can offer richer and more powerful alternatives to maths routines which emerge in non-school settings. The major question appears to centre on the proper pedagogical point of departure, i.e. where to start. We suggest that educators should question the practice of treating mathematical systems as formal subjects from the outset and should instead seek ways of introducing these systems in contexts which allow them to be sustained by human daily sense.

NOTES

1 In the present report the term 'class' is employed loosely, without a clear distinction from the expression 'socio-economic stratum'.
2 (. . .) is used here to mark ascending intonation suggestive of the interruption, and not completion, of a statement.

REFERENCES

Berlinck, M. T. (1977) *Marginalidade Social e Relações de Classe em São Paulo*, Petrópolis, RJ, Brazil: Vozes.

Bruner, J. (1972) *Relevance of Education*, London: Penguin.
Carraher, T., Carraher, D. and Schliemann, A. (1982) 'Na vida dez, na escola zero: Os contextos culturais da aprendizagem da matemática', *Cadernos de Pesquisa* 42: 79–86. (São Paulo, Brazil, special UNESCO issue for Latin America.)
Carraher, T. and Schliemann, A. (1985) 'Computation routines prescribed by schools: Help or hindrance?', *Journal for Research in Mathematics Education* 16: 37–44.
Cavalcanti, C. (1978) *Viabilidada do Setor Informal. A Demanda de Pequenos Serviços no Grande Recife*, Recife, PE, Brazil: Instituto Joaquim Nabuco de Pesquisas Sociais.
Cavalcanti, C. and Duarte, R. (1981a) *A Procura de Espaço na Economia Urbana: O Setor Informal de Fortaleza*, Recife, PE, Brazil: SUDENE/FUNDAJ.
Cavalcanti, C. and Duarte, R. (1980b) *O Setor Informal de Salvador: Dimensões, Natureza, Significação*, Recife, PE, Brazil: SUDENE/FUNDAJ.
Donaldson, M. (1978) *Children's Minds*, New York: Norton.
Gay, J. and Cole, M. (1976) *The New Mathematics and an Old Culture: A Study of Learning Among the Kpelle of Liberia*, New York: Holt, Rinehart & Winston.
Johnson-Laird, P. N., Legrenzi, P. and Sonino Legrenzi, M. (1972) 'Reasoning and a sense of reality', *British Journal of Psychology* 63: 395–400.
Lave, J., Murtaugh, M. and de La Rocha, O. (1984) 'The dialectical construction of arithmetic practice', in B. Rogoff and J. Lave (eds) *Everyday Cognition: Its Development in Social Context*, pp. 67–94, Cambridge, MA: Harvard University Press.
Lunzer, E. A., Harrison, C. and Davey, M. (1972) 'The four-card problem and the development of formal reasoning', *Quarterly Journal of Experimental Psychology* 24: 326–39.
Luria, A. R. (1976) *Cognitive Development: Its Cultural and Social Foundations*, Cambridge, MA: Harvard University Press.
Reed, H. J. and Lave, J. (1981) 'Arithmetic as a tool for investigating relations between culture and cognition', in R. W. Casson (ed.) *Language, Culture and Cognition: Anthropological Perspectives*, New York: Macmillan.
Wason, P. C. and Shapiro, D. (1971) 'Natural and contrived experience in a reasoning problem', *Quarterly Journal of Experimental Psychology* 23: 63–71.

14 How domain-general and domain-specific knowledge interact to produce strategy choices

Robert S. Siegler
Source: *Merrill-Palmer Quarterly* (1989), January, 35(1): 1–26. Reprinted by permission of the Wayne State University Press.

Views of the relative impact of domain-general and domain-specific processes have shifted radically in the past 20 years. When Piaget's influence was strongest, great emphasis was placed on processes that were believed to influence all of cognition, such as accommodation and assimilation. More recently, the importance of domain-specific knowledge has been increasingly emphasized; as Chi (1978) demonstrated, a child with sufficient domain-specific knowledge can generate more advanced performance than an adult with lesser knowledge. The importance of both domain-general and domain-specific process has been amply demonstrated now, and the current challenge is to illustrate how general and specific processes interact to produce cognitive functioning.

The context within which I consider interactions of domain-general and domain-specific knowledge involves children's choices among strategies. Children often know and use many strategies for solving a class of problems. Knowing diverse strategies adds to the children's flexibility in solving problems, but creates a problem for investigators: How do children choose among the strategies? This article describes one strategy choice mechanism that, at least in the areas in which it has been tested, yields strategy choices quite similar to children's. The mechanism combines domain-general and domain-specific properties. The choice process is similar across quite varied domains, but the outcomes of the process, the strategy choices that are made, are highly dependent on domain-specific knowledge. Together, these domain-general and domain-specific properties have proved to be sufficient to produce adaptive strategy choices in numerous domains.

In the past, cognitive developmental models have avoided the need to explain how children choose among strategies by depicting children of a particular age as always using a particular strategy. This assumption has been common to stage and nonstage theories, and has been made about many different areas of cognitive development. For example, in the area of memory development, 5-year-olds have been said not to use rehearsal as a strategy for remembering, 8-year-olds to use a simple form of rehearsal, and 11-year-olds to use a sophisticated version of it (Flavell, Beach and Chinsky 1966; Ornstein, Naus and Liberty 1975). In the area of addition of small numbers, preschoolers have been said to use the strategy of counting from 1, first and second graders to count-on from the larger number (e.g. to solve 3 + 5 by counting-on from 5), and older children to retrieve answers from memory (Ashcraft 1982; Groen and Parkman 1972; Ilg and Ames 1951). In the area of problem solving, children below the age of 6 have been said to centre on a single dimension, whereas older children have been said to consider multiple dimensions (Case 1985; Piaget 1952). In language development, Stage I children have been said to generate past tense forms of verbs through rote repetition of what they have heard, whereas Stage II children have been said to do so by over-generalizing the *ed* rule (Brown, Cazden and Bellugi 1969).

It is becoming increasingly apparent that in all of these areas and many others, equating age and strategy use has produced too simple a portrayal of children's thinking. For example, Maratsos (1983) noted that at no age do children uniformly use the *ed* rule to produce past tenses. In the extreme case, a child will say *went* in one sentence, *goed* in the next, and *wented* in a third.

Recognizing the diversity of children's strategies is important not only for increasing the accuracy of descriptions of children's thinking, but also for raising a number of new questions. What advantages do children gain by using diverse strategies rather than just a single strategy? How does a child choose among the strategies that he or she has available? How do strategy choices change over time? Which aspects of strategy choices are unique to particular domains, and which are general across domains?

All of these questions are based on the assumption that children do, in fact, use multiple strategies. The next section examines evidence for such strategy diversity in one situation where evidence supporting the view that children consistently used a single strategy seemed particularly strong.

EVIDENCE THAT CHILDREN USE DIVERSE STRATEGIES

Groen and Parkman (1972) observed that the size of the smaller addend (the smaller of the two numbers being added) was an excellent predictor of first graders' solution times on simple addition problems. This finding led these researchers to postulate that children of this age consistently use the min strategy to solve such problems. This *min strategy* involves counting up from the larger addend the number of times indicated by the smaller addend. For example, a child using the min strategy to solve the problem of 3 + 6 would start at 6 and count upward three counts (the child would think '6, 7, 8, 9'). Groen and Parkman hypothesized that the only source of variation in solution times for different problems was the number of counts upward from the larger addend that were needed to solve the problem. Thus, 4 + 3, 3 + 7, and 6 + 3 would all produce the same solution times, because all required three upward counts.

A variety of findings have supported the view that young children add through the type of process depicted in the min model. The size of the smaller addend has consistently been the best predictor of first and second graders' solution times (Ashcraft 1982; 1987; Kay, Post, Hall, and Dineen 1986; Svenson 1975). It is a good predictor in absolute as well as relative terms, accounting for 60% to 75% of the variance in solution times in a number of studies. These studies have included children in special classes for poor students as well as children in standard classes, and children in Europe as well as in North America (Svenson and Broquist 1975). The model fits individual children's solution times as well as group averages (Groen and Resnick 1977; Kaye *et al.* 1986; Svenson 1975).

Despite all this support, the model is at best oversimplified. In a recent experiment, Siegler (1987a) examined young children's simple addition, using both the usual solution-time and error measures and children's self-reports of what they had done, obtained immediately after each trial. The results were striking. When data were averaged over all trials (and over all strategies), as in earlier studies, the results closely replicated the previous finding that solution times and percentage of errors were a linear function of the smaller addend. If these analyses were the only ones conducted, the usual conclusion would have been reached, namely, that first and second graders consistently use the min strategy to add.

However, the children's verbal reports suggested a quite different picture. The min strategy was but one of five approaches that they

Table 14.1 Percentage of use of each strategy by children of each age

Grade	Strategy				
	Retrieval	Min	Decompo-sition	Count-all	Guess or no response
Kindergarten	16	30	2	22	30
Grade 1	44	38	9	1	8
Grade 2	45	40	11	0	5
Overall	35	36	7	8	14

Source: Data from Siegler 1987a.

reported using (Table 14.1). They also said that they used the count-all strategy (counting from 1); decomposition, that is, dividing a problem into two easier ones, such as 12 + 3 = 10 + (2 + 3); retrieval; and guessing. This report of diverse strategies characterized individual as well as group performance; most children reported using at least three approaches. Not only did children not report using the min strategy on every trial, they only said they had used it on 36% of trials. At no age did they report using it on more than 40% of trials.

Dividing the error and solution time data according to what strategy children said they had used on that trial lent considerable credence to the children's verbal reports. As shown in Table 14.2, on trials where they reported using the min strategy, the min model was an even better predictor of solution times than in past studies or in the present data set as a whole; it accounted for 86% of the variance in solution times. In contrast, on trials where they reported using one of the other strategies, the min model was never a good predictor of performance, either in absolute terms or relative to other predictors. It never accounted for as much as 40% of the variance. A variety of measures converged on the conclusion that children used the five strategies that they reported using, and that they employed them on those trials where they said they had. Thus, it appeared that the min model misrepresented what children were doing on almost two-thirds of trials. (Statistical reasons for the min models' excellent fit to the data, despite not being used on most trials, are provided in Siegler 1987a).

There is no reason to think that variability of strategy use within a single person is limited to children or to arithmetic. Rather, it is becoming apparent that in domains as varied as referential communication, series completion, causal reasoning, and decision making, individuals often use multiple strategies to solve a single class of problems (Kahan and Richards 1986; LeFevre and Bisanz 1986;

Table 14.2 Best predictor of median solution time on each problem

Strategy	Best predictor	R^2
All trials	Smaller addend	76
Retrieval	Sum	30
Min	Smaller addend	86
Decomposition	Sum squared	42
Count-all	Sum	35
Guessing	No significant predictors	

Source: Data from Siegler 1987a.

Payne, Bettman and Johnson 1988; Shultz, Fisher, Pratt and Rulf 1986). The next issue is their reason for doing so.

THE ADAPTIVE VALUE OF USING DIVERSE STRATEGIES

Considering the patterns of speed and accuracy produced by different strategies suggests that children derive substantial advantages from using multiple approaches. This can be seen especially clearly in the choice of whether to state a retrieved answer or to use a backup strategy. A *backup strategy* is defined as any strategy other than retrieval; thus, probability of backup strategy use is always 1 minus probability of retrieval. Examples of backup strategies include counting fingers to add, sounding out words to read, looking up a word's spelling in a dictionary, counting by 5s from the hour to tell the time, and rehearsing a telephone number.

Both retrieval and use of backup strategies have clear, though different, advantages. Retrieval can be executed much faster. Backup strategies can yield accurate performance on problems where retrieval cannot. Ideally, children would use retrieval on problems where that fast approach could be executed accurately, and would use backup strategies where they were necessary for accurate performance.

In fact, children's strategy choices have followed exactly this pattern in all of the domains we have studied. On easy problems, children rely primarily on retrieval; on difficult problems, they rely primarily on backup strategies. This pattern can be seen in Figure 14.1. The more difficult the problem, defined here in terms of percentage of errors, the more often children use backup strategies.

Comparing children's behavior under conditions where they are allowed to use backup strategies to conditions where they are not allowed to do so reveals just how adaptive the children's strategy choices are. Children perform more accurately on all problems when allowed to use backup strategies. However, children use backup strategies most often where they do them the most good. That is, on problems where children's percent correct is much higher on backup strategy trials than on retrieval trials, they use backup strategies very often. On problems where children are only slightly more accurate when they use backup strategies, they use them much less often (Siegler 1987b).

This pattern of strategy use allows children to strike an effective balance between concerns of speed and accuracy. They use the fastest strategy, retrieval, most often on problems where they can do so accurately, and use slower backup strategies when such strategies are necessary for accurate performance. The question is how children are able to make such adaptive strategy choices.

MODELS OF STRATEGY CHOICE BASED ON RATIONAL CALCULATIONS

Underlying most research on how children choose strategies is the plausible belief that they consider task demands and available strategies and then rationally choose which strategy to use. Illustratively, when confronted with a problem, a child might reason, 'This is a difficult problem, too difficult to solve without a powerful strategy such as X, I'd better use X.'

Doubtless, children sometimes go through such rational decision processes. However, as a general explanation of strategy choice, this approach has run into serious problems. On an empirical level, research has often revealed only modest correlations between children's knowledge about cognition, on which their rational calculations would be based, and performance measures. Theoretically, there is considerable lack of clarity about how and when metacognitive knowledge would exercise its effects on strategy choices (Brown, Bransford, Ferrara and Campione 1983; Wellman 1983).

Children's strategy choices may be less subject to conscious, rational control than often thought. An experiment I recently conducted illustrates this point. Second graders were presented subtraction problems under one of three conditions. In one condition, children were told that all that was important was that they answer correctly, regardless of how long it took. In another condition, they were told that all that was important was that they answer as fast as possible, even if they were sometimes wrong. In the third condition, they were told that both speed and accuracy were important. In the accuracy

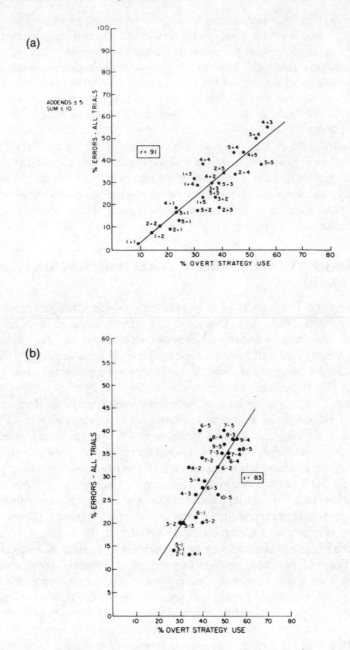

Figure 14.1 Correlations between percentage of errors and percentage use of overt (backup) strategies in addition and subtraction (parts a and b), and multiplication and reading (parts c and d)

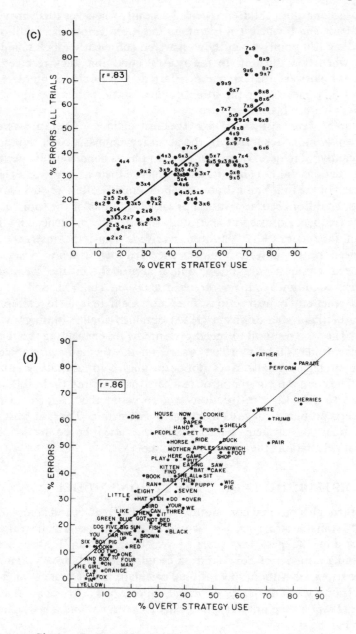

Source: Siegler, R. S. (1986) 'Unities across domains in children's strategy choices', in M. Perlmutter (ed.) *Minnesota Symposium on Child Development*, vol. 19. Copyright 1986 by Erlbaum Associates. Reprinted by permission.

emphasis condition, children received 6 points whenever their answer was correct and 0 when it was not. In the speed emphasis condition, they received 6 points when they answered sufficiently quickly and 0 points when they did not. In the neutral condition, they received 6 points for answers that were both fast and accurate, 3 points for answers that had one or the other quality, and 0 points for answers that were neither fast nor accurate.

Children were influenced by the instructions. They answered significantly more accurately in the accuracy emphasis condition and significantly more quickly in the speed emphasis condition. However, the instructions did not significantly influence their strategy use. They used each of the four main strategies about equally often, regardless of whether speed or accuracy was emphasized. In none of the four cases was the frequency of use of the strategy significantly influenced by the type of instructions that children received. Thus, the instructions influenced the way in which children executed each strategy – faster in the speed emphasis condition, more accurately in the accuracy emphasis condition – but not which strategy the children used.

This reaction to instructions does not seem unique to children. Payne, Bettman, and Johnson (1988) obtained similar findings with adults. They too respond to speed pressure by first executing the same strategies faster. Only as a last resort did the Payne *et al.* subjects change strategies. It also does not seem unique to laboratory situations. The common complaint of teachers that children find all kinds of ways to defy their instructions not to count their fingers to do arithmetic problems suggests a similar phenomenon. Thus, at least in some situations, strategy choices may less often be controlled by rational calculations then we often assume.

THE DISTRIBUTIONS OF ASSOCIATIONS MODEL

If not through a rational consideration of task demands and characteristics of available strategies, how would children choose which strategy to use? For the past few years, my colleagues and I have been developing a model of how children could choose adaptively among diverse strategies without any rational calculation. The model, labeled the *distributions of associations model*, is described in greater detail in Siegler (1986). In the present space, only an overview and a few salient details can be provided.

The two main parts of the model are a representation of knowledge about particular problems and a process that operates on this representation to produce answers. The answers, in turn, reshape the knowledge in the representation; the model learns by doing. Thus, factors that influence which answers are generated on a particular trial also determine the later contents of the knowledge representation. Backup strategies, knowledge of related tasks, and frequency of encountering problems, all contribute to development through their influence on current behavior.

First consider the representation. As shown in Figure 14.2, children are hypothesized to associate responses, both correct and incorrect, with specific problems. For example, 3 + 5 would be associated not only with 8 but also with 6, 7, and 9. The representations of particular problems can be classified along a dimension of the *peakedness* of their distribution of associations with various answers. In a peaked distribution, such as that on the left in Figure 14.2, most of the associative strength is concentrated in a single answer, ordinarily the correct answer. At the other extreme, in a flat distribution, such as that on the right of Figure 14.2, associative strength is dispersed among several answers, with none of them forming a strong peak.

The process that operates on this representation involves three sequential phases, any one of which can produce an answer and thus terminate the process: retrieval, elaboration of the representation, and application of an algorithm. When trying to add numbers, a girl might first try to retrieve an answer; if not sufficiently confident of any answer, she might put up fingers representing the two addends and see if she recognized how many fingers there were; if she still did not know the answer, she might count the fingers and advance the number corresponding to the last count as the answer. All distributions of associations models include these three phases. The way in which retrieval occurs is also constant across the models, though the other two phases are specific to each task.

The way in which the retrieval process works is central within the model. Probability of retrieving any given answer to a problem is proportional to that answer's associative strength relative to the total associative strengths of all answers to the problem. For example, if a given answer had an associative strength of 0.4, and the total associative strength of all answers was 0.8, then that answer would be retrieved on 50% of retrieval efforts. Once retrieved, an answer is stated if its associative strength exceeds a response threshold known as the *confidence criterion*. In Figure 14.2, the confidence criterion is depicted as 0.15. Thus, if a girl had a distribution of associations and a confidence criterion like that shown for 3 + 5 in Figure 14.2, she would state the answer if she retrieved 6, 7, or 8, but not if she retrieved any other answer.

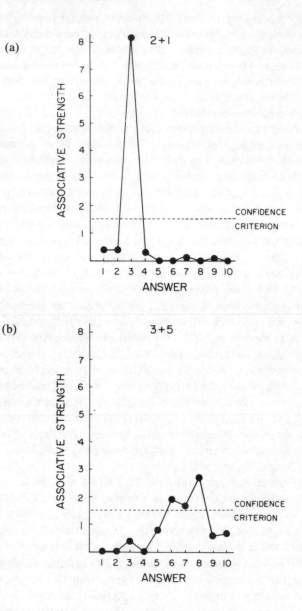

Figure 14.2   A peaked (a) and a flat (b) distribution of associations

Source: Siegler, R. S. (1986) 'Unities across domains in children's strategy choices', in M. Perlmutter (ed.) *Minnesota Symposium on Child Development*, vol. 19. Copyright 1986 by Erlbaum Associates. Reprinted by permission.

If the answer's associative strength does not exceed the confidence criterion, the child can again retrieve an answer from the distribution of associations, and state it if its associative strength exceeds the confidence criterion. If the retrieval process fails to yield a statable answer within the allocated time, the child proceeds to use a backup strategy, such as counting fingers in addition or sounding out a word in spelling, to generate an answer.

As discussed in previous articles (Siegler 1986; Siegler and Shrager 1984), this model accounts for a broad range of children's behavior, including which strategies they use, the relative frequency of errors and length of solution times on different problems, and the particular errors that they make. To illustrate the model's workings, consider its account of the adaptive quality of children's strategy choices, that is, its accounts of how children come to use backup strategies most often on the most difficult problems. The reason suggested by the model is that the same factor that determines problem difficulty also determines whether retrieval of a backup strategy is used. This factor is the peakedness of the distribution of associations. To understand this hypothesis, it is useful to compare the model's workings on problems with peaked and flat distributions of associations.

Relative to a peaked distribution, a flat distribution will elicit a higher percentage of use of backup strategies (because flat distributions, by definition, lack a strongly-associated answer that has a high probability of being retrieved and a high probability of exceeding the confidence criterion once it is retrieved; the absence of such a strongly-associated answer will lead to children being unable to state any retrieved answer and instead using a backup strategy). The flat distribution will also elicit a higher percentage of errors (because the difference between the strength of association of correct and incorrect answers will be smaller in the flatter distribution). Finally, the flatter distribution will lead to longer solution times (because the flatter the distribution, the less likely that an answer whose associative strength exceeds the confidence criterion will be retrieved and stated on an early retrieval attempt). Thus, within this model, backup strategies will be used primarily on the most difficult problems because the peakedness of the distribution of associations determines both problem difficulty and strategy choices.

This model focuses on how children make the particular strategy choice of whether to retrieve or use a backup strategy. What of the more general case of choosing among a variety of backup strategies together with retrieval? Chris Shipley and I are currently working on a computer simulation that solves this problem in the same way as the current simulation solves the problem of which, if any, retrieved answer to state.

The new simulation is based on the assumption that just as children associate a number of answers with each problem, they also may associate a number of strategies with each problem. Further, strategy choices on a given problem may also be influenced by associations of the strategy with related problems and with the class of problems as a whole. For example, in addition of small numbers, the min strategy might be associated to varying degrees with the problem 9 + 2, with related problems such as 10 + 2 and 2 + 9, and with addition problems in general. The strength with which a given strategy is associated with a given problem is assumed to be a function of the speed and accuracy with which that strategy has been executed in the past on the particular problem, on related problems, and in the domain in general.

An additional feature of the new simulation is that newly generated strategies have *novelty points* that temporarily add to their associative strength and thus allow them to be tried even when they have little or no track record. The associative strength conferred by these novelty points would be gradually lost as experience with the strategy provided an increasingly informative data base about it. This feature was motivated by the view that people are often interested in exercising newly developed cognitive capabilites (Piaget 1970), and by the realization that without a track record, a newly-developed strategy would otherwise be unlikely to be chosen, especially if previously developed strategies had been reasonably successful.

How might this novelty-points mechanism function? This part of the simulation is not yet entirely implemented, but the plan is reasonably well worked out. The initial number of novelty points is set as a percentage of the total associative strength of all strategies and answers associated with the problem; for example, as 20% of the total associative strength. For purposes of selecting a strategy, these novelty points are equivalent to the strategy having an amount of associative strength equal to the number of novelty points. Thus, if the number of novelty points of a new strategy is 20% of the total associative strength of all strategies and answers, the new strategy would have a 20% probability of being selected. Unlike the usual associative strength, however, the novelty points would decrease with each use of the strategy. If the strategy led to quick and accurate responding on a trial, the associative strength that it would gain through use on that trial would more than offset the amount lost through the decrease in novelty points. If it proved to generate inaccurate and/or slow responding on the trial, the novelty points would be gradually used up without compensating gains in associative strength.

The new simulation's process involves two phases: strategy choice and strategy execution. Within the strategy choice phase, strategies are retrieved with probability that is proportional to their associative strength relative to the associative strength of all of the strategies. If the strategy that is retrieved has associative strength that exceeds the confidence criterion, the child attempts to execute the strategy. If not, the child repeats the strategy choice phase until a sufficiently promising strategy is found (with guessing as a default option). Once a strategy is chosen, the child attempts to execute it. If the strategy can be executed, it will be used to generate an answer. If it cannot be executed (for example, if retrieval is chosen but no answer with associative strength exceeding the confidence criterion can be retrieved), the process returns to the strategy choice phase. The cycle continues until the model chooses a strategy that can be executed, at which point it executes that strategy and states the answer. The goal of this model is to demonstrate that the same principles that have proved effective in describing the choice between retrieval and backup strategies will prove useful in describing the choice among a wider variety of strategies as well.

CHANGES IN THE REPRESENTATION OVER TIME

As described earlier, the peakedness of a problem's distribution of associations is viewed as a key determinant of the probability of use of backup strategies and of problem difficulty. This view raises the question of how some problems come to have more peaked distributions than others, that is, why some problems elicit higher percentages of errors, longer solution times, and higher percentages of backup strategies than others. The basic assumption of the model here is that people associate whatever answer they state, correct or incorrect, with the problem on which they state it. This assumption reduces the issue of what factors lead children to develop a particular distribution of associations on each problem to what factors lead them to state particular answers on each problem.

Three factors that seem influential in some problems developing peaked distributions and others flat ones are (a) difficulty of executing backup strategies on the problem, (b) frequency of encountering the problem, and (c) knowledge of related problems. Consider how each of these would affect beginning multiplication. The influence of the first two factors can be seen in the particular errors made by children just learning to multiply. The primary backup strategy in multiplication is repeated addition, in which children add one multiplicand to itself the number of times indicated by the other multiplicand (i.e. on 4 × 8, they would add four 8s or eight 4s). Use of repeated addition generates two primary types of errors: errors in which a multiplicand is added too many or too few times (e.g. 8 × 4 = 36), and errors in which a small addition error is made (8 × 4 = 33). These are also the two most common errors in children's multiplication, even when children are not allowed to use any backup strategy (Siegler 1988a). Under speeded conditions, such errors frequently appear in adults' multiplication as well (Campbell 1987; Campbell and Graham 1985).

The influence of related operations is particularly apparent in intrusions of addition facts into multiplication. Surprisingly frequently, children confuse the two operations; for example, by saying that 5 × 3 = 8 (Siegler 1988a). Again, adults show a similar pattern under speeded conditions (Miller, Perlmutter and Keating 1984; Winkelman and Schmidt 1974).

The third influence on the development of the distribution of associations is frequency of problem presentation. Examination of textbooks and of parental behavior indicates that parents and textbooks present some problems more frequently than others. This pattern does not produce any particular type of error, but does result in the frequently-presented problems being easier than would otherwise be predicted (Hamann and Ashcraft 1986; Siegler 1988a).

The effects of these variables have been examined empirically in addition, subtraction, and multiplication. In these areas, regression analyses have shown that each of the three factors hypothesized to contribute to these transitions does so. In addition, all three hypothesized factors accounted for significant independent variance in frequency of errors to that which could be accounted for by the other two factors; in subtraction and multiplication, two of the three did so. The three factors together account for at least 80% of the variance in frequency of errors on each of the three operations (Siegler 1987b; 1988a; Siegler and Shrager 1984).

My colleagues and I have built computer simulations of the learning of addition, subtraction, and multiplication in which these three hypothesized influences on development play a central role (Siegler 1987b; 1988a; Siegler and Shrager 1984). The basic operating procedures of the simulations are:

1 The simulation is presented problems in accord with their relative frequency in parental input or textbooks.

2 Before each problem, the simulation generates a confidence criterion, with the criterion varying randomly within the limits set by the simulation.

3 The probability of retrieving an answer is proportional to its associative strength compared to the associative strengths of all answers to the problem. A retrieved answer is stated if its associative strength exceeds the current confidence criterion. Retrieval attempts continue until either the associative strength of a retrieved answer exceeds the confidence criterion or the number of searches matches the number that are allowed.

4 If no answer has been stated and the end of the retrieval phase has been reached, the program generates an elaborated representation. The particular elaboration varies with the operation being modeled; in all cases, though, it may lead directly to a statable answer.

5 If no answer has been stated, the model uses an algorithmic backup strategy, which again is specific to the operation being modeled. This algorithmic strategy will always yield a statable answer.

6 Every time the system advances an answer, the association between that answer and the problem increases. The increment is twice as great for correct answers, that presumably are reinforced, as for incorrect answers, that presumably are not.

The simulations not only produce performance, their performance improves with experience. In terms of immediate performance, the simulations' output closely resembles that of children in a number of ways. The strategies produced by the simulations, the relative solution times of the strategies, and the particular errors all are similar to those of children. Most striking are the high correlations in all three simulations between the children's and the simulations' percentage of errors, length of solution times, and percentage use of backup strategies on each problem. As shown in Table 14.3, all of these correlations have been at least $r = 0.80$.

The changes over trials in the simulations' performance also parallel the changes in children's performance with age and experience. For example, within the multiplication simulation, retrieval increased from 24% on the first 200 trials of the simulation's run to 77% on the last 200. As the distributions of associations became more peaked, use of backup strategies fell off and use of retrieval increased. Trends toward decreasing percentages of errors and shorter solution times were equally pronounced. For example, in the multiplication simulation, errors decreased from 39% on the first 200 trials to 11% on the last 200. Overall, then, both the model's performance at any one time

Table 14.3 Correlations between children's and computer simulation's performance

	Arithmetic operation		
Variables correlated	*Addition*	*Subtraction*	*Multiplication*
Percentage of errors produced by model and by children	0.88	0.80	0.90
Percentage of overt strategy use produced by model and children	0.92	0.84	0.90
Mean solution times produced by model and by children	0.87	0.81	0.95

and the path of changes over time closely resemble those of children.

This model of performance and change reflects both domain-general and domain-specific aspects. The basic organization of the model is hypothesized to be general across all tasks in which children have substantial experience with particular items. The workings of the retrieval process, and the way in which strategy choices are made, are also hypothesized to be general across this range of tasks. These general features have allowed the model to be applied not only to arithmetic but to other tasks as varied as reading (word identification), spelling, and time-telling (Siegler 1986; Siegler and McGilly 1989). The three factors hypothesized to influence development of the distribution of associations – difficulty of executing backup strategies, frequency of encountering problems, and knowledge of related operations – are also hypothesized to be general across this range of tasks. As noted earlier, they have been shown to be influential in addition, subtraction, and multiplication. These common aspects of the strategy choice procedure and of the influences on development result in some aspects of performance being constant across tasks; for example, the strong correlations among percent errors, length of solution times, and percent backup strategies on each problem.

The model also contains domain-specific aspects. The particular backup strategies that are used obviously are specific to each task; counting fingers is not helpful in spelling, and dictionaries are not helpful in arithmetic. Particular associations between problems and answers also are obviously specific to each task, and tendencies to form peaked or flat distributions probably are as well. A child may form very peaked distributions of associations in spelling, yet form only flat ones in arithmetic. This pattern could occur through more accurate execution of the backup strategies in spelling, through more practice in spelling, or through greater transfer from related operations such as reading. These domain-specific influences can lead to the same basic strategy choice procedure producing radically different strategy choices on different tasks.

ACQUISITION OF NEW STRATEGIES

The computer simulations generate a fair range of transitions in children's arithmetic, but by no means all of them. Perhaps the most conspicuous gap is in the account of how new strategies are acquired. Thus, Eric Jenkins, a graduate student at Carnegie-Mellon, and I recently conducted a longitudinal study of acquisition of the min strategy. Past studies indicate that children ordinarily acquire this strategy at age 5 or 6, and that 4-year-olds can learn it if given extensive addition experience (Groen and Resnick 1977).

Jenkins and I first pretested a group of 4- and 5-year-olds to identify children who gave no evidence of prior knowledge of the min strategy. Once such children were identified, we presented each child with problems on many days over a 2-month period. After each problem, we asked the child how he or she had solved the problem. The self-report, together with the videocassette of the child's overt behavior while solving the problem, was used to identify the child's strategy on each trial. This method gave us a way of identifying the exact trial on which the child discovered the min strategy, and thus to analyze what led to the discovery. It also allowed us to examine how the strategy, once discovered, was extended to new problems.

The data are still being analyzed, but several findings appear clear. Seven of the eight children receiving the addition experience discovered the min strategy. In none of these seven cases did the min strategy become the child's sole strategy; this finding is consistent with the Siegler (1987a) cross-sectional findings that most kindergartners, first graders, and second graders used multiple strategies. Also consistent with the cross-sectional findings, children continued frequently to use the count-all strategy after discovering the min strategy, even though the count-all strategy requires more counting on all problems than the min strategy.

The trial-by-trial method of observation in this longitudinal study enabled us to obtain a qualitative sense of the children's discovery process. The following protocol of the trial on which one child discovered the min strategy exhibits the kind of insight that accompanied some children's discovery process.

E: OK, how much is 2 + 5?

S: 2 + 5? Six, seven . . . it's seven.

E: How did you know that?

S: Never counted.

E: You didn't count?

S: Just said it . . . I just said after six something . . . seven . . . six, seven.

E: You did? Why did you say six, seven?

S: Cause I wanted to see what it really was?

E: OK . . . you didn't count one, two, three, you just said 'six, seven'?

S: Yeah . . . smart answer.

Other children seemed to start using the min strategy without any single insightful experience. They counted on from the larger number, but could not verbalize what they had done; often they denied counting altogether, even when their overt behavior made it plain that they had counted.

Children's ability to describe the new strategy verbally seemed to influence their subsequent extension of it to new problems. The four children who described clearly what they had done used the min strategy much more on later problems that did the three children who did not describe what they had done. This finding suggests that conscious realization of having used a new strategy may be related to later generalization of the strategy to new problems.

The trial-by-trial method of observation in this study also allowed us to detect short-lived transitional strategies that may have mediated discovery of the min strategy. One such transitional strategy involved an abbreviated version of the sum strategy (also called the 'counting all strategy'), that we labeled the *shortcut sum* strategy. The usual sum strategy involves two rounds of counting, one to represent the addends and one to combine them. Thus, on 5 + 2, a child would count out '1, 2, 3, 4, 5' fingers, then would count out '1, 2' fingers, and finally would count '1, 2, 3, 4, 5, 6, 7'. In contrast, in the shortcut sum strategy, the child would just continue counting; on 5 + 2, the child would count out '1, 2, 3, 4, 5,' fingers and then would continue by saying '6, 7' while putting up the last two fingers. This procedure is like the usual sum strategy in that the count starts with 1, but is like the min strategy in that counting of the second set continues from the end of the first set, without any recounting of the first set.

The shortcut sum strategy was quite widely used; 7 of the 8 children used it. For 5 of these 7, discovery of the min strategy occurred within two sessions of discovery of the shortcut sum strategy. The frequency of children generating the shortcut sum approach shortly before generating the min strategy, together with the fact that shortcut sum incorporates features of both the min and the standard sum strategy, suggests that it may be a key contributor to the discovery of the min strategy. Note, though, that the data also indicate that different children follow different paths to discovery of the min strategy. For example, one child used the shortcut sum strategy 140 times before discovering the min approach, and another child discovered the min strategy without ever having used the shortcut sum approach. Models of the strategy discovery process will need to account for both the regularities and the variability of paths leading to discoveries.

This example, like previous ones, points to the interplay of domain-specific and domain-general knowledge. The domain-specific aspect is evident in the particular transitional strategy that is discovered. It is a more efficient version of the sum strategy that children already knew. Yet the general tendency to construct more efficient strategies, even when existing strategies yield consistently correct answers, has been noted in a number of domains. Markman (1978) noted such a tendency in the context of class inclusion, Siegler (1981) in the context of number conservation, and Klahr and Wallace (1976) proposed that it was a general feature of cognitive development. Thus, the search for new, more efficient strategies may be general across domains, but the particular contents of the new strategies may depend heavily on what is already known in the particular domain.

INDIVIDUAL DIFFERENCES IN STRATEGY CHOICES

Studying individual differences across tasks provides one of the most direct ways of addressing the relation between domain-general and domain-specific knowledge. Performance that is characteristic of an individual over many tasks, but that differentiates that individual's performance from that of other people, argues for domain-general influences. Performance that varies widely on different tasks argues for domain-specific influences.

To examine individual differences and consistencies in strategy choices, Siegler (1988b) had first graders perform each of three tasks where the present model of strategy choice had been found previously to apply: addition, subtraction, and reading (word identification). The addition and subtraction items were basic fact problems involving numbers no greater than 18; the reading words were presented individually on a card, and were drawn from the words in the children's reading textbook. The types of arithmetic backup strategies that young children use were described earlier; the main backup strategy in reading was letter-by-letter sounding out.

Correlations of individual performance on each of the three possible pairs of tasks were computed for measures of mean solution times, percent errors, and percent use of backup strategies. The results of these analyses can be summarized quite simply. Children's performance on the two arithmetic tasks was significantly related on all dependent measures. Their performance on the word identification task was significantly related on some measures to performance on the two arithmetic tasks, but the relation was less consistent and less strong.

However, the most revealing analysis of the data was a cluster analysis, conducted to indicate whether children's performance fell into characteristic patterns. The input to the cluster analysis was the percentage use of retrieval, the percentage correct on retrieval trials, and the percentage correct on backup strategy trials on each of the three tasks. Thus, the input for each child involved 9 data points.

On the basis of this input, the clustering program (PKM) divided children into three groups, with 12, 9, and 15 children, respectively. The differences among the three groups' performance were readily interpretable. The three groups were labeled the *good students*, the *not-so-good students*, and the *perfectionists*.

The contrast between the good and not-so-good students was evident along all the dimensions that might be expected from the names. As shown in Figure 14.3, the good students were correct more often on both retrieval and non-retrieval trials on all three tasks. They also used retrieval more often on both addition and subtraction. The good students were also faster in executing the overt strategies on all three tasks, and were faster in retrieving answers on addition and subtraction problems.

The relation of the performance of the perfectionists to that of children in the other two groups was more complex. Despite their being by all measures at least the equals of the good students, they used retrieval even less than did the not-so-good students. As shown in Figure 14.3, the perfectionists used retrieval much less often than either the good or the not-so-good students on the addition and subtraction tasks; the three groups were indistinguishable in their percentage of retrieval in reading. When the perfectionists did use retrieval, however, they were the most accurate of the three groups on all three tasks, and were also the fastest on all three.

To provide convergent validation for the groupings that emerged from the cluster analysis, the three groups yielded by it were also

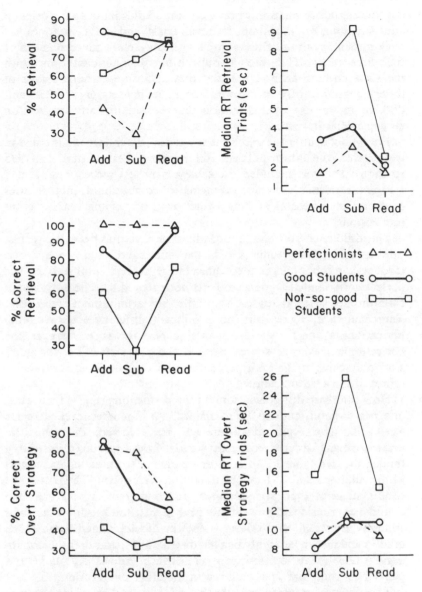

Figure 14.3 Performance of perfectionists, good students, and not-so-good students in addition, subtraction, and reading (word identification)

Source: Siegler, R. S. and Campbell, J. I. D. (1990) 'Diagnosing individual differences in strategy choice procedures', in N. Fredriksen (ed.) *Diagnostic Monitoring of Skill and Knowledge Acqusition*. Copyright by Erlbaum Associates. Reprinted by permission.

contrasted on two measures that were not used as input to the original analysis: solution times on retrieval trials and solution times on backup strategy trials. These two measures were examined on each of the three tasks. The three groups differed significantly on both measures on both arithmetic tasks; they also were extremely close to differing significantly on retrieval times in reading ($p = 0.06$), and differed in the expected direction, but nonsignificantly, in backup strategy times in reading.

Four months after the experiment was run, all children in the school were given the Metropolitan Achievement Test (Form L, 1985 revision). This test included six achievement test scores that seemed relevant: total mathematics, mathematics computation, mathematics problem solving, total reading, word recognition, and reading comprehension.

The differences on the standardized test scores between perfectionists and good students, on the one hand, and not-so-good students, on the other, echoed those in the experimental setting. The perfectionists and the good students both scored significantly higher than the not-so-good students on all of the achievement scores that were examined; there were no significant differences between the perfectionists' and the good-students' scores. Across the six tests, the perfectionists' average scores were at the 81st percentile, the good students' scores at the 80th percentile, and the not-so-good students' scores at the 43rd percentile.

How can these differences among the perfectionists, good students, and not-so-good students be explained? At a general level, it seems likely that two types of differences are involved: differences in knowledge and differences in motivation. In the specific terms of the model, the two types of differences involve differences in peakedness of distributions and differences in confidence criteria. The pattern of results suggests that perfectionists are children who set very high confidence criteria and have highly peaked distributions; that the good students are children who set somewhat less stringent confidence criteria and also have highly peaked distributions; and that the not-so-good students set less stringent confidence criteria and have less peaked distributions than children in the other two groups.

That the perfectionists were both the fastest and the most accurate of the three groups on retrieval trials (Figure 14.3) indicates that they had the most peaked distributions. That in spite of these peaked distributions, they used retrieval the least often of children in any group, attests to their setting very stringent confidence criteria for stating a retrieved answer. Conversely, the fact that the not-so-good students produced the least accurate and slowest performance on retrieval trials suggests that they had the least peaked distributions of associations. Their relatively high percentage of retrieval, in spite of these relatively flat distributions, suggests that they set quite loose confidence criteria. The good students seemed to possess quite peaked confidence criteria, but to set only moderately stringent confidence criteria. (For more details of this analysis, see Siegler 1988b.)

A possible mechanism by which differences in peakedness could arise was also apparent – the accuracy of execution of backup strategies. Recall that within the strategy choice model, the more accurately that backup strategies are executed, the more peaked distributions of associations become. Supporting this assumption, on all three tasks in the present experiment, a child's accuracy in executing backup strategies was significantly correlated with the child's accuracy in using retrieval. For addition, the correlation was $r = 0.43$; for subtraction, it was $r = 0.55$; for reading, it was $r = 0.57$. The perfectionists were the most accurate of the three groups in executing the backup strategies and the not-so-good students the least accurate (Figure 14.3).

This analysis also has an intriguing instructional implication. In this study of individual differences, accuracy of execution of backup strategies paralleled stringency of confidence criteria. Perfectionists were the most accurate in executing backup strategies and set the highest criteria; not-so-good students were the least accurate in executing backup strategies and set the lowest criteria; good students were in the middle on both measures. The parallels may not be coincidental. If a child cannot execute backup strategies accurately, there is little reason to set high confidence criteria. The child may as well set low criteria, and at least be able to answer quickly. This analysis implies that teaching not-so-good students to execute backup strategies more accurately might lead to their setting higher confidence criteria, because there would be more payoff for taking the extra time needed to execute the backup strategies. More accurate execution of the backup strategies also would have the advantage of contributing to the building of more peaked distributions of associations, which ultimately would allow retrieval to be executed more accurately as well.

In conclusion, this research illustrates how domain-specific and domain-general properties can work together to produce both performance and cognitive change. It appears that across a variety of domains, strategy choices are produced by a domain-general process operating on domain-specific associative knowledge. The effectiveness

260   *Context and cognition*

of executing backup strategies influences performance in all of these domains, but the particular backup strategies that are executed, and the efficiency with which they are executed, are specific to each individual domain. Consistent individual differences in strategy choices are present across addition, subtraction, and reading, but the similarities between performance on the two arithmetic tasks are closer than those between performance on the reading task and either arithmetic task. Clearly, both domain-general and domain-specific knowledge influence children's thinking; only by specifying how they work together can it fully be understood how they contribute to cognitive development.

REFERENCES

Ashcraft, M. H. (1982) 'The development of mental arithmetic: A chronometric approach', *Developmental Review* 2: 213–36.

Ashcraft, M. H. (1987) 'Children's knowledge of simple arithmetic: A developmental model and simulation', in C. J. Brainerd, R. Kail, and J. Bisanz (eds) *Formal Methods in Developmental Psychology*, pp. 302–38, New York: Springer-Verlag.

Brown, A. L., Bransford, J. D., Ferrara, R. A., and Campione, J. C. (1983) 'Learning, remembering, and understanding', in J. H. Flavell and E. M. Markman (eds) *Handbook of Child Psychology: vol. 3. Cognitive Development*, 4th edn, pp. 77–166, New York: Wiley.

Brown, R., Cazden, C., and Bellugi, U. (1969) 'The child's grammar from I to III', in J. P. Hill (ed.) *Minnesota Symposium on Child Psychology* pp. 28–74, Minneapolis: University of Minnesota Press.

Campbell, J. I. D. (1987) 'Production, verification, and priming of multiplication facts', *Memory & Cognition* 15: 349–64.

Campbell, J. I. D. and Graham, D. J. (1985) 'Mental multiplication skill: Structure, process, and acquisition', *Canadian Journal of Psychology* 39: 338–66.

Case, R. (1985) *Intellectual Development: Birth to Adulthood*, Orlando, FL: Academic Press.

Chi, M. T. H. (1978) 'Knowedge structures and memory development', in R. S. Siegler (ed.) *Children's Thinking: What Develops?*, pp. 73–96, Hillsdale, NJ: Erlbaum.

Flavell, J. H., Beach, D. R., and Chinsky, I. M. (1966) 'Spontaneous verbal rehearsal in a memory task as a function of age', *Child Development* 37: 283–99.

Groen, G. J. and Parkman, J. M. (1972) 'A chronometric analysis of simple addition', *Psychological Review* 79: 329–43.

Groen, G. J. and Resnick, I. B. (1977) 'Can preschool children invent addition algorithms?', *Journal of Educational Psychology* 69: 645–52.

Hamann, M. S. and Ashcraft, M. H. (1986) 'Textbook presentations of the basic addition facts', *Cognition and Instruction* 3: 173–92.

Ilg, E. and Ames, L. B. (1951) 'Developmental trends in arithmetic', *Journal of Genetic Psychology* 79: 3–28.

Kahan, I. D. and Richards, D. D. (1986) 'The effects of context on children's referential communication strategies', *Child Development* 57: 1,130–41.

Kaye, D. B., Post, T. A., Hall, V. C., and Dineen, I. T. (1986) 'The emergence of information retrieval strategies in numerical cognition: A developmental study', *Cognition and Instruction* 3: 137–66.

Klahr, D. and Wallace, J. G. (1976) *Cognitive Development: An Information Processing View*, Hillsdale, NJ: Erlbaum.

LeFevre, J. and Bisanz, J. (1986) 'A cognitive analysis of number-series problems: Sources of individual differences in performance', *Memory & Cognition* 14: 287–98.

Maratsos, M. P. (1983) 'Some current issues in the study of the acquisition of grammar', in J. H. Flavell and E. M. Markman (eds) *Handbook of Child Psychology: vol. 3. Cognitive Development*, 4th edn, pp. 707–86, New York: Wiley.

Markman, E. M. (1978) 'Empirical versus logical solutions to part-whole comparison problems concerning classes and collections', *Child Development* 49: 168–77.

Miller, K., Perlmutter, M., and Keating, D. (1984) 'Cognitive arithmetic: Comparison of operations', *Journal of Experimental Psychology: Learning, Memory, and Cognition* 10: 46–60.

Ornstein, P. A., Naus, M. J., and Liberty, C. (1975) 'Rehearsal and organizational processes in children's memory', *Child Development* 26: 818–30.

Payne, J. W., Bettman, J. R., and Johnson, E. J. (1988) 'Adaptive strategy selection in decision making', *Journal of Experimental Psychology: Learning, Memory, and Cognition* 14: 534–52.

Piaget, J. (1952) *The Child's Concept of Number*, New York: W.W. Norton.

Piaget, J. (1970) *Psychology and Epistemology*, New York: Viking Press.

Shultz, T. R., Fisher, G. W., Pratt, C. C., and Rulf, S. (1986), 'Selection of causal rules', *Child Development* 57: 143–52.

Siegler, R. S. (1981) 'Developmental sequences within and between concepts', *Monographs of the Society for Research in Child Development* 46(2), serial no. 189.

Siegler, R. S. (1986) 'Unities across domains in children's strategy choices', in M. Perlmutter (ed.) *Minnesota Symposium on Child Development*, pp. 1–48, Hillsdale, NJ: Erlbaum.

Siegler, R. S. (1987a) 'The perils of averaging data over strategies: an example from children's addition', *Journal of Experimental Psychology: General* 116: 250–64.

Siegler, R. S. (1987b) 'Strategy choices in subtraction', in J. A. Sloboda and D. Rogers (eds) *Cognitive Processes in Mathematics*, pp. 81–106, Oxford: Clarendon Press.

Siegler, R. S. (1988a) 'Strategy choice procedures and the development of multiplication skill', *Journal of Experimental Psychology: General* 117: 258–75.

Siegler, R. S. (1988b) 'Individual differences in strategy choices: Good students, not-so-good students, and perfectionists', *Child Development* 59: 833–51.

Siegler, R. S. and McGilly, K. (1989) 'Strategy choices in time telling', in I. Levin and D. Zakay (eds) *Psychological Time: A Life Span Perspective*, North Holland: Elsevier.

Siegler, R. S. and Shrager, J. (1984) 'A model of strategy choice', in C. Sophian (ed.) *Origins of Cognitive Skills*, pp. 229–93, Hillsdale, NJ: Erlbaum.

Svenson, O. (1975) 'Analysis of time required by children for simple additions', *Acta Psychologica* 39: 289–302.

Svenson, O. and Broquist, S. (1975) 'Strategies for solving simple addition problems: A comparison of normal and subnormal children', *Scandinavian Journal of Psychology* 16: 143–51.

Wellman, H. M. (1983) 'Metamemory revisited', in M. T. H. Chi (ed.) *Trends in Memory Development Research*, pp. 31–51, New York: Karger.

Winkelman, J. and Schmidt, J. (1974) 'Associative confusions in mental arithmetic', *Journal of Experimental Psychology* 102: 734–6.

15 A study of consistency in the use of students' conceptual frameworks across different task contexts

E. E. Clough and R. Driver

Source: *Science Education* (1986) 70(4).

INTRODUCTION AND RATIONALE

Recent studies have indicated that individuals construct informal theories which they use in interpreting a range of natural events. Perhaps the most well-researched topic is that of intuitive mechanics, where a number of studies have shown that most people have ideas about force and motion which may differ substantially from accepted physics theory.

For example, individuals commonly attribute a force to any moving object and suggest that an object requires a constant force to maintain it in motion. (Viennot 1979; Sjoberg and Lie 1981; Watts 1983). Studies of students' ideas about gravity, falling objects, and projectiles have also indicated that the same naive theories tend to be used by different individuals (Caramazza, McCloskey and Green 1981; Gunstone and White 1981) and that these theories persist despite formal instruction in physics even up to college level. Studies of other topics such as the Earth concept (Nussbaum and Novak 1976; Nussbaum 1979, Mali and Howe 1979) and the nature of heat (Albert 1978; Andersson 1980; Erickson 1979; Strauss 1977; Tiberghien 1980; Engel 1982) also indicate a similarity in the kinds of conceptions or beliefs used by people over a wide age range. These conceptions, which have been referred to as alternative frameworks (Driver 1981) in children's science or naive principles (Caramazza *et al.* 1981), sometimes reflect ideas which have held sway among scientists in the past; indeed, it has been proposed that 'the historical persistence of these beliefs suggests that they are a natural outcome of experience with the world.' (Caramazza *et al.* 1981: 122).

The existence of these beliefs presents problems for science educators. From an educational perspective it has been argued that it may be necessary to take account of the ideas and beliefs that young people bring to their formal study of science, if these ideas are to be successfully modified by instruction. A model for learning as conceptual change has been proposed by Hewson (1982) and a number of studies reporting attempts to promote conceptual change in classroom settings have been undertaken (Champagne *et al.* 1982, 1983; Nussbaum and Novick 1981, 1982; Rowell and Dawson 1981, 1983).

In most cases, studies of this kind have been based on the assumption that the intuitive ideas that students hold prior to teaching are both identifiable and stable and have enough commonality to make it worth planning instructional sequences designed to change them. Other researchers, while acknowledging the importance of students' current conceptions in determining learning activities, are more skeptical about the stability or generality of these intuitive ideas (West and Sutton 1982) and this may lead, therefore, to different educational strategies being advocated.

This study explored the issues of the consistency of use of students' conceptions across a number of different tasks which probed understanding of aspects of pressure, heat, and biological evolution. Children's conceptions about these three content areas have been investigated by other researchers: Erickson (1979), Strauss (1977), and Albert (1978) have reported studies of children's ideas about aspects of heat phenomena; studies on evolution have been reported by Brumby (1979), Deadman and Kelly (1978), and Kargbo *et al.* (1980); and children's ideas about air pressure have been reported by Sere (1982). These studies have tended to focus on documenting the range of conceptions used by a particular age group of students.

The purpose here was not only to document student's ideas or conceptual frameworks, but to investigate the consistency with which the ideas were used by individuals in different contexts. This is an important question for a number of reasons. There is considerable research evidence to suggest that the context or phenomenal setting of a task or problem influences an individual's performance. This demonstration of the dependence of thinking skills on the context of the task has provided a powerful argument for those who question the usefulness of Piagetian stage theory as a model for learning (Brown and Desforges 1977; Driver 1978). Donaldson (1978) has demonstrated that young children's reasoning needs the prop of contexts which make what she calls 'human sense' to the individual. Her experiments show that three- to four-year-olds frequently find the procedures of a task perplexing, but that when the same problem is couched in a familiar and realistic guise, dramatic improvements in performance result. Wason (1977) reports exactly the same influence with intelligent adults undertaking tasks which require, in Piagetian terms, formal operational thought. The learner's interpretation of a task will, of course, depend on preexisting notions which arise from experience-based intuition, as well as more formally acquired concepts. Studies which document children's conceptions have certainly acknowledged the base of experiential knowledge underlying learning, but like earlier Piagetian studies they tend not to address critically the question of task context. Yet this is likely to be an important issue in any assessment of the cognitive status of student frameworks identified in interviews which are structured around tasks or problems. Indeed this status has been challenged in a fundamental way by McClelland (1984) who suggests that many physical phenomena (presumably in whatever context they are presented) have little 'salience' to people, and that they, therefore, find no compelling reason to spontaneously theorize about them. He argues that since many physical phenomena are 'neither particularly pleasant nor unpleasant and so are not particularly emotionally charged' most people can live happily without understanding them. Many frameworks identified from interview transcripts would presumably then be little more than artifacts of the methodology, transient solutions devised in an interview where an answer of some kind is a social imperative. It can be argued, however, that the use of the same intuitive ideas across contexts which are different, but which scientists construe similarly, would offer some support for the validity of student frameworks as commonly available ways of thinking. We based our study on this premise and presented students with tasks which were similar to scientists, that is, they required understanding of the same scientific ideas for their solution. In the discussion section at the end of this paper we question this approach and acknowledge that tasks which may be similar to scientists may not appear that way to students.

The particular issues which the study addressed were the following:

1 Was there any commonality in students' conceptions and, if so, what frameworks were identified?
2 What was the prevalence of these frameworks among students of different ages?
3 To what extent were the same frameworks used in different contexts by the sample as a whole?
4 To what extent were the same frameworks used in different contexts by individual students?

THE TASKS

The three areas selected for investigation were chosen so as to represent both the physical and the biological sciences, as well as being areas of interest from an educational point of view and to be among those in which students would probably have developed intuitive ideas from everyday experiences.

The following ideas were investigated in the study:

1 changes in pressure with depth in a fluid,
2 pressure in different directions in a fluid,
3 movement of fluids from regions of higher to lower pressure,
4 the conduction of heat energy through solids,
5 variations acquired during an organism's lifetime are not inherited,
6 as the environment changes, organisms with favorable variation survive and leave more descendants.

At least two tasks were devised to probe the understanding of each idea. These tasks were constructed to reflect either experiences commonly encountered in school science or in everyday experience and were designed for individual administration in an interview setting. Each task presented the student with a phenomenon; as far as possible actual events were demonstrated, but where this was not possible, as in the case of some of the biological questions, photographs were used. The purpose of the tasks was to elicit each individual's conception of the phenomenon in question. In general the tasks were set in familiar contexts and were presented in such a way as to avoid introducing vocabulary which could suggest taught scientific ideas or principles.

THE STUDENTS IN THE SAMPLE

Once the tasks had been developed, 84 students consisting of 30 12-year-olds, 30 14-year-olds, and 24 16-year-olds, were selected to take part in the study. The students were drawn from three schools in one urban area. In order to obtain a comparable spread of ability in each age group in the study a stratified random sample was drawn based on the results of a short relational reasoning test (Shipley 1941).

PRESENTATION OF THE TASKS

Each student was interviewed about the tasks in two sessions, each session lasting about 45 minutes. The tasks were administered in the same fixed order to each student. In each task the students were asked to make predictions and give explanations about the phenomenon presented. Each student's conception of the phenomenon was elicited by asking for verbal predictions and explanations of the observed event or situation. The interviewer probed responses to ascertain, as far as possible, the student's meaning for terms and details of the nature of the theoretical relationships postulated. The interview setting provided an opportunity to probe the reasons behind the initial responses offered. It also gave an opportunity to check students' meanings by making reference to the physical system. Since the purpose of the study was to characterize each student's conception of the phenomena presented, the interviewer made every attempt to avoid using terminology which could prompt the use of specific ideas or concepts. Scientific terminology in the presentation of questions was, therefore, avoided and use was made of the terms introduced by students themselves during the interview. All the interviews, which were conducted by the first author, were audiotaped and notes were made on students' actions as they proceeded. Most of the audiotaped interviews were transcribed.

Two years later the two younger age groups were represented with the same tasks in a second round of interviews. These longitudinal data are analyzed, together with commentary on individuals' development of thinking, and presented elsewhere (Engel 1982). The results from the second round of interviews have been amalgamated with those from the first for some of the analyses reported here (see Tables 15.1–15.7), so increasing the size of the 14-year-old group to 59 and that of the 16-year-old group to 53.

ANALYSIS OF THE INTERVIEW DATA

The data obtained in the interviews were analyzed in two stages. In the first stage the responses given to each task were grouped into mutually exclusive categories based on the type of reason of explanation offered. Some categories contained the accepted scientific explanation, others incorporated ideas which were partially correct, and others contained alternative yet distinguishable interpretations. Where only one type of reason was included in a student's response the categorization was unambiguous. In some cases, however, students gave protracted responses which included more than one type of reason. In such cases it would have been possible to categorize each of the reasons given. However, since the study was investigating the stability of individual student's conceptions it was necessary to allocate each student's response to a unique category. Ground rules were established in order to handle such responses consistently. In cases where students changed their mind during an interview and appeared to be convinced by the later reason given, it was this later reason that was coded. Where the response contained a number of reasons which were either confused or where the student did not indicate a clear preference then the response was designated 'uncodeable'.

This approach differs from that used in some other studies in which a similar content analysis of students' ideas had been undertaken (Osborne and Gilbert 1980; Watts 1983) in that it is the student's performance rather than the ideas which are categorized. This is an important distinction since the degree of consistency at the individual level is the issue under investigation here. The process of allocating student responses to the categories was repeated by a second trained rater as an independent check. A level of agreement between the raters of over 90 per cent for the three concept areas was obtained.

The analysis was then taken to a second stage in which category sets for the responses to parallel tasks, that is to tasks relating to the same scientific ideas, were compared. Where a category of response occurred in more than one task then it was called a framework. A framework, therefore, is being taken to be a description of a perspective which, at the very minimum, should have been demonstrated in more than one question context, though not necessarily by the same student. It is thus assumed to be a way of thinking which is not simply question-dependent and which has some generality within a population of students. Additional factors, such as the reporting of the same idea in other research studies, influenced the process of the establishment of frameworks.

This two-stage process of analysis is illustrated in the appendix to this article using two tasks on the movement of fluids. Sample transcripts are presented and their categorization is discussed. The complete set of response categories for the two tasks is then given together with the main frameworks which were identified. This process involved a considerable reduction in the data. Clearly it is not possible to document here in the same level of detail the range of the conceptions used by students to all the other tasks – these are described fully elsewhere (Engel 1982).

We identified frameworks which occurred across question contexts for all groups of questions, indicating the existence of certain general but alternative conceptions about the phenomena investigated. Once the frameworks used in parallel contexts had been identified, then the consistency of responses across contexts at the individual and group level were investigated.

In the next section the data for each group of questions are presented in two ways. First for each group of questions, the prevalence of each of the main frameworks identified is documented by tabulating the percentage of students of each age using each identified framework. These tables give some indication of the consistency with which particular frameworks were used across task contexts by the group as a whole and describe trends across the age groups. However, the tabulations give no indication of the consistency with which frameworks were used in different contexts by individuals. To explore this issue two tasks from each group were selected, a contingency table indicating the responses of individuals in the two contexts was drawn up and the contingency coefficient for responses to each pair of tasks was calculated. (One contingency table is given as an example (Table 15.4); in the interest of economy of space for other pairs of tasks the contingency coefficient only is given.)

INCIDENCE OF FRAMEWORKS IN DIFFERENT QUESTION CONTEXTS AND CONSISTENCY OF INDIVIDUAL RESPONSES

In general the proportion of students using each framework was similar in the different task contexts relating to a given idea. However, consistency of the use of frameworks by individuals was not always as apparent as would be expected. It was more likely to occur for phenomena for which there were a limited number of alternative frameworks and where these were congruent with intuition. As data presented later will indicate, there was evidence for consistency of use of both accepted and alternative frameworks, although the degree of consistency appeared to depend on contextual aspects of the tasks.

In order to document these general findings, the kinds of responses given to each group of questions is presented and commented on. It is hoped that this will give some flavor of the ideas students have used and indicate factors which affected the variability in types of responses.

Idea 1: Pressure in a fluid increases with depth

Two tasks were presented to probe understanding of this idea. In the first, students were required to predict which of two goldfish (at different depths in a tank of water) had more pressure on it, and to

Table 15.1 Student responses to tasks related to pressure/depth relationship in fluids

Framework	% Students					
	12 years n = 30		14 years n = 59		16 years n = 53	
	'fish'	'sub'	'fish'	'sub'	'fish'	'sub'
Pressure in a fluid increases with depth	60	67	64	80	83	87
Pressure in a fluid decreases with depth	17	17	8	12	4	9
Other	10	0	7	0	3	0
No identifiable framework	13	17	20	8	6	9
Contingency coefficient (3 × 3 table) C = 0.52						

Note: In this and all subsequent tables which summarize results of 142 responses it should be noted that 53 16-year-olds include 29 of the 30 original 14-year-olds and 59 14-year-olds include 29 of the 30 original 12-year-olds.

explain their answer. For the second task, students were presented with a drawing of a submarine lying on the seabed; given the information that 12 atmospheres of pressure were exerted on the craft they were asked to predict and explain any pressure change when the submarine moved halfway up to the surface of the sea. Results in Table 15.1 indicate the percentage of students giving each type of response at different ages for the two tasks.

The majority of students used the scientifically accepted framework in their explanations; in this case it clearly coincides with intuition for this idea. The percentages of students using the two frameworks in the three age groups were similar for the two tasks. A degree of consistency was apparent when responses of individual students were examined as indicated by the contingency coefficient; for example, 69 per cent of the 84 students in the sample gave the scientifically correct responses to both tasks. However, there was less evidence for the consistent use of the alternative framework.

Table 15.2 Student responses to tasks related to pressure/direction in a fluid

Framework	% Students					
	12 years n = 30		14 years n = 59		16 years n = 53	
	'fish'	'sub'	'fish'	'sub'	'fish'	'sub'
Pressure acts equally in all directions	13	13	15	19	31	34
Pressure downwards greater than pressure across	53	63	47	47	27	23
Other	3	3	7	2	6	0
No identifiable framework	30	20	31	32	37	43

Contingency coefficient (3 × 3 table) C = 0.53

Idea 2: Pressure at a point in a fluid is the same in all directions

The two task contexts – the goldfish and the submarine – were used to ask questions about pressure in different directions in a fluid. The results are presented in Table 15.2.

Here the scientifically accepted framework, which is counter to intuition, was not popular, whereas many pupils subscribed to the alternative framework that pressure downwards is greater than pressure across (possibly based on their experiences with rigid bodies). Again the percentage of students using each of the frameworks is similar in the two question contexts. At the level of the individual, more than a third of the 84 students interviewed subscribed to the view that pressure in a downwards direction is greater than pressure across in response to both the questions. In other words, the degree of consistency at an individual level was considerable.

Idea 3: Atmospheric pressure

Three tasks were presented in the interview to test students' understanding of the idea that fluids tend to move from regions of higher to lower pressure. Two of these, the straw and the syringe questions, are given in the Appendix (p. 284). The third task concerned a boy washing up and his difficulty in lifting hot, soapy, upturned glasses from a flat surface. The results shown in Table 15.3 indicate the percentage of pupil responses at different ages and the range of these across the three tasks.

Three frameworks were identified in response to these questions; the accepted response in terms of pressure differences, a response in terms of atmospheric pressure on the outside with no mention of pressure on the inside, and an alternative framework in terms of vacuums or suction.

For this idea the range of responses across question contexts was much greater. Percentages of students subscribing to frameworks in response to the 'syringe' and 'washing up' tasks were similar, but the response pattern to the 'straw' task was markedly different. In this latter question students were invited to 'use the idea of atmospheric pressure' to explain the phenomenon. This may account for the larger proportion of students giving a partially correct answer to the straw question and the correspondingly small numbers drawing on the idea of a vacuum sucking. It is possible that students were unable to use the correct scientific explanation, but that the question wording which included reference to atmospheric pressure precluded the use of the intuitive notion of actively sucking vacuums (a popular framework for the other two tasks).

More than half the students using the scientifically correct framework did so in at least two question contexts. Similarly, as Table 15.4 indicates, just over half the students who used the notion that pressure or a vacuum sucks or pulls gave a consistent response to the 'syringe' and 'washing up' tasks. In this case then, there seems to be some consistency of frameworks held by individuals across different tasks. It suggests that the notion of vacuum or suction as an active pulling agent, for example, is not simply question-dependent, but has the status of an informal theory for the individual, a theory which guides responses to a class of tasks. As with the case of the relationship between pressure and depth in fluids, the idea of vacuum is based on sensory experience with the world.

Idea 4: Conduction of heat

Such experience is also seen to play a part in students' responses to the conductivity tasks. Three tasks probed student understanding of this idea. In the first one, four spoons made of different materials were soaked in a cup of hot water and students were asked to explain why the handle of the metal spoon felt hot sooner than the others. In another task students were asked to feel metal and plastic plates and to

Table 15.3 Student responses to tasks related to atmospheric pressure

Framework	12 years n = 30			14 years n = 59			16 years n = 53		
	'straw'	'syr'[a]	'wash up'[b]	'straw'	'syr'	'wash up'	'straw'	'syr'	'wash up'
Atmosphere exerts a pressure observable when there is a pressure difference	17	13	7	7	10	17	23	21	15
Atmosphere exerts pressure on surfaces	27	10	14	32	7	0	23	6	0
Pressure or vacuum actively sucks or pulls	0	50	44	12	51	49	6	45	43
Other	0	0	0	0	0	0	0	0	0
No identifiable framework	57	27	34	49	31	34	49	28	42

% Students

Notes: [a] 'syr' = syringe; [b] 'wash up' = washing up

Table 15.4 Contingency table of responses to two tasks on atmospheric pressure

'Syringe' 'washing up'	Pressure of atmosphere	Vacuum/ suction	Other	Total
Pressure of atmosphere	10	0	4	14
Vacuum/ suction	1	22	18	41
Other	6	16	7	29
Total	17	38	29	84

Contingency coefficient (3 × 3 table) for 'syringe' and 'washing up' C = 0.54

explain why the metal one felt colder. In the third task explanations were sought for the fact that, on a cold day, the metal part of the handlebars of a bicycle feels colder than the plastic grips. Table 15.5 gives the frameworks which emerged from explanations of these tasks.

In this case the question dependence of response may be due to the perceptual dissimilarity of these tasks. The pattern of results for tasks involving a sensation of 'coldness' was different from that involving a 'hot sensation'. In the spoons question, where the perception of 'hotness' is in keeping with a notion of the flow of heat, much higher percentages of the scientifically accepted framework were elicited in all age groups. However, few students drew on the notion of differences in observable properties of materials (such as 'metal is shiny, wood is not') to explain difference in conductivities of the spoons, though this was a popular framework for the other two tasks. At the individual level, as the contingency coefficient indicates, there was evidence of some consistency of response across the 'plates' and 'handlebars' tasks; two-thirds of the students who used alternative frameworks to explain these phenomena used the same one across these two tasks.

It is apparent that tasks which are related to the same scientific phenomenon may not be construed in the same way by students. Whereas there was considerable consistency across the two tasks which involved a sensation of 'coldness', this was not the case where perceptual differences obtruded, as in the case of the 'spoons' task on one hand the 'plates' and 'handlebars' tasks on the other.

Table 15.5 Student responses to tasks related to conductivity of heat

Framework	% Students								
	12 years n = 30			14 years n = 59			16 years n = 53		
	'spns'[a]	'plts'[b]	'hbs'[c]	'spns'	'plts'	'hbs'	'spns'	'plts'	'hbs'
Heat energy travels through different materials at different rates	27	3	0	54	2	2	79	19	19
Metal attracts/conducts coldness	0	3	23	0	15	34	0	4	25
Conductivities depend on some observable property of material	3	37	20	2	20	19	0	8	4
Metals let heat in and out more easily	33	20	10	36	17	10	8	26	19
Other	13	0	0	0	2	0	2	2	0
No identifiable framework	23	37	47	8	44	36	11	42	34

Contingency coefficient (5 × 5 table for 'plates' and 'handlebars') C = 0.69

Notes: [a] 'spns' = spoons; [b] 'plts' = plates; [c] 'hbs' = handlebars

Idea 5: Acquired characteristics are not inherited

Students were asked to predict and comment on the possibility of the inheritance of variations acquired during organisms' lifetimes in three different question contexts: taillessness in mice; athletic ability in humans, and rough skin due to gardening in humans. Table 15.6 indicates the frameworks and percentages of students subscribing to each across these three tasks.

In response to follow-up questions about the influence of time on the process of inheritance many students suggested that acquired characteristics are not inherited immediately, but may be over several generations (see Table 15.7).

The tables indicate a similar prevalence of the frameworks identified across the different tasks, particularly for the well-subscribed framework that noninheritance can be adequately explained by drawing on the idea of the 'unnaturalness' of the process. This probably represents little more than an intuitive hunch that acquired characteristics are not inherited. Similarly, the percentage of students who subscribed to the view that the passage of time would influence phenotypic change was very similar across question contexts. At the level of the individual student, the low contingency coefficient indicates a low overall level of consistency across contexts. However, this general measure masks some unevenness in the data – with a higher level of consistency in the use of frameworks that acquired characteristics would not be inherited than in the use of the alternative framework.

Idea 6: As the environment changes, organisms with favorable variations survive and leave more descendants

Three tasks, illustrated with photographs, were discussed with students in the interview. In the first one, explanations were sought for the distribution of light and dark caterpillars on tree trunks of different color; why were most of the pale ones to be found on pale trees and most of the dark ones on dark trees? In the second task, students were asked to predict what might happen to the dark caterpillars if the dark trees became gradually paler over the years. In the third task, students were asked to explain the origin of the thick fur of the Arctic fox, an important characteristic in its survival at low temperatures. Table 15.8 indicates the frameworks which emerged from responses and the range of incidence of these across the tasks.

The figures in Table 15.8 indicate that few students explained biological adaptive processes and that there was a considerable range

Table 15.6 Student responses to tasks related to acquired characteristics

Framework	% Students								
	12 years n = 30			14 years n = 59			16 years n = 53		
	'mice'[a]	'aths'[b]	'gdnr'[c]	'mice'	'aths'	'gdnr'	'mice'	'aths'	'gdnr'
Acquired characteristics are not inherited because there is no genetic change	10	7	10	17	14	7	43	25	21
Acquired characteristics are not inherited because it is 'unnatural'	63	67	70	58	54	66	36	45	57
Acquired characteristics are inherited	27	13	6	17	12	9	15	9	10
Other	0	0	0	0	0	0	0	0	0
No identifiable framework	0	13	13	8	20	19	6	21	13

Contingency coefficient (4 × 4 table for 'mice' and 'gardener') C = 0.38

Notes: [a] 'mice' = mice; [b] 'aths' = athletes; [c] 'gdnr' = gardener

Table 15.7 Student responses to tasks related to acquired characteristics over time

Framework	% Students					
	12 years		14 years		16 years	
	'mice' n = 24	*'athletes'* n = 26	*'mice'* n = 52	*'athletes'* n = 53	*'mice'* n = 46	*'athletes'* n = 50
Acquired characteristics not inherited immediately but may be over several generations	42	42	38	45	43	32

of response across the different question contexts. The fox question yielded large percentages of responses which drew on the notion of reaction to a generalized need, presumably because the image of a cold, adverse climate engendered this response, whereas there were no similar explanations for the caterpillar tasks. For these latter tasks, on the other hand (but not for the fox task), larger percentages of students suggested that the animals' response would be to move to a more favorable environment.

The contingency coefficient for responses to this idea is high which is partly explained by the large number of students who fell into the 'other' category in response to both tasks. A detailed breakdown of results at the individual level indicates considerable consistency also in the use of the accepted scientific framework, but little consistency in use of identifiable alternative frameworks.

THE CONSISTENCY OF ACCEPTED AND ALTERNATIVE RESPONSES

An overall indication of the consistency of response at the individual level to the parallel tasks is given by the contingency coefficients in Table 15.9.

It is of both theoretical and practical interest to compare the consistency with which accepted and alternative responses were used by students. In order to obtain an indication of the consistency with which accepted responses were given across contexts, the responses were dichotomized (accepted versus other) and 2 × 2 contingency

Table 15.8 Student Responses to Tasks Related to Biological Adaptation

Framework	% Students								
	12 years			14 years			16 years		
	$c1^a$ $n = 30$	$c2^b$ $n = 26$	fox^c $n = 30$	$c1$ $n = 59$	$c2$ $n = 52$	fox $n = 59$	$c1$ $n = 53$	$c2$ $n = 47$	fox $n = 52$
Biological adaptation results from natural selection operating on a population	3	0	3	8	8	7	30	28	21
Animals consciously change in response to a changed environment	3	4	27	19	15	12	13	11	8
Animals adapt in response to a need for change	0	0	37	0	0	46	0	0	38
Adaption is a natural process	7	15	0	12	15	7	15	21	8
Animals seek out a more favourable environment in response to a changed environment	37	62	3	14	40	0	2	21	0
No identifiable framework	50	19	30	47	21	29	40	19	25

Contingency coefficient (5×5 table for 'caterpillar 1' and 'fox') C = 0.72

Notes: [a] c1 = caterpillar 1; [b] c2 = caterpillar 2; [c] fox = fox

Table 15.9 Consistency of response across context

Ideas/tasks	Contingency coefficients
Pressure and depth 'fish' 'sub'	0.52
Pressure and direction 'fish' 'sub'	0.53
Pressure difference 'straw' 'syringe'	0.54
Conduction of heat 'plates' 'handlebars'	0.69
Acquired characteristics 'mice' 'athletes'	0.38
Adaptation 'fox' 'caterpillars'	0.72

tables were set up for two parallel tasks concerned with each idea. The ϕ coefficient (the product–moment correlation coefficient for dichotomous data) was computed for each pair of tasks for each age group. The same procedure was also undertaken for the alternative frameworks used. (In cases where more than one alternative framework was identified the most commonly used one was selected.) The values of ϕ thus computed are given in Table 15.10.

As the results in Table 15.10 indicate, no general pattern emerges from this table. For a number of tasks the alternative framework appears to be used more consistently than the accepted one. This was particularly noticeable where very few, if any students used the accepted ideas, as in the tasks concerned with conduction of heat and acquired characteristics. Overall, however, accepted responses appear to be used more consistently than alternative responses. At least for most of the ideas investigated in this study it seems that students are more likely to use an accepted idea across different question contexts than they are to use an alternative idea.

SUMMARY AND IMPLICATIONS

For the groups of students studied, frameworks occurred in similar proportions for some of the ideas across different question contexts. Where this occurred, a degree of consistency was detectable in the responses of individuals. This was the case for responses to tasks

Table 15.10 Consistency of accepted and alternative responses across contexts

Ideas/tasks	Age (years)	n	φ accepted framework	φ alternative framework
Pressure and depth	12	30	0.58	0.54
'fish' 'sub'	14	30	0.30	0.11
	16	24	0.42	0.55
Pressure and direction	12	30	0.71	0.54
'fish' 'sub'	14	30	0.52	0.11
	16	23	0.25	0.55
Pressure difference	12	30	0.47	0.00
'straw' 'syringe'	14	29	0.55	0.25
	16	24	0.59	0.30
Conduction of heat	12	30	0.00	0.39
'plates' 'handlebars'	14	30	0.00	0.11
	16	24	0.87	0.41
Acquired	12	21	0.15	0.43
characteristics	14	21	0.22	0.22
'mice' 'athletes'	16	21	0.28	0.26
Adaptation	12	30	0.69	0.31
'fox' 'caterpillars'	14	30	1.00	0.26
	16	23	0.81	0.27

related to the pressure/depth and pressure/direction relationships in fluids and to the noninheritance of acquired characteristics.

For other ideas, however, responses varied much more across question contexts both at population and individual levels. It seems likely that the way the questions are framed, and particularly whether terms are used with are suggestive of particular models, will influence responses. This point is illustrated by responses to the 'straw' question, where the inclusion of scientific terminology in the question appeared to generate a different distribution in the pattern of response. Secondly, when tasks probing the same scientific idea are perceived differently by students, and seem not to address the same phenomenon, no consistency of response across contexts is apparent. This difference may be based on actual experience (as in the opposite sensations of 'hot' and 'cold' in the tasks related to conduction of heat) or on differences in the way situations are construed (as in the case of the fox and caterpillars tasks related to adaptation).

The results obtained in this study have caused us at least to question the assumption that if students do not apply the same intuitive principles across contexts which scientists construe similarly, then they do not have any systematic conceptual framework. It may be that we need to ask 'What are the situations which students construe in similar ways?' since they may categorize situations according to different principles than scientists.

Evidence for common patterns of conceptual frameworks was obtained in all the areas investigated which suggests that it would be possible for educators to anticipate some of the common frameworks likely to occur in teaching students of a particular age group. Research could, therefore, raise teacher awareness of the possible perspectives students may bring to their scientific learning and enable more effective classroom communication to take place.

The results suggest that there is a range of ways in which given phenomena may be conceptualized. Although in some cases there are very clearly identified single alternative frameworks, in other cases the situation is more complex. This suggests that a model of learning as a process of conceptual change from a single identifiable naive view to the accepted view may be too simplistic.

The complexity of the situation is further indicated by the fact that, despite some consistency in the use of frameworks at the level of the individual student, the evidence for this is much more equivocal. For some of the ideas students were using different alternative frameworks in response to parallel questions.

There was some evidence that alternative ideas are not as consistently used by individuals as are accepted responses. This could be interpreted as a hopeful finding for science educators – it suggests that once students learn and use a correct scientific explanation in one context they are more likely to employ it in others.

In general, the results also indicate a relatively small change towards a more scientific understanding of phenomena at both population and individual levels in the age range studied. It may be that some of the variation in results across the different scientific ideas can be accounted for by differences in the nature of the ideas themselves. There is some evidence that students' alternative frameworks related to ideas which would be informed by experiential knowledge, such as air pressure and heat conductivity, are more persistent that others. It is possible that the stability of the former is attributable to their derivation from and reinforcement through sensory experience (Strauss 1981). If the correct scientific explanation does not accord with an individual's existing 'working theory' built up from sense experiences, then it seems that it is less likely to be assimilated.

Frameworks related to other ideas, such as inheritance (Engel Clough and Wood-Robinson 1985), may be derived partly from general experience (e.g. the observations of inheritance patterns in humans and pets) and partly from planned learning experience (such as TV programs, books, early sex education). Alternative ideas derived in these ways may be more amenable to change.

The suggestion that curriculum development should take account of the structure of a child's thought is of course an ancient one, but nevertheless it has gone largely unheeded in secondary-school science teaching. However, the question of exactly how a teacher can usefully respond to student ideas is still very much an open one. What this may involve in practice is just beginning to be considered in secondary-school science courses and a number of teaching strategies designed to promote conceptual change have been proposed and evaluated (Driver and Erickson 1983).

This study indicates that children do have alternative frameworks in all areas investigated in this study, and that the prevalence of these is reasonably predictable across similar contexts, but that the frameworks are used less consistently at the individual level. The consistency with which ideas are used also appears to depend on the topic area. This would need to be taken into account in curriculum planning. Science curricula could be developed in such a way as to pay explicit attention to these various ideas, to provide other opportunities for students to make their ideas explicit so they are open to inspection, and to provide counter examples to stimulate conceptual change.

Unfortunately, there is evidence that some alternative conceptions are resistant to instruction even when the teaching has been deliberately structured to incorporate or confront children's ideas (Nussbaum and Novick 1981, 1982; Champagne *et al.* 1983). Clearly, detailed classroom-based research is needed to devise appropriate teaching strategies to deal with this problem.

APPENDIX: MATERIALS TO ILLUSTRATE ANALYSIS PROCEDURES (STRAW AND SYRINGE)

Appendix includes:

1 description of straw and syringe task designed to probe understanding of air pressure,
2 transcripts of two students' responses to straw and syringe tasks, together with notes on coding of these responses,
3 categories derived for straw and syringe,
4 frameworks derived for atmospheric pressures.

1 Two parallel tasks relating to the idea of air pressure

The student was presented with a bottle containing some orange squash.

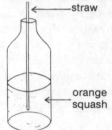

Question: Use the idea of *atmospheric pressure* to explain how you can drink orange squash through a straw.

The plunger of the syringe was depressed and, with a finger firmly over the end under the water, the plunger was then pulled upwards. The finger was then removed and water rushed into the syringe.

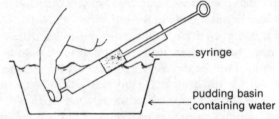

Question: What makes the water rush in like that?

2 Transcript of a 12-year-old student's response to the straw and syringe tasks

A

Interviewer: In this question you were asked to use the idea of atmospheric pressure, now can you tell me what happens when you drink squash through a straw?

Student: Well, either the straw breaks or because you suck out all the air out from the straw – it will stop . . . it will . . . Nature hates anything to be empty and that's why in space if you went out without an oxygen suit your lungs would be turned inside out with the pressure – because the pressure is zero. You know, it is nothing.

Interviewer: What about the pressure in the straw, then, when you suck?

Student: Well, that's precisely what would break the straw – that's why you don't have a lot of paper straws nowadays because they break easily – when you suck hard they sort of . . . go . . . .

Interviewer: So . . . would the pressure be . . . increased or decreased in the straw?

Student: It would be decreased and that's what would make the straw go down . . . it would decrease and so the orange would fill up in the straw to balance the atmospheric pressure . . . .

Interviewer: Balance the atmospheric pressure' . . . can you explain that a bit?

Student: Well, here (pointing to the straw) it's low and outside it's high . . . so the orange would flow into the straw to level it out.

Interviewer: Where is the atmospheric pressure . . . where is it being exerted?

Student: It's everywhere, inside the straw it's pretty low, outside the straw it's what we know so . . . with a difference something has to level it out.

B

Interviewer: . . . my finger over the end under the water and pull up the plunger . . . what is inside the syringe, do you think?

Student: Nothing.

Interviewer: I'll let my finger off . . . is that what you expected?

Student: Well I've never seen it that way – a vacuum happen – but yes, I would expect it to react that way. Well, because the air has been pulled out and it was such a strong cylinder it hadn't been destroyed by the pressure on it – it hadn't collapsed inwards. So there's nothing whatever inside it or if there was anything – *very* low pressure, and so when you let the water in it came in with a lot of force to quickly balance it out and once the water was in there is was just the same.

Interviewer: You say it came in with a lot of force?

Student: Because I said Nature hates anything to be empty and the atmospheric pressure . . . the suction would be so much . . .

Interviewer: When you say 'suction' . . .?

Student: Well, there's nothing inside that glass tube so the suction pulling things in would be so much that the water would really go in fast. The pressure (inside the tube) is low, but the suction is a pull to make the water or whatever it is go into the glass.

Interviewer: You mentioned also atmospheric pressure?

Student: . . . the atmospheric pressure is zero . . . because there's no air in . . . now it has nothing in – the suction would pull the water in, but when you let your finger off the . . . that's all really.

Transcript of a 16-year-old student's response to the straw and syringe tasks

A

Interviewer: You were told here to use the idea of atmospheric pressure to explain about drinking orange juice. Now can you tell what happens when you drink squash through a straw?

Student: Er – well, when you suck up there, you suck all the air out of your straw, so it creates like a vacuum in the straw. And so where the vacuum is, it sucks the drink up. And also there'd be pressure pushing down, probably. And your drink'd go up the straw into the vacuum and so into your mouth.

Interviewer: And so you mentioned two things. You said that the vacuum would . . .?

Student: Pull it up.

Interviewer: Would pull it up, and you said something about pushing . . .? Can you explain that a bit?

Student: Em no, I don't think that's right now. I just think that'll pull it up.

Interviewer: The vacuum in the straw will pull it up?

Student: Yeah. The vacuum in the straw will pull it up.

B

Interviewer: O.K. Fine. Let me show you something else interesting. There is a syringe – an ordinary syringe. O.K. If I put my finger tightly over the end and put it under the water, and pull up the plunger, what do you think is inside the syringe now?

Student: Just air.

Interviewer: Just air. O.K. Now I'm going to take my finger off the end. Watch.

Student: Ahh. There's nothing in it. Cos I'd forgotten you'd got your finger over the end, so when you push it – pull it up there's nothing in it – it's just a vacuum.

Interviewer: Well, let's do it again. Put my finger over the end and pull it up. Now you think there's nothing there?

Student: There's nothing there. It's a vacuum pulling it.

Interviewer: Take my finger off . . .

Student: And the vacuum pulls it up.

Interviewer: It comes up with quite a whoosh, doesn't it? That's the vacuum pulling the water up, is it?

Student: Yeah. It's like in the straw.

Notes on coding these responses

The 12-year-old student:

(Straw task)

This student (Andrew) focuses first on what is happening inside the straw but later draws on the idea of pressure difference to explain the rise of the orange up the straw.

His response was categorized as 'Atmospheric pressure outside is greater than pressure in the mouth/straw (therefore, orange rises)' – i.e., the scientifically accepted explanation.

(Syringe task)

Andrew explains that a vacuum is an area of no (or very low) pressure; he also refers to 'a lot of force quickly balancing it out' and introduces the notion of atmospheric pressure. However perhaps because he was very impressed with the practical demonstration of 'a vacuum happening' he focuses his explanation entirely on what is happening inside the syringe and describes the suction of the vacuum pulling the water in.

His response was categorized as 'Vacuum pulls/sucks water up.'

The 16-year-old student

(Straw task)

The student (Lynne) starts (marker *A* in the protocol) by offering two explanations: (1) the vacuum created in the straw sucks the drink up, and (2) pressure is pushing down. When the interviewer pointed out that she had given two reasons Lynne decided that the vacuum in the straw was the preferred one. (It is possible that the cue in the question to 'use the idea of atmospheric pressure' caused her to suggest pressure pushing down as an additional explanation.)

This response was categorized as 'vacuum in straw sucks orange up.'

(Syringe task)

Lynne's response here (marker *B* in the protocol) is clearly drawing again on the notion of a sucking vacuum. At the end she recognizes the similarity of the two tasks 'it's like in the straw' – and indicates that she is still using the idea of vacuums in her thinking about both tasks.

The response was categorized as 'vacuum pulls/sucks water up'.

3 Response categories derived for straw and syringe tasks

Straw Task		Syringe Task	
Description of category	*% responses (n = 84)*	*Description of category*	*% responses (n = 3)*
Suction (force in straw causes the orange to go up the straw	44	Air (under high pressure)/pressure in the syringe pulls the water in	28
Atmospheric pressure inside bottle causes orange to go up	21	Vacuum pulls/sucks water up	18
Atmospheric pressure outside is greater than pressure in the mouth/straw (therefore, orange rises)	17	As air goes out water goes/is pulled in	14
Vacuum in straw sucks orange up	4	Atmospheric pressure outside is greater than pressure inside (therefore water enters)	13
Air in bottle responsible for orange rising	4	Atmosphere presses on surface of the water and pushes water up	7
Miscellaneous and uncodeable	11	Water enters to fill space	6
		Miscellaneuos and uncodeable	13

4 Frameworks derived for atmospheric pressure

(from response categories for straw, syringe, and washing up tasks):

1 Atmosphere exerts a pressure observable when there is a pressure difference.
2 The atmosphere exerts a pressure on surface.
3 Vacuum or pressure inside actively sucks or pulls.
4 No identifiable framework.[1]

NOTE

1 Frameworks represent perspectives which were identifiable in the sample of students studied. Unlike response categories for tasks, frameworks are *not* allocated to individual students.

REFERENCES

Albert, E. (1978) 'Development of the concept of heat in children', *Science Education* 62: 389–99.

Andersson, B. (1980) 'Some aspects of children's understanding of boiling point', in W. F. Archenhold, R. H. Driver, A. Orton and C. Wood-Robinson (eds) *Cognitive Development Research in Science and Mathematics*, pp. 252–9, Leeds: University of Leeds.

Brown, G. and Desforges, C. (1977) 'Piagetian psychology and education: Time for revision', *British Journal of Educational Psychology* 47: 7–17.

Brumby, M. (1979) 'Problems in learning the concept of natural selection', *Journal of Biology Education* 13(2): 109–22.

Caramazza, A., McCloskey, M. and Green, B. (1981) 'Naive beliefs in "sophisticated" subjects: Misconceptions about trajectories of objects', *Cognition* 9: 117–23.

Champagne, A. B., Klopfer, L. E. and Gunstone, R. F. (1982) 'Cognitive research and the design of science instruction', *Educational Psychologist* 17: 31–53.

Champagne, A. G., Gunstone, R. F. and Klopfer, L. E. (1983) 'Effecting changes in cognitive structures amongst physics students', paper presented at the symposium on Stability and Change in Conceptual Understanding, annual meeting of the American Education Research Association, Montreal, PQ, Canada.

Deadman, J. A. and Kelly, P. J. (1978) 'What do secondary school boys understand about evolution and heredity before they are taught the topics?', *Journal of Biology Education* 12(1): 7–15.

Donaldson, M. (1978) *Children's Minds*, London: Fontana/Collins.

Driver, R. (1978) 'When is a stage not a stage?', *Education Research* 21(1): 54–61.

Driver, R. H. (1981) 'Pupils alternative frameworks in science', *European Journal of Science Education* 3(1): 93–101.

Driver, R. and Erickson, G. (1983) 'Theories-in-action: Some theoretical and empirical issues in the study of students' conceptual frameworks in science', *Studies in Science Education* 10: 37–60.

Engel, M. E. T. (1982) 'The development of understanding of selected aspects of pressure heat and evolution in pupils aged between 12–16 years', unpublished Ph.D. thesis, Leeds: University of Leeds.

Engel Clough, E. and Wood-Robinson, C. (1985) 'Children's understanding of inheritance', *Journal of Biology Education* 19, 304–10.

Erickson, G. L. (1979) 'Children's conceptions of heat and temperature', *Science Education* 63: 221–30.

Gilbert, J. K., Osborne, J. and Fensham, P. J. (1982) 'Children's science and its consequences for teaching', *Science Education* 66(4): 623–33.

Gunstone, R. and White, R. (1981) 'Understanding of gravity', *Science Education* 65(3): 291–9.

Hewson, P.W. (1982) 'A case study of conceptual change in special relativity: The influence of prior knowledge in learning', *European Journal of Science Education* 4(1): 61–78.

Kargbo, D. B., Hobbs, E. D. and Erickson, G. L. (1980) 'Children's beliefs about inherited characteristics', *Journal of Biology Education* 14(2): 137–46.

Mali, G. B. and Howe, A. (1979) 'Development of Earth and gravity concepts among Nepali children', *Science Education* 63: 685–91.

McClelland, J. A. G. (1984) 'Alternative frameworks: Interpretation of evidence', *European Journal of Science Education* 6(1): 1–6.

Nussbaum, J. (1979) 'Children's conceptions of the Earth as a cosmic body: A cross age study', *Science Education* 63: 83–93.

Nussbaum, J. and Novak, J. D. (1976) 'An assessment of children's concepts of the Earth utilizing structured interviews', *Science Education* 60: 535–50.

Nussbaum, J. and Novick, S. (1981) 'Brainstorming in the classroom to invent a model: A case study', *School Science Review* 62: 771–8.

Nussbaum, J. and Novick, S. (1982) 'A study of conceptual change in the classroom', paper presented at the annual meeting of the National Association for Research in Science Teaching, April.

Osborne, R. and Gilbert, J. (1980) 'A method for the investigation of concept understanding in science', *European Journal of Science Education* 2(3): 311–21.

Rowell, J. and Dawson, C. (1981) 'Volume, conservation and instruction: A classroom based Solomon Four group study of conflict', *Journal of Research in Science Teaching* 18(6): 533–46.

Rowell, J. A. and Dawson, C. J. (1983) 'Laboratory counter examples and the growth of understanding in science', *European Journal of Science Education* 5(2): 203–16.

Sere, M. (1982) 'A study of some frameworks used by pupils aged 11–13 years in the interpretation of air pressure', *European Journal of Science Education* 4(3): 299–309.

Shipley, W. C. (1941) 'A self administering scale for measuring intellectual impairment and deterioration', *Journal of Psychology* 9: 371–7.

Sjoberg, S. and Lie, S. (1981) 'Ideas about force and movement among Norwegian pupils and students', Report 81-11, Institute of Physics Report Series, Oslo: University of Oslo.

Strauss, S. (1977) 'Educational implications of U-shaped behavioural growth', A position paper for the Ford Foundation, Tel-Aviv: Tel-Aviv University.

Strauss, S. (1981) 'Cognitive development in school and out', *Cognition* 10: 295–300.

Tiberghien, A. (1980) 'Modes and conditions of learning. An example: the learning of some aspects of the concept of heat', in W. F. Archenhold, R. H. Driver, A. Orton and C. Wood-Robinson (eds) *Cognitive Develop-*

ment Research in Science and Mathematics, pp. 288–309, Leeds: University of Leeds.

Vicentini-Missoni, M. (1982) 'Earth and gravity: Comparison between adults' and children's knowledge', in *Problems Concerning Students' Representation of Physics and Chemistry Knowledge*, pp. 234–54. Proceedings of an International Workshop on Students' Representations, Ludwigsburg, Germany, September.

Viennot, L. (1979) 'Spontaneous reasoning in elementary dynamics', *European Journal of Science Education* 1(2): 205–22.

Wason, P. C. (1977) 'The theory of formal operations – a critique', in B. A. Gerber (ed.) *Piaget and Knowing*, London: Routledge.

Watts, D. M. (1983) 'A study of school children's alternative frameworks of the concept of force', *European Journal of Science Education* 5(2): 217–30.

West, L. and Sutton, C. (1982) 'Investigating children's existing ideas about science', occasional paper, School of Education, University of Leicester.

16 Development viewed in its cultural context

Barbara Rogoff, Mary Gauvain and Shari Ellis
Source: Bornstein, M. and Lamb, M. (eds) (1984)
Developmental Psychology: An Advanced Textbook,
Hillsdale, NJ: Lawrence Erlbaum, pp. 533–71.

INTRODUCTION

Cross-cultural research permits psychologists a broader perspective on human development than is available when considering human behavior in a single cultural group. This expanded view holds important implications for a psychology that has grown out of Western thought and has been tested almost exclusively on Western societies.[1] By allowing psychologists to view variations on human behavior not normally found in mainstream US or Western European society, cross-cultural observation aids in the understanding of human adaptation. Cross-cultural research may allow psychologists to disentangle variables highly associated in one culture but less so in another. In addition, cross-cultural investigations can make use of variations within a single society to examine naturally occurring cause–effect relationships that cannot be manipulated experimentally. Most importantly, cross-cultural research forces psychologists to look closely at the impact of their own belief systems (folk psychology) on scientific theories. When subjects and researchers are from the same population, interpretations of development may be constrained by implicit cultural assumptions.

Some of the broad questions that have been consistently emphasized in cross-cultural work include whether certain mental abilities are universal or vary across cultures, and how individual personality may relate to cultural characteristics such as subsistence methods or value systems. These lines of research have yielded interesting results, which are reviewed in detail in a number of excellent sources: Bornstein (1980); Dasen (1977); Field, Sostek, Vietze and Leiderman (1981); Laboratory of Comparative Human Cognition (1979, 1980); Leiderman, Tulkin and Rosenfeld (1977); Munroe and Munroe (1975); Munroe, Munroe and Whiting (1981); Serpell (1976);

Triandis and Heron (1981); Wagner and Stevenson (1981); and Werner (1979). In this chapter we do not review the extensive research examining cultural universals and variations in human thinking, personality, and behavior. However, we do briefly describe some investigations of universality and variation that refine our understanding of human functioning.

The bulk of this chapter discusses the way in which research involving culture has led psychologists to conceptualize the relationship between culture and thought or behavior. In much cross-cultural research to date, this relationship has been examined using a model in which culture serves as an independent variable (or a set of independent variables) and behavior (or thought) is regarded as the dependent variable, or outcome, of variation in cultural variables. Culture and behavior are conceived as separate variables, rather than mutually embedded aspects of cultural and individual systems. The influence of culture on the individual is frequently studied by correlating an aspect of culture with an aspect of individual functioning. For example, the correlation between the complexity of social structure in the culture and the personality characteristics of its members may be examined. Then investigators may undertake a closer examination of the contexts in which behavior occurs or is taught in varying cultural settings, in the interest of understanding how a particular aspect of culture may influence a particular aspect of individual behavior. For example, how might participation in a technological society encourage children to be more or less nurturant, aggressive, or competitive. This kind of close examination focuses attention on *how* culture can channel development. Whiting (1976) urges that we attempt to 'unpackage' independent variables such as culture, social class, schooling, and gender. Because developmental psychologists have similarly become concerned with the process of change rather than simply correlating broad categories of experience and behavioral outcomes (Brown 1982), this chapter stresses the guidance provided for the field of developmental psychology by cross-cultural emphasis on the contexts in which culture meets individual.

Our primary theme is that human development is guided by the opportunities provided by culture to learn and practice particular skills and behavior. We stress the cultural and contextual basis of development, from the perspective that culture and context are meshed with development rather than separate from it. We argue that to understand children's actions (or to compare them with those of other children of a different age or culture), it is essential to place these actions in the context of the children's interpretation of the task to be accomplished, the goal in performing the activity, and the broader social context of such activities in the children's experience. Although many of our examples are taken from research on cognitive development, we include studies of the role of context in children's social skills wherever possible. In fact, the incorporation of contextual considerations in the study of development de-emphasizes the distinction between cognitive and social development, because thinking occurs in social settings, and socialization occurs in problem-solving situations.

In this chapter, we first refer to the usefulness of cross-cultural research for testing the universal applicability of existing theories and for examining and refining empirical relationships between sociocultural variables and human development. We then focus on concerns raised in cross-cultural research with how to conceptualize the role of the context of human activity. We review studies that suggest the impossibility of understanding human nature without considering the context in which people develop and use their skills. We contrast concepts of development and indicate recent theoretical directions and empirical studies that attempt to integrate aspects of context with conceptions of human activities and development.

CROSS-CULTURAL TESTING OF WESTERN THEORIES AND FINDINGS

This section briefly describes some ways that cross-cultural research can revise existing theories and refine our understanding of the relation between experience and human functioning.

Testing existing theories

Cross-cultural research has been useful in testing psychological theories based on observations in Western cultures for their applicability under other circumstances. Such research may provide crucial counter-examples demonstrating limitations or challenging the basic assumptions of a theory. For example, Malinowski's investigations with Trobriand Islanders (1927) calls into question the foundations of the Oedipal complex in Freud's theory. Freud's theory developed in a society in which the father played both the role of mother's lover and of child's disciplinarian. Among the Trobrianders, however, the roles are separated: the mother's lover is her husband, and the child's disciplinarian is his maternal uncle. Since the Trobriand boys' resentment is directed toward their uncle and not their mother's husband, it appears that the sexual relationship between mother and father may not be related to young boys' resentment toward their father as postulated in the Oedipal complex. This finding illustrates that cross-cultural research can raise questions not only about the universal applicability of a theory, but also about the postulates of the theory itself.

Another theoretical approach that has received considerable attention in cross-cultural tests of universality is Piaget's (1971) theory of cognitive development (see reviews by Dasen 1977; Dasen and Heron 1981; Greenfield 1976; Price-Williams 1980). This research has demonstrated great variation in the rate of Piagetian cognitive development and has examined the question of whether Piaget's stages appear in the same order in different cultures. Cross-cultural research demonstrating the rarity of formal operational performance among non-literate adults has led to widespread concern that this stage represents a culturally specific course of development, perhaps best represented by the 'Western scientist.'[2] Largely because of the cross-cultural evidence, Piaget revised his stance on the formal operational stage, stating in 1972 that this stage may be one that appears only in specific familiar domains rather than being a structured ensemble. Later research conducted in the US investigating performance on formal operational tasks across domains supports this reformulation (Kuhn and Brannock 1977).

These examples illustrate the ways in which cross-cultural research may suggest refinements in a theory or raise questions to be addressed in further theoretical development. Findings such as these reaffirm the complexity of psychological phenomena and highlight the importance of the cultural context in which psychological phenomena occur and in which psychological theories develop.

Cross-cultural research may also discover impressive regularities across cultures in developmental phenomena. For instance, there is marked similarity across cultures in the sequence and timing of sensorimotor development as well as in the age of onset of smiling and separation distress (Gewirtz 1965; Goldberg 1972; Konner 1972; Super 1981); the order of stages in language acquisition is also constant across a large variety of cultural groups (Bowerman 1981; Slobin 1973). Through cross-cultural research, we may become aware of patterns of variation and similarity in human activity, advancing our understanding of human development and of the ways in which experience relates to behavior.

Refining relationships between experience and behavior

Cross-cultural research can be useful in calling attention to the assumptions regarding human 'nature' which go unnoticed by researchers who share the cultural background of the people they study. Doing research in another culture can make one aware of aspects of human behavior which are not noticeable until they are missing or differently arranged, as with the fish who reputedly is unaware of water until removed from it. The fact that human activities are often arranged differently in other cultures allows researchers to examine the pattern of particular variables when they fit differently with other variables in the cultural system.

Cross-cultural research helps to clarify the relationship between experience and behavior by extending the range of variation beyond that available for study in the researcher's own culture and by rearranging variables which may be highly correlated in one culture but not in another. For example, Sears and Wise (1950, reported in Whiting and Child 1953) conclude that the older a baby is when weaned, the greater the associated emotional disturbance. However, their Kansas City sample was weaned very early: only 5 out of 70 children had not been weaned by the age of 7 months. Using a worldwide sample of 52 societies, Whiting and Child (1953) found that the age at weaning ranged from 6 months to 5½ years with 2½ years the median. In only one culture were the children weaned as early as those of the Kansas City sample. What is particularly interesting is that with this worldwide variation in the age of weaning, it was possible to modify Sears and Wise's conclusion: Up to age 13–18 months, it appeared to be true that the older the baby was, the more it became disturbed. But after this peak, weaning became easier as children grew older, with older children frequently weaning themselves as their interests diversified. Given the narrow range of variation available in this US sample, the developmental progression would have been predicted inaccurately.

Other investigations of the relationship between experience and behavior are available in studies of mother–infant contact and relationships on the Israeli kibbutz. In some kibbutzim, children live separately from their parents and are tended in a children's house from early infancy by a children's nurse. Research suggests that infants separated daily from their mothers nevertheless evidence greater interest in staying close to their mothers than to the caretakers with whom they spend great amounts of time (Fox 1977). It is also interesting that the babies develop strong bonds with their infant roommates (Zaslow 1980). This suggests that, with extensive contact, infants show a level of social involvement presumed beyond their maturational level in studies (Maudry and Nekula 1939; Parten 1933) using US infants who tend to be relatively isolated from other infants (Zaslow and Rogoff 1978).

Cross-cultural studies also allow investigators to vary factors that cannot be disentangled in one culture but that are less highly associated in other cultures, allowing a form of 'natural experiment'. For example, studies of mother–child households carried out in the US have, in addition to the absence of the father in the household, a stigma of 'broken household', which labels the family structure as aberrant and undesirable. In other cultures (e.g., in polygynous settings), however, mother–child residence patterns are the usual family structure and their effects could be studied without being confounded by a public attitude of undesirability. For example, low male salience in polygynous households has been related to boys' sex-role development and to societal practices such as masculine-oriented initiation rites and the institutionalization of male participation in pregnancy (the *couvade*, see Munroe and Munroe 1975).

Another example of covarying factors that are difficult to disentangle in US research is the relation between children's chronological age and the amount of schooling they have received. US researchers commonly use age (Wohlwill 1970) as a proxy for maturation or for some sort of general experience with the world. But, as the Laboratory of Comparative Human Cognition (1979) notes, 'to some people it seems that cognitive developmental research in the United States has been measuring *years of schooling*, using *age* as its proxy variable' (p. 830). Developmental studies often find a discontinuity in various skills and knowledge structures about age 5–7 (White 1965), which happens to be the age of the onset of schooling in the US. If we are to understand development without confounding maturation with amount of schooling, it is very useful to examine the development of skills in cultures in which schooling is not mandatory or where age and schooling are not so tightly related (see Rogoff 1981).

A third example of the opportunity that cross-cultural research provides for disentangling intertwined variables is available in observations of children's companionship. It has been noted that Americans emphasize children's peer relations over sibling relations (Ruffy 1981; Wolfenstein 1955). Lack of companionship between siblings may not relate to their kinship but to other differences characterizing siblings versus unrelated peers in Western societies. In Western cultures, sibling interaction implies cross-age relations, since children born of monogamous marriages are unlikely to be very close in age. But in polygynous families there are likely to be same-age siblings living within the same compound. In addition, Western children are separated from siblings through age-graded institutions such as school, while children in non-Western cultures are less subject to the age-grading of schools and are highly involved in caring for younger siblings (Weisner and Gallimore 1977). However, even in the US sibling interaction may be common if families are isolated from other families, if children are responsible for tending siblings, or if children are not attending school (Ellis, Rogoff and Cromer 1981; Gump, Schoggen and Redl 1963; Hicks 1976; Young 1970). Cross-cultural observations of prevalence and preference for sibling interaction suggest that age differences between siblings, age grading, and availability of siblings and unrelated companions may be at least as important to consider as the relatedness variable in accounting for a child's choice of companions.

The preceding discussion illustrates how cross-cultural research has modified developmental theories and provided fresh perspectives on the relation between experience and human behavior and development. Through extensive work focusing on cultural variation in human development, the attention of researchers has been drawn to the role of context in human activity. Next we discuss how cross-cultural research has focused the attention of developmentalists on the role of context in human development. By context we mean any physical or social feature of an activity that channels behavior.

THE ROLE OF CONTEXT IN DEVELOPMENT

Although most approaches in psychology have considered aspects of context to be relevant to the study of the person (e.g., in the need to specify the stimulus or describe the task), understanding the role of context has generally been secondary to examining characteristics of the person. This is true of developmental as well as cross-cultural psychology, in that the basic research strategy is to search for the influence of broad classes of experience (e.g., culture, SES, age, gender) that influence broad classes of individual outcome (e.g., IQ, personality, cognitive level). The focus generally had been on the individual as the basic unit of analysis, with human activity explained in terms of motives, personality, and social and cognitive traits and capacities. Characteristics of the person have been assumed to be relatively stable across situations.

Recently, however, psychologists have become increasingly concerned with the role of context (Bronfenbrenner 1979; Cole, Hood, and McDermott 1978; Gelman 1978; Rogoff 1982; Siegel 1977). This concern was sparked to a significant extent by some early cross-cultural observations of the variability of people's performances in differing contexts. Cross-cultural researchers who supplemented their 'experimental' measures of performance with ethnographic observations of people's everyday activities have been struck by the fact that people who have difficulty with a particular task in the laboratory may spontaneously use the skill of interest in their everyday activities (see discussion in Cole, Hood, and McDermott 1978; Laboratory of Comparative Human Cognition 1979; Rogoff 1981). Gladwin (1970) reports that Micronesian navigators who show extraordinary skills in memory, inference, and calculation in sailing from island to island perform abominably on standard tests of intellectual functioning. Scribner (1976) points out that subjects who perform poorly on logical syllogisms in a test situation often can be observed using elegant reasoning in other situations, such as giving hypothetical arguments for avoiding answering logical reasoning problems. Cole (1975) and Labov (1970) similarly describe people who seem to lack communicative abilities in a testing situation but who exhibit very skillful and logical persuasive skills in everyday social interaction, such as talking the experimenter into buying a beer.

Contextual variation is increasingly noted in US research indicating that children's behavior in their familiar environments and in the laboratory differs (DeLoache 1980; Kessel 1979; Laboratory of Comparative Human Cognition 1979; Neisser 1976; Todd and Perlmutter 1980). For example, young children routinely have difficulty with egocentrism in referential communication tasks (Erickson 1981; Glucksberg, Krauss, and Higgins 1975), yet in everyday situations they adjust their communication to meet the needs of their listeners (Gleason 1973; Shatz and Gelman 1977). Similarly, toddlers have difficulty in laboratory memory tests but demonstrate impressive memory for locations of objects hidden in their own homes (DeLoache and Brown 1979) and impressive recall and strategic capacities in other quasi-naturalistic tasks (Wellman and Somerville 1980). Infants use an egocentric frame of reference in looking for an object in the laboratory, but use a non-egocentric frame of reference when tested at home (Acredolo 1979). Babies are more likely to display separation protest when left by their mothers in a laboratory situation than in the home (Ross, Kagan, Zelazo and Kotelchuck 1975). Such findings indicate that children's behavior often differs in laboratory tasks compared to more familiar contexts.

A common reaction to the findings that laboratory skills appear different from behavior outside the lab is to encourage the study of people's actions in their natural environments. It is assumed that valid measures of people's real psychological processes will be found only in natural environments (Charlesworth 1976). While it is important to examine activities outside of the laboratory, the dichotomy of laboratory versus 'natural' behavior is an oversimplification. Focusing the issue on a field versus laboratory distinction (McCall 1977; Parke 1979; Weisz 1978; Wohlwill 1981) overlooks the fact that there is no one situation in which people's *real* capabilities and processes can be uncovered. This view assumes that it is possible, under ideal circumstances, to attribute underlying capacities or processes to internal functioning of people without concern for the context of their activity.

Thinking as well as acting, however, are intricately interwoven with the context of the activity underway. For example, children's communication skills appear to vary depending on whether their listener is a peer or a teacher (Steinberg and Cazden 1979) or whether they are at home or at school (Shultz, Florio and Erickson 1982). One parent's interactions with an infant decrease in the presence of the other parent (Lamb 1978), and children's peer interactions are more negative when their mothers or teachers are present (Abramovitch, Pepler and Corter 1982; Cook-Gumperz and Corsaro 1977; Field 1979; Huston-Stein, Friedrich-Cofer and Susman 1977). Fifth graders are more likely to evidence altruism when they know they are observed by an experimenter (Zarbatany, Hartmann, Gelfand and Ramsey 1982). One must attend to the context in order to understand psychological processes. This is the case for any situation in which development is studied, including the laboratory context, which is not context-*free* as researchers frequently seem to assume. Context is a complex and structured feature of psychological events, one that is not separate from the activity of the person (Rogoff 1982).

These concerns are crucial in cross-cultural comparisons (or any comparisons based on group membership, e.g., age or gender comparisons), because such comparisons assume that the factor compared is equivalent for the groups compared, and that other factors do not simultaneously vary. Cross-cultural psychologists distinguish degrees of sensitivity to the broad contexts of human functioning in discussions of *emic, imposed etic*, and *derived etic* research strategies (Berry 1969). In an emic approach, an investigator attempts to maintain the rich interplay of all aspects of the cultural context in the description of a cultural group. Such research may make use of ethnographic observation and participation in the activities of the culture studied.

In an imposed etic approach, an investigator attempts to make general statements about human functioning across cultural groups, but with insufficient attention to the cultural contexts used to support the generalization. Thus, by definition the investigator carrying out an imposed etic study is too quick to impose a culturally inappropriate understanding of the phenomenon of interest, usually uncritically importing theory and measures from research done in Western settings. The ideas and procedures are not sufficiently adapted to the culture being studied, and although the researcher may 'get data,' the researcher is in jeopardy of misinterpreting the results. The imposed etic approach could involve applying questionnaires, behavioral coding systems, or experimental procedures without modifying them to fit the culture and without seeking evidence that the behavior observed means the same thing to the subjects as to the foreign experimenter.

In contrast, in the derived etic approach the researcher adapts general statements regarding human functioning to fit each cultural group studied. The resulting statements are informed by emic approaches in each culture and are sensitive to the cultural context and the varying meaning of the variables across cultures. Clearly, cross-cultural psychologists aspire to use the derived etic research strategy by coming to understand the cultural contexts studied, adapting procedures to fit the cultures studied, and adapting theories to fit the sensitive tests and observations made in a variety of cultures. Even when the variable of interest requires little inference to observe (e.g., touching, eye contact, carrying practices), some understanding of the cultural milieu is necessary to determine the contexts in which the data are to be gathered (e.g., place in daily routine, cast of characters present) and how the behavior is to be interpreted (e.g., in terms of stimulation or sensitivity).

In the following sections we summarize cross-cultural evidence suggesting that in order to understand behavior it is necessary to attend to the immediate physical and interactional context of the activity, to the person's goal and understanding of the activity, and to the appropriate means of reaching the goal. These goals and means are to a large extent socially defined as well as socially managed. The familiarity of the task materials, purpose of the activity, and features of the social situation are intertwined with culture in ways making it difficult to assume that comparisons of an individual's performance can be made without consideration of the complexity of the context of the performance. Cultural differences may reflect varying exposure to activities differing in their organization, purpose, and social function.

Task materials and meaningfulness of the activity

The relative familiarity of task materials to different populations has obvious relevance to attempts to ensure cultural appropriateness of tasks (Price-Williams 1962). Irwin and McLaughlin (1970) found that nonliterate Liberian adults were more successful in classifying bowls of rice than classifying geometric stimuli (both differing in color, shape, and number). A sequel to that study (Irwin, Schafer, and Feiden 1974) reported that US undergraduates responded to requests to sort bowls of rice with the same hesitation and bewilderment as shown by Liberian nonliterates when asked to sort cards decorated with squares and triangles. Both groups, when tested with unfamiliar materials, sorted in a manner considered less advanced than when tested with familiar materials.

But as Cole, Sharp, and Lave (1976), Greenfield (1974), and Lave (1977) have argued, it is not only familiarity of materials that must be considered in comparisons of groups. If the materials are familiar but the task to be performed on the materials is unfamiliar, or if both materials and task are familiar but performing that particular task with those particular materials is unfamiliar, the activity is likely to be perceived as foreign.

The importance of the familiar relation of materials and task is illustrated by several studies in which developmental or cross-cultural differences disappear when the task materials are related in a meaningful, familiar way. Memory research has traditionally tried to minimize the relationships between items (e.g. in free recall, memory span, or paired-associates tasks) in an attempt to equate the circumstances of memory tests given to different people because associations between items are differentially affected by prior experience. However, sophisticated subjects (especially those who have experienced formal schooling) invent connections between items, for example, by clustering by category or elaborating associations. Young children or people from non-Western cultures are usually less familiar with schooling and consequently with associational strategies developed in practice with the lists of decontextualized items associated with literacy (Goody 1977). Hence, they experience difficulty remembering lists with little or no familiar or meaningful relations among items (Flavell 1977; Rogoff 1981).

List-memory tasks may be contrasted with everyday memory

problems such as remembering the plot of a story or the location of a store downtown. The information in everyday memory problems is meaningfully interrelated. The familiar organization of the materials or contextual organization can be used by the subject as a structure for recall, rather than requiring organization to be imposed on unrelated items. Research involving contextually organized verbal or spatial information, such as recall of stories or of scenes, has found cross-cultural similarities rather than differences in performance by children and adults (Mandler, Scribner, Cole, and DeForest 1980; Rogoff and Waddell 1982). Cultural differences in memory performance may be limited to tasks which exclude reliance on contextual organization of materials for structuring memory performance.

The use of unfamiliar or meaningless materials and tasks may be an important feature accounting for some findings of developmental and cultural differences in laboratory tasks. Greenfield and Childs (1977) and Kelly (1977) have found impressive performance by non-Western children using an indigenous kinship system to explore relational thinking and an indigenous botanical classification system to test class inclusion concepts.

Familiarity of materials and tasks is intimately related to the activities that are usual for the subjects. Serpell (1979) contrasted Zambian and English children's ability to copy visual displays in four activities differing in familiarity for the two cultures. The Zambian children performed better when asked to copy two-dimensional figures formed of strips of wire (an activity that Serpell observed Zambian children engaging in frequently), whereas the English children surpassed the Zambians in copying two-dimensional figures with paper and pencil (a common activity of English but not Zambian children). No differences were found in activities to which the two groups had similar exposure: copying positions of adults' hands and modeling figures out of clay. The results support the conclusion that cultural differences reflect varying exposure to particular activities, rather than a general cognitive difference between groups.

Problems of representativeness of task do not disappear in research relying on naturalistic observations. Zaslow and Rogoff (1981) argue that the choice of context for observation and the interpretation of behavior observed provides a crucial problem for cross-cultural comparisons of early interaction:

Although studies of early social interaction do not necessarily involve introducing unfamiliar materials, tasks, or contexts, the fact that these studies involve *sampling* behavior makes it necessary to consider comparability of the situation (social and otherwise) sampled and of the behaviors selected for observation. Identical contexts (e.g. mother–infant interaction without others present) may not sample equally representative proportions of the infant's experience in different cultures. Behaviors chosen for observation on the grounds that they sample the range of social interactions in one culture may sample behaviors incompletely in another, providing a distorted view of interaction. Identical behaviors need not have the same connotations in different cultures.

(p. 249)

For example, in cultures in which it is rare for a caregiver and infant to be alone together, the imposition of dyadic interaction might yield data confounded by the reactions of both child and caregiver to being isolated from the usual social group (Sostek, Vietze, Zaslow, Kreiss, van der Waals, and Rubinstein 1981). Bowerman (1981) similarly notes that the traditional technique of taping mother–child interaction to elicit children's speech is unsuited to cultures in which children are seldom conversational partners with adults. In cross-cultural comparisons of observed behavior it is essential to consider the equivalence of the segment of behavior sampled and the meaning of the activity and behaviors to the participants in each culture. Price-Williams (1975) notes that:

Among Hausa mothers, the custom in not to show affection for their infants in public. Now those psychologists who are concerned with nurturance and dependency will go astray on their frequency counts if they do not realize this. A casual ethnographer is likely to witness only public interaction; only when much further inquiry is made is the absence of the event put into its proper perspective.

(p. 17)

Perhaps the most crucial aspect of a task that makes it or its components meaningful is the presence of a meaningful purpose for the activity. Brown (1975), Lave (1980), Leont'ev (1981), and Smirnov and Zinchenko (1969) point out that cognitive research has concentrated on memory or thinking as a goal in itself, rather than as the means to a practical goal, e.g., to remember something of importance or to solve a real problem. The arbitrariness of performance as a goal in itself may account for many developmental and cultural differences. Istomina (1977) found that preschool children's recall of a list of items was much better when the children were asked to remember items to bring back from a play store than in standard free recall tasks.

It is often difficult to ascertain the subject's idea of the purpose of an experimental task. People unfamiliar with experiments may invoke a purpose for the activity that is at odds with the experimenter's intent. The potential mismatch between the experimenter's and the naive subjects' approach to a task is illustrated by an anecdote provided by Glick (1975). He found that in a classification task Kpelle subjects sorted 20 objects into functional groups (e.g. knife with orange, potato with hoe) rather than categorical groups and would often volunteer, on being questioned further, that that was the way a wise man would do things. 'When an exasperated experimenter asked finally, "How would a fool do it", he was given back sorts of the type that were initially expected – four neat piles with food in one, tools in another, and so on' (p. 636). Super, Harkness, and Baldwin (1977) and Skeen, Rogoff, and Ellis (1983) suggest that the classification of real items in everyday life (e.g., in organizing a kitchen or dresser drawers) is not as exhaustive or taxonomic as laboratory researchers expect to find with mature classifiers. Categorization in real life, in contrast to that which occurs in the laboratory, is primarily functional and varies with the purpose of the activity. In the laboratory, the practical goal is typically removed and the subjects are left with their knowledge and inferences regarding what the experimenter is likely to consider an appropriate classification scheme.

The appropriate solutions, goals, tasks, and materials represented in traditional laboratory studies of cognition bear a marked resemblance to activities familiar in the school situation. Several authors have suggested that the difficulty met by young children and relatively traditional peoples in laboratory tests is due to their limited experience with formal schooling (Rogoff 1981; Sharp, Cole, and Lave (1979). People who have more schooling, such as older children and Western peoples, may do better on cognitive tests because tests are usually a sample of the activities specifically taught in school. As Cole, Sharp, and Lave (1976) and Charlesworth (1976) point out, versions of most traditional cognitive tasks can be found in Binet's early measures predicting school performance. In addition, familiarity with performing a task merely for the purpose of being evaluated may relate to experience with Western schooling, a particular social setting.

Social situation

The social context of an activity organizes materials and tasks in meaningful ways. As emphasized by Vygotsky (1978), the social context affects development at both the institutional and material level, as well as at the interpersonal level. At the institutional level, cultural history provides organizations and tools useful to cognitive activity (through institutions such as school and inventions such as the calculator or literacy) and practices facilitating socially appropriate solutions to problems (e.g., norms for the arrangement of grocery shelves to aid shoppers in locating or remembering what they need; common mnemonic devices). The society provides organization for human activity in institutions such as schools and political systems, in which particular forms of behavior are encouraged.

Social institutions

An example of the role of societal institutions in psychological functioning comes from research on moral development, which may relate to the political system of an individual's society. Kohlberg (1969) takes the position that moral development stages are comparable across cultures, with 'higher' performance on moral development interviews indicating 'more adequate' morality. The first two stages in Kohlberg's hierarchy of moral development focus on avoiding punishment and getting reward, and the third emphasizes achieving the approval of others. The fourth stage is defined in terms of obedience to the laws set down by those in power, i.e., to be a good citizen and keep social order. The firth and sixth stages emphasize moral principles established through mutual agreement or on the basis of universal ethical principles; if social rules conflict with moral principles, individuals may morally decide not to follow the rules of society.

Edwards (1981) contests this view, arguing that the bureaucratic systems' perspective of Stage Four is appropriate for people whose political frame of reference is a large industrialized society, but inappropriate for people in small traditional tribal societies: 'The two types of social systems are very different (though of course both are valid working types of systems), and thus everyday social life in them calls forth different modes of moral problem solving whose adequacy must be judged relative to their particular contexts (p. 274).' Stages Five and Six are rare in cross-cultural studies and Edwards proposes that these 'metaethical reflections on morality' should be eliminated from the system, leaving a sequence of moral development with three universal stages and a fourth present for some adults in large industrialized societies with formal institutions. The political institutions of a society may channel individual moral reasoning by providing standards for the resolution of moral problems.

An important cultural institution is Western schooling, which similarly structures behavior by providing norms and strategies for performance that are considered advanced in cognitive tests. Schooling may provide students with a common view of what is 'clever' (e.g. classification of objects by taxonomic category rather than by their function). An emphasis on fast performance, as in a timed test, may be unusual in many cultures. Goodnow (1976) suggests that differences between cultural groups may be ascribed largely to the interpretation of what problem is being solved in the task, and to different values regarding 'proper' methods of solution (e.g. speed, reaching a solution with a minimum of moves or redundancy, physically handling materials versus 'mental shuffling').

The cultural tools and techniques used in school involve certain conventions and genres, such as Western conventions for representing depth in two-dimensional pictures; the common format of test items (e.g., multiple choice); and the genre of the story problem (similar to the logical syllogism), in which one must rely only on information given in the problem to reach the answer. Luria (1976) found that Central Asian subjects did not treat verbal logical problems (syllogisms) as if the premises constituted a logical relation, but as if they were unrelated judgments requiring verification from direct experience. While Luria (and others) take the peasants' responses as indicative of logical shortcomings, it is clear from transcripts that the subjects did not conceive the problem in the same manner as the experimenter. The syllogism was handled by the subjects as a request for an opinion. Many nonliterate subjects refused to answer, not accepting the problem as a self-contained puzzle with the truth determinable from the stated premises. They protested that they 'could only judge what they had seen' or 'didn't want to lie.' Here is an example of the interaction between a peasant and the experimenter (Luria 1976):

[Syllogism:] In the Far North, where there is snow, all bears are white. Novaya Zemlya is in the Far North and there is always snow there. What colour are the bears there?
. . . 'We always speak only of what we see; we don't talk about what we haven't seen.'
[E:] But what do my words imply? [The syllogism is repeated.]
'Well, it's like this: our tsar isn't like yours, and yours isn't like ours. Your words can be answered only by someone who was there, and if a person wasn't there he can't say anything on the basis of your words.'
[E:]. . . But on the basis on my words – in the North, where there is

always snow, the bears are white, can you gather what kind of bears there are in Novaya Zemlya?
'If a man was sixty or eighty and had seen a white bear and had told about it, he could be believed, but I've never seen one and hence I can't say. That's my last word. Those who saw can tell, and those who didn't see can't say anything!' (At this point a young Uzbek volunteered, 'From your words it means that bears there are white.')
[E:] Well, which of you is right?
'What the cock knows how to do, he does. What I know, I say, and nothing beyond that!'

(pp. 108–9)

The subject and the experimenter seem to disagree about what kind of evidence one should accept as truth. The subject insists that truth should be based on first-hand knowledge, or perhaps on the word of a reliable, experienced person. (He obviously does not include the experimenter in the latter category.) Given differing criteria for determining truth, the peasant's treatment of the syllogism cannot be taken as evidence of his logical functioning. Luria notes that the nonliterate subjects' reasoning and deduction were excellent when dealing with immediate practical experience. However, in a system of 'theoretical thinking,' they showed several differences from literate subjects. They refused to accept the premise as a point of departure for subsequent reasoning; they treated the premise as a message about some particular phenomenon rather than as 'a priori', and they treated the syllogism as a collection of independent statements rather than as a unified logical problem.

Cole, Gay, Glick, and Sharp (1971) found that when the problem format was changed to evaluating someone else's conclusion from the premises, rather than personally answering a question on the basis of the premises, nonschooled subjects had much less difficulty. This supports the argument that nonschooled subjects were uncomfortable having to answer a question for which they could not verify the premises. When the subjects did not need to assert that a conclusion was true, they were willing to consider whether that answer was a logical conclusion and examined the hypothetical premises and conclusion to see if they fit logically.

Scribner (1977) suggests that verbal syllogisms represent a specialized language genre that is recognizably different from other genres. Through practice with the genre, individuals become able to handle more complex versions of it and understand the form of the problem. In Western schooling, people may become familiar with the genre through experience with story problems and other verbal problems in which the answer must be derived from the relationships presented in the problem. Hence, it appears that logical reasoning practices cannot be separated from the formats developed for such thinking in cultural institutions such as schools. Other institutions such as courts, markets, and families may share these formats or have their own conventions in different cultures.

Social interaction

In addition to considering the influence of social institutions on development, Vygotsky (1978) also emphasizes the immediate social interactional context of activity. Social interaction structures individual activity, especially as information regarding tools and practices is transmitted through interaction with more experienced members of society during development. Particular patterns of interpersonal relations are organized by institutional conventions and the availability of cultural tools. Social aspects of experimental and observational situations are unfamiliar to some groups. For example, the relationship between Experimenter and Subject in an experiment may be rapidly grasped by Western children familiar with testing in school, but may be highly discrepant from familiar adult–child interactions for non-Western children and adults. In addition, schooling provides familiarity with having to answer questions on content material before it has been fully mastered. The practice of testing school children at an arbitrary point in the learning process may be unusual in cultures where learners begin to participate in an activity only when they feel competent at the skill being learned (Cazden and John 1971).

Schooled children are likely to have had more practice figuring out what an adult is really asking when the adult does not reveal all aspects of performance that will be evaluated. Sharp, Cole, and Lave (1979) found that schooled subjects were more sensitive to the nuances of their experimental instructions. Pinard, Morin, and Lefebvre (1973) found that with minimal training in conservation task, nonschooled children showed far more spontaneous switches to conserving responses than did nonconserving schooled children, supporting the idea that the nonschooled children were simply learning what it was that they were being asked, whereas the schooled children may have already understood the question even if they could not answer it correctly. Nonschooled children, having less experience with a testing situation, may be more concerned with showing respectful behavior to the tester and trying to figure out the tester, than with trying to figure out the problem. Kiminyo (1977) points out that the non-schooled child will be more likely to change an answer when asked 'why?' by an adult, as this traditionally means the adult considers the child's answer incorrect rather than indicating that the child should explain his or her reasoning. Kiminyo argues that Western education in African settings teaches skills and rules for such performance in examinations, making schooled African children better prepared to justify their answers in Piagetian tests.

Schooled people are more familiar with an interview or testing situation in which a high-status adult, who already knows the answer to the question, requests information of a lower-status person, such as a child. It is not uncommon in traditional societies for the interaction between adults and children to be characterized in terms of commands by the adult and compliance by the child (Harkness and Super 1977). Traditional adults seldom ask children's opinions (Blount 1972). In a traditional society, a year of school dramatically increases a child's ability to finish an experiment – regardless of the correctness of the answers – and increases the number of words used in responding (Super 1977).

An example of how conventions of social interaction influence cognitive test performance is provided by Rogoff and Mistry (1985), who note that it is culturally inappropriate for Mayan children to speak freely to an adult. When carrying messages to adults, they must politely add the word 'cha' ('so I have been told'). In a recall task, when asked to tell a story to an adult, the Mayan children's excessively bashful utterances were frequently punctuated with the word 'cha'. Their performance also indicated that they were responding as if being grilled rather than narrating a story. Although the Mayan children usually mentioned a fact from each of the main episodes of the story, they did so in a disjointed fashion as if they were listing the answers to questions regarding the facts of the story. The experimenter found it continually necessary to ask 'What happened next?' In contrast, the US children's more fluent recalls were marked by much more narrative connections between pieces of information and less need for prompting questions, suggesting that they were more familiar with the social situation of the task.

Irvine (1978) notes that findings of Piagetian nonconservation by nonschooled Wolof adolescents and adults (Greenfield 1966) might be due to the test-like social features of the experimental setting:

Outside the schoolroom, it is rare for a Wolof adult to ask another adult, or even a child more than six or seven years old, a question to which he or she already knows the answer. Where this kind of questioning does occur it suggests an aggressive challenge, or a riddle with a trick answer. . . . [S]ubjects unaccustomed to schoolroom interrogation would be in a poor position to understand the researcher's motives or to guess what sort of response was wanted of them.

(Irvine 1978: 304)

The nonschooled children may simply be responding to a strange situation involving a powerful adult by trying to give an answer that the adult might be presumed to expect, since she had crossed the ocean to ask what, to her, must be an important question. This idea is supported by the fact that Greenfield's nonschooled Wolof subjects gave conservation responses essentially equal to those of the schooled subjects when they themselves poured the water in the conservation test.

Irvine (1978) informally investigated adults' conservation responses by modifying the setting of examination. Her subjects were informants who dropped in to visit her in the familiar setting of a village household. She presented the task in the context of questions about language (explaining to the ignorant language-learner words like 'more' and 'the same' using water and beakers for illustration), rather than as a test. Irvine paused and waited for elaborations of initial responses or indicated that she did not understand. Several of the informants' initial responses suggested nonconservation, with responses strikingly similar to the ones recorded by Greenfield. However each informant subsequently elaborated with a response clearly reflecting conservation (e.g., 'The glasses are not the same, but the waters are the same' p. 306). Although discrepancies between Irvine's and Greenfield's observations are not resolved (see Greenfield 1979), the work clearly illustrates that the cultural institutions which organize social interaction must be considered in order to interpret the skills displayed.

Even in naturalistic observations, the behavior of those observed is influenced by their interpretation of the social situation. Like the experimenter, the observer plays a social role which must be taken into account when considering the constraints on the interaction observed. The observer may be regarded as an intruder, a visitor, or a strange alien, but it is not likely that the observer's presence is ignored: 'It seems likely that one influence of the observer on parents is to produce a heightened frequency of behavior that the participants judge to be more socially desirable and inhibit behavior considered socially undesirable' (Pedersen 1980: 181). Field and Widmayer (1981) note that mothers' objectives for interaction vary across cultures, with Cuban American mothers interested in 'educating' their children and Black American mothers concerned about not spoiling their children by giving them too much attention. Such agendas might be differentially exhibited in the presence of an observer from another culture, depending on the presumed similarity between the mothers' and the observer's cultures.

The reports of researchers observing early interaction in other cultures indicate that the presence of an observer leads to changes in behavior and that subjects interpret the observational context differently in diverse cultures. Among the Zinacantecos, a group of Mayan Indians living in Mexico, Brazelton (1977) describes fear of the observer in both adults and infants:

> We were automatically endowed with 'the evil eye' until I assured mothers that I was a 'curer' and could counteract it if I had it. However the effects of stranger anxiety in the baby were powerfully reinforced by his parents' constant anxiety about our presence. We were unable to relate to babies after nine months of age because the effect was so powerful.
>
> (p. 174)

Brazelton expresses concern about the impact on the data of such an intense reaction to the observer.

On the other hand, the appearance of an observer may produce great interest rather than fear, which nevertheless disrupts the observation. Munroe and Munroe (1971) report that in Logoli (East African) households, as soon as the observer arrived, the infant was readied for display. It was picked up and brought to the observer for inspection. This cooperation on the part of the Logoli mothers made for difficulty observing the usual caretaking of the infants. Hence, the Munroes changed their observational procedure to data taken from a first glance (a 'snapshot') of the infant and its surroundings, before the observer's presence was noticed and disrupted the ongoing activity.

A study of Graves and Glick (1978) suggests how American middle-class mothers interpret what is expected of them when being observed. Graves and Glick contrasted behaviors of mothers with their 18- to 25-month-old children when the mothers thought they were being observed (video equipment was conspicuously running) and when they thought they were simply waiting in an observation room (repairs were 'being made' on the video equipment; in fact, observations were made from behind a one-way mirror). The mothers' behavior when they thought they were being observed seemed to reflect their concept of 'good mothering'. Speech to the children doubled when the mothers thought they were being observed; mothers used more indirect directives, produced more test questions, engaged in more naming and action routines, made more evaluative comments, asked more questions, and spent more time in joint interactive focus with their children, than when they thought they were not being observed.

Clearly, there is a problem of comparability in studies contrasting the observed behavior of two groups whose responses to, or even tolerance for, the presence of an observer differ substantially. Researchers must be alert to the fact that being observed or interacting with an experimenter is not a context-free situation. It is a social context with meaning varying for different populations.

Familarity of the activity and its goals, as well as the social context of behavior, influence the behavior of individuals. To compare the characteristics of individuals across cultures (or ages or gender), it is necessary to consider their behavior as embedded in a complex system of activities and social situations usual in their experience. To interpret differences, the context of the behavior observed must receive considerable attention. In the next section, we compare concepts of development that differ in how they handle the relation between an individual's previous experience and current behavior.

CONCEPTS OF DEVELOPMENT

The relation between cultural variables and individual functioning has often been cast in terms of the effects of broad aspects of culture on broad aspects of individual characteristics. Attempts to understand *how* the culture meets the individual (or how the individual develops in culture) suggest that the relation of culture and behavior resides in the particular learning experiences of individuals. While there should be nothing surprising in the idea that people learn what they know or develop skills through practice, there are differences in how general the learning experiences and the resulting performances are expected to be, and therefore in how cultural differences are explained.

The Laboratory of Comparative Human Cognition (1980) has drawn a distinction between two models of learning, the 'Central Processor Model,' which they suggest characterizes the assumptions of existing developmental theory and research, and the 'Specific Learning Model,' which they offer as a substitute. The two models are diagrammed in Figure 16.1.

In the Central Processor Model, the person experiences a variety of

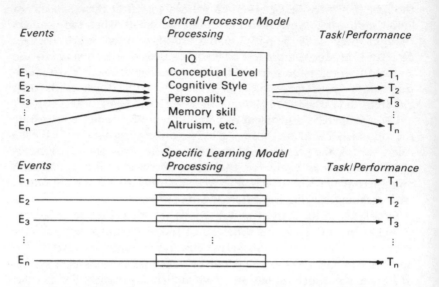

Figure 16.1 Diagrams of Central Processor Model and Specific Learning Model of learning and performance

Source: Adapted from the Laboratory of Comparative Human Cognition 1980.

events, each of which contributes some strength or power to a central processor, which is conceived as consisting of somewhat general abilities or skills. When a subject is faced with a particular task, he or she makes use of the general ability contained in the central processor to perform the task. The central processor is assumed to function similarly on a large variety of tasks. As an example we may take the construct 'intelligence'. The individual's 'intelligence' is developed through a variety of experiences which strengthen it, and the person deploys intelligence in a similar way when solving a number of tasks that are presumed to require intelligence for successful performance. It is worth noting that the background experience that builds intelligence does not necessarily bear an obvious relation to the task the subject is asked to perform. Thus, researchers may ask whether maternal employment or number of siblings influence 'intelligence,' as evidenced on a task requiring people to remember a string of numbers backwards. A correlation may be found, and the researchers would then try to identify a mechanism by which the independent variable could conceivably influence task performance. For example, research based on Berry's (1976) ecocultural theory focuses on determining which ecological and childrearing variables (e.g., hunting and gathering for subsistence, nomadic versus sedentary settlement pattern, level of sociopolitical stratification, restrictiveness in socialization) promote 'psychological differentiation', which is assumed to be characteristic of an individual across a variety of social, perceptual, and cognitive tasks. The Central Processor Model represents views of development that assume that context plays little role in thinking or behavior and that personality, behavioural propensities, and skills are general.

The Specific Learning Model has grown out of cross-cultural attempts to understand developmental processes. Recognizing that behavior and skills are closely tied to the context of practice, researchers in cross-cultural human development are currently developing the Specific Learning Model as an alternative to the Central Processing Model. (See especially Laboratory of Comparative Human Cognition 1980; Rogoff and Lave 1984). The Specific Learning Model has a much closer tie between the events experienced by individuals and the tasks on which their performance is observed[3]. In this model, the individual develops skills in particular tasks through experience in related activities. Skills are customized to the particular task. There is no assumption that experience in Event E_1 builds skills that generalize broadly to performance in Task T_3. Research focuses on specific relations between performance on tasks and previous experience in similar events. For example, an investigation may relate performance on a test requiring people to remember a string of words with experience memorizing strings of foreign words in Qur'anic schooling (Scribner and Cole 1981; Wagner 1978). The problem with this alternate model is that we are left with the question of how far and by what means generalization occurs.

Experience in a variety of similar events builds skills that, although specifically groomed in practiced activities, may be applied to related but novel tasks. Each task we perform is both somewhat novel and somewhat similar to previously experienced events, either in the form presented or in the way we reorganize it for solution. It would be a gross oversimplification to assume that because there is contextual variation in performance, the specificity of skill is infinitely narrow. The problem here is to determine to what extent there is transfer from one experience to performance on a somewhat novel task and how such transfer occurs. What prediction can be made from successful performance on, say, a logical syllogism? That the individual (1) will do well on the next syllogism? (2) will do well on other kinds of logic problems? (3) will be logical in many situations? or (4) is smart? The question of generality is an empirical one that has received little attention due to the predominance of the Central Processor Model in developmental psychology. This problem is not solved but instead posed by the alternate Specific Learning Model. We return to this question after a more complete discussion of the two models.

The Central Processor Model and questions of context

Psychologists have long debated the amount of transfer expected from specific activities to other activities (Vygotsky 1962). Thorndike's (1914) discussion of 'mental discipline' described the common view that:

> The words accuracy, quickness, discrimination, memory, observation, attention, concentration, judgment, reasoning, etc., stand for some real and elemental abilities which are the same no matter what material they work upon; that . . . in a more or less mysterious way learning to do one thing well will make one do better things that in concrete appearance have absolutely no community with it.
>
> (p. 272)

Most depictions of stages (e.g., Piaget's concrete operational stage), capacities (e.g., spatial skill, metamemory), or personality traits (e.g., competitiveness, altruism) assume that the stage, capacity, or trait characterizes the child's thinking and behavior across a large number of task situations (Ekehammar 1974; Feldman 1980; Fischer 1980; Lewis 1978; Mischel 1979; Piaget 1971). Usually the existence of the stage, capacity, or trait is evaluated through the use of a single task or a small sample of tasks assumed to be representative of the domain of problems that children meet. However, when multiple tasks are given, the assumption of widespread generality of stage, capacity, or trait is usually not upheld (Brainerd 1978; Fischer 1980; Fowler 1980; Siegler 1981). Skills that are logically similar appear at different ages or do not cluster together on similar tasks performed by the same individuals (Feldman 1980; Reese 1977).

Piaget's theory contends that task performances relate to each other in an interrelated structure (*structure d'ensemble*), but it requires the concept of *décalage* to account for time lags in tasks that are formally similar. Piaget (1971) considered it impossible to develop a general theory of time lags in, for example, class inclusion problems involving two different sets of objects. He claimed the time lags were due to variation in the 'resistances' of the different types of object.

Cross-cultural research has borrowed tests, interpretations of performance, and the concept of developmental stages from Piaget. The research uses the tests Piaget developed to probe the thinking of Western European children. For example, the test for liquid conservation involves pouring equal amounts of liquid into identical containers, having the child verify that they contain the same amount, then pouring the contents of one of the containers into another of a different shape. A child who answers that they are still the same amount is considered a conserver, and one who maintains that there is more water in one container is considered a nonconserver. Piaget was most interested in understanding how the child reasoned, rather than in whether the child knew the right answer. He used a 'clinical method' in which children's answers were probed and questions reworded in an individual fashion in order to understand *how* the children reached their answers. Cross-cultural research using Piaget's tests has generally not followed the clinical method, but has standardized the questions and sometimes not even asked the children to explain their answers. This facilitates comparison of populations, but uses Piaget's tasks as intelligence test items in which reasoning is not probed but explanations are simply assessed for correctness.

Researchers have also borrowed Piaget's interpretation of what Piagetian tests indicate; underlying development in logical thinking. There is reason to doubt that comparing quantities of water necessarily taps the same process in all cultures. Since the child's reasoning is seldom explored, all one can safely conclude from most studies is that the child has compared two glasses of water and answered 'the same' or 'not the same'. Whether this tests the child's understanding of the world is another matter.

In addition to borrowing the specific tests and the interpretation of performance, cross-cultural researchers have made use of the theoretical concept of developmental progression. If nonschooled 9-year-olds do not conserve and nonschooled 13-year-olds do conserve, the researcher concludes that it is not until the age of 13 that nonschooled children enter the stage of concrete operations, which implies more than simply whether a child can conserve or not. It implies, in addition, a generalized structure of thought that is assumed to permeate much, if not all, of the child's intelligence. This is a far bigger inferential leap than simply concluding that it is not until the age of 13 that nonschooled children learn a particular skill or concept (e.g. to impose organization spontaneously on material to be remembered, to explain the dimensions used in classifying geometric stimuli). Borrowing the concept of generalized cognitive development along a time line, the researcher may claim that one population is retarded relative to another, or even that one population is stunted in cognitive development (if adults do not pass the test either). Such analyses result in unwarranted conclusions about the logical stage of people, on the basis of their performance on a few tests in which their opinions about the quantity of deformed materials is obtained.

Psychologists apparently assume that it is possible to examine psychological processes without concern for the content or context of what is being processed; that is, to neutralize the task so that performance reflects 'pure process' (see Cole and Scribner 1975; Price-Williams 1980; Rogoff 1982). The research reviewed in previous sections of this chapter suggests that behavior does not involve abstract, context-free competences that may be used generally across widely diverse problem domains; rather, it involves skills tied to somewhat specific types of activity in particular contexts. Behavior in one situation may not generalize to another, even though we may be able to name some process (e.g., role-taking, sharing, competing, remembering, problem-solving) that both activities have in common. People with experience in one type of problem will be able to apply the skill to that kind of problem, but not necessarily to another problem with which they are less familiar.

The Specific Learning Model and questions of transfer

In order to make use of previously learned skills or information, people must be able to generalize some aspects of knowledge and skills to new situations which differ in at least some details from the problems they have previously experienced. People would be very limited if they could only apply what they learn to identical problems met repeatedly. Thus, while performance is somewhat specific to the context of practice, the notion of strict specificity of skills will not account for the flexibility of application of skills from one problem to another. Accounting for transfer in terms of a mechanical process of generalization from one problem to another on the basis of formal or physical similarities of the problems themselves does not take into account the systems nature of contexts, involving not only the form of the problem but also the purpose of solving it and the social context in which the activity is embedded.

People transform novel problems, making them resemble familiar situations by actively – but not necessarily consciously – seeking analogies across problems. A person's interpretation of a problem in any particular activity may be important in applying skills already developed in another context. The person uses the context of the problem to apply familiar information and skills to the novel problem, metaphorically transferring aspects of the familiar context to the new problem (Burstein 1981; Petrie 1979). Bartlett (1958) asserts that generalization 'is not in the least likely to occur . . . unless there is active exploration of the situation that offers it an opportunity' (p. 95). Gick and Holyoak (1980) demonstrate that with story problems that differ but have the same structure and logically isomorphic solutions, subjects do not transfer relevant information from one problem to another unless they first notice the underlying similarity, even though the transfer is relatively simple once the similarity is suggested. And Duncker's (1945) experiments on functional fixedness demonstrate that the ease with which subjects employ materials in unconventional uses in problem solving depends on the relation of the problem to the familiar context of use of the materials.

Even more important than the active role of the individual in bridging contexts is the part played by other individuals and cultural scripts for problem solution in guiding the individual's application of information and skills to a new situation. We discuss this process in some detail in the next section, in which we summarize some theoretical frameworks that provide an appealing solution to the problem of context's role in development and in the application of knowledge and skills to new situations.

FUNCTIONAL APPROACHES TO DEVELOPMENT

Theoretical formulations

In this section we review some theories that emphasize that ways of thinking and behaving are not characteristics of the person separate from the context in which the person functions. We focus on Soviet work influenced by Vygotsky (1962, 1978; Wertsch 1979a, 1979b) and work by the Laboratory of Comparative Human Cognition (1979, 1980). Some similar ideas are contained in Gibson's (1979) ecological theory but without the focus on culture contained in the Vygotsky and LCHC frameworks. While several other theories (Feldman 1980; Fischer 1980) have attempted to involve context in explanations of cognitive development, their consideration of context has been limited to the structure or features of the task or to the domain of knowledge. They have not incorporated the purpose of the activity or the interpersonal and cultural context in which an activity is embedded. The functional approaches we discuss in this section emphasize that behavior is directed toward accomplishing goals and that these goals are socially defined and mediated by other members of the culture.

Vygotsky's theory stresses the adaptation of behavior to fit the context and the structuring of context to support behavior. This perspective focuses on the social adaptation of humans to their environments through cultural history. As such, the study of development and the cultural context are both central to the examination of the processes of human functioning. To understand how culture relates to individual psychological functioning, the process of development or adaptation is examined rather than simply studying outcomes or static states. Development is not assumed to take a fixed, unidimensional course toward a unique or ideal end point; rather, the individual is expected to differentiate to fit the niche or cultural setting.

Rather than focusing on individual responses to environmental stimuli as the unit of analysis, the Vygotskian approach focuses on the concept of *activity*, Leont'ev (1981) has elaborated the Vygotskian concept of activity, a molar unit of analysis involving goals, means, and conditions that mediates between the individual and the context. The cultural practice theory of the LCHC (1980) also focuses on activity by identifying 'socially assembled situations' as the unit of analysis rather than working from characteristics of individual persons or cultures. 'Socially assembled situations' are cultural contexts for action and problem solving that are constructed by people as they interact with one another. Cultural practices employed in socially assembled situations are learned systems of activity in which knowledge consists of standing rules for thought and action appropriate to a particular situation, embodied in the cooperation of individual members of a culture. The Laboratory of Comparative Human Cognition argues that descriptions of what people 'know-to-do' are distorted if they do not consider the social circumstances in which that knowledge is displayed and interpreted. In such an approach, the distinction between social and cognitive functioning fades.

Both the Laboratory of Comparative Human Cognition and Vygotskian approaches emphasize the *practice* of socially constructed modes of thinking, where cognition involves *doing* goal-directed action. In related work, Scribner and Cole (1981) define practice as 'a recurrent, goal-directed sequence of activities using a particular technology and particular systems of knowledge' (p. 236).

In a functional approach, thought and action are integrated. Both mental and physical processes are means by which an organism achieves practical results that are relevant in particular contexts. The purpose of cognition is not to produce thoughts but to guide intelligent action. Leont'ev (1981) objects strongly to the dualism of mental and physical processes, on the basis that mental activity develops from processes that put the agent in 'practical contact with objective reality'. Similarly, ecological psychologists (see Gibson 1979; Michaels and Carello 1981) emphasize the confluence of perception and action, integrating perceptual learning and the acquisition of motor skills. Perception tailors the animal's actions to its environment. The point of perception is appropriate action; to act adaptively, the person needs to perceive the environment accurately; to perceive effectively requires putting oneself in a position to obtain information (Gibson 1982).

In the Vygotskian approach, thought develops from experience in socially structured activity through the internalization of the processes and practices provided by society and its members. As discussed earlier, the social context influences the individual's patterns of behavior through cultural institutional tools of action and thought (and norms for the use of those tools), such as arithmetic systems and electronic calculators, and mnemonic strategies, writing systems, and paper. Such tools – indeed all objects – are socially developed and defined. Social and nonsocial objects are not distinguished, because even with 'natural' objects, their significance for people is socially determined.

The Vygotskian view of cognition emphasizes that the social unit in which the child is embedded channels development, and suggests that, rather than deriving explanations of activity from the individual plus secondary social influences, we should focus on the social unit of activity and regard individual functioning as its product. This stance makes it of foremost importance to consider the role of the formal institutions of society and the informal interactions of its members as central to the process of development. In order to understand development, we must attend to the role played by such influences as formal schooling, television, the characteristics of children's toys, and the formal and informal instructional roles played by adults and other individuals expert in the activity and by peers as they coordinate joint activities.

The cultural institutional context reaches the individual largely through interaction with other members of the society. The social interaction of children with people who are proficient with the skills and tools of society is essential to development. Indeed, the child's individual social and cognitive activity derives from his or her interactions with other people. Vygotsky (1962, 1978) emphasizes that development occurs in situations where the child's problem solving is guided by an adult who structures and models the appropriate solution to the problem (in the 'zone of proximal development' – the region of sensitivity to instruction where the child is not quite able to manage the problem independently and can benefit most from guidance). Cole (1981) argues that the zone of proximal development is 'where culture and cognition create each other'. Through experience in the zone of proximal development, the child's individual mental functioning develops. Adults are instrumental in arranging the occurrence of cognitive tasks for children, and they facilitate learning by regulating the difficulty of the task and providing a model of mature performance. Formal instruction and informal social interaction embed the child in the application of appropriate background information for a new problem, thereby providing experience in generalizing knowledge to new problems.

The process of interaction requires the creation of a common framework for the coordination of action and the exchange of information. Communication relies on the establishment of an intelligible context of interaction; this coordination facilitates generalization, in that new information has to be made compatible with the newcomer's (novice's, child's) existing knowledge. In the process, the child is led toward an understanding of this new information or situation. For example, in observations of mothers teaching their children how to perform classification tasks, Rogoff, Gauvain, and Gardner (in preparation) observe that 84 percent of the mothers guided the child in transferring relevant concepts from more familiar settings to a relatively novel laboratory task with statements such as 'we're going to organize things by categories. You know, just like we don't put the spoons in the pan drawer and all that stuff.' The language used in communication removes some of the complex alternative interpretations of an event by coding it in a particular way. In this way, cultural expectations are transmitted by linguistic labels in which events regarded as similar are coded similarly by a cultural group. The structuring provided in communication serves as a 'scaffold' (Wood 1980) for the novice, providing bridges between the old knowledge and the new. In making new information compatible with the child's current knowledge and skills, an adult guides the child in generalization to the new problem.

The answer offered, then, by a functional approach to the problem of how generalization from specific contexts occurs, is that individuals actively seek bridges from one situation to another and are greatly assisted by others who have more or different experience and make the analogy intelligible to the newcomer. Development and learning are not spontaneous but guided and channeled by other people experienced in the culturally developed modes of handling situations.

In the next section, we review some cross-cultural research that is consistent with the functional approaches we have described. Although some of these investigations of the relation between cultural experience and individual functioning have been influenced by Vygotsky's theories, others have not. Nevertheless, they have in common an emphasis on examination of the process of adaptation of people in their wider social/cultural milieux.

Research on the functional fit of cultural experience and individual development

Several recent lines of investigation illustrate the functional relation between learning experiences and the cognitive skills developed. In the following sections, we review some examples of the development of particular skills in domains of practice encouraged or structured by the cultural milieu. Along with the many studies previously reviewed in this chapter, they form the empirical basis of the sociocultural, functional theories of development we have described.

Cognitive skills

Lave (1977) examined arithmetic skills used by Liberian tailors varying in amount of schooling and in amount of tailoring experience. She designed the problems to involve identical arithmetic skills, but to vary in resemblance to arithmetic problems met in school and in tailoring. The results showed a specific relation between the type of math experience obtained and skill in the different types of math problems. Neither arithmetic skills learned in school nor those learned in the practical problems of tailors generalized to arithmetic problems different from either type.

Scribner (1984) investigated arithmetic calculation by US dairy workers whose day-to-day experiences provide them with practice in calculations involving numbers of single cartons and cases (full of cartons) of milk products. The workers' responsibilities varied, either manipulating numbers of cartons and cases to fill orders, accounting for deliveries using numbers of computer forms, or billing for the product using entirely symbolic numerical representations. Scribner gave calculation problems in these different formats, and found that calculation skill and strategies corresponded to the daily use to which the individual habitually applied such calculation. Scribner argues that skilled practical thinking is goal-directed and adapted to the changing properties of problems and task conditions.

Rogoff and Gauvain (1983) tested Navajo women with varying amounts of experience in weaving and in formal school. They gave tests of pattern continuation that varied in resemblance to weaving processes (continuing yarn patterns on small looms) and school procedures (continuing paper-and-pencil patterns in workbooks). The results showed a specific relationship between experience and pattern continuation skill: Experience as a weaver related to performance on patterns resembling the process of weaving, and experience in school related only slightly to performance on any patterns.

Literacy effects

Scribner and Cole (1981) expected a specific functional relation between the practice of literacy and consequent cognitive skills. To test this, they studied 'general' and 'specific' cognitive skills used by the Vai people of Liberia, who varied in use of several types of literacy. The Vai people independently developed a phonetic writing system, widely available throughout the society, consisting of a syllabary of 200 characters with a common core of 20–40. Vai individuals may also be literate in Arabic or in English or not literate in any script. English is the official national language and is learned in Western-style schools; Arabic is the religious script and is learned in traditional Qur'anic schools emphasizing the rote memorization of religious passages usually without understanding; Vai script is used for the majority of personal and public needs and is transmitted outside any institutional setting, with a nonprofessional literate teaching a friend or relative over a period of two weeks to two months.

Scribner and Cole predicted that literacy in the Vai script would not have the general intellectual consequences that have been suggested to be the result of high levels of school-based literacy, as Vai literacy does not involve new knowledge or the examination of ideas. To test for general cognitive consequences of literacy, Scribner and Cole studied performance on logic and classification tasks and found little difference between nonschooled Vai literates and Vai people not literate in any script.

To test for specific effects of learning and using the various scripts, they examined the component skills involved in Vai people's literacy in Vai script, Arabic, and English, compared with nonliteracy. (Note that English literacy is confounded with Western-style schooling.) In describing a board game in its absence, Vai literates (who frequently write letters requiring communication carried in the test and not supported by context) were more successful than Arabic literates and people not literate in any script. The English literates (high school students) were highly successful in this task as well.

Since Vai script is written without word division, the authors suspected that Vai literates might be skilled in the integration of syllables into meaningful linguistic units. Vai literates were better at comprehending and repeating sentences broken into slowed syllables than were Arabic literates and nonliterates. When the sentences were presented word by word instead of syllable by syllable, the Vai literates had no advantage over the other literates.

The authors demonstrated specific consequences of Qur'anic schooling with a memory task resembling learning of the Qur'an (learning a string of words in order, adding one word to the list on each trial). On this task, English students ranked first, but here the Arabic literates showed better performance than either the Vai literates or the nonliterates. On other memory tests (Scribner and Cole 1981; Wagner 1978), Arabic literates showed no superiority in performance over the Vai literates and the nonliterates, suggesting a very specific transfer of learning rather than general transfer.

Also consistent with the conclusion that literacy promotes specific skills is Olson's (1976, 1977) statement that human intellect cannot be separated from the technologies (e.g. writing, speech, numerical systems) invented to extend cognitive processes. He argues that the conception of a general quality of mind (underlying ability) is useless, as it is only in the interaction with the technology (writing, navigational system, and so on) that cognitive processes operate:

> All tasks or performances that we require from children in intelligence tests reflect competence with our technologies. They assess the level of competence of a child or an adult in using some artifact that we find important in our culture. . . . If it is agreed that our measures of intelligence reflect different kinds of symbolic competencies, it is perfectly legitimate to measure this level of competence to determine, for example, if a child requires more practice, but it is illegitimate to draw any inferences about so-called underlying abilities.
>
> (Olson 1976: 195)

Infant development

Super (1981) and Kilbride (1980) argue that the controversy over 'precocious' sensorimotor development in African infants is best resolved by considering the practices of the cultural system in which the babies develop. They present evidence that the items on tests of infant development do not function uniformly, and that the variation from item to item is meaningful. African infants routinely surpass US infants in their rate of learning to sit and to walk, but not in learning to crawl or to climb stairs. They report that African parents provide experiences for their babies that are intended to teach sitting and walking. Sitting skills are encouraged by propping very young infants in a sitting position supported by rolled blankets in a hole in the ground. Walking skills are encouraged by exercising the newborn's walking reflex and by bouncing babies on their feet. But crawling is discouraged, and stair-climbing skills may be limited by the absence of access to stairs. Infant sensorimotor tests assess an aggregate of skills varying in rate of development according to opportunity or encouragement to practice them, rather than involving a general skill or a uniform set of skills.

Super (1981) also suggests that infant sleep patterns vary as a function of culturally determined sleeping arrangements. In the US, the common developmental milestone of sleeping for eight uninterrupted hours by 4–5 months of age is regarded as a sign of neurological maturity. In other cultures, however, the infant often sleeps with the mother and is allowed to nurse on demand with minimal disturbance of adult sleep. In this arrangement, there is less parental motivation to enforce 'sleeping through the night,' and Super reports that in this arrangement, the developmental course of sleeping is at variance with that observed in the US. Babies continue to wake about every four hours during the night to feed, which is about the frequency of feeding during the day. Thus, it appears that this developmental milestone, in addition to its biological basis, is culturally mediated; that is, it is adapted to the context in which it develops.

Personality and sex role development

Whiting and Whiting (1975) observe that the social behaviors displayed by children in six cultures varied according to the age and gender of the people with whom they were interacting. Children displayed nurturance in the company of infants, aggression with peers, and dependence with adults. Analyses of sex differences in these behaviors revealed worldwide trends in which older girls (age 7 to 11 years) were more nurturant than boys of their age; younger girls (age 3 to 7 years) were more responsible than their male counterparts; and boys were more aggressive than girls (Whiting and Edwards 1973). Whiting and Edwards discuss these sex differences in terms of the tasks usually assigned girls and boys in the six cultures. The nurturant behavior of the older girls was probably related to the fact that they were far more likely to be assigned infant care than were boys. Girls of all ages were assigned chores near or inside the home, requiring compliance to mother, while boys were allowed to play or work (e.g., herd animals) farther from home and in the company of peers. In addition, girls were assigned chores at a younger age than were boys.

The impact of task assignment on social behavior is examined by Ember (1973) in a study of sex differences among children in a Luo community in Kenya. While Luo mothers attempted to assign girls and boys chores that were culturally defined as feminine and masculine, respectively, the absence of an elder sister in some homes required boys to undertake some of the feminine chores. Ember found that Luo boys who were assigned feminine work in the home, especially infant care, were less aggressive and more prosocial than boys who did not have these task assignments. The importance of Ember's finding is that the nurturance exhibited by Luo boys with experience in tending infants generalized to their interactions with other individuals. Hollos (1980) similarly reports that Hungarian 6- to 8-year-olds who began school later and spent more time after school at home tending siblings were less competitive than children who spent their time with same-age peers in a collective educational setting beginning at about age 2.

Whiting's (1980) model for the development of patterns of social behavior stresses the importance of setting variables, especially the characteristics of individuals and activities that occupy a setting. Children are assigned to different settings on the basis of their sex, age, kinship, and relative status. In turn, different settings are marked by varying activities and amounts of time spent with infants, peers, adults, siblings, teachers, etc. Whiting hypothesizes that the patterns of social behavior learned and practiced in the most frequented settings may transfer to new settings or to individuals of different status. Certainly one task of childhood is to learn which patterns of social behavior are appropriate to transfer to novel settings.

Summary of functional approaches to development

In this section we discussed theoretical approaches and empirical studies that focus on the functional relation of cultural experience and individual development. To understand the process of children's development in their cultural context, functional approaches emphasize examining the adaptations to particular contexts made by children and those around them. It is assumed that since development is adapted to the cultural context, the course of development is multidirectional; there is no unique end point or developmental trajectory for children in general. Children's skills in thinking and acting are regarded as developing for the purpose of solving practical problems, which vary according to the cultural context. This development involves children's adapting and adopting the tools and skills of their culture, aided by other people.

CONCLUSION

We have argued that research and theory focusing on how culture channels development provides important perspectives on variation and universal patterns of human development. One of the most important lessons of the cross-cultural perspective is that the development of personality, cognitive skills, and behavioral patterns is intimately related to the immediate social and physical contexts and the broader cultural contexts in which children are embedded.

We have suggested that the particular contexts forming culture be examined in order to understand the process of child development. This contrasts with the treatment of culture simply as an unexamined independent variable, or child development as the general progression of the child's skills without regard for the contexts in which these skills are developed and employed. It is necessary to 'unpackage' culture and the skills children practice in order to place their actions in the context of their interpretation of the tasks to be accomplished, the goals in performing the activities, and the broader sociocultural contexts of children's activities.

We discussed functional approaches to development which are presently being developed, influenced by cross-cultural perspectives and by Vygotsky's theory. These approaches emphasize that in development, children adapt their cognitive and social skills to the particular demands of their culture through practice in particular activities. Children learn to use physical and conceptual tools provided by the culture to handle the problems of importance in routine activities, and they rely on more experienced members of their culture to guide their development.

A major contribution that cross-cultural research and theorizing have made to developmental psychology is the notion that the meaningfulness of the materials, demands, goals, and social situation of an activity channels an individual's performance on a task. Sociocultural experience and individual functioning are fundamentally tied to one another and are, thus, companions in human behavior and development.

NOTES

1 In cross-cultural psychology, the term 'Western' is used to refer to technological, industrialized, modern cultures such as the United States, Canada, Western Europe, or Russia. While it is not geographically appropriate, it is more satisfactory than its substitutes which generally carry unwarranted value judgements regarding degree of civilization, development, or cultural advancement.

Please note that our use of the term culture is intentionally broad. While we focus on comparisons of groups differing in their societal membership and examinations of the workings of culture within groups, we believe our arguments are appropriate for groups differing in other background experiences (e.g., age or gender). We also note that Western cultures and non-Western cultures are not homogeneous; societal and subcultural variation of all sorts provide valuable material for comparisons among groups or examination of patterns within groups.

2 It should be noted, however, that only 30 percent of US undergraduates perform in a formal operational way (Ashton 1975).

3 The LCHC also refers to this model as the 'Functional Practice' or 'Cultural Practice' Model.

REFERENCES

Abramovitch, R., Pepler, D., and Corter, C. E. (1982) 'Patterns of sibling interaction among preschool children', in M. E. Lamb and B. Sutton-Smith (eds) *Sibling Relationships: Their Nature and Significance Across the Lifespan*, Hillsdale, NJ: Lawrence Erlbaum Associates.

Acredolo, L. P. (1979) 'Laboratory versus home: The effect of environment on the nine-month-old infant's choice of spatial reference system', *Developmental Psychology* 15: 666-7.

Ashton, P. T. (1975) 'Cross-cultural Piagetian research: An experimental perspective', *Harvard Educational Review* 45: 475-506.

Bartlett, F. C. (1958) *Thinking: An Experimental and Social Study*, New York: Basic Books.

Berry, J. W. (1969) 'On cross-cultural comparability', *International Journal of Psychology* 4: 119–28.

Berry, J. W. (1976) *Human Ecology and Cognitive Style*, New York: Wiley.

Blount, B. G. (1972) 'Parental speech and language acquisition: Some Luo and Samoan examples', *Anthropological Linguistics* 14: 119–30.

Bornstein, M. H. (1980) 'Cross-cultural developmental psychology', in M. H. Bornstein (ed.) *Comparative Methods in Psychology*, Hillsdale: NJ: Lawrence Erlbaum Associates.

Bowerman, M. (1981) 'Language development', in H. C. Triandis and A. Heron (eds) *Handbook of Cross-cultural Psychology*, vol. 4, Boston: Allyn & Bacon.

Brainerd, C. J. (1978) 'The stage question in cognitive-development theory', *Behavioural and Brain Sciences* 1: 173–81.

Brazelton, T. B. (1977) 'Implications of infant development among the Mayan Indians of Mexico', in P. H. Leiderman, S. R. Tulkin and A. Rosenfeld (eds) *Culture and Infancy*, New York: Academic Press.

Bronfenbrenner, U. (1979) *The Ecology of Human Development*, Cambridge, MA: Harvard University Press.

Brown, A. L. (1975) 'The development of memory: Knowing, knowing about knowing and knowing how to know', in H. W. Reese (ed.) *Advances in Child Development and Behavior*, vol. 10, New York: Academic Press.

Brown, A. L. (1982) 'Learning and development: The problem of compatibility, access, and induction', *Human Development* 25: 89–115.

Burstein, M. H. (1981) 'Concept formation through the interaction of multiple models', *Proceedings of the Third Annual Conference of the Cognitive Science Society*, Berkeley, CA: August.

Cazden, C. B. and John, V. P. (1971) 'Learning in American Indian children', in M. L. Wax, S. Diamond, and F. O. Gearing (eds) *Anthropological Perspectives in Education*, New York: Basic Books.

Charlesworth, W. R. (1976) 'Human intelligence as adaptation: An ethnological approach', in L. B. Resnick (ed.) *The Nature of Intelligence*, Hillsdale, NJ: Lawrence Erlbaum Associates.

Cole, M. (1975) 'An ethnographic psychology of cognition', in R. W. Brislin, S. Bochner, and W. J. Lonner (eds) *Cross-cultural Perspectives on Learning*, New York: Wiley.

Cole, M. (1981) *The Zone of Proximal Development: Where Culture and Cognition Create Each Other*, Univesity of California San Diego, Center for Human Information Processing report 106, September.

Cole, M., Gay, J., Glick, J. A., and Sharp, D. W. (1971) *The Cultural Context of Learning and Thinking*, New York: Basic Books.

Cole, M., Hood, L., and McDermott, R. P. (1978) 'Concepts of ecological validity: Their differing implications for comparative cognitive research', *The Quarterly Newsletter of the Institute for Comparative Human Development* 2: 34–7.

Cole, M. and Scribner, S. (1975) 'Theorizing about socialization of cognition', *Ethos* 3: 250–68.

Cole, M., Sharp, D. W., and Lave, C. (1976) 'The cognitive consequences of education', *Urban Review* 9: 218-33.

Cook-Gumperz, J. and Corsaro, W. (1977) 'Social-ecological constraints on children's communicative strategies', *Sociology* 11: 411-33.

Dasen, P. R. (ed.) (1977) *Piagetian Psychology: Cross-cultural Contributions*, New York: Gardner Press.

Dasen, P. R. and Heron, A. (1981) 'Cross-cultural tests of Piaget's theory', in H. C. Triandis and A. Heron (eds) *Handbook of Cross-cultural Psychology*, vol. 4, Boston: Allyn & Bacon.

DeLoache, J. S. (1980) 'Naturalistic studies of memory for object location in very young children', *New Directions for Child Development* 10: 17-32.

DeLoache, J. S. and Brown, A. L. (1979) 'Looking for big bird: Studies of memory in very young children', *The Quarterly Newsletter of the Laboratory of Comparative Human Cognition* 1: 53-7.

Duncker, K. (1945) 'On problem solving', *Psychological Monographs* 58: 85-93.

Edwards, C. P. (1981) 'The comparative study of the development of moral judgment and reasoning', in R. H. Munroe, R. L. Munroe and B. B. Whiting (eds) *Handbook of Cross-cultural Human Development*, New York: Garland.

Ekehammar, B. (1974) 'Interactionism in personality from a historical perspective', *Psychological Bulletin* 8: 1,026-48.

Ellis, S., Rogoff, B., and Cromer, C. C. (1981) 'Age segregation in children's social interactions', *Developmental Psychology* 17: 399-407.

Ember, C. R. (1973) 'Feminine task assignment and the social behavior of boys', *Ethos* 1: 424-39.

Erickson, F. (1981) 'Timing and context in everyday discourse: Implications for the study of referential and social meaning', in W. P. Dickson (ed.) *Children's Oral Communication Skills*, New York: Academic Press.

Feldman, D. H. (1980) *Beyond Universals in Cognitive Development*, Norwood, NJ: Ablex.

Field, T. (1979) 'Infant behaviors directed toward peers and adults in the presence and absence of mother', *Infant Behavior and Development* 2: 47-54.

Field, T. M., Sostek, A. M., Vietze, P., and Leiderman, P. H. (eds) (1981) *Culture and Early Interactions*, Hillsdale, NJ: Lawrence Erlbaum Associates.

Field, T. M. and Widmayer, S. M. (1981) 'Mother–infant interactions among lower SES Black, Cuban, Puerto Rican and South American immigrants', in T. M. Field, A. M. Sostek, P. Vietze, and P. H. Leiderman (eds) *Culture and Early Interactions*, Hillsdale, NJ: Lawrence Erlbaum Associates.

Fischer, K. W. (1980) 'A theory of cognitive development: The control and construction of hierarchies of skills', *Psychological Review* 87: 477-531.

Fitchen, J. M. (1981) *Poverty in Rural America: A Case Study*, Boulder, CO: Westview Press, Inc.

Flavell, J. H. (1977) *Cognitive Development*, Englewood Cliffs, NJ: Prentice-Hall.

Fowler, W. (1980) 'Cognitive differentiation and developmental learning', in H. W. Reese and L. P. Lipsitt (eds) *Advances in Child Development and Behavior*, vol. 15, New York: Academic Press.

Fox, N. A. (1977) 'Attachment of Kibbutz infants to mother and metapelet', *Child Development* 48: 1,228–39.

Gelman, R. (1978) 'Cognitive development', *Annual Review of Psychology* 29: 297–332.

Gewirtz, J. L. (1965) 'The course of infant smiling in four child-rearing environments in Israel', in B. M. Foss (ed.) *Determinants of Infant Behavior*, vol. 3, London: Methuen.

Gibson, E. J. (1982) 'The concept of affordances in development: The renascence of functionalism', in W. A. Collins (ed.) *Minnesota Symposium on Child Psychology*, vol. 15, Hillsdale, NJ: Lawrence Erlbaum Associates.

Gibson, J. J. (1980) *The Ecological Approach to Visual Perception*, Boston: Houghton Mifflin.

Gick, M. L. and Holyoak, K. J. (1980) 'Analogical problem solving', *Cognitive Psychology* 12: 306–55.

Gladwin, T. (1970) *East is a Big Bird*, Cambridge, MA: Belknap Press.

Gleason, J. B. (1973) 'Code switching in children's language', in T. E. Moore (ed.) *Cognitive Development and the Acquision of Language*, New York: Academic Press.

Glick, J. (1975) 'Cognitive development in cross-cultural perspective', in F. Horowitz *et al.* (eds) *Review of Child Development Research,* vol. 4, Chicago: University of Chicago Press.

Glucksberg, S., Krauss, R. M., and Higgins, E. T. (1975) 'The development of referential communication skills', in F. D. Horowitz (ed.) *Review of Child Development Research*, vol. 4, Chicago: University of Chicago Press.

Goldberg, S. (1972) 'Infant care and growth in urban Zambia', *Human Development* 15: 77–89.

Goodnow, J. J. (1976) 'The nature of intelligent behavior: Questions raised by cross-cultural studies', in L. B. Resnick (ed.) *The Nature of Intelligence*, Hillsdale, NJ: Lawrence Erlbaum Associates.

Goody, J. (1977) *The Domestication of the Savage Mind*, Cambridge: Cambridge University Press.

Graves, Z. R. and Glick, J. (1978) 'The effect of context on mother–child interaction', *The Quarterly Newsletter of the Institute for Comparative Human Development* 2: 41–6.

Greenfield, P. M. (1966) 'On culture and conservation', in J. S. Bruner, R. R. Olver, and P. M. Greenfield (eds) *Studies in Cognitive Growth*, New York: Wiley.

Greenfield, P. M. (1974) 'Comparing dimensional categorization in natural and artificial contexts: A developmental study among the Zinancantecos of Mexico', *Journal of Social Psychology* 93: 157–71.

Greenfield, P. M. (1976) 'Cross-cultural research and Piagetian theory: Paradox and progress', in K. F. Riegel and J. A. Meacham (eds) *The Developing Individual in a Changing World*, vol. 1, Chicago: Aldine.

Greenfield, P. M. (1979) 'Response to Wolof "magical thinking": Culture and conservation revisited' by Judith T. Irvine', *Journal of Cross-cultural Psychology* 10: 251–6.

Greenfield, P. M. and Childs, C. P. (1977) 'Understanding sibling concepts: A developmental study of kin terms in Zinacantan', in P. R. Dasen (ed.) *Piagetian Psychology: Cross-cultural Contributions*, New York: Gardner Press.

Gump, P., Schoggen, P., and Redl, F. (1963) 'The behavior of the same child in different milieus', in R. C. Barker (ed.) *The Stream of Behavior*, New York: Appleton-Century-Crofts.

Harkness, S. and Super, C. M. (1977) 'Why African children are so hard to test', in L. L. Adler (ed.) *Issues in Cross-cultural Research Annals of the New York Academy of Sciences*, vol. 285, pp. 326–31.

Hicks, G. (1976) *Appalachian Valley*, New York: Holt, Rinehart & Winston.

Hollos, M. (1980) 'Collective education in Hungary: The development of competitive, cooperative and role-taking behaviors', *Ethos* 8: 3–23.

Huston-Stein, A., Friedrick-Cofer, L., and Susman, E. J. (1977) 'The relation of classroom structure to social behavior, imaginative play and self-regulation of economically disadvantaged children', *Child Development* 48: 908–16.

Irvine, J. T. (1978) 'Wolof "magical thinking": Culture and conservation revisited', *Journal of Cross-cultural Psychology* 9: 300–10.

Irwin, M. H., and McLaughlin, D. H. (1970) 'Ability and preference in category sorting by Mano school-children and adults', *Journal of Social Psychology* 82: 15–24.

Irwin, M. H. Schafer, G. N. and Feiden, C. P. (1974) 'Emic and unfamiliar category sorting of Mano farmers and US undergraduates', *Journal of Cross-cultural Psychology* 5: 407–23.

Istomina, Z. M. (1977) 'The development of voluntary memory in preschool-age children', in M. Cole (ed.) *Soviet Developmental Psychology*, White Plains, NY: Sharpe.

Kelly, M. (1977) 'Papua New Guinea and Piaget – An eight-year study', in P. R. Dasen (ed.) *Piagetian Psychology: Cross-cultural Contributions*, New York: Gardner Press.

Kessel, F. S. (1979) 'Research in action settings: A sketch of emerging perspectives', *International Journal of Behavioral Development* 2: 185–205.

Kilbride, P. L. (1980) 'Sensorimotor behavior of Baganda and Samia infants', *Journal of Cross-cultural Psychology* 11: 131–52.

Kiminyo, D. M. (1977) 'A cross-cultural study of the development of conservation of mass, weight, and volume among Kamba children', in P. R. Dasen (ed.) *Piagetian Psychology: Cross-cultural Contributions*, New York: Gardner Press.

Kohlberg, L. (1969) 'Stage and sequence: The cognitive-developmental approach to socialization', in D. Goslin (ed.) *Handbook of Socialization*, New York: Rand McNally.

Konner, M. (1972) 'Aspects of the developmental ethnology of a foraging people', in N. Blurton-Jones (ed.) *Ethnological Studies of Child Behavior*, Cambridge: Cambridge University Press.

Kuhn, D. and Brannock, J. (1977) 'Development of the isolation of variables scheme in experimental and "natural experiment" contexts', *Developmental Psychology* 13: 9–14.

Laboratory of Comparative Human Cognition (1979) 'Cross-cultural psychology's challenges to our ideas of children and development', *American Psychologist* 34: 827–33.

Laboratory of Comparative Human Cognition (1980) 'Culture and cognitive development', unpublished manuscript, University of California, San Diego.

Labov, W. (1970) 'The logic of non-standard English', in F. Williams (ed.) *Language and Poverty*, Chicago: Markham.

Lamb, M. E. (1978) 'The effects of social context on dyadic social interaction', in M. E. Lamb, S. J. Suomi, and G. R. Stephenson (eds) *Social Interaction Analysis: Methodological Issues*, Madison, WI: University of Wisconsin Press.

Lave, J. (1977) 'Tailor-made experiments and evaluating the intellectual consequences of apprenticeship training', *The Quarterly Newsletter of the Institute for Comparative Human Development* 1: 1–3.

Lave, J. (1980) 'What's special about experiments as contexts for thinking', *Quarterly Newsletter of the Laboratory of Comparative Human Cognition* 4: 86–91.

Leiderman, P. H., Tulkin, S. R., and Rosenfeld, A. (eds) (1977) *Culture and Infancy*, New York: Academic Press.

Leont'ev A. N. (1981) 'The problem of activity in psychology', in J. V. Wertsch (ed.) *The Concept of Activity in Soviet Psychology*, Armonk, NY: Sharpe.

Lewis, M. (1978) 'Situational analysis and the study of behavioral development', in L. A. Pervin and M. Lewis (eds) *Perspectives in Interactional Psychology*, New York: Plenum.

Luria, A. R. (1976) *Cognitive Development: Its Cultural and Social Foundations*, Cambridge, MA: Harvard University Press.

Malinowski, B. (1927) *The Father in Primitive Psychology*, New York: Norton.

Mandler, J. M., Scribner, S., Cole, M., and DeForest, M. (1980) 'Cross-cultural invariance in story recall', *Child Development* 51: 19–26.

Maudry, M. and Nekula, M. (1939) 'Social relations between children of the same age during the first two years of life', *Journal of Genetic Psychology* 54: 193–215.

McCall, R. B. (1977) 'Challenges to a science of developmental psychology', *Child Development* 48: 333–44.

Michaels, C. F., and Carello, C. (1981) *Direct Perception*, Englewood Cliffs, NJ: Prentice-Hall.

Mischel, W. (1979) 'On the interface of cognition and personality: Beyond the person–situation debate', *American Psychologist* 34: 740–54.

Munroe, R. H. and Munroe, R. L. (1971) 'Household density and infant care in an East African society', *Journal of Social Psychology* 83: 3–13.

Munroe, R. H., Munroe, R. L., and Whiting, B. B. (eds) (1981) *Handbook of Cross-cultural Human Development*, New York: Garland.

Munroe, R. L. and Munroe, R. H. (1975) *Cross-cultural Human Development*, Monterey, CA: Brooks/Cole.

Neisser, U. (1976) 'General academic, and artificial intelligence', in L. B. Resnick (ed.) *The Nature of Intelligence*, Hillsdale, NJ: Lawrence Erlbaum Associates.

Olson D. R. (1976) 'Culture, technology, and intellect', in L. B. Resnick (ed.) *The Nature of Intelligence*, Hillsdale, NJ: Lawrence Erlbaum Associates.

Olson, D. R. (1977) 'The languages of instruction: The literate bias of schooling', in R. C. Anderson, R. J. Spiro, and W. E. Montague (eds) *Schooling and the Acquisition of Knowledge*, Hillsdale, NJ: Lawrence Erlbaum Associates.

Parke, R. D. (1979) 'Interactional designs', in R. B. Cairns (ed.) *The Analysis of Social Interactions*, Hillsdale, NJ: Lawrence Erlbaum Associates.

Parten, M. B. (1933) 'Social play among preschool children', *Journal of Abnormal and Social Pshcyology* 28: 136–47.

Pedersen, F. A. (1980) *The Father-Infant Relationship: Observational Studies in the Family Setting*, New York: Praeger.

Pertrie, H. G. (1979) 'Metaphor and learning', in A. Ortony (ed.) *Metaphor and Thought*, Cambridge: Cambridge University Press.

Piaget, J. (1971) 'The theory of stages in cognitive development', in D. R. Green, M. P. Ford, and G. P. Flamer (eds) *Measurement and Piaget*, New York: McGraw-Hill.

Piaget, J. (1972) 'Intellectual evolution from adolescence to adulthood', *Human Development* 15: 1–12.

Pinard, A., Morin, C., and Lefebvre, M. (1973) 'Apprentissage de la conservation des quantités liquides chez des enfants rwandais et canadiens-français', *International Journal of Psychology* 8: 15–23.

Price-Williams, D. R. (1962) 'Abstract and concrete modes of classification in a primitive society', *British Journal of Educational Psychology* 32: 50–61.

Price-Williams, D. R. (1975) *Explorations in Cross-cultural Psychology*, San Francisco: Chandler & Sharp.

Price-Williams, D. R. (1980) 'Anthropological approaches to cognition and their relevance to psychology', in H. C. Triandis and W. Lonner (eds) *Handbook of Cross-cultural Psychology*, vol. 3, Boston: Allyn & Bacon.

Reese, H. W. (1977) 'Discriminative learning and transfer: Dialectical perspectives', in N. Datan and H. W. Reese (eds) *Life-span Developmental Psychology: Dialectical Perspectives on Experimental Research*, New York: Academic Press.

Rogoff, B. (1981) 'Schooling and the development of cognitive skills', in

H. C. Triandis and A. Heron (eds) *Handbook of Cross-cultural Psychology*, vol. 4, Boston: Allyn & Bacon.

Rogoff, B. (1982) 'Integrating context and cognitive development', in M. E. Lamb and A. L. Brown (eds) *Advances in Developmental Psychology*, vol. 2, Hillsdale, NJ: Lawrence Erlbaum Associates.

Rogoff, B. and Gauvain, M. (1983) 'The cognitive consequences of specific experiencs: Weaving versus schooling among the Navajo', unpublished manuscript, University of Utah.

Rogoff, B., Gauvain, M., and Gardner, W. (1986) 'Guidance in cognitive development: Structural analyses', in J. Valsiner (ed.) *The Individual Subject and Scientific Psychology*, New York: Plenum.

Rogoff, B. and Lave, J. (1984) *Everyday Cognition: Its Development in Social Context*, Cambridge, MA: Harvard University Press.

Rogoff, B. and Mistry, J. (1985) 'Memory development in cultural context', in M. Pressley and C. Brainerd (eds) *Cognitive Learning and Memory in Children*, New York: Springer-Verlag.

Rogoff, B. and Waddell, K. J. (1982) 'Memory for information organized in a scene by children from two cultures', *Child Development* 53: 224–8.

Ross, G., Kagan, J., Zelazo, P., and Kotelchuck, M. (1975) 'Separation protest in infants in home and laboratory', *Developmental Psychology* 11: 256–7.

Ruffy, M. (1981) 'Influence of social factors in the development of the young child's moral judgments', *European Journal of Social Psychology* 11: 61–75.

Scribner, S. (1976) 'Situating the experiment in cross-cultural research', in K. F. Riegel and J. A. Meacham (eds) *The Developing Individual in a Changing World*, vol. 1, Chicago: Aldine.

Scribner, S. (1977) 'Modes of thinking and ways of speaking: Culture and logic reconsidered', in P. N. Johnson-Laird and P. C. Wason (eds) *Thinking*, Cambridge: Cambridge University Press.

Scribner, S. (1984) 'Studying working intelligence', in B. Rogoff and J. Lave (eds) *Everyday Cognition: Its Development in Social Context*, Cambridge, MA: Harvard University Press.

Scribner, S. and Cole, M. (1981) *The Psychology of Literacy*, Cambridge, MA: Harvard University Press.

Serpell, R. (1976) *Culture's Influence on Behavior*, London: Methuen.

Serpell, R. (1979) 'How specific are perceptual skills? A cross-cultural study of pattern reproduction', *British Journal of Psychology* 70: 365–80.

Sharp, D., Cole, M., and Lave, C. (1979) 'Education and cognitive development: The evidence from experimental research', *Monographs of the Society for Research in Child Development*, 44: (1–2, serial no. 178).

Shatz, M. and Gelman, R. (1977) 'Beyond syntax: The influence of conversational constraints on speech modifications', in C. E. Snow and C. A. Ferguson (eds) *Talking to Children*, Cambridge: Cambridge Univesity Press.

Shultz, J. J., Florio, S., and Erickson, F. (1982) 'Where's the floor? Aspects of the cultural organization of social relationships in communication at home and in school', in P. Gilmore and A. A. Glatthorn (eds) *Children In and Out of School*, Washington, DC: Center for Applied Linguistics.

Siegel, A. W. (1977) "Remembering" is alive and well (and even thriving) in empiricism', in N. Datan and H. W. Reese (eds) *Life-span Developmental Psychology: Dialectical Perspectives on Experimental Research*, New York: Academic Press.

Siegler, R. S. (1981) 'Developmental sequences within and between concepts', *Monographs of the Society for Research in Child Development* 46(2) serial no. 189.

Skeen, J., Rogoff, B., and Ellis, S. (1983) 'Categorization by children and adults in communication contexts', *International Journal of Behavioral Development* 6: 213–20.

Slobin, D. I. (1973) 'Cognitive prerequisites for the development of grammar', in C. A. Ferguson and D. I. Slobin (eds) *Studies of Child Language Development*, New York: Holt, Rinehart & Winston.

Smirnov, A. A. and Zinchenko, P. I. (1969) 'Problems in the psychology of memory', in M. Cole and I. Maltzman (eds) *A Handbook of Contemporary Soviet Psychology*, New York: Basic Books.

Sostek, A. M., Vietze, P., Zaslow, M., Kriess, L., van der Walls, F., and Rubinstein, D. (1981) 'Social context in caregiver–infant interaction: A film study of Fais and the United States', in T. M. Field, A. M. Sostek, P. Vietze, and P. H. Leiderman (eds) *Culture and Early Interactions*, Hillsdale, NJ: Lawrence Erlbaum Associates.

Steinberg, Z. D. and Cazden, C. B. (1979) 'Children as teachers – of peers and ourselves', *Theory into Practice* 18: 258–66.

Super, C. M. (1977) 'Who goes to school and what do they learn?', paper presented at the meeting of the Society for Research in Child Development, New Orleans.

Super, C. M. (1981) 'Behavioral development in infancy', in R. H. Munroe, R. L. Munroe, and B. B. Whiting (eds) *Handbook of Cross-cultural Human Development*, New York: Garland.

Super, C. M., Harkness, S., and Baldwin, L. M. (1977) 'Category behavior in natural ecologies and in cognitive tests', *The Quarterly Newsletter of the Institute for Comparative Human Development* 1: 4–7.

Thorndike, E. L. (1914) *Educational Psychology*, New York: Teachers College.

Todd, C. M. and Perlmutter, M. (1980) 'Reality recalled by preschool children', *New Directions for Child Development* 10: 69–85.

Triandis, H. C. and Heron, A. (eds) (1981) *Handbook of Cross-cultural Psychology*, vol. 4, Boston: Allyn & Bacon.

Vygotsky, L. S. (1962) *Thought and Language*, Cambridge, MA: MIT Press.

Vygotsky, L. S. (1978) *Mind in Society*, Cambridge, MA: Harvard University Press.

Wagner, D. A. (1978) 'Memories of Morocco: The influence of age, schooling, and environment on memory', *Cognitive Psychology* 10: 1–28.

Wagner, D. A. and Stevenson, H. W. (1982) *Cultural Perspectives on Child Development*, San Francisco: Freeman.

Weisner, T. S. and Gallimore, R. (1977) 'My brother's keeper: Child and sibling caretaking', *Current Anthropology* 18: 169–90.

Weisz, J. R. (1978) 'Transcontextual validity in developmental research', *Child Development* 49: 1–12.

Wellman, H. M. and Somerville, S. C. (1980) 'Quasi-naturalistic tasks in the study of cognition: The memory-related skills of toddlers', *New Directions for Child Development* 10: 33–48.

Werner, E. E. (1979) *Cross-cultural Child Development*, Monterey, CA: Brooks/Cole.

Wertsch, J. V. (1979a) 'A state of the art review of Soviet research in cognitive psychology', unpublished manuscript, Northwestern University.

Wertsch, J. V. (1979b) 'From social interaction to higher psychological processes: a classification and application of Vygotsky's theory', *Human Development* 22: 1–22.

White, S. H. (1965) 'Evidence for a hierarchical arrangement of learning processes', in L. P. Lipsitt and C. C. Spiker (eds) *Advances in Child Development and Behavior*, vol. 2, New York: Academic Press.

Whiting, B. B. (1976) 'The problem of the packaged variable', in K. F. Riegel and J. A. Meacham (eds) *The Developing Individual in a Changing World*, Chicago: Aldine.

Whiting, B. B. (1980) 'Culture and social behavior: A model for the development of social behavior', *Ethos* 8: 95–116.

Whiting, B. B. and Edwards, C. (1973) 'A cross-cultural analysis of sex differences in the behavior of children aged 3 to 11', *Journal of Social Psychology* 91: 171–88.

Whiting, B. B. and Whiting, J. W. M. (1975) *Children of Six Cultures*, Cambridge, MA: Harvard University Press.

Whiting, J. W. M. and Child, I. L. (1953) *Child Training and Personality*, New Haven: Yale University Press.

Wohlwill, J. F. (1970) 'The age variable in psychological research', *Psychological Review* 77: 49–64.

Wohlwill, J. F. (1981) 'Ecological representativeness in developmental research: A critical view', paper presented at the meetings of the Society for Research in Child Development, Boston, April.

Wolfenstein, M. (1955) 'French parents take their children to the park', in M. Mead and M. Wolfenstein (eds) *Childhood in Contemporary Cultures*, Chicago: University of Chicago Press.

Wood, D. J. (1980) 'Teaching the young child: Some relationships between social interaction, language, and thought', in D. R. Olson (ed.) *The Social Foundations of Language and Thought*, New York: Norton.

Young, V. H. (1970) 'Family and childhood in a Southern Negro community', *American Anthropology* 72: 269–88.

Zarbatany, L., Hartmann, D. P., Gelfand, D. M., and Ramsey, C. (1982) 'The ecological validity of experiments on children's charitable behaviour', paper presented at the meeting of the American Psychological Association, Washington, DC, August.

Zaslow, M. (1980) 'Relationships among peers in kibbutz toddler groups', *Child Psychiatry and Human Development* 10: 178–89.

Zaslow, M. and Rogoff, B. (1978) 'A framework for considering cross-cultural differences in children's peer interactions', paper presented at the meetings of the Society for Cross-Cultural Research, New Haven, February.

Zaslow, M. J. and Rogoff, B. (1981) 'The cross-cultural study of early interaction: Implications from research in culture and cognition', in T. Field, A. Sostek, P. Vietze, and H. Leiderman (eds) *Culture and Early Interactions*, Hillsdale, NJ: Lawrence Erlbaum Associates.

Name index

Subject index